*"Winds
Can
Wake up the Dead"*

"Winds Can Wake up the Dead"

AN ERIC WALROND READER

Edited by Louis J. Parascandola

Wayne State University Press Detroit

AFRICAN AMERICAN LIFE SERIES

A complete listing of the books in this series can be found at the back of this volume.

LIBRARY OF CONGRESS CATALOGING-IN-PUBLICATION DATA

Walrond, Eric, 1898–1966.
Winds can wake up the dead : an Eric Walrond reader / edited by
Louis J. Parascandola.
p.   cm. — (African American life series)
Includes bibliographical references (p.   ).
ISBN 0-8143-2709-5 (pbk. : alk. paper)
1. West Indian Americans—Literary collections.   2. Afro-
Americans—Literary collections.   3. West Indies—Literary
collections.   4. Blacks—Literary collections.   5. Afro-Americans—
Civilization.   6. Blacks—Civilization.   I. Parascandola, Louis
J., 1952–   .   II. Title.   III. Series.
PS3545.A5826A6   1998
98-34550

The author wishes to thank the Crisis Publishing Co., Inc.,
the Magazine of the National Association for the Advancement of
Colored People for authorizing the use of "El Africano"
and "By the River Avon."

Other acknowledgments are indicated on the first page of each piece.
Any errors or omissions are unintentional. The publisher, if notified,
will be pleased to make any corrections at the earliest opportunity.

DESIGNER: S.R. TENENBAUM

Contents

ᛩ
PART I: APPRENTICE WORK

Journalism

Fiction

◯

PART IV: BRITISH PERSPECTIVES

Journalism

Fiction

Acknowledgments

I first encountered Eric Walrond several years ago while reading David Levering Lewis's *When Harlem Was in Vogue*. Since that time, Walrond, as anyone who has spent much time around me will surely attest, has been a passion in my life. But my work has not been in isolation. I am grateful to the following people for their support with this project:

THE NUMEROUS PUBLICATIONS THAT GAVE PERMISSION TO REPRINT
WALROND'S WORK

G. Thomas Tanselle and the staff at the John Simon Guggenheim Memorial Foundation for providing material pertaining to Walrond and for allowing me permission to quote from letters written by the Foundation's staff;

Minnie H. Clayton, Charles Freeney, and Vanessa Weaver of the Robert W. Woodruff Library at Atlanta University Center for providing the Walrond photo and the Roundway Material;

Diana Lachantere and the staff at the Schomburg Center for Research in Black Culture for assisting me in locating a number of pertinent items;

The staff at the Harmon Foundation at the Library of Congress for providing material relating to Walrond's application and award;

The staff at the James Weldon Johnson Collection at Yale University;

Janet Sims-Woods and the staff at the Moorland-Spingarn Research Center at Howard University;

The staff at the Copyright Office at the Library of Congress who helped in locating copyright holders;

My friends at Mid-Manhattan Library;

My colleagues at Long Island University;

L.I.U.'s Research Released Time Committee, which helped to provide the time to complete this work;

My Creole experts, Mom Stels and Aunt Vera;

Susan Rothschild, for her advice;

The late Camille E. Beazer, whose spirit is always with me;

My sisters Maryann and Judy and their families;

My brother John, for his advice and invaluable research assistance, and his family;

My parents, Louis and Ann, whose help I can never repay;

Sarah Griffin, for proofreading;

The several blind reviewers of the manuscript, who urged some ultimately necessary changes to the introduction and the arrangement of the text;

The staff at Wayne State University Press, including Mary Beth O'Sullivan, who initially read the manuscript, copyeditor Mary Gillis for her sharp eye and helpful suggestions, and especially my editor Kathryn Wildfong for patiently answering my unending queries and guiding me along each step;

Professor Emeritus Robert Bone of Columbia University, who generously and unfailingly provided his vast expertise on Walrond.

Special thanks to Shondel Nero, whose wisdom, guidance, encouragement, and love helped get me through many "hard guava days"; this book would not exist without her.

May you all walk good.

To the spirit of Eric Walrond—on the centennial of his birth.

*I*ntroduction

In a letter from Arna Bontemps to Langston Hughes dated September 1, 1966, Bontemps tells Hughes that Eric Walrond had died a couple of weeks earlier from "a heart attack (about his 5th) on a street in London" (474). Bontemps's casual remark is one of the few signs that anyone even noticed Walrond's passing, a sad indication of the fate that had befallen this remarkable figure. This neglect has been unfortunate. Walrond's work as an editor for Marcus Garvey's *Negro World* and Charles S. Johnson's *Opportunity* helped foster the Harlem Renaissance, and his collection *Tropic Death* (1926), in addition to other stories, essays, and reviews, provides great insight into that significant literary and cultural movement. He is especially important for his depiction of Black immigrant life during the 1920s, a subject that has not yet received the attention it deserves. Furthermore, the three issues that dominated his work—migration, discrimination, and racial pride—are still relevant to present-day readers, and the creative tension caused by the intersection of these issues in his literary output often results in his best writing.

Eric Derwent Walrond was born December 18, 1898, in Georgetown, British Guiana (now Guyana), to a Guyanese father and a Barbadian mother. He moved with his mother and siblings to Barbados in 1906, after a devastating fire in Georgetown in 1905. Walrond's father had gone to seek work in Panama during the building of the Canal, and Ruth

Walrond, alone with her children, wanted to be near her family. Once in Barbados, Walrond was educated at St. Stephen's Boys' School, located near Black Rock (outside the capital, Bridgetown), not far from where his grandfather owned a small settlement. Gerald Bright, the young boy in the semi-autobiographical story "Tropic Death," vividly describes his memories of the island in one of Walrond's typically opulent passages:

> He was back in Black Rock; a dinky backward village; . . . the crops of dry peas and cassava and tannias and eddoes, robbed, before they could feel the pulse of the sun, of their gum or juice; the goats, bred on some jealous tenant's cane shoots, or guided some silken black night down a planter's gully—and then only able to give a little bit of milk; the rain, a whimsical rarity. And then [there were] the joys, for a boy of eight—a dew-sprayed, toe-searching tramp at sunrise for "touched" fruit dropped in the night by the epicurean bats, almonds, mangoes, golden apples . . . [.]

Despite the beauty of the environment, however, these were difficult financial times for the family, a fact that is reflected in Walrond's fiction. In "The Black Pin," a story from *Tropic Death*, the protagonist, by herself, must turn a crumbling shack inhabited by scorpions and centipedes into a suitable home for her family. These hard times are also reflected in "Drought," from *Tropic Death*, where the family struggles to eke out a wretched existence. The glimpses in these stories mirror the harsh reality of Walrond's life. With few resources of their own and having had no word from the father for several months, the Walrond family was forced to sell their property and, in 1911, moved to Colón, in the Panama Canal Zone.

The Walronds arrived in Panama at a crucial point in its history. It had only declared its independence from Colombia in 1903 after prompting from the United States government. The area had been a magnet for Caribbean migrants since the 1880s when the French first made attempts to build a canal; however, the number of laborers increased dramatically after the Unites States government began overseeing the Canal Zone project in 1904. Some twenty-five to thirty thousand Caribbean people migrated to Panama between 1904 and 1914, when the Canal was completed. Life there was difficult for Black laborers since the Canal Zone was extremely segregated along color and class lines, with Blacks being paid in silver while whites received gold. It was even harder for families, such as Walrond's, headed by females (Watkins-Owens 12–17).

The move to Colón, a rapidly developing Spanish-speaking city, must have been a shock to young Walrond, a frail, overprotected anglophone child who was used to a more rural life in Barbados. The West Indian area of the city was disease-ridden, the inhabitants suffering especially from yellow fever and malaria; moreover, poverty was rampant. The tenements in which Blacks lived are described in the story "Tropic Death" as "a row of lecherous huts." "Bottle Alley," literally paved with old wine bottles and the setting for a number of Walrond's stories, was notorious for gambling and prostitution (McCullough 147).

There was also racial bias against West Indians. In an essay, "White Man, What Now?" Walrond recalls that in his childhood in Panama he endured "prejudice on the basis of [his] British nationality." He was ridiculed as a "chumbo" (a Black West Indian). This race hatred often manifested itself in violence. In one story from *Tropic Death*, "Subjection," a Black man is killed for trying to prevent the torment of another man by an American marine. The police, often of Spanish descent, are also portrayed as being brutal to West Indians in several stories. However, despite these problems, Walrond felt a fondness for Panama. In a biographical note included with his short story "Godless City," Walrond said, "I am spiritually a native of Panama. I owe the sincerest kind of allegiance to it."

In Panama, Walrond became fluent in Spanish and continued his education in public and private schools and with tutors in Colón. He then accepted a position as a clerk in the Health Department of the Canal Commission in Cristobal before working as a reporter, from 1916 to 1918, for the important Latin American newspaper, *The Panama Star and Herald*, which began its run in 1849 and continues to this day. Walrond said he "used to write up brawls, murders, political scandals, voodoo rituals, labor confabs, campaigns, concerts, dramatic affairs, shipping intelligence, etc." for the paper ("Godless City"[1]). Unfortunately, it is difficult to evaluate the extent of Walrond's contributions to the *Star and Herald* since the paper seldom gave bylines; however, his experience with the periodical prompted him to seek new challenges. An American working for the paper gave Walrond "graphic pictures of work and opportunity 'up the States'" ("Adventures in Misunderstanding" *World Tomorrow* April 1926: 110). For Walrond, America "was lurking" and on June 30, 1918, he arrived in the United States, where he lived for the next ten years, a time that would constitute the most productive literary period of his life.

When Walrond arrived in New York City, the wave of West Indian immigrants was reaching its peak. Between 1900 and 1914 over 76 percent of the Black immigrants to the U.S. came from the Caribbean, largely the British West Indies (Walter 523). There were over 36,000 foreign born Blacks, mostly West Indians, in Harlem in 1920, up from 3,552 in 1900 (Holder 9). The peak years for West Indian immigration were 1911–24 (Watkins-Owens 4). The reasons these immigrants came at this time were varied. Inexpensive, regular means of transportation to America, first offered in the 1890s by the United Fruit Company, and a combination of poverty, overcrowding, and natural disasters at home all contributed to this influx (Holder 7–9). Whatever their background, West Indians saw the United States as a land of economic opportunity, and the more immigrants that came, the more those at home wanted to come, often because of the favorable reports from those who had preceded them.[2]

Although they may have come to America with great optimism, many West Indian immigrants encountered their first experience with racial prejudice once they arrived here. Jamaican W. A. Domingo wrote that "while color and caste lines tend to converge in the islands, it is never-theless true that because of the ratio of population, historical background and tradition of rebellions before and since their emancipation, West Indians of color do not have their activities, social, occupational and otherwise, determined by their race" (650). West Indians often did not know how to respond to racial bias, and there were stories of them, when facing discrimination, crying out in anger and confusion, "I am a British subject, I will report this to my consulate" (quoted in Kasinitz 48). Walrond was shocked by the racial prejudice he experienced in New York, and he would carry its scars for the remainder of his life. In "The Color of the Caribbean," he writes:

> On coming to the United States, the West Indian often finds himself out of patience with the attitude he meets here respecting the position of whites and Negroes. He is bewildered—that is, if he is not "clear" enough to pass as a Greek or Spaniard or Italian—at being shoved down certain blocks and alleys "among his own people." He is angry and amazed at the futility of seeking out certain types of employment for which he may be specially adapted. And about the cruelest injury that could be inflicted upon him is to ask him to submit to the notion that because he is black it is useless for him to aspire to be more than a trap drummer at Small's, a Red Cap in Pennsylvania Station, or a clerk in the Bowling Green Post Office.

In addition to racial prejudice, Walrond often felt bias from Blacks born in the United States. After the Civil War, but particularly after 1890, Blacks from the South had begun migrating North in large num-bers. The convergence of Southern Blacks and West Indians in Harlem was not always harmonious; indeed, there were tensions between most native-born Americans and immigrants in the years shortly after World War I. West Indians, brought up to value self-respect, hard work, and thrift, were often thought to be arrogant, pushy, and miserly by many Americans. Their food, clothes, language, and culture were sometimes ridiculed as strange, but they clung to these ways, often failing (like Walrond) to become citizens. Walrond poignantly records his own feelings as an outsider in "White Man, What Now?":

> I went on to New York. I settled in the Harlem Negro quarter. I found the community fairly evenly dominated by Southern Negroes and West Indian emigrants. A wide cleavage existed between the two groups. The West Indian with his Scottish, Irish or Devonshire accent, was to the native Black who has still retained a measure of his African folk-culture, uproariously funny. He was joked at on street corners, burlesqued on the stage and discriminated against in business and social life. His pride in his British heritage and lack of racial consciousness were contemptuously put down to "airs."

Despite his considerable experience as a journalist, Walrond had a difficult time finding a newspaper position, largely because of discrimination. Out of necessity, he worked as, among other occupations, a porter, a secretary, a stenographer, and a janitor. The racism he encountered in his employment experiences is described in "On Being Black" and "On Being a Domestic." Eventually, he obtained work with *The Brooklyn and Long Island Informer* and Marcus Garvey's *The Weekly Review*.

Walrond won a contest sponsored by Garvey's Universal Negro Improvement Association (U.N.I.A.) for a fictional work entitled "A Senator's Memoirs," published in the December 17, 1921, issue of Garvey's weekly, *Negro World*. The sketch is set in a future after Garvey's utopia of a united Africa has been achieved, with Garvey being depicted as a wise, almost godlike leader. The piece is a fantasy demonstrating Walrond's youthful adulation of Garvey. Soon after it appeared, Walrond became an assistant and then an associate editor with the periodical, between 1921 and 1923. This was Walrond's first real break in America, putting him in an important post at an early age. At its zenith in the early 1920s, *Negro World* had a circulation of 200,000 (Martin *Fundamentalism* xv) and boasted of contributors such as Claude McKay, Arthur Schomburg, Carter G. Woodson, Alain Locke, W. A. Domingo, Hubert H. Harrison, and Zora Neale Hurston. As Cary D. Wintz points out, "[t]he years of Walrond's involvement with the paper corresponded with the peak of Garvey's literary activity, some of which anticipated the developments several years later that launched the Harlem Renaissance" (148).

Initially, Walrond was attracted to his fellow West Indian's message, especially Garvey's interest in Black pride, Pan-Africanism, and his defiance of white racism. He wrote several favorable pieces about him and the U.N.I.A. In "Marcus Garvey—A Defense," for instance, Walrond justifies the "czar-like methods" used by Garvey to weed out those less than 100 percent loyal to him. Walrond's essays, reviews, and sketches in the paper tended to stress racial pride, whether he was describing a visit (with Zora Neale Hurston) to bibliophile Arthur Schomburg's library or praising talented Blacks such as performer Bert Williams. Racial pride would remain a major topic for Walrond throughout his life.

Shortly after joining the paper, Walrond's views of Garvey began to change. To some scholars such as Tony Martin, Walrond's eventual rejection of the Garveyite cause made him an opportunist, or worse, a traitor (Garveyism 124–32). However, Walrond's shift was probably less determined by opportunistic impulses than by some genuine philosophical differences between himself and Garvey. First, the exact nature of Walrond's relationship with the U.N.I.A. is unclear. The urbane Walrond, raised by a genteel mother and largely privately educated, likely always felt some distance from the more humbly-born Garvey and his mass movement. Furthermore, Walrond in his essays and reviews consistently felt that literature should be judged for its aesthetic quality, not for its political message. As Martin says, "[f]or Walrond, propaganda tended to detract from good art" (Garveyism 16). This "anti-propaganda" view of literature often seemed at variance with the rest of the Negro World editorial staff. In addition, Walrond's own fiction contributions to Negro World, including a series of vignettes praising the beauty of women from a variety of racial backgrounds, were disconcerting to some staff and readers of the periodical. It should also be noted that Walrond was not the only member of Garvey's circle to question his leadership at this time. Garvey's continuing squabbles with other Black leaders, his theatrics, his fiscal troubles over U.N.I.A. funds, his disastrous meeting with members of the Ku Klux Klan in 1922, and the federal investigation of his activities (culminating in his eventual imprisonment in 1925 and deportation in 1927 on charges of mail fraud) all eroded his base of support (Lewis 40–45).

While working with Negro World, Walrond began to publish in several white-owned periodicals. "On Being Black," a series of three vignettes portraying racial prejudice, appeared in The New Republic. An article praising Black authors, "Developed and Undeveloped Negro Literature," was published in Henry Ford's *Dearborn Independent*. Initially, *Negro World* editors William H. Ferris and Robert L. Poston felt that Walrond's emergence in mainstream periodicals would increase the visibility of Garveyite issues. Ferris, in praising "On Being Black," said that Walrond "is keen and wide-awake, has the gift of expression, and we expect great things from him in the future" (*Negro World* Nov. 18, 1922). However, the *Dearborn* article displays Walrond's increasing disenchantment with the U.N.I.A. The subtitle of the *Dearborn* essay, "Writers Desert Great Field of Folk-Life for Propagandism," shows Walrond's preference for folk literature, not generally featured in *Negro World*, over literature he believed had a more overt political message.

Another essay, "The New Negro Faces America" (*Current History*), clearly marks Walrond's growing rift with Garveyism. Here Walrond is critical of Booker T. Washington (as represented by his successor at Tuskegee, Major Robert Moton), W. E. B. Du Bois, and Garvey. Moton is chastised for his emphasis on obtaining white acceptance and for stressing the need for learning "industrial efficiency." Du Bois is derided for being pompous and for his lack of awareness of the conditions of most Blacks; furthermore, he appears to be someone who "hates to be black." Garvey towers "head and shoulders above these two"; however, Walrond believes that Garvey does things "for theatrical effect," makes "preposterous mistakes," and is "a megalomaniac." Most important, he feels that American Blacks have no desire to return to Africa, the cornerstone of Garvey's philosophy. In rejecting all the major Black leaders, Walrond offers his own hopeful view of the New Negro, recounting the economic progress made by the race. This New Negro does not want "to be like the white man." He seeks new leadership. "He is pinning everything on the hope, illusion or not, that America will some day find its soul, forget the negro's black skin, and recognize him as one of the nation's most loyal sons and defenders." It is probably Walrond's most optimistic statement about race relations in America, an optimism that was to be short-lived. Not surprisingly, after the article appeared, Walrond's involvement with *Negro World* virtually ceased and his name was dropped from the editorial staff by August 1923.[3]

After leaving *Negro World*, Walrond reexamined his political perspectives and his literary style. As a result, he published in a variety of venues and experimented with different literary forms between 1923 and 1926. His choice of publications seems intentionally designed to make as emphatic a break from Garvey as possible. One of Walrond's earliest post-*Negro World* pieces (August 1923) was an essay on an artist known as "El Africano" in *Crisis*, the journal of Garvey's bitter opponent,

W. E. B. Du Bois. This was the only work Walrond ever published in *Crisis* while Du Bois was the editor, not surprising considering Walrond's earlier criticism of him. Du Bois's view that "all Art is propaganda" ("Criteria" 66) was also in opposition to Walrond's theory of art. Du Bois, who believed that literature should depict the lives of the "Talented Tenth," the small group of professional Blacks who would advance the race, had many differences with Garvey, but he would agree with the *Negro World* editor that literature should portray positive images of Blacks. While Walrond was also extremely interested in "uplifting" the Black race, he felt the need to display all aspects of Black life, even unfavorable ones. His praise, for example, of Carl Van Vechten's *Nigger Heaven* (1926) and Claude McKay's *Home to Harlem* (1928) would further distance him from Du Bois and Garvey, who each wrote blistering reviews of these novels depicting the unsavory side of Harlem life.

In the early 1920s, there were also indications that Walrond was beginning to espouse an interest in socialism. This was signaled by his contributions to the leftist periodical *The Messenger*, edited by A. Philip Randolph and Chandler Owen. In "The Black City" Walrond forcefully speaks of the contradictions in Harlem, "a sociological *el dorado*" of vibrant creativity and crushing poverty. Walrond would later become a contributing editor of the communist journal *New Masses* from 1926 to 1930, though he never published in it. His links with radical political movements, albeit apparently without ever officially joining the socialist or communist parties, are not surprising considering his ties with the Harlem Caribbean community, where such prominent personalities as Claude McKay, Cyril Briggs, Grace Campbell, Hubert H. Harrison, Richard B. Moore, and Frank R. Crosswaith belonged to such groups. W. A. Domingo, a socialist, was on the editorial staff of *Negro World* until 1919. In fact, there was a popular notion that a Harlem radical by definition was "an over-educated West Indian without a job" (quoted in Watkins-Owens 104). Perhaps these radical tendencies hastened Walrond's break with Garvey, one West Indian leader who was generally opposed to leftist politics.

Besides his essays and reviews, Walrond tried his hand at the short story, penning "Miss Kenny's Marriage" for the *Smart Set*, edited by H. L. Mencken. Walrond's tale warns of the dangers of cultural assimilation as the prosperous but poorly connected Miss Kenny, newly arrived in Brooklyn, tries to marry her way into a long-established but hard up Brooklyn family. Miss Kenny's life is all show. Instead of thinking of herself as a hairdresser, she considers herself "a beauty culturist" and spices up her language with words like "trichological." She is an aspiring social climber who believes she is above most Blacks, saying "[t]here ain't none of the nigger in me." Yet despite her flaws, Miss Kenny is a likeable character. She has many friends and is beloved by her customers. When her young husband runs off with all her money, one feels some pity for her. As an outsider trying to fit into a new environment, her situation arouses our sympathy. No doubt Walrond was thinking of his own immigrant experience. Miss Kenny simply gets caught up in the trap of trying to gain happiness through money and status, ironically by selling hair relaxers and skin lighteners that might aid in the assimilation process. Fittingly, her shop is described as a "cobwebby parlor." Unfortunately for her, she has been caught in her own snare.

At the same time that "Miss Kenny's Marriage" was published, Walrond began writing for Charles S. Johnson's magazine *Opportunity*, an organ of the National Urban League. Johnson, a prominent sociologist, was national director of Research and Investigation for the Urban League and would go on to become the first Black president of Fisk University. No one was further removed from Garvey, a staunch Black separatist, than Johnson, who believed in the necessity of improving interracial relationships and felt that publishing literature displaying the intellectual capabilities of Blacks could help dispel white stereotypes. Johnson's importance to the literary movement was so strong that Langston Hughes said that he "did more to encourage and develop Negro writers during the 1920's than anyone else in America" (quoted in Lewis 125). Johnson's appreciation of literature for its aesthetic qualities appealed to Walrond, although he ultimately questioned Johnson's optimistic view of race relations.

Walrond began to hone his skills at fiction, writing six stories for *Opportunity*: four brief sketches relating encounters with racial discrimination and two pieces set in Panama that are precursors to the stories in *Tropic Death*. He even won a third prize in *Opportunity*'s 1925 literary contest for "The Voodoo's Revenge." The most intriguing of these pieces are "Vignettes of the Dusk" and "The Stone Rebounds." Walrond's work for *Opportunity*, as with other publications, often seemed contrary to the goal of the journal and the organization that supported it. His independent views would not allow him to adhere strictly to a particular party line.

"Vignettes of the Dusk" is a series of five short scenes depicting prejudice in a myriad of forms. The most fully-developed of the vignettes is the first piece, set in the middle of New York's financial district. The nameless narrator has some money and seeks a more upscale eatery than is his usual wont, dreaming of mingling with the wealthy and marveling at "the beauty that is America." He is in awe of the fancy restaurant and is almost afraid to enter. When he does, he feels he does not belong and is only able to whisper his order: "Oyster salad—and vanilla temptation." The "vanilla temptation" so tentatively ordered is symbolic of the "weirdly enchanting" lure of the restaurant, and to a larger extent, white America. Oysters, often thought of as an aphrodisiac, perhaps allude to sexual stereotypes of Blacks or the narrator's own repressed desires. The waiter hands him the bag "as if its contents were leprous." The man meekly leaves, but he realizes that he's been essentially "sho[o]ed out." The message seems to be that white America wants no part of integration between the races and that if Blacks aspire to the "vanilla temptation," they will only face rejection.

Jay Berry believes that in "The Stone Rebounds" Walrond "assumes the persona of a white writer who has been ostracized by his colleagues for bringing a black playwright to an all-white literary gathering. Later in the story the black playwright is implicitly and indirectly criticized by his black friends for bringing the white writer into a Harlem cabaret" (298). However, the story conveys a more subtle message than mere mutual racial intolerance. Kraus, the egotistical white narrator (an attribute immediately apparent when he uses the word "I" thirty-one times in the opening paragraph), lacks any insight. He can blithely declare, "I haven't any prejudices." When Earl, his Black friend, suggests that they go to Harlem, Kraus jumps at the suggestion. He had never before visited it, but he immediately feels "[i]t is so—Bohemian." After badgering some guests with a discussion of race, there is an awkward silence while he tries "to think up clever things to say." Clearly he does not belong here, but he is too self-absorbed to realize it: "I look around. On me a houseful of eyes is cast. I do not feel out of place. I rejoice in the reaction. I know why they are staring at me. I am white." Unlike the nameless narrator in "Vignettes of the Dusk," who appears ashamed of his race, Kraus exults in his whiteness.

Kraus is an armchair radical who knows little about the people or causes he purports to advance. He merely wants to be seen as avant-garde. Interestingly, the guests at the party think that he is an anthropologist, probably there to study them. They believe the only whites interested in Blacks are ones that can get something out of them. In Kraus's case, they have good reason to be suspicious. He exhibits the most superficial understanding of interracial relationships, reveling in the "exotic" differences between Blacks and whites, and ultimately he has a smug sense of superiority in being white. It is a fascinating piece, especially in a journal attempting to advance better relationships between the races.

Eric Walrond, Toulon, France, 1931.
From the Countee Cullen–Harold Jackman Memorial Collection, Archives and Special Collections Department, Atlanta University Center Robert W. Woodruff Library, Atlanta, Georgia.

Walrond's Harlem
residence in the
1920s. Photo taken
in 1988.
*Courtesy, Robert
Bone.*

Marcus Garvey.
Photographs and Prints Division, Schomburg Center for Research in Black Culture, The New York Public Library, Astor, Lenox and Tilden Foundations.

Charles S. Johnson.
Photographs and Prints Division, Schomburg Center for Research in Black Culture, The New York Public Library, Astor, Lenox and Tilden Foundations.

In an interview with Jacques Lebar in 1933, Walrond said he had little interest in writing about whites. This devastating critique is one of his few examinations of the white psyche.

Walrond's affiliation with *Opportunity* thrust him into the progressive, race-building New Negro Movement. The affable West Indian made a great hit at social events. Ethel Ray Nance, Charles S. Johnson's secretary, recalled Walrond: "He had flashing eyes; his face was very alert and very alive" (quoted in Lewis 128). He moved to Harlem (108 West 144th St.) from Brooklyn to be closer to the center of the New Negro Movement and soon became "the 'rage' of the early and mid-1920s" (Arthur P. Davis cited in Bogle 475). Through Johnson, he met and established friendships with many significant figures of the Harlem Renaissance, including Howard University professor Alain Locke and writers Gwendolyn Bennett, Countee Cullen, and Langston Hughes.[4]

Walrond's contributions to the Harlem Renaissance were significant during his time as business manager of *Opportunity* (August 1925 to February 1927). His careful monitoring of the financially fragile periodical helped assure its solvency. He was also instrumental in obtaining the support of the wealthy West Indian-born numbers banker Casper Holstein, who helped to sponsor *Opportunity's* writing contests; Walrond would later dedicate *Tropic Death* to Holstein. Furthermore, Walrond helped to broaden the international scope of the journal. He was largely responsible for a special November 1926 issue focusing on the Caribbean, which included work by Holstein, McKay, and Domingo. An editorial praises Walrond's contribution: "To his thorough acquaintance with the spokesmen of the Caribbean in this country, we are indebted for the section of special articles which appear in these pages" (334).

In addition to these achievements, Walrond recommended the inclusion of many of the younger New Negro writers in *Opportunity*. A number of these authors were represented in Alain Locke's anthology *The New Negro* (1925), considered by many literary historians to be one of the most significant cultural manifestos of the Harlem Renaissance. Walrond contributed a short story, "The Palm Porch," later included in *Tropic Death*.[5] He had great respect for Locke, a very proper, highly educated man, the first Black to be awarded a Rhodes scholarship. Locke's reaction against literature "*about* the Negro rather than of him" (Foreword *The New Negro* xxv) rang true with Walrond. The Howard professor's interest in Black folklore and in the depiction of Blacks other than just the "Talented Tenth" also appealed to Walrond.

Walrond enjoyed socializing with Locke and others in the "Talented Tenth." He belonged to the very formal Harlem Eclectic Club, a "dickty" (high society) organization that was appalled when Claude McKay failed, as he said in his autobiography, to "put on a dress suit to appear before them" (114). However, Walrond's fiction rarely deals with the lives of the New Negro elite. In his earlier *Dearborn* essay, Walrond expresses his admiration for folk literature, especially singling out for praise Paul Laurence Dunbar. He expands upon this interest in the common folk in his essay, "The Negro Literati." Walrond, discussing depictions of upper-class Black life in fiction, argues, "if there is a society that is more stilted, more snobbish, that is harder to break into, than the Negro society these tales depict, then I've yet to hear about it." He believes that many Black authors, afraid of having whites see Blacks in a disparaging light, create an unrealistic, sterile atmosphere in their works. Instead of writing about the "Talented Tenth," as does someone like Jessie Fauset, Walrond advises the Black author to "paint pictures of people— of tantalizing black people—he knows." The authors whom he most admires, such as Dunbar, Hughes, Zora Neale Hurston, and Jean Toomer, all write in this Black folk tradition.[6] Therefore, it is not surprising that his major literary work, *Tropic Death*, concerns itself with the lives of ordinary folk in Barbados, Panama, and British Guiana. And, like the work of Dunbar, Hughes, Hurston, and Toomer, these stories are told in the vernacular. The title *Tropic Death* suggests Walrond's Caribbean: lush, beautiful, and teeming with life, but death looms behind every corner, no matter how blissful things may appear.

The ten stories in *Tropic Death* hold a unique place in Black literature. One of the book's most important aspects is its focus on Blacks outside the United States, displaying the Pan-African element of the Harlem Renaissance. Kenneth Ramchand calls the collection "one of the startling treasures in the lost literature of the West Indies" (67). Robert A. Hill goes further, saying it is "probably the greatest short story work in the entire body of West Indian literature" (Introduction to Garvey's *Black Man* 19). In *Tropic Death*, Walrond writes of the migratory nature of many Caribbean people, the oppressive colonial system which had been established in the area, the colorism that white racism had facilitated, the changes being wrought by industrialization, the beauty and harshness of the land, and the maintenance of traditional culture such as folklore, songs, and obeah (a folk belief in magic).

He is particularly concerned with the languages of the people, and he takes great pains to recreate the many dialects of the region, generally succeeding with remarkable dexterity.[7] Jamaican-born writer Michelle Cliff describes how in her writing she alternates "the King's English with *patois*, not only to show the class background of characters, but to show

how Jamaicans operate within a split consciousness" (59–60). Walrond does much the same in *Tropic Death*, using language to probe both the European and the African aspects of Caribbean identity. Walrond, a Black immigrant living in America, often felt a duality somewhat akin to the split consciousness Du Bois ascribed to African Americans. Walrond took great pride in his heritage, celebrating his culture and language, yet he was also aware of the potential rewards (and the frequent dangers) of identifying with the language and ways of white folks. Challenging the stereotypical American view of a monolithic Caribbean, Walrond depicts a complex area rich in linguistic and cultural diversity. An examination of four representative stories in the book suggests the range of subjects Walrond explores.

"Drought," like the other stories in *Tropic Death*, does not present a romantic, idealized version of the Caribbean. Walrond had witnessed firsthand the devastating consequences of droughts, which periodically plagued Barbados in the early twentieth century (Richardson 15). The Barbadian peasants described in the story struggle against the forces of nature and man. The sun is seen not as a life-giving source but as an adversary, having "robbed the land of its juice, squeezed it dry." The people pray to an unfeeling God to ease the suffering caused by the drought. They are insignificant compared to the forces of nature; the protagonist, Coggins Rum, named after one of the island's major commodities, is "a black, animate dot" on the white marl road.

The harsh environment is not the only obstacle with which the natives must contend. The effects of British colonialism are also felt. Throughout the story whiteness is linked with oppression and death. The road is for the benefit of the colonizers. The road crew is led by a buckra (white) "driver" (reminiscent of the days of slavery) who has a Black mistress. However, despite the grinding poverty endured by the peasants, there is a deadly appeal in the white colonial system. The natives must wrench "themselves free of the lure of the white earth." They still follow such British rituals as having high tea at dusk, clinging "to the utmost vestiges of the Crown," but, as demonstrated in the tragic case of Coggins's six-year-old daughter Beryl, who rejects the family food and dies after stuffing herself with marl, contact with whiteness can lead to destruction. There is a suggestion, in fact, that the light-complexioned girl, with "white, shiny, appealing" eyes, "the only one of the Rum children who wasn't black as sin," may have been the result of an extramarital liaison of her mother. Ironically, the child dies at dusk, obtaining relief through death from her hard life just as the land gains relief from "the livid sun."

A frequent concern of Walrond's, as George Hutchinson remarks, is "the North American obsession with racial definability" (409). Jamaican-born Miss Buckner, in "The Palm Porch," is one of Walrond's many characters with such an obsession. She is the proprietor of a bordello in Colón in which she employs her own daughters. In many ways, Miss Buckner is like her establishment. Just as the palm porch keeps "out eyes effectively," so too is Miss Buckner cloaked in secrecy. Wild rumors swirl through the city about this "half-white" woman, but no one knows the "mystical heritage" of her or her five daughters.

The palm porch is described as being "opulent" but filled with "illusion," again appropriate descriptions for Miss Buckner. She dresses in elaborate Victorian garb, but her clothing holds hidden danger, a dagger which she is not averse to using on unruly clients. After having killed one such patron with the dagger, she can calmly debate what type of dessert to have for lunch.

Miss Buckner's life is ruled by a rigid code of decorum which dictates that her daughters cannot take up with those she feels are beneath them. Obsessed with colorism, the haughty Miss Buckner (we never learn her given name) is appalled that two daughters have run off with darker complexioned men. She would much rather that they become involved with the olive-skinned Spanish captain who comes to the palm porch.

In Miss Buckner's world, one can have "manners" and display "proper" behavior despite engaging in murder and prostitution. Although Miss Buckner's actions certainly cannot be condoned, she is not without her virtues. She is an enterprising, forceful woman; in fact, she is reminiscent (with some obvious differences) of Mrs. Mooney in James Joyce's story "The Boarding House," a woman who "dealt with moral problems as a cleaver deals with meat." Again, Walrond, as an outsider, could feel some sympathy for an independent person struggling to survive in a hostile, unfamiliar environment.

In "The Vampire Bat," Walrond effectively uses folklore in recounting the story of Bellon Prout, a white plantation owner who has just returned to Barbados after fighting the Boers. Prout, "a solid pillar of the Crown," refuses to take the advice of an old mulatto who warns him not to travel at night. He also dismisses the story of a frightened Black woman who tells of having seen a "man in de [sugar] canes." Continuing his journey, he sees a Black child in the burning cane fields. Prout, assuming it is an innocent victim left to die, picks up the babe; however, in the morning, Prout's bloodless body is found with a small mark on the forehead.

"The Vampire Bat" may appear to be a slight story, even if chillingly told. It is, in fact, a gothic tale, a form at which Walrond could excel.

Tales of obeah, duppies (spirits), and fire hags (spirits "shedding their skins and waltzing forth at night as sheep and goats, on errands of fiery vengeance") are woven throughout the story. However, "The Vampire Bat" is more than just a potboiler. The story is almost allegorical in nature, amounting to a warning to the colonizers of the West Indies. Prout's destination, Mount Tabor, is "a garden of lustrous desolation," a fallen Eden, mirroring the destruction of Barbados brought on by the British as well as a harbinger of Prout's (and by extension the plantation system's) own demise. Prout's home is near Locust Hall, appropriate for the destructive nature of the colonizers; in fact, it was one of the central sugar cane factories on the island (Beckles 148). In this case, however, the British (normally the parasites) become the hosts. Prout fails to recognize the significance of the burning of the cane field, an act of rebellion against the plantocracy. He sees the child and thinks of "[a]nother of the colony's lurking evils, the desertion—often the murder of illegitimate Negro babes." Yet the plantation owner, in his arrogance, has ignored the warnings he has been given. He dismisses the customs and beliefs of the natives as mere superstition. As a result, his body is drained "utterly white and bloodless," the victim of a culture he has denigrated. It is a striking story of vengeance on those who exploit the islands of the West Indies, using the people and land for their own selfish purposes.

Walrond describes the migration of Barbadians to Panama in "Tropic Death," perhaps his most autobiographical story. Walrond, like the young protagonist Gerald Bright, did emigrate from Barbados to a poor area in Panama. He, like Bright, did have a fierce love for his mother. Walrond wrote, "I owe everything to the encouragement of my mother and her determination" (note to "Godless City"). His mother, like the mother in the story, was a devout follower of the Plymouth Brethren, a Christian fundamentalist group Walrond describes in several stories. Walrond's family, too, went in search of a father who had gone to work in the Canal Zone. Indeed, the bond between mothers and sons, particularly when fathers are absent, is a recurrent theme in Walrond's work (Bogle 479–80).[8]

The tripartite setting of the story—in Barbados, on shipboard, and in Panama—mirrors the psychological passage of Gerald Bright from innocence to knowledge of evil and finally to forgiveness. The story is filled with religious imagery. When we first see Gerald, he is a sheltered child, one who had joyfully played in the hills of his small village in Barbados. Though poor, he has been spared the kind of existence lived by the street urchins of Bridgetown. Gerald feels veneration toward his mother for having saved him from such a life: "He wanted . . . to breathe the lovely, holy beauty of her." During the hideous Middle Passage to Panama, "[t]he sun baptized the sea." On the crowded, fetid ship, Gerald listens to a religious zealot calling for God's forgiveness. Upon his arrival in Panama, the boy is reunited with his father, Lucian (reminiscent of the fallen angel, Lucifer), who is a womanizer and a drunkard, living in a "noisy and vulgar" place. Lucian is diseased, spiritually as well as physically, and is about to be put in a leper colony. Despite his initial anger at his father, Gerald gradually comes to love him. Although he has lost social status because of the father's desertion of the family, the boy has gained "a new resiliency, a greater maturity, and a wider experience of life" (Bone 198). It is a lesson he has learned from his mother. In contrast to her half-brother Charlie, who believes that all sinners must be condemned, Sarah maintains her belief that it is possible to obtain God's forgiveness. Despite the strictness of her religious beliefs, she shows kindness toward her husband, which prompts him to show concern, per-haps for the first time, for his family: "An' yo' mus' tek good cyah o' yo'self, heah Sarah, an' don't le' nobody tek exvantage o' yo', yo' heah, dis is a bad country—." Fittingly, this, the final story in *Tropic Death*, is the only piece in the collection that allows for some possibility of redemption.

Walrond's generally sympathetic portrayal of the Plymouth Brethren in the story suggests his own inner turmoil. Although Walrond enjoyed the pleasures of life too much to embrace such a harsh religion, he found it difficult to criticize the Brethren because of his feelings toward his mother. In addition, there was likely at least some appeal to Walrond in the religion, which encouraged Black leadership in the church, advo-cated the concerns of poorer Barbadians, and allowed the incorporation of African culture into traditional Anglican rituals (Richardson 221–23; Beckles 154).[9]

Walrond's treatment of such subjects as prostitution, colorism, pov-erty, crime, and vengeance in *Tropic Death* caused controversy. Wallace Thurman, the radical leader of the younger New Negro writers, warned that if Walrond turned his focus to America, he would "be blacklisted in polite colored circles" ("Negro Artists" 37). Indeed, as Chidi Ikonné notes, "[m]ost of the subjects treated by Walrond are matters which a large part of the black literati of the West Indies and the United States would have liked to leave unrevealed" (179). Therefore, it is not surprising that Du Bois ("Books" 152) offers a mixed evaluation of the book (although his quarrels are more with the use of dialect and the impressionistic style rather than the subject matter). Generally, however, the book was well received. Langston Hughes writes, "[t]he throbbing life

29

and sun-bright hardness of these pages fascinate me" (9), while Benjamin Brawley believes "it is the most important contribution made by a Negro to American letters since the appearance [in 1896] of [Paul Laurence] Dunbar's 'Lyrics of Lowly Life'" (179). Even Du Bois concedes that "on the whole, it is a human document of deep significance and great promise" ("Books" 152). The favorable response of the critics prompted Walrond's publisher, Boni and Liveright, to issue a second printing and provide an advance for another book, *The Big Ditch*, on the building of the Panama Canal. *Tropic Death* secured Walrond's reputation, and many people felt he would write the great novel of the Harlem Renaissance, a pressure that would weigh heavily on him.[10]

"City Love," published in the anthology *American Caravan* (1927), added to Walrond's stature. The story is perhaps the finest literary work depicting the lives of West Indian immigrants during the Harlem Renaissance. Primus, the main character, tries to seduce a woman, Nicey, taking her to a hotel where they are rejected because they have no baggage. Primus goes home to get bags and has a row with his wife. He goes to another hotel with Nicey, but again they are refused, this time because Nicey does not have a hat. Determined to fulfill his desires, he buys a hat for her and they are finally admitted. Primus's pursuit of his mistress is filled with irony. First, we see that there is no love in this city, only lust. The lure of the city, indeed of America, for the immigrant turns out to be false. City life is sordid, squalid, and ultimately frustrating. Primus pretends to have status, but in reality, he comes from "de Back Swamp" and in New York lives in a broken-down apartment building. He is desperate to assimilate into his new surroundings, perhaps one reason why he pursues Nicey, whose speech is far less creolized than that of Tiny, his wife; in fact, the more excited he gets, the more his own accent comes out.

Primus thinks of himself as being experienced and in charge of his life; however, we see that he is a greenhorn who is powerless in his relationships with his wife, his lover, his coworkers, and the hotel workers where he brings Nicey. Instead of taking out his anger at its real sources, he rages ineffectively at his infant son. The immigrant Primus is, as Robert Bone suggests, treated as a child by the society around him and so, in frustration, he bullies his own son in a futile attempt to gain power (183). It is altogether fitting that this story, mocking a West Indian man unable to master the rules of life in the United States, was Walrond's last significant work published in America.

Walrond's success as an author may be measured by three major awards he received in 1927–28: a Harmon Award in Literature, a Zona Gale scholarship at the University of Wisconsin,[11] and a Guggenheim Award to "[t]ravel and study in the West Indies for the purpose of obtaining material for a series of novels and short stories depicting native life there" (Henry Allen Moe letter, March 13, 1928). After winning the Guggenheim award, Walrond left for Panama in September 1928, and he diligently reported his travels to Panama, Haiti, the Dominican Republic, St. Kitts, Barbados, and the Virgin Islands over the next two years to Henry Allen Moe, the secretary for the Guggenheim Foundation. He would scarcely return to America after this time. Walrond pursued many projects during his travels, perhaps being overwhelmed by possible material for study. A brief trip to Haiti, for example, caused him to consider writing a book on the country's history from 1804 to 1915 and another on the American occupation of the country beginning in 1915. These works, however, never appeared. Neither did the "series of novels" mentioned in his award, although no doubt some of his experiences became the grist for a handful of later stories. Instead, Walrond's attention turned to *The Big Ditch*, particularly the French involvement in the Panama Canal, and he requested permission from Guggenheim officials to continue his research and writing in France (letter to Moe, April 2, 1929).

Walrond arrived in Paris in July 1929, and he stayed in France until 1932. French interest in African culture, particularly its masks, dances, and oral literature, had been growing steadily since the turn of the century. A thriving Black community existed in France and several of Walrond's literary friends, including Countee Cullen and Gwendolyn Bennett, had spoken with him about life there. The ever-sociable Walrond easily fit into French society, and he was seen at many parties (Stovall 65, 98). He took an interest in French literature, especially the works of Gustave Flaubert and Blaise Cendrars. However, his extravagant lifestyle put him in constant need of money, and although he received a six-month extension of his Guggenheim grant, it was feared by his friends that he was quickly using up his resources.

Canadian and West Indian author John Hearne, in reflecting on Walrond, is puzzled that there is so little evidence documenting his time in France (cited in Bogle 476). There are, however, some tantalizing morsels from these years. In 1931, Walrond became part of the entourage of British steamship heiress Nancy Cunard (Crowder 132). Cunard, who shocked "polite" society with her political and social views (she was a communist and lived with Black musician Henry Crowder for several years), assembled and published a massive anthology of Black literature and culture, *Negro* (1934). Although Walrond was asked to contribute to this collection, he refused unless he received payment (Kellner 90).

Also during this period, Walrond shared an apartment for a time with Countee Cullen. The two men had long been friends, working together briefly on *Opportunity*, and Walrond had favorably reviewed Cullen's volume *Color* for the *New Republic*, writing "if there ever was a poet ordained by the stars to sing of the joys and sorrows attendant upon the experience of thwarted black folk placed in wretched juxtaposition to our Western civilization, that poet is Countee Cullen." Walrond appreciated the strength, beauty, and grace of Cullen's poetry, and Cullen returned this admiration. One of his most famous poems, "Incident," is dedicated to Walrond. Appropriately, it is perhaps Cullen's most biting racial poem, for as Blanche E. Ferguson observes, Walrond's "militant outgoing personality was a helpful contrast to Cullen's introspection" (120–21).

Walrond's writings in Europe, though not abundant, do add to our knowledge of Black expatriate life on the Continent in the 1930s and 1940s. In the early 1930s, he published several articles on Harlem and the Panama Canal for French and Spanish periodicals (Fabre 138–39). "Harlem" (1933) is a sketch that depicts "the Black capital" as a lively, exciting but wildly hedonistic place. Black Harlemites, like most Americans, are seen as being obsessed with making money, but because of discrimination, they can only get it through buying on credit or obtaining stolen goods. The desire for wealth led to numerous illegal activities, such as theft, prostitution, and bootlegging, frequently conducted with the tacit approval of white law officers.

The articles on the history of the Panama Canal, particularly "Como de Hizo el Canal de Panama" in the Madrid magazine *Ahora* (1934), are also intriguing, giving us a glimpse of *The Big Ditch*. Walrond continued to work on the book, and still hoped to publish it. In fact, there seemed to be enough material for two books, one "a story of the French attempt to construct a canal through Nicaragua" and another "telling the story of the American construction of the Panama Canal" (Moe to Horace Hitchcock, letter, Sept. 17, 1931).

In France, Walrond felt less of the racial discrimination he had experienced in the United States or would later encounter in England. Upon returning to America briefly in 1931, he said, "there's no particular thrill in being here again. . . . Only urgent business brought me back to this country." In commenting on his life in France, he remarked that "[n]one of the difficulties and interruptions which infest Harlem are present here" ("Eric Walrond" 11). Jacques Lebar's interview with

Walrond reveals some of his feelings on the conditions for Blacks in America and France. Walrond remarks that it is easier for Blacks to assimilate in France than in America, yet one conjectures that even in the relatively benign atmosphere of France, Walrond believes that fragmentation occurs. He tells Lebar it is "your country," and he cannot remain in France any more than he could in America. He needed to come full circle. The British subject must finally venture to the "homeland."

Walrond moved to England in 1932 and, except for some years traveling, spent his remaining years there. Although Walrond's years in England remain shrouded in mystery, the following sketch may provide seeds for future research. Once in England, he was reunited with Garvey in the mid-1930s and contributed several articles to Garvey's periodical, *The Black Man*. Their reconciliation is not completely surprising. First, Garvey had never been too harsh on Walrond. His strongest words against him came in an article criticizing Claude McKay (*Negro World* Sept. 29, 1928). Walrond had been grouped with other Black writers, including Walter White and James Weldon Johnson, whom Garvey felt had been used by white publishers to cast Blacks in a disparaging light. Garvey knew that Walrond could still be useful as an author and editor in the attempt to resuscitate the flagging U.N.I.A. Walrond, in fact, published more in *The Black Man* than anyone other than Garvey himself. He was still attracted to Garvey's fighting spirit and, not finding a great deal of success in placing his works elsewhere, saw he might obtain steady employment with *The Black Man*. In addition, Walrond, soured by the racism he had encountered in America and in England, was even more receptive to Garvey's warnings about the dangers of assimilation than he had been in his younger days.[12]

Several of Walrond's *Black Man* pieces chronicle his disenchantment with the position of Blacks in England. As a youth, Walrond saw "England through a romantic and illusive veil" ("The Negro in London"). Upon his arrival in the "Mother Country," however, he felt alienation and discrimination because of prejudice based on race and class. This was a devastating experience for Walrond. Like many West Indians, Walrond valued many aspects of British culture, which he felt was a large part of his own identity. Encountering prejudice in Panama or America was insulting enough, but having to face it in England must have been particularly heinous for him. Perhaps this disillusionment and alienation caused the increasing militancy in these later essays. In "The Negro before the World," for example, he inveighs against capitalism and imperialism, which he believes fatten off the working class only to benefit a small privileged group. In "On England," Walrond attacks the rigid British class system in which "any person of gentle birth, any unborn candidate for the playing fields of Eton, any suave, gilt-edged rascal may be a gentleman." While these scamps run the government, those in the Empire are left "a crushed, unorganized and completely voiceless mass." Walrond's radical politics would continue in his articles for the *People's Voice*, edited by Harlem activist Reverend Adam Clayton Powell Jr. in the 1940s.[13]

Several of Walrond's articles in the *People's Voice* deal with the treatment of Blacks in the Royal Air Force. Walrond's anger over the lack of respect given to British soldiers in Britain is apparent in the short story "By the River Avon," set in Bradford-on-Avon, in Wiltshire, where Walrond had moved in 1939. The piece, about a Black GI in England, denounces the hypocrisy of British "egalitarianism."[14]

A biographical note with "By the River Avon" indicated that Walrond had another collection of fiction "under his hat." Two such stories, "Wind in the Palms" (Sept. 1954) and "Success Story" (Feb.–May 1954), were published in *Roundway Review*.[15] Both pieces deal with memories from Walrond's youth in the Caribbean. The protagonist, Coolie, in "Wind in the Palms" is a "dougla" (a mixed race child of Black and East Indian ancestry) growing up in Colón. Although he does not know his Indian father and his name itself is a racial slur against Indians, Coolie looks down upon Blacks, vowing never to marry a woman with a wide nose. As in a number of earlier writings, Walrond is critical of the destructiveness of racism and self-loathing.

"Success Story" is, after "Tropic Death," Walrond's longest published piece. Like "Tropic Death," it is largely autobiographical, narrating the life of Jim Prout from his birth in British Guiana through his migrations to Barbados, Panama, and the United States. Although the story is filled with references to Walrond's own life, the process of assimilation Prout undergoes could describe any number of new immigrants to America. The story ends with Prout finally gaining employment in the shipping department of a soap company, a job Walrond himself once held.

In September 1957, Walrond returned to London. Along with Rosey E. Pool, a Dutch professor, he selected poems for a program of African American poetry presented at the Royal Court Theatre in London on October 5, 1958. The poems were published as a book entitled, like the program, *Black and Unknown Bards* by the Hand and Flower Press in 1958. The poems were selected to depict the history and conditions of Black life in America. Walrond worked diligently researching the material to be used for the recital, including spirituals, older writers such as McKay, Hughes, and Cullen, but also younger artists like Robert Hayden, Margaret Walker, and Gwendolyn Brooks. The work helped to bridge the gap between the different generations and draw attention to some poets who were not well known in England at the time.

Walrond worked on several projects for the remainder of his life. He selected photographs of African sculpture for a book on African art by Boris de Rachewiltz published in 1959. He also vowed, in a letter to Henry Allen Moe from 1960, to pursue his writing (cited in Ramchand 74–75). He sought, without success, a publisher for his book on the French involvement with the Panama Canal (entitled *The Second Battle*). In addition, even up until his final years, Walrond resiliently explored ideas for new fiction and expressed interest in republishing *Tropic Death* with revisions he had made.

Despite all his plans, Walrond's literary output decreased in his later years. Perhaps a sense of self-doubt that had long plagued him stifled his genius. Walrond seems to have been driven to excel as a writer. He says, "I have got to get there—there are so many reasons why I must find my place in the sun!" (note to "Godless City"). His letters often speak, though, of the brooding nature that sometimes prevented him from writing. As early as 1924, he laments in several letters to Alain Locke (Moorland-Spingarn, Howard University) that he is feeling anxiety and depression that inhibit his creativity. He constantly chides himself for not fulfilling his capabilities. His letters late in life to Henry Allen Moe continue to voice this same concern. He could well have been burdened by his youthful success and his own and other people's expectations. Or perhaps he was just tired, tired of a life of constant migration and of continually fighting the prejudice he encountered wherever he went. It is this fatigue that may account for his remaining in England for over thirty years despite often feeling discrimination. In any event, Walrond was largely forgotten by the time of his death in August 1966.

Walrond's life was filled with paradox. His links at various times with different movements may seem contradictory or self-serving, but his gradual evolution reflects stages also experienced by Claude McKay. Walrond and McKay, as West Indian Blacks, never felt completely at home in the United States or Europe. Exiles, as Edward Said has indicated, often feel a strong need to belong and join organizations in an attempt to fit in their new land (150). Walrond and McKay sought a place in Garveyism, the New Negro Movement, and socialism, but none of these movements adequately addressed the authors' concerns with race and identity. Ultimately, Walrond abhorred any movement that he felt was doctrinaire, one which stressed politics over art. Inevitably, as he became more closely involved with different political, social, and literary movements, he became disenchanted with the dogma that frequently accompanied them. As the fictional Cedric Williams, a West Indian short story writer modeled after Walrond in Wallace Thurman's *roman à clef, Infants of the Spring* (1932), says, "There is ample room for everyone to follow his own individual track. . . . Only in that way will anything at all be achieved" (240). The view expressed by Williams, that the Black artist is best served by keeping an independent mind rather than slavishly following any one specific ideology, is one with which Walrond would concur.

The dominating force in Walrond's life was not so much any political or literary "movement" as actual geographic "movement." The history of the Caribbean is one built on migration, both voluntary and enforced. It is a pattern that continues to this day.[16] Walrond felt this migration in his own life, having spent considerable time in six countries, four by the time he was twenty. Not surprisingly, the movement of Blacks within and to the Caribbean, the United States, and Europe is a major focus in his work.[17] As Robert Bone states, "[h]uman transplantation is Walrond's essential theme" (177). Although shortly after leaving America he would tell people in the Virgin Islands that he felt more American than West Indian (Gereau 1), he generally identified the Caribbean as "home." Therefore, he can look at himself in the United States as a "foreigner" (a term by which he defines himself in "Negro Literati"). The same is true of his life in France and England. That is why his work constantly returns to the area of his youth. Like many people from the Caribbean, Walrond became a permanent migrant, always having a sense of home while simultaneously feeling the loss of it. This contradiction is what often adds power and poignancy to his work. Despite the torture of living in an American or European society in which he faced racism he could neither understand nor accept, he returned to the Caribbean only for short visits. For this reason, perhaps, his work, as critics such as Hugh Gloster (181–83) have pointed out, is detached, enabling him to write objectively about the area. Such detachment is often true for writers in exile (Said 150–51).[18]

As Guyanese-born author Jan Carew notes, "[t]he Caribbean person is subjected to successive waves of cultural alienation from birth—a process that has its origins embedded in a mosaic of cultural fragments—Amerindian, African, European, Asian" (91). Michelle Cliff echoes this sentiment when she states, "[w]e are a fragmented people . . . coming from a culture of colonialism, a culture of Black people riven from each other" (60). Walrond throughout his adult life was fragmented wherever he lived because of his position as a racial and ethnic outsider. Edward Said, citing Theodor Adorno, expresses the belief that through writing, often of their native lands, many exiles attempt to gain wholeness. They are motivated "by the belief that the only home truly available now, though fragile and vulnerable, is in writing" (150). Walrond, recognizing the fragmentation in his life, felt the need to build a home. There is often an urgency in his writing to confront his own homelessness and that of people like him. His need to document their stories, record their achievements, and pass on their heritage is, in fact, his response to the fragmentation caused by migration and the pain caused by racial and ethnic prejudice. No other element resonates more strongly in Walrond's writing than this sense of racial consciousness. In his interview with Jacques Lebar he concludes: "My duty and my *raison d'être* are to give an accurate portrayal of my race, its history, its sufferings, its hopes and its rebellions. Therein lies a rich source of emotion and pain. It is there that I draw the essence of my work, and I will dedicate my energy as a writer to serving the Black race."[19]

Rebecca Chalmers Barton believes that Walrond and McKay are writers "of local color" (108). As such, they are trying to preserve in writing a vibrant oral tradition, a history the authors feel needs to be passed on. David Anderson, in a call for papers toward a book on Claude McKay, expresses the opinion "that McKay has been unjustly ignored, partly because his multinational career does not fit the nationalist criteria used to construct African American and Caribbean literary canons and partly because his multifaceted literary output over several decades does not fit within the narrow historical and cultural boundaries accorded such literary movements as the Harlem Renaissance" (158). These words also can be aptly applied to Walrond, who has been summarily dismissed in many studies of both African American and Caribbean literature, in large part because of the difficulty in categorizing him. Margaret Perry, for example, in her survey of Harlem Renaissance literature *Silence to the Drums*, says "Eric Waldrond's [sic] best stories were uniquely West Indian; hence, they should be examined as Caribbean literature" (111). However, Walrond's work, like that of McKay and many others born outside the United States, speaks forcefully for a large segment of America's population. It represents a voice that must not be forgotten.

NOTES

1. See the note to the story "Godless City," pp. 332–33 in this volume.

2. Statistics on Black immigrants are difficult to break down since no distinction tends to be made for place of origin. I have used Kasinitz's term to define West Indian: "people of African descent from the English-speaking Caribbean, including the mainland nations of Guyana and Belize, as well as their descendants from the English-speaking black diaspora communities in officially Spanish- and Dutch-speaking countries" (14).

3. Walrond criticizes Garvey more severely in "The Hebrews of the Black Race" (*International Interpreter* July 14, 1923). In this essay he condemns Garvey for stirring America's anti-West Indian sentiment. Walrond calls him "crude, blatant, egocentric, a mental lilliputian" who "by virtue of his upbringing, training, and early environment, is not representative of the best the West Indian Negroes have to offer."

Walrond wrote one final essay on Garvey, "Imperator Africanus" (1925). There he praises Garvey for his oratorical skills and his strong resistance to white racism, but in terms of business sense, he "is a hopeless nincompoop." Still, Walrond has some sympathy for Garvey, who remains "[u]daunted, unswerved" by the sniping of Du Bois and other Black leaders.

4. Walrond's move also marked another change in his life: his divorce from his Jamaican-born wife, Edith, with whom he had three daughters, Jean, Dorothy, and Lucille. According to Enid Bogle, Walrond remarried while in Europe (476).

5. The version of "The Palm Porch" contained in *The New Negro* seems very much like a draft. It is far less subtle in its usage of language and treatment of its subject matter than the story published a year later in *Tropic Death*. A comparison of the two pieces demonstrates Walrond's growth as a writer and also gives one an insight into Walrond's writing process.

6. Several of Walrond's letters to Countee Cullen are housed in the Countee Cullen Papers at the Amistad Research Center (Tulane University). Walrond discusses a number of his contemporaries in these missives. Particularly revealing is a letter dated October 26, 1925, in which he expresses his feelings on Fauset, Toomer, Hughes, McKay, Rudolph Fisher, and Cullen himself.

7. Linguists define a dialect as a variety of a language, characterized by a specific pronunciation, syntax, and vocabulary. However, the word "dialect" has become stigmatized in some non-linguistic quarters. I use "dialect" in the linguistic sense throughout my discussion of Walrond. For more on the subject, see Peter A. Roberts, *West Indians and Their Language*.

8. The story, however, mixes fictional elements with autobiography. Walrond, for example, emigrated to Panama when he was about thirteen, not eight, which is Gerald's age.

9. Walrond is more critical of the Plymouth Brethren in "Success Story."

10. For a list of reviews of *Tropic Death*, see John E. Bassett's *Harlem in Review: Critical Reactions to Black American Writers, 1917–1939* (Selinsgrove, Pa.: Susquehanna UP, 1992): 65–67.

11. Walrond attended Wisconsin in the spring of 1928. Earlier, he had

taken courses in creative writing and literature at City College of New York (1922–24) and Columbia University (1924–26). However, he never received a degree from any of these schools.

12. There is little documentation about the relationship between the two men while they were in England. However, if Garvey's letter to his wife Amy Jacques Garvey from May 25, 1937, is any indication, the Jamaican still had some concerns about Walrond's behavior: "The fellow Walron[d] I have here seems to have been making love to all of them [Garvey's housekeepers] at one and the same time. . . . All of them had a kind of masonry and I knew nothing about it" (Papers 7: 743).

13. Walrond was engaged in work besides writing in the mid-'30s. He was also touring Europe with a vaudeville troupe. According to one account, he served "as publicity manager of a Negro revue" (Daily Gleaner Apr. 5, 1935). It was reported that the act included a number of "old West Indian melodies," an indication that Walrond's interest in preserving Black culture remained intact.

14. An article stated that Walrond had been lost in a German air raid while serving in the Royal Air Force ("Eric Waldron [sic], Novelist, Lost in Air Raid," Chicago Defender April 29, 1944). The report of his being lost was apparently unfounded (Kaiser Index 5: 303).

15. The Roundway stories are available in the Countee Cullen/Harold Jackman collection at Atlanta University. The Review, a monthly publication of Roundway Hospital and Old Park House in Devizes, Wiltshire, circulated beyond the immediate hospital environs, and Walrond, in addition to contributing several pieces, served as assistant editor. He was a patient, voluntarily, at Roundway, a psychiatric hospital, from 1952 to September 1957. See his correspondence with Erica Marx, editor of the Hand and Flower Press, especially his letter from May 20, 1957 (box 12, folder 6, Hoyt William Fuller Collection, Atlanta University). For information on Roundway Hospital in the 1950s, see the Hospitals' Directory: England and Wales 1955 (London: Ministry of Health, 1956) and The Medical Directory 1954 (London: J. A. Churchill Ltd., 1954). Thanks to Cherryl Cooper for informing me that Roundway has since changed its name to Green Lane Hospital.

16. For example, three of the five largest sources of legal immigrants to New York City between 1990 and 1994 were Caribbean nations. Walrond's birthplace, Guyana, a country of only three-quarters of a million people, was fifth on this list (Dugger, New York Times Jan. 9, 1997).

17. Possibly because of his own migratory experiences, Walrond had an abiding interest in the movement of American Blacks to the North. In addition to "The Negro Comes North" and "From Cotton, Cane, and Rice Fields," Walrond published two other articles on the subject: "The Negro Migration to the North" (International Interpreter Aug. 18, 1923) and "The Negro Exodus from the South" (Current History Sept. 1923). Walrond's interest in migration was no doubt stimulated by his growing involvement with sociologist Charles S. Johnson beginning in 1923. As with much of his other writing, Walrond's essays

on migration emphasize the achievements of Blacks despite the obstacles they faced.

18. Said makes interesting distinctions between exiles, expatriates, émigrés, and refugees (147–48). Many West Indian writers have described themselves as exiles and written extensively on the topic (e.g., George Lamming's *The Pleasures of Exile* and V. S. Naipaul's *The Enigma of Arrival*).

19. "Mon devoir et ma raison d'être sont de peindre l'existence de ma race, son histoire, ses souffrances, ses espoirs et ses révoltes. Il y a là une source féconde d'émotions et de peines. C'est là que je puise les éléments de mon oeuvre et c'est au service de la race noire que je consacrerai mon activité d'écrivain." Thanks to Shondel Nero and Pascale Lavenaire for translating from the French.

WORKS CITED

Anderson, David. "Claude McKay." *PMLA* 113 (1998):158.

Barton, Rebecca Chalmers. *Black Voices in American Fiction, 1900–1930*. Oakdale, N.Y.: Dowling College P, 1976.

Beckles, Hilary. *A History of Barbados: From Amerindian Settlement to Nation-State*. New York: Cambridge UP, 1990.

Berry, Jay. "Eric Walrond." *Dictionary of Literary Biography*, vol. 51: *Afro-American Writers from the Harlem Renaissance to 1940*. Ed. Trudier Harris. Detroit: Gale, 1987. 296–300.

Bogle, Enid E. "Eric Walrond." *Fifty Caribbean Writers: A Bio-Bibliographical Critical Sourcebook*. Ed. Daryl Cumber Dance. Westport, Conn.: Greenwood, 1986. 474–82.

Bone, Robert. *Down Home: Origins of the Afro-American Short Story*. New York: Columbia UP, 1975.

Bontemps, Arna, and Langston Hughes. *Arna Bontemps–Langston Hughes Letters, 1925–1967*. Ed. Charles H. Nichols. New York: Dodd, Mead & Co., 1980.

Brawley, Benjamin. "The Negro Literary Renaissance." *The Southern Workman* 56 (Apr. 1927): 177–84.

Carew, Jan. *Fulcrums of Change: Origins of Racism in the Americas and Other Essays*. Trenton, N.J.: Africa World P, 1988.

Cliff, Michelle. "A Journey into Speech." *The Graywolf Annual Five: Multicultural Literacy*. Eds. Rick Simonson and Scott Walker. Saint Paul, Minn.: Graywolf P, 1988. 57–62.

Crowder, Henry, with Hugo Speck. *As Wonderful as All That?: Henry Crowder's Memoir of His Affair with Nancy Cunard, 1928–1935*. Navarro, Calif.: Wild Trees, 1987.

Domingo, W. A. "The Tropics in New York." *Survey Graphic* (Mar. 1, 1925): 648–50.

Du Bois, W. E. B. "Criteria of Negro Art." *Within the Circle: An Anthology of African American Literary Criticism from the Harlem Renaissance to the Present*. Ed. Angelyn Mitchell. Durham: Duke UP, 1994. 60–68.

————. "Five Books." *Crisis* 33 (Jan. 1927): 152.

Dugger, Celia W. "City of Immigrants Becoming More So in 90s." *New York Times* (Jan. 9, 1997): 1+.

"Eric Waldron [sic], Novelist, Lost in German Aid Raid." *Chicago Defender* (April 29, 1944): 1.

"Eric Walrond, Back in City, Feels No Homecoming Thrill." *New York Amsterdam News* (Sept. 9, 1931): 11.

Fabre, Michel. *From Harlem to Paris: Black American Writers in France, 1840–1980*. Urbana: U of Illinois P, 1991.

Ferguson, Blanche E. *Countee Cullen and the Negro Renaissance*. New York: Dodd, Mead & Co., 1966.

Garvey, Marcus. *The Marcus Garvey and Universal Negro Improvement Association Papers*. 7 vols. Ed. Robert A. Hill. Berkeley: U of California P, 1983–1990.

————, ed. *Black Man: A Monthly Magazine of Negro Thought and Opinion*. Comp. and ed. Robert A. Hill. Millwood, N.J.: Kraus-Thomson, 1975.

Gereau, Adolph. "With Eric Waldron [sic] at the Eureka." *Emancipator* (St. Thomas, Virgin Islands) (Apr. 3, 1929): 1.

Gloster, Hugh. *Negro Voices in American Fiction*. Chapel Hill: U of North Carolina P, 1948.

Holder, Calvin B. "The Causes and Composition of West Indian Immigration to New York City, 1900–1952." *Afro-Americans in New York Life and History* (Jan. 1987): 7–26.

Hughes, Langston. "Marl-Dust and West Indian Sun." *New York Herald Tribune* (Dec. 5, 1926): 9.

Hutchinson, George. *The Harlem Renaissance in Black and White*. Cambridge: Harvard UP, 1995.

Ikonné, Chidi. *From Du Bois to Van Vechten: The Early New Negro Literature, 1903–1926*. Westport, Conn.: Greenwood P, 1981.

The Kaiser Index to Black Resources, 1948–1986: From the Schomburg Center for Research in Black Culture of the New York Public Library. 5 vols. Brooklyn: Carlton Pub. Co., 1992.

Kasinitz, Philip. *Caribbean New York: Black Immigrants and the Politics of Race*. Ithaca, N.Y.: Cornell UP, 1992.

Kellner, Bruce. *The Harlem Renaissance: A Historical Dictionary for the Era*. Westport, Conn.: Greenwood P, 1984.

Lewis, David Levering. *When Harlem Was in Vogue*. New York: Oxford UP, 1981.

Locke, Alain, ed. *The New Negro*. 1925; rpt. New York: Atheneum, 1992.

McCullough, David. *The Path between the Seas: The Creation of the Panama Canal, 1870–1914*. New York: Simon & Schuster, 1977.

McKay, Claude. *A Long Way from Home*. New York: Lee Furman Inc., 1937.

Martin, Tony, ed. *African Fundamentalism: A Literary and Cultural Anthology of Garvey's Harlem Renaissance*. Dover, Mass.: Majority P, 1991.

————. *Literary Garveyism: Garvey, Black Arts and the Harlem Renaissance*. Dover, Mass.: Majority P, 1983.

Perry, Margaret. *Silence to the Drums: A Survey of the Literature of the Harlem Renaissance*. Westport, Conn." Greenwood P, 1976.

Ramchand, Kenneth. "The Writer Who Ran Away: Eric Walrond and *Tropic Death*." *Savacou* 2 (Sept. 1970): 67–75.

Richardson, Bonham C. *Panama Money in Barbados, 1900–1920*. Knoxville: U of Tennessee P, 1985.

Roberts, Peter A. *West Indians and Their Language*. New York: Cambridge UP, 1988.

Said, Edward. "Reflections on Exile." *Inventing America: Readings in Identity and Culture*. Eds. Gabriella Ibieta and Miles Orvell. New York: St. Martin's, 1996. 147–51.

Stovall, Tyler. *Paris Noir: African Americans in the City of Light*. Boston: Houghton Mifflin, 1996.

Thurman, Wallace. *Infants of the Spring*. 1932; rpt. Boston: Northwestern UP, 1992.

———. "Negro Artists and the Negro." *New Republic* (Aug. 31, 1927): 37–39.

Walrond, Eric. "Avec . . . Eric Walrond." Interview. By Jacques Lebar. *Lectures du Soir* (Jan. 14, 1933).

Walter, John C. "The Caribbean Immigrant Impulse in American Life: 1900–1930." *Revista/Review Interamericana* 11 (1981/1982): 522–44.

Watkins-Owens, Irma. *Blood Relations: Caribbean Immigrants and the Harlem Community, 1900–1930*. Bloomington: Indiana UP, 1996.

Wintz, Cary D. *Black Culture and the Harlem Renaissance*. Houston: Rice UP, 1988.

$\mathcal{A}$ Note on the Text

Most critics imply that Walrond wrote a relatively small amount; however, he actually compiled a fairly sizable body of work. He is, of course, best known for *Tropic Death* and I am grateful to Liveright, the present copyright holder, for allowing me to reprint the bulk of that volume. I have also tried to choose a representative sampling of his other fiction, essays, and reviews on a variety of topics relevant both to his time and our own. Walrond was a man filled with paradoxes. The selections in this volume reflect his shifting political and cultural impulses and his often conflicted status as a person of Caribbean heritage residing in America and Europe. Finally, the inclusion of several pieces written while he was in Europe may help to dispel the common assumption that he stopped writing entirely after he left the United States in 1928.

Walrond contributed to numerous publications, each with its own editorial policies. I have silently edited several minor punctuation discrepancies. A list of other emendations is provided on page 349. My general goal, however, has been to adhere to the texts as they were originally published. Several small omissions have been made, indicated in the text by three asterisks, when it was felt material would be irrelevant or confusing to readers. I have selectively provided annotations for terms (marked with an asterisk) that will likely be unfamiliar to a late twentieth-century American reader, at the end of the text.

Some Notes on Caribbean English

In his *Dictionary of Caribbean English Usage*, Richard Allsopp describes the English language in the Caribbean as "the oldest exportation of that language from its British homeland in the present fraternity of World English" (xli). The exportation of a language is not a static phenomenon, for a language must necessarily adapt itself to the place, time, and, of course, lived experience of the people who use it. Such is the case of Caribbean English—a linguistic mosaic of sub-varieties of English which emanates from the complex history, culture, and ecology of the Caribbean region.

Caribbean English emerged from a language contact situation whereby European colonizers imposed British English on a largely enslaved labor force who spoke a variety of ethnic languages. The result is what is commonly referred to in linguistics as a *creole continuum*, which includes a continuous spectrum of speech varieties ranging from the *basilect* (the most creolized form) to the *mesolect* (mid-range, less creolized varieties) to the *acrolect* (the standard variety—in this case, a Caribbean standard). To be sure, no clearly demarcated boundaries can be claimed along the continuum nor can strict homogeneity be established in regard to language use in the various Caribbean countries. Caribbean natives engage in a great amount of bidirectional style shifting along the continuum based on the interplay of a host of factors including social class, ethnicity, education, rural/urban provenance, formality/informality of the context, topic, audience, and so forth.

In trying to capture the range, cadences, and texture of Caribbean speech, Walrond undertook a monumental task. Not only are his characters as diverse as their language, but their experiences reach beyond the anglophone Caribbean into the francophone islands and Spanish-speaking Panama; hence the need to include the language of those territories. Add to this the fact that Walrond was writing at a time when very few writers dared to put Caribbean folk speech—a language with no standardized orthography—into written form. Yet Walrond, living outside of the Caribbean, captures the colorfulness of Caribbean speech with remarkable accuracy.

To the untrained ear or eye, Caribbean folk speech on the page can be disconcerting. While there is a wide variety of features that characterize Caribbean dialects, there are certain salient features that are common to most of them. Many of these features occur frequently in Walrond's stories. The following guide is offered to help the reader understand Walrond's representation of his characters' dialects. All examples are taken from Walrond's stories.

Syntax

1. Subject, object, and possessive pronouns are used in various sentence positions:

(a) Tek um back to *she* (Take it back to *her*).

(b) *'Im* bruk *'im* wheel barrow (*He* broke *his* wheelbarrow).

(c) *Me* too tiad (*I'm* too tired).

2. There is often no plural inflection /s/ in Creole when the noun is modified by a number greater than one, e.g.:

(a) "Me 'fraid say me can't give yo' mo' dan fifty pound o' ice."

Plurality can also be indicated by using "dem" either before or after the noun, e.g.:

(a) "dem low-neck dress she ah wear"

(b) "Oh, le' de picknee dem go."

3. Standard English regular past tense inflection "ed" as in "turned" is usually deleted. Tense in Creole English is indicated by context.

4. *Front focusing.* This phenomenon occurs when the speaker wants to emphasize a point. The main verb or clause of a sentence is introduced, then repeated in the sentence in normal position: "Is *rob* you want *rob* me" (meaning you seriously intend to rob me).

5. *Functional shift.* Because of a tendency toward economy of expression, Caribbean English maximizes its stock of vocabulary by having words take on multiple syntactic functions; thus, adjectives can function as adverbs and vice versa, nouns as verbs, and so forth. For example, "teef" (thief), normally a noun, functions as a verb (meaning "steal") in the following sentence: "Some people can *teef* an' got so much mout' besides."

6. *Phrasing.* Words are often repeated for emphasis: "a sulky, *cry cry,* suck-finger boy."

Pronunciation

CONSONANTS

Consonant clusters of all kinds, in any position in the word, tend to be reduced. The most common ones are:

1. /ŋ/ or *ng* as in "talking" is reduced to /n/ = "talkin'."

2. /ð/ or *th* as in "there" or "other" is reduced to /d/ = "dere," "odda."

3. /θ/ or *th* as in "thief" or "mouth" is reduced to /t/ = "teef," "mout'."

4. /st/ as in "best" or "just" is reduced to /s/ = "bes'," "jes'."

5. /n/ plus one or more consecutive consonants as in "don't" or "pound" is reduced to /n/ = "don'," "poun'."

6. In the case of /r/ plus one or more consecutive consonants as in "thirty," "first," "turn," or horse," the /r/ tends to be dropped: "thutty," "fuss," "tun," "hoss."

7. *Special case:* Barbadian speech often uses retroflexion, a strong rolling /r/: e.g., "Lorrd."

8. *Palatalization:* The insertion of the /y/ sound between any of the consonants /p,t,k,d,g/ and a following vowel, usually /a/. For example, "cyah" (care). This feature is common in Barbados, Guyana, and Jamaica.

9. *Special case: word-initial /h/.* /h/ in initial position tends to be dropped or added incorrectly, especially in Jamaican English. When /h/ is dropped "home" and "him" are pronounced "'ome" and "'im." Word-initial

additions of /h/ occur in the following examples: "hunions" (onions); "hice" (ice); "hawfissah" (officer).

VOWELS

1. After a vowel, an /r/ sound tends to be dropped:

(a) for = fo'

(b) your = yo'

(c) mister = mistah

2. In Jamaican Creole English, though, "her" is pronounced " 'ar."

3. The /o/ before some consonants is pronounced as /a/: e.g., "promise = "pramise."

Vocabulary

Caribbean English encompasses a wide vocabulary including words from standard World English as well as African, Creole, Indic, French, Spanish, Dutch, Portuguese, and Amerindian words.

1. *False friends.* In Walrond's stories there are several examples of standard English words that carry Creole meanings:

(a) tea = any hot beverage.

(b) hand = the part of the body from the shoulders to the fingers.

2. Preference for concrete, graphic descriptions: "water mout' " = "dribble."

Range of Speech

The range of speech in Caribbean English, measured loosely by the degree of "creoleness" or "standardness," is remarkably wide, such that the same person can sound decidedly different depending on the context. The aspiring socialite Miss Buckner, in the story "The Palm Porch," provides a good example. The following sentences were both addressed to her children:

1. "Mek fun, an' be a dam set o' fools all yo' life."

2. "Yo' think yo' don't! But don't fool yourselves, children, there is more to make the mare go than you think—I see that now."

The examples above are by no means exhaustive but should shed some light on the complexity of Caribbean dialects.

Shondel J. Nero

Assistant Professor of TESOL and Applied Linguistics

St. John's University

PART I

APPRENTICE WORK

*W*alrond's apprenticeship as a writer was served largely during his editorship of two widely different periodicals, the Universal Negro Improvement Association's (U.N.I.A.) *Negro World* and the National Urban League's *Opportunity*. His work with *Negro World* reflects his early attraction to the Garveyite movement. However, there are indications even then of his resistance to Garvey's use of writing for "propaganda." The selections included here demonstrate the conflicting feelings Walrond had toward Garvey and his philosophy, eventually leading to Walrond's departure from the movement.

Walrond's writings for *Opportunity* mark a change in direction from the days of his affiliation with the U.N.I.A. His association with Charles S. Johnson was in many ways the beginning of his New Negro days. Nevertheless, Walrond's fictional pieces for *Opportunity* (as well as for *Negro World* and *New Republic*) belong to this apprentice period, often demonstrating his experimentation with the permeable boundaries between journalism and fiction. At times, as in "On Being Black" and "Vignettes of the Dusk," Walrond loosely presents a series of different scenes, leaving it to the reader to connect them. In these sketches, we see him experimenting with the impressionistic technique which he would master in *Tropic Death*. Pieces such as "I Am an American" and "The Voodoo's Revenge" demonstrate his early interest in the Caribbean. The latter story, with its focus on *obeah* and revenge, is a harbinger of what would come in the more fully realized stories of *Tropic Death*.

Journalism

*A*rt and Propaganda

Ernest Boyd in the Literary Review criticizes the judges who awarded the coveted "Prix Goncourt" to Rene Marin, the Martiniquan Negro, whose "Batouala"* they adjudged the best French novel of the year. Tied to the conventions of literature, Boyd found too many African words in the book; it is replete with crotchets and quavers and demi semi-quavers. Ignoring the rules of rhetoric, the author plunges along at a desperate rate, forgetful of the landmarks of style, form, clarity. With all these things Mr. Boyd finds fault. Also, he sniffs at the introduction to the work, which is a carping, merciless indictment of the brutal colonial system of France. As far as Mr. Boyd can see, what on earth has all this to do with a work of art, a penetrating study of a savage chieftain? Incidentally, Mr. James Weldon Johnson throws a ray of light on the subject. Mr. Johnson tells us there is a tendency on the part of Negro poets to be propagandic. For this reason it is going to be very difficult for the American Negro poet to create a lasting work of art. He must first purge himself of the feelings and sufferings and emotions of an outraged being, and think and write along colorless sectionless lines. Hate, rancor, vituperation—all these things he must cleanse himself of.

From *Negro World* December 31, 1921.

But is this possible? The Negro, for centuries to come, will never be able to divorce himself from the feeling that he has not had a square deal from the rest of mankind. His music is a piercing, yelping cry against his cruel enslavement. What little he has accomplished in the field of literature is confined to the life he knows best—the life of the underdog in revolt. So far he has ignored the most potent form of literary expression, the form that brought Marin the Goncourt award. When he does take it up, it is not going to be in any half-hearted, wishy washy manner, but straight from the shoulder, slashing, murdering, disemboweling! In the manner of H. L. Mencken!*

$\mathcal{M}$arcus Garvey—A Defense

The favorite parting shot of "dishonorably discharged" officers of the Universal Negro Improvement Association is to yelp and howl about the "dictatorship" of Mr. Marcus Garvey. "The Great I Am," "Imperialist," "Czar," etc., are epithets familiar to those editors and journalists who delight in wallowing in the mire of scandal and vituperation. Of the methods and administrative policies of Mr. Garvey they say a "mouthful." It is unfortunate that he is so iron-fisted and damning in his relations with his associates. For this reason the personnel of his organization is "inferior" in point of "culture" and "refinement" and "education." There is no comparison with it and other organizations with better trained men in them, with staffs which boast of college professors and competent experts.

All along the line criticism is directed against him because he demands of those about him 100 per cent loyalty above everything else. It is even gossiped that men of "brains" and "experience" have been passed up in preference to men who have shown a maximum of interest in Africa's redemption! Why not? This policy is the outgrowth—the direct psychological reaction—of the tragedy, as the black world knows,

From *Negro World* February 11, 1922.

55

of appointing men of "brains" and "experience" to positions of trust and responsibility. From the beginning it was Mr. Garvey's rule to pick out the ablest men he could find and place them in executive office. Experience had taught him that to succeed, to carry out his monster program, brains, and brains of the highest order, had to be pressed into service. With that in mind, he went about the formation of a cabinet, examining, selecting, rejecting. In those days it mattered not where a man had come from, what church he attended, what association he was a member of. Only one thing counted—his fitness. After a rigorous investigation of his character and qualifications he was brought in, appointed according to his ability, and left to do his bit in the mighty cause of Africa's freedom. But what did the majority of them do? Did they start to work with the idea of rendering service to the cause, of subordinating personal greed and power to the larger interests of the movement? No. To them affiliation with it meant a means to a very definite personal end. Money, and as much of it as they could lay their hands on, was their purpose. Apart from that they had no interest in Mr. Garvey and his "crazy organization." In time exposures, expulsions and prosecutions followed.

The man's eyes began to open. Were all Negroes—so-called "educated" Negroes—crooks and liars? With his comparative analytical mind he dismissed that as Anglo-Saxon. That was the white man's way of summing up the whole race. But he had learned his lesson— a pretty dear one, indeed—and he was going to profit by it. What did he do? The fastidious smart-Aleck who drops into his office and overwhelms him with his "cultured" ways and courtly manners and his protestations of love for the Motherland is seen in his true colors. If necessary, czar-like methods are adopted to exclude rogues and traitors from the organization. "Once bitten, twice shy." Can you blame him?

The Dice of Destiny

Once in a while we hear of a white employer truculently discharging a Negro who is in sympathy with the radical doctrines of Mr. Marcus Garvey. "Go to Garvey," screams the irate capitalist; "go and let him give you a job." The upshot of the matter is a minority of colored people are of the opinion that Mr. Garvey's philosophy is untimely and premature and inimical to the prosperity of the race. But these people, unfortunately, are misguided. They ought to remember that whenever a white man opposes a movement started by black people in the interest of black people, it is the best proof of that movement's virtue and timeliness. And when a white employer vents his spleen in such a high-handed manner, he unconsciously betrays fear of the awful potentialities of such a movement. White-like, he thinks of self-preservation, and the easiest way to gratify that is to "take it out of" his Negro help. But this ought to be a scorching lesson to the Negro. It ought to fortify him, to bring to his mind's eye the tragedy of what it is to be black, and upstanding. It ought to send him out in the world with the film torn from his eyes, seeing the red monster labeled race prejudice in all his grizzly colors. And then, when he comes to

From *Negro World* March 11, 1922.

retrospect, to think of casting the dice of destiny, he is convinced that the organization that brings terror to the hearts of white men is the one for him!

$\mathcal{V}$isit to Arthur Schomburg's Library Brings out Wealth of Historical Information

A visit to Arthur Schomburg's library! It is easy to appreciate why writers and artists, poets and anthologists, of both races, flock to the unpretentious little dusty-brown house on Kosciusko street. Not only is it famous for its golden treasures, but the man, the mighty human spirit behind it, is the most precious, the most interesting curio of all.

The young lady* in our party is a Columbia student who abominates what she contemptuously calls "form" and "useless ceremony." She has had experience with Negro celebrities. She knows what to expect; therefore, she went armed. Armed to her pearl-white teeth. As we put our feet on the hollowed ground and the warm glitter of Mr. Schomburg's brown-black eyes shone down upon us, she gave way to a characteristic weakness—whispering—whispering out of the corner of her beautiful mouth.

"Well, I declare," stamping a petulant foot. "Why, I am flabbergasted. I expected to find a terribly austere giant who looked at me out of withering eyes. But the man is human, ponderously, overwhelmingly human, a genuine eighteen karat."

From *Negro World* April 22, 1922.

We enter a sitting room that exudes a classic odor. On the walls are a mezzotint of St. George, a water color drawing of a Negro drum-major in Queen Anne's army, a sylph-like sketch of an Ethiopian princess, prints and pictures, paintings and daguerreotypes.

"What would you like to do first?" It was Mr. Schomburg's amiable voice. "Here I have a set of books on Hayti. I'd like to show you Baron De Vastey's 'Cry of the Fatherland in the Interest of all Haytians,'* which is, of course, a very valuable work. Spencer St. John* wrote a famous book on the black republic, too. Yes, miss, help yourself. Here is Madison's 'History of Hayti,' in three volumes. Oh, yes, Japan vellum is expensive, but I believe in expensive printing.

"Over here is a book I'd like to call your attention to. It is Henry Calloway's personal copy of 'Zulu Folk Lore,'* bound in morocco. It proves that the Zulus, like the Jews and Russians, had a folk lore of their own, and— How did I get it? Oh, well, that is neither here nor there—"

"But tell us," went up a chorus.

"You see Calloway presented it to Ralston, president of the Folk Lore Society of London; and Ralston, upon his death, willed it to Andrew Long,* the celebrated writer. Later it strayed into the library of a famous Lord Somebody in London and I got it at a sale. As you see, it was set up and run off by Negro printers in Springvale, Natal, in 1868. That was the beginning of folk lore in Africa."

"I imagine," breathed one of us, "he must have a lot of money to be able to buy all these books."

But Mr. Schomburg had overheard.

"That is the mistake a lot of people make. Because I buy a lot of books it does not mean that I have a lot of money. I can't spend it and have it too.

"Here is something I'd like you to make note of. Our friend James Weldon Johnson has just got out a 'Book of American Negro Poetry,'* but it seems as if he has neglected a very important poet, and that is Leo, of British Guiana. Here is his 'Poetical Works.'" ***

"Why, Leo is one of the greatest Negro poets in history. I can't for the life of me see why Mr. Johnson overlooked him.

"There are two other things I don't like in that 'Book of American Negro Poetry,'" continued Mr. Schomburg, "and they are, one, the part about Negro music, and, two, the inclusion of Dr. DuBois as a poet. DuBois is no poet. If Johnson wanted to write on music, he should not mix it up with poetry."

Asked to approximate the total number of books by Negro authors in his possession, and the subjects about which they wrote, Mr. Schomburg replied: "I think I've got about 2,000 books by Negro writers, and they cover every imaginable subject under the sun—science, mathematics, religion, philosophy, psychology, finance—everything. ***

"Say Miss Hurston, I don't suppose you know who Francis Baker* was—"

"Oh, yes, I read Bacon's essays at Howard."

"Not Bacon. Barker—Francis Barker. Barker was private secretary to Samuel Johnson. Here is a letter I received a few years ago from the author of Barker's Life. Barker was a slave, and Johnson, so impressed was he with his literary and aesthetic sense, made him his amanuensis. Read it." ***

But all of this was very fine, interesting, and all that. It is certainly heartening to be able to look Gertrude Atherton* in the eye and inform her that Alex. Hamilton was unquestionably a Negro. Did we not have our hands on a copy of "The Afro-American Magazine," published in 1859 at 48 Beekman street, New York, by a descendent of Hamilton— Thomas Hamilton—and reputed to be the most literary periodical by Negroes in America? Of course. But the motif, the raison d'etre, the whys and wherefores, the philosophy, the spirit of the man—that is the thing I wanted to get at. I communicated my desire to him.

"Ah, my boy, I don't as a rule, submit to interviews. Interviewers are always lying about me. How I started? Oh, I think it was way back in my school days in Porto Rico. I used to attend el Instituto Nacional, and it was a passion for us boys to collect books about poets. Of course, the white boys would collect books about the white poets, and I decided I'd fish out all the books I could by black poets. And I am still doing it. Not so very long ago my lodge, Prince Hall, gave me a beautiful gold medal," and he showed it to us, "for my services to the lodge. I came to America thirty years ago with the intention of studying medicine. But I perished by the wayside. Instead, I became interested in the struggle for independence in Cuba and Porto Rico. I was secretary of one of the revolutionary clubs, Las Dos Antillas, and charter member of the Porto Rican Revolutionary Party until it was dissolved by order of the U.S. Government. At present I am employed as chief of the mailing department of the Bankers Trust Company."

Developed and Undeveloped Negro Literature

WRITERS DESERT GREAT FIELD OF FOLK-LIFE FOR PROPAGANDISM

*** We now come to Paul Laurence Dunbar, dean of American Negro writers. Born in Dayton, in 1872, Dunbar worked as an elevator operator; his education was limited. His first volume, "Oak and Ivy," was published in 1893 at his own expense. Peddling his own poems became so distasteful that he swore he would prefer to go unsung rather than do it again. And he did not have to. William Dean Howells took an interest in him and wrote an introduction to "Lyrics of Lowly Life," which appeared a few years later. In his dialect poems, irresistible in humor and pathos, and his short stories of southern Negro life, a master of his art, Dunbar depicted the Negro as he is. Yet that does not mean that he was not capable of classic prose. Realizing that a Negro poet is expected to sing the songs of the cotton fields in the language of the cotton fields, Dunbar wrote dialect. ***

There is only one Negro writer with whom we may compare Dunbar, and that is the late Charles W. Chestnutt,* the novelist. Not so very long ago a book reviewer for a New York paper told us he thought "it was time for the Negro to return to the age of Chestnutt; that there is so much bite and venom and vituperation in his work." Exactly. But why Chestnutt?

From *The Dearborn Independent* May 13, 1922.

Why not Dunbar? Author of "The Conjure Woman," a volume of short stories: "The Wife of His Youth and Other Stories of the Color-Line," a biography of Frederick Douglass, and three novels, Chestnutt not only did not interpret the soul-movements of the black race, as Dunbar did, but he was—especially in "The Marrow of Tradition"—a purpose novelist, a propagandist. Indeed, Chestnutt, from his lofty pedestal, saw the red monster of race prejudice in all its sordid colors and leveled his javelin at it. It is regrettable for there is not the slightest doubt that Chestnutt knew how to write, and wrote trenchantly.

Another Negro novelist who fell by the wayside is Dr. W. E. B. DuBois, editor of the *Crisis*. It is no idle cant to state that Dr. DuBois is one of the most brilliant prose writers in America today. Oh, if he would only stop writing history and sociology and stick to the art of fiction! Then critics like Charles Hanson Towne would not be able to talk—as he does in his review of T. S. Stribling's Negro novel, "Birthright"*—about the decadence of black writers; of the inability of the Negro to write a great novel about himself. But DuBois, a wizard at words, is probably serving his race best in his present position. ***

One reason why the Negro has not made any sort of headway in fiction is due to the effects of color prejudice. It is difficult for a Negro to write stories without bringing in the race question. As soon as a writer demonstrates skill along imaginative lines he is bound to succumb to the temptations of reform and propaganda. That is why it was possible for Alexandre Dumas and Pushkin in Russia to write colorlessly; and it also explains why Negro poets and novelists in Spanish-America are not limited by the narrowness of color. It is not a strange thing to find educated Negroes objecting strenuously to stories that do not depict the "Higher Form" of Negro life, stories whose characters are not all Negroes.

Friends of the Negro, like Miss Ovington,* sigh at the vast patches of color open to the Negro fictionist—the soft rhythmic stream of life in the Negro Quarter. From Dixie issues the murmur of voices—the melodies of black millions—crying for a dusky satirist, a DuBois, to pen a tragic epic on "The Glory and Chivalry of the South."

*B*ert Williams Foundation
Organized to Perpetuate Ideals
of Celebrated Actor

On March 4, 1922, at the very
height of his career, Bert Williams, the Negro star actor, died—a martyr
to his art. This and other illuminating facts are graphically set forth
in a volume just issued by the English Crafters, 12 West Sixty-ninth
street, New York city, called "Bert Williams, Son of Laughter." The
author, Mabel Rowland, for sixteen years was the comedian's publicity
expert and secretary. More than any one who had the distinction of
being closely associated with him, she knows the ups and downs of
his celebrated career—the bitter and the sweet portions of it. In a
richly sympathetic volume Miss Rowland has preserved for posterity
the priceless heirlooms of Bert Williams' character, both on and off the
stage, and as an actor, a partner, a husband and a celebrity. Through it
all there runs a poignant strain—a strain of melancholy—a nostalgia
of the soul—of the blackface comedian who wanted to follow in the
footsteps of celebrated Negro actors like Ira Aldridge,* who wanted to
play "Othello" and other non-comical pieces. In this book Williams is
made to live. One sees him, a handsome youth, just from Antigua, West

From *Negro World* April 21, 1923.

Indies, where he was born, coming to America; later shuffling about San Francisco as a singer, a cabaret entertainer.

On to Chicago and later to New York as a headliner. Crowning it all is the command to present "In Dahomey"* for the artistic tasting of the late King Edward of England. It is a biographic treasure. For—there is no doubt about it—Bert Williams will go down in history alongside the great artists of the theatre of all time. To us, to whom he meant so much as an ambassador across the border of color, his memory will grow richer and more glorious as time goes on. For Bert Williams blazed the trail to Broadway for the Negro actor. It was he who made it possible for shows like "Shuffle Along," "The Plantation Revue," "Liza" and "Strut Miss Lizzie"* to go on Broadway. Not only that, but serious dramas of a tragic-superstitious nature which require a great deal of emotional acting, like "Taboo" and "The Emperor Jones," of which Charles Gilpin,* a contemporary of Williams, was star—plays of this sort Bert Williams was directly responsible for bringing to Broadway.

One of the things that we get on reading this book is Bert Williams' dominant melancholia. Some day one of our budding story writers ought to sit down and write a novel with a Negro protagonist with melancholia as the central idea. Bert Williams had it. Although it was his business to make people laugh, there were times when he would go into his shell-like cave of a mind and reflect—and fight it out.

"Is it worth it?" One side of him would ask, "Is it worth it—the applause, the financial rewards, the fame? Is it really worth it—lynching one's soul in blackface twaddle?"

"But it is the only way you can break in," protests the other side of the man. "It is the only way. That is what the white man expects of you—comedy—blackface comedy. In time, you know, they'll learn to expect serious things from you. In time."

With that Bert Williams bore the brunt of ridicule—of ridicule from the Negro press—and fought his noble fight. Today the results are just coming to light. The demand for Negro shows on Broadway is taking a number of Negro girls and men out of kitchens and pool rooms and janitor service.

Bert Williams' tree—to him one of gall—is already beginning to bear fruit, and there is no telling how long the harvest will last. ***

$\mathcal{E}$l Africano

Henry O. Tanner, the Negro artist whose paintings adorn the Louvre in Paris, and Alfred Smith,* whose etchings of Toussaint L'Ouverture, Frederick Douglass, Paul Lawrence Dunbar, Phyllis Wheatley and other Negro Immortals are at present on exhibition at the 135th Street of the New York Public Library, are so far the two most outstanding painters of color of note known to us on this side of the Atlantic.

In Spain, however, there is a painter in whose veins runs the noble blood of Africa who is conceded by the foremost art critics of Europe to be the greatest imaginative painter in the world. The story of this Negro artist, who has never had a lesson in his life, reads like a chapter from a richly woven romance by Poushkin or Dumas. Born on the Canary Isles but thirty years ago Nestor Martin Fernandez de la Torré as a very young man became famous as a swimmer in the sea between the Canary Islands and the Moroccan coast. Idolized as the peer, by reason of the lofty reach of his imagination, of such internationally famous painters as Sorrolla and Zuloaga,* de la Torré is adored by the nobility of Old Spain as "El Africano." Some of his mural paintings actually take one's

From *The Crisis* August 23, 1923. Reprinted with permission.

breath away. For superb skill, originality, deftness of execution, and sheer gorgeousness, they are unparalleled. Some of the shrewdest art critics of Europe, like Antonio Zarraga, are overwhelmed at the mighty sweep of his imagination. Only Montecelli* whose canvases are still a mystery to civilization, flung paint on in that way. This, this utter disregard for convention, plus an uncanny genius for color, is even astonishing to sophisticated Spain. The secret of it is that de la Torré is a genius of the rarest water who looks out on the boulevard of life from the romantic point of view of a Negro. Were he a literary artist he would be a combination of Balzac, Pierre Loti, Lafcadio Hearn,* Joseph Conrad and de Maupassant.

Nobody paints or has painted the sea as he is painting it today. In every artist's life it is inexorable that environment—early environment—play a determining part. This is particularly true in de la Torré's case. His masterpiece, "The Dream of Life On Lost Atlantis," is the result of years of dreaming and exotic languoring on the lovely coast of Morocco. It is pagan in its beauty. There is nothing like it in all art—this gorgeous bit of oriental tapestry.

Some of his work, a series of four mural paintings, are soon to be privately exhibited in America. These are said to be as magnificent as anything done by Gustav de la Touche.* No one has painted the land as he is painting it, except, possibly, the Chinese draftsmen in the days of Ming and a few of the Japanese when they showed us the moon above Fujiyama. Besides that, de la Torré, when he is not painting the nobility of Old Spain or celebrities like Guerra, the actress, Granada, the composer, and others, goes to the great centers of Europe designing magnificent dresses for women of princely rank. He also designs jewelry, necklaces, and gowns, and in this field he is said to be the equal of Erte.*

Fiction

$\mathcal{A}$ Senator's Memoirs

As I turn back to the period of adolescence in the history of the darker races; as I behold the strong men of the earth flying at each other's throats over the spoils of a wretched war; as I gaze upon the spectacle of nations born and bred in the cradle of chivalry sinking their claws into the treasure-chests of bedridden Africa; as I observe white men banking—laying out actual cash—on the perpetual inertia of the black race—God, how the memory of this oppresses me!—as I imagine a pageant of the crimes and blasphemies perpetuated against us for ages and ages—I shudder at the thought of the fate and future of a "backward" race.

Thanks to Jehovah, I am a free man—free to traverse the surface of the earth—free to stop and dine at any hostelry I wish—free! As I sit here and dash off these notes I cannot but think it all a massive dream. Twenty years ago, as a stranded emigrant on the shores of Egypt, if I had been told that I'd be out here, on my own estate, drinking of the transcendent beauty of the Congo, a master of my people, to be honored and respected, I'd have discounted it as an overworking of the imagination. ***

From *Negro World* December 17, 1921.

Ah, as I give way to retrospection, to think that after all those years of oppression—to think that a "trifling incident" as the outraging of a dark-skinned maiden on the streets of Harlem would lead to such a turbulent conflagration. Then, as if the hand of Providence was back of it all, a self-willed statesman at the London Conference, in a moment of fury, boxed the ears of the Nipponese prince.

For a moment the fate of civilization rested in the palm of a yellow man's hand. But Tokugawa, as cool as a cucumber, packed his grip and quietly set sail for the Orient.

Three months later, as the shadows of darkness fell and a million mud-fires sparkled on the banks of the Island Empire, three men—a Japanese, an East Indian and a Maroon descendant—knelt, and plotted the doom of the white world.***

Liberty Square. This is a place that always brings me back to the age of freedom. There is a spirit of love and equality and righteousness about it that thrills me. It is a huge park, a bandstand or speakers' gallery in the center, and for three miles I saw nothing but myriad brown-faced people. From the banks of the Zambesi, from across the Nile, from South Africa, Liberia, Hayti, America—they stood, a free and redeemed people!

As Senator from the Congo, I was escorted to the gallery. To think that I, a cabinet officer, unaware of the significance of the occasion! May tenth! Ten years of African independence! Assets? Ah, tortuous memory, a stable government, an army second to none, a place among the powers of the earth—but, no, let me get off the stage of action and present the prince of men to you.

A chorus of cheers deafens us as a little man, in a white tunic, stepped forward on the principal speakers' rostrum. A life packed with dramatic climaxes, a man whose mental fiber ripens with the avalanche of time—there he stood—grim in the sunlight —there—hail him, boys— Garvey!

"Citizens of Africa Redeemed, I come once more before you to give an account of ten years of my administration as President of the Republic of Africa. First, I wish it to be known that despite what the political economists had to say about us as a race of shiftless parasites, we've been able to organize and operate successfully a chain of national banks throughout the continent of Africa. Also, as far as I can gather from the Minister of Commerce, the exports of Africa to foreign countries for the ten years of native rule amount to $500,000,000,000. Incidentally, the merchandise in question, which consisted of balata, cocoa, gold, diamonds, sheep skins, steel, coal, etc., was shot to all parts of the globe in the ships of the Black Star Line.*

"The promulgation of the Civil Service act and the organization of a modern system of public education throughout the land, I believe, will tend to eliminate corruption, inefficiency and graft in the governmental departments. At present, in spite of all that is being said in the enemy press, the rights of African citizens abroad are being safeguarded by a competent diplomatic corps. Only a few days ago the government of Australia was forced to abrogate its infamous exclusion laws as a result of action brought by our ambassador at Sydney.

"As regards the matter of land armament, the Republic of Africa voted at an extraordinary session of the cabinet on February 6 to appropriate £10,000,000 yearly for the maintenance of a standing army of 1,000,000 men. This is independent of naval construction, as Liberia, as you all know, is virtually a shipbuilding base, and the construction of battle cruisers is proceeding at a phenomenal rate."

Tears trickled down my enflamed cheeks as I forced my way out of the intense multitude. If the God of Hosts had come down on earth the transfiguration could not have been more complete. The Bishop of West Africa then leaped to the platform, and, as one man, the mighty arena of freemen sank down on their knees and sang hosannahs to Him.

$\mathcal{A}$ Black Virgin

Yesterday I strode into the library and had a glimpse of her. I cross over to the table next to the paper rack so as to be able to get a good look at her. She sat simply at her task, not ten yards from me, her eyes fixed on the writing she was doing. Her eyelids are long—and fluttering. Entranced, I gaze, not impudently, as becomes a street urchin, but penetratingly, studying the features of this exquisite black virgin. Her hair is black—a mass of shining curls. Bobbed. She is not what F. Scott Fitzgerald or the editors of Mr. Hearst's "American" would call a flapper. The pink in the pigment of her velvety black skin is evident. I can see it boring its way to the front. My inquisitive mind sends me farther. I look at her throat. It is long and slender and beautiful. It is not confusing in its color, as are her eyes. It brings about a sort of equilibrium of her entire exotic being. What shall I call it? Olive? Too misleading a word. Or ripe star-apple?* That's more like it. . . . For a long time I sit there dreaming—dreaming—dreaming. Of what? Of the fortunes of the flower of youth? Of the curse of bringing a girl of her color into the world? Of fight, of agitation, of propaganda? No. Clearly separating my art from my propaganda, I sit and prop my chin on my palm

From *Negro World* February 11, 1922.

and wish I were an artist. On my canvas I'd etch the lines of her fleeting figure, I'd know to a T the right shades of color to use to transform her madonna-like face for the world to look and sigh at. Her eyes, her hair, her teeth, her lips—God, those lips! . . . The place is close and I start to go. But before I do that a strange temptation seizes me. Her voice. I wonder what it is like? I go to her. "Will—will—you please tell me where I can find a copy of 'Who's Who in America?'" I startle her. Like a hounded hare she glances at me. Shy. Self-conscious, I think of my unshaved neck and my baggy trouser knees. I fumble at the buckles of my portfolio. Those eyes! I never saw anything so intensely mystical, so appealing, so full of pathos and the emotions of a soul. "Why, yes, I think there is one over there." Her voice falls on my ear as the ripple of a running stream. Her face I love—her voice I adore. It is so young, so burdened with life and feeling. I follow the swish-swish of her skirt, I get the book and she is gone—gone out of my life!

On Being Black

I go to an optician and ask for a pair of goggles. My eyes are getting bad and my wife insists upon my getting them. For a long time I have hesitated to do so. I hated to be literary—that is, to look literary. It is a fad, I believe. On an afterthought I am convinced she is right; I need them. My eyes are paining me. Moreover, the lights in the subway are blindingly dark, and head swirling. Again, the glitter of spring sends needles through my skull. I need the things badly. I decide to go to the optician's. I go. It is a Jewish place. Elderly is the salesman. I put my cards on the table. . . . "Fine day, isn't it?" He rubs and twists his pigmy fingers and ambles back to the rear. A moment later he returns. With him is a tray of jewelry—lenses and gold rings, diamonds and silver frames. Fine, dainty, effeminate things.

"Here is a nice one," chirps the old gentleman in a sing-song tone, as he tries to fit it on to my nose. "Just the right kind of goggles to keep the dust from going into your eyes. Only the other day I sold—"

At first I feel as if it is one of these confounded new fangled things. Overnight they come, these new styles. Ideas! Here, I whisper to myself,

From *The New Republic* November 1, 1922.

is a new one on me. But I look again. It has a perforated bit of tin on either side of it, like the black star-eyed guard on a horse's blinker.

"Oh, I can show you others, if you don't like that one. Want one with a bigger dust piece? I have others back here. Don't be afraid, I'll fix you up. All the colored chauffeurs on Cumberland Street buy their glasses here."

"But I am not a chauffeur," I reply softly. Were it a Negro store, I might have said it with a great deal of emphasis, of vehemence. But being what it is, and knowing that the moment I raise my voice I am accused of "uppishness," I take pains—oh such pains, to be discreet. I wanted to bellow into his ears, "Don't think every Negro you see is a chauffeur." But the man is overwhelmingly amused. His snow-white head is bent—bent over the tray of precious gold, and I can see his face wrinkle in an atrociously cynical smile. But I cannot stand it—that smile. I walk out.*

II

I am a stenographer. I am in need of a job. I try the employment agencies. I battle with anaemic youngsters and giggling flappers. I am at the tail end of a long line—only to be told the job is already filled. I am ignorantly optimistic. America is a big place; I feel it is only a question of time and perseverance. Encouraged, I go into the tall office buildings on Lower Broadway. I try everyone of them. Not a firm is missed. I walk in and offer my services. I am black, foreign-looking and a curio. My name is taken. I shall be sent for, certainly, in case of need. "Oh, don't mention it, sir. . . . Glad you came in. . . . Good morning." I am smiled out. I never hear from them again.

Eventually I am told that that is not the way it is done here. What typewriter do I use? Oh,—. Well, go to the firm that makes them. It maintains an employment bureau, for the benefit of users of its machine. There is no discrimination there; go and see them. Before I go I write stating my experience and so forth. Are there any vacancies? In reply I get a flattering letter asking me to call. I do so.

The place is crowded. A sea of feminine faces disarms me. But I am no longer sensitive. I've got over that—long since. I grind my teeth and confidently take my seat with the mob. At the desk the clerks are busy telephoning and making out cards. I am sure they do not see me. I am just one of the crowd. One by one the girls, and men, too, are sent out after jobs. It has been raining and the air is frowsy. The Jewish girls are sweating in their war-paint. At last they get around to me. It is my turn.

I am sitting away down at the front. In order to get to me the lady is obliged to do a lot of detouring. At first I thought she was about to go out to go past me. But I am mistaken. She takes a seat right in front of me, a smile on her wrinkled old-maidish face. I am sure she is the head of the department. It is a situation that requires a strong diplomatic hand. She does not send one of the girls. She comes herself. She is from Ohio, I can see that. She tries to make me feel at home by smiling broadly in my face.

"Are you Mr.—?"

"Yes."

"That's nice. Now how much experience you say you've had?"

She is about to write.

"I stated all that in the letter, I think. I've had five years. I worked for—"

"Oh yes, I have it right here. Used to be secretary to Dr.—. Then you worked for an export house, and a soap manufacturer. Also as a shorthand reporter on a South American paper. That is interesting; quite an experience for a young man, isn't it?"

I murmur unintelligibly.

"Well," continues the lady, "we haven't anything at present—"

"But I thought you said in your letter that there is a job vacant. I've got it here in my pockets. I hope I haven't left it at home—"

"That won't suit you. You see it—it—is a post that requires banking experience. One of the biggest banks in the city. Secretary to the vice-president. Ah, by the way; come to think of it, you're just the man for it. You know Mr.— of Lenox Avenue? You do! I think the number is—Yes, here it is. Also one of his cards. Well, if I were you I would go and see him. Good day."

Dusk is on the horizon. I am once more on Broadway. I am not going to see the man on Lenox Avenue. It won't do any good. The man she is sending me to is a pupil of mine!

III

My wife's health is not very good and I think of sending her to the tropics. I write to the steamship company and in reply I receive a sheaf of booklets telling me all about the blueness of the Caribbean, the beauty of Montega Bay,* and the fine a la carte service at the Myrtle Bank Hotel. I am intrigued—I think that is the word—by a three months' cruise at a special rate of $150.00. I telephone the company in an effort to get some information as to sailing dates, reservations, and so forth.

"I understand," I say to the young man who answers the telephone, "I understand that you have a ship sailing on the tenth. I would like to reserve a berth at the $150.00 you are at present offering."

"White or colored?"

"Colored."

Evidently the clerk is consulting someone. But his hand is over the mouthpiece and I can not hear what he is saying. Presently—

"Better come in the office and make reservations."

"What time do you close?"

"Five o'clock."

"What time is it now, please?"

"Ten to."

"Good," I hurry, "I am at Park Place now. Do you think if I hop on a Broadway trolley I can make it before five?"

"I don't know," unconcernedly.

I am at the booking desk. It is three minutes to five. The clerks, tall, lean, light-haired youths, are ready to go home. As I enter a dozen pairs of eyes are fastened upon me. Murmuring. Only a nigger. Again the wheels of life grind on. Lots are cast—I am not speaking metaphorically. The joke is on the Latin. Down in Panama he is a government clerk. Over in Caracas, a tinterillo,* and in Mexico, a scientifico. I know the type. Coming to New York, he shuns the society of Spanish-Americans. On the subway at night he reads the New York Journal instead of La Prensa.* And on wintry evenings, you can always find him around Seventy-second Street and Broadway. The lad before me is dark, has crystal brown eyes, and straight black hair.

"I would like," I begin, "to reserve a passage for my wife on one of your steamers to Kingston. I want to get it at the $150.00 rate."

"Well, it is this way." I am positive he is from Guayaquil.* "It will cost you $178.00."

"Why $178.00?"

"You see, the passage alone is $170.00—"

"A hundred and seventy dollars! Why, this booklet here says $150.00 round trip. You must have made a mistake."

"You see, this $150.00 rate is for three in a room, and all the rooms on the ship sailing on the tenth are already taken up."

"All right," I decide, "the date is inconsequential. What I want is the $150.00 rate. Reserve a berth for me on any ship that is not already filled up. I don't care how late in the summer it is. I have brought a deposit along with me—"

I am not truculent. Everything I say I strive to say softly, unoffensively —especially when in the midst of a color-ordeal!

"Well, you'd have to get two persons to go with her." The Peruvian is independent. "There are only three berths in a stateroom, and if your wife wants to take advantage of the $150.00 rate, she will have to get two other colored persons to go with her."

"I s-e-e!" I mutter dreamily. And I did see!

"Come in tomorrow and pay a deposit on it, if you want to. It is five o'clock and—"

I am out on the street again. From across the Hudson a gurgling wind brings dust to my nostrils. I am limp, static, emotionless. There is only one line to Jamaica, and I am going to send her by it. It is the only thing to do. Tomorrow I am going back, with the $178.00. It pays to be black.

I Am an American

I had deserted the languor of the prado* to explore the depths of those labyrinthian callecitas* one associates instinctively with the mystic lore of brujeria.* It was two o'clock in the morning. Along el Avenida Italia old ragged brown women smoking Ghanga weed—"It mek you smaht lek a flea"—huddled up against the picturesque dwellings. Taxis filled with carnivalling crowds sped by. Foreign seamen staggered half-drunk out of Casas Francesas. Doggoning the heat Babbitt* and silk-sweatered Myra clung desperately to flasks of honest-to-goodness Bacardi. Bewitching senoritas in opera wraps of white and orange and scintillating brown stept out of gorgeous limousines.

Nostalgically I dug into the bowels of the dingy callecitas. Something, I don't know what, drew me, led me on. Was it the glamor of the tropical sky, the hot, voluptuous night, the nectar of Felipe's cebada?* Or, maybe, the intriguing echo of Mademoiselle's "Martinique! Hola, Martinique!" as the taxi skiddadled around the corner? It was all of these and more. Yonder, in those open cafes (doesn't it ever rain in Habana?) scores of youths tranquilly sipt rum and wine and anisette. In the parque scores

From *Negro World* April 7, 1923.

more sat on benches and softly talked—not of the overwhelming cares of this world, not of the relative fitness of Ambassador Crowder,* but talk, talk, for the sheer beauty of it.

On I drifted. In the middle of every block I saw native laborers sleeping on the piazzas. In dark shadowy halls, black folk, ulcered, leprous, unwashed, victims of the hideous wiles of brujeria, sang and crooned and rocked their knees while they fondled statuettes of the Virgin. Half an hour later I emerged on a boulevard of Andalusian architecture—El Paseo Malecon. It overlooked the sea. For miles a wall fringed it. On the wall I sat and dreamt and gazed across the bay at the dark outlines of Morro Castle. Violet-like was the blueness of the Caribbean. It licked the black rocks at my feet. Above stars of silver glittered in an ebony sky. It was an ideal night.

Not a soul was in sight. The paseo was deserted. Reluctantly I tore myself away and started back. I walked as in a nightmare up the silent paseo. In the distance I espied a figure. No, the paseo was not deserted, after all. There was a man coming towards me. He had on sandals and dragged his feet after him as he walked, as if they were swollen. Nearer I closely examined him. He had on a sailor jacket, crocus bag* trousers, and a woolen cap pulled over his eyes. I stopped him and asked him to show me the way back. He threw back his head—he had to—to answer me. I could not see his eyes. I saw, or thought I saw, two bits of coal blazing at me. No mistake about his cheeks, however. They were round as apples and black as jet. But the amazing thing about my derelict friend was the first words that came out of his mouth, "I am an American, I am. I came from—" He mentioned a rural town in Georgia.

On down the boulevard we tramped in silence. He piloted me down to the prado, where, at the edge of a fountain, he rhythmically talked to me.

"How long have you been in Cuba?" I asked him.

"Oh," he replied, "on to eight years. I left my home town in Georgia about eight years ago. Just eight. I hit it for Florida where I worked in a grease factory. Then I came on here. That was before the war, you know."

"In the first place, I like Cuba," he vouchsafed, "it ain't like the States. You ain't got to do no hustling. Of course a lot of people say niggers are shiftless anyhow and all that, but that isn't all. A man who slaves from six to six—what time has he got to look about himself? Now look at me. I ain't got a hell of a lot, but I live just the same. What more do I want? I am happy. I and three other fellows—all of us from back home—the four of us live in a house down by the railroad station and we get along pretty good. Of course, if I had a family, maybe things would be different, but

I haven't. Yes, I get a little to do now and then—working on buildings and in factories. I am a plasterer. But there ain't much money in Habana. Six dollars a week. No, there ain't much money in Habana."

"But the Spaniards treat you all right, don't they?"

"Oh, so-so. I tell you. When I came here first I had a hell of a time. New, green—you know. Called me 'Negro Jamaicano.' Sure got it in for the Jamaicans here. Say they bring things down—make labor cheap. But them black folks from Kingston ain't to be blamed. The English government is at fault. Jamaica's got as much chance as Cuba—but it ain't developed.

"Yes, now I can jabber the language and I get on all right. I am treated like a regular native. For instance, if I went in to the Hotel Inglaterra or the Hotel Plaza or the Centro Gallego—they wouldn't just let me stand there without asking me what I want and freeze me out, like they do in the States. They'd come to me and I'd get everything I want, like a white man.

"I tell you. I meet a lot of fellows and they try to get me on ships to work my way back to the States, but the way I figure it out, I can't see it. I tell 'em nothing doing. Nothing doing. I ain't going to leave Habana. I am not going back to the States. You don't hear of any niggers getting lynched in Habana. Nor any black and white laws—laws for the white folks and laws for the black folks. All look alike in Habana.

"Well, there you are! That's how it is in a nut-shell. I ain't got no kick coming. If I am a bum they treat me like a bum. If I am a man they treat me like a man. It's up to me entirely. It is up to me. That's the way it is in Habana."

And, quite sepulchrally, I said, yes, yes, yes.

On Being a Domestic

"Ousman?" he asked.

"Yes," I replied, dodging a cataract of saliva.

"Work the blazes out of you, too. Last nigger they had quit the very day they took him on."

"That's fair enough."

"Nearly worked him to death. That housekeeper—she's a pippin. Work—work—they'll kill you with work in this place. Why, nobody stays here longer than three days."

"I'll quit if they work me too hard," I retorted.

"Well, you're sure—you're bound to quit."

And I did, really. Surely a laborer—a galley slave—has that much left to him. The prerogative of quitting! The ease, the luxury, the beautiful freedom of it!

Still, it wasn't for the reason put forward by my voluble pearl diver. It was this—simply this.

It was morning. The housekeeper, a fragile lady—herself an inflated galley slave—wrote and ladled out memos as she talked.

From *Opportunity* August 1923. Reprinted by permission of the National Urban League.

"Run up," she flung at me, "to 301 and tidy it up. And when you get through go to 303–307–309–411–633–714–."

Up to 301 the elevator shot me. On the door I rapt.

"Who is it?"

"Houseman."

"Come back in about an hour. I am not ready for you yet."

I went to 303. I swept and dusted and mopt and scrubbed and threw at times a misty eye at the poet at the sun-baked window, tugging at his unruly brain. Surreptitiously I sipt of the atmospheric wine. At least, he would let me stay—and live. So unlike that other place on the top floor where I had forgot my pail. I went back for it. The lady, the lady of the scenarios, on opening the door and depriving me of the aesthetic privilege of at least hearing her voice, poised on the threshold like an icily petrified thing—and pointed with Joan-of-Arc-like fingers at it— my pail—nestling under the writing table. Audibly, loudly her fingers articulated, "There it is! Come and get—you coon!"

In bewilderment I groped my way back to earth—and reason.

II

Back to 301 I went.

"Who is it?"

"Houseman."

Follows a pause. Then, briskly the door opens. The lady, horn-eyed, street attired, is cross, crimson, belligerent.

"I told you to come back over two hours ago. I can't waste my time waiting on you. Why didn't you do as I told you? I told you to come back in an hour. Why, I've been out almost two hours. And now I return, and the place is still dirty. You go in and clean up and lock the door when you come out. I am going out for lunch now and I won't be back for an hour, so you'll have plenty of time to clean up. I don't want to be alone in the room with you while you're cleaning up—."

I am tongue-tied. I drop the broom and the pail and out of eyes white with the dust of emotion, watch the figure chastely going down the steps. Aeons of time creep by me. It is years before I come to. But when I do it is with gargantuan violence. There rises up within me, drowning all sense of reason and pacification, a passionate feeling of revolt—revolt against domestic service—against that damnable social heirloom of my race.

It is low, mean, degrading—this domestic serving. It thrives on chicanery. By its eternal spirit-wounds, it is responsible for the Negro's enigmatic character. It dams up his fountains of feeling and expression. It is always a question of showering on him fistfuls of sweets, nothings, tips,—"With us, it matters not that you are colored. We don't care what color you are. Our firm opens its arms to everybody. Why, who knows, we might in time put you in charge of a bench. Who knows?" Only when the crucial moment comes, the usual aftermath—subterfuge is "Yes, niggers are so doggone lazy. They won't work! They expect as much consideration as white people."

Or—

"Now that colored fellow was all right, but I couldn't make him shipping clerk! Porter to shipping clerk! Ridiculous! Imagine me doing that. Why, it'd ruin my business. It'd break up the morale of my help. I told him so, but he said he'd quit just the same—let him quit. I can't help it. I'll get another one like him in the morning."

Or, again, this,—taken from the NEW YORK TIMES, May 27, 1923,—". . . . If they (the Negroes) have worked a few days, they lay off and loaf until their money is exhausted. They shift from place to place in the slightest cause or pretext. . . ."

And still they wonder why. Still, but what's the use?

It is hell, I say, to be a domestic!

$\mathcal{T}$he Stone Rebounds

It is night. I am in dark Harlem. I am walking along Seventh Avenue, in company with a Negro playwright. I had met him at a radical forum downtown. I pride myself on being an intellectual anarchist; I haven't any prejudices. I am interested in the Negro problem. Interested in it the same as I am interested in Russia and India and Corea. I want to see Society take on a different shape. I am a radical. I stick to my Negro friend. I take him around with me. I run the risk of being ostracized. I remember once I took him to Barrett Manor. Barrett Manor is an art colony. Flappers and broken-down celebrities hang out there. It is a nice place. It is full of Dore's illustrations.* I like it. Always I am lionized by the crowd. Of love and death, poetry and pragmatism, sex and the eternal will—of all these things I would talk. They would hang around and anticipate the words as they came from my lips, especially the girls. I was such a favorite there. Then I took my Negro friend there. Why not? My friend is more intellectual than I. I realize it. I am big enough to admit it. In the old days as soon as I opened the wire-screened door they would all flock to greet me—but that day,

From *Opportunity* September 1923. Reprinted by permission of the National Urban League.

I shall never forget it. I let my friend in first. I went in afterward. What a change! I was no longer the idol, the master conversationalist; no, I had fallen. Fallen from grace; fallen like Lucifer. That entire day I felt a pang of remorse at what it was to be white. Earl, superman that he is, did not seem to notice it. Why should he? It was his first visit there. But it galled me. I have tabooed Barrett Manor. I haven't been there since.

I think of all these things as I swing up the avenue. And my confession! As much as I had tried, I couldn't conceal it. At first I used to blame it on the bourgeoise; but Earl was wise. I could see it in the way he'd smile. Smiling out of the corner of his mouth!

So I decided to tell him. I laid my cards on the table. It is useless, I said, trying to run up against a stonewall—a Gibraltar of prejudice. Useless! I didn't have any difficulty bringing him to my point of view. Yes, he said, he had felt it all along—at the restaurant, the theatre, on the bus, in Greenwich Village; yes, it had followed us, like a starving wolf. But my friend, non-combatant that he is, suggested a way out. Why not let us meet up in Harlem, Black Harlem? Surely—. No, I hadn't any objection, I hastily assured him. Truth is, the idea thrilled me. I long wanted to visit the place. I had heard so much about it.

"It is in here."

I am jerked out of my reverie. I am on a dark, maple-shaded street. I don't know how Earl manages it, but I suppose he knows the place very well. I follow him. It is down in a basement. A sheet of purple is over everything. Dimly I make it out. Witch-like silhouettes belt it. Over the fireplace is a white peacock.* A majestic-looking bird. On the wall, over the piano, is a girl sitting on the bough of a huge cypress, playing a harp. Sunset shines thru the branches. Beside the piano is a bookcase, and on the center table is a medieval lamp. Its chimney is daubed with Oriental flowers. Quaint as can be. At once I take to it. I like the atmosphere. But the people in it! At a jut-like table is a girl, I don't know whether she is white or colored, talking to a man. I can not see his face—it is away from me. But his neck I can see. It is black. I am being introduced around. I can not always see their faces. The place is so romantically dark. It is a long time before I adjust my sight to the light. I am invited to a seat at the center table, and talk—group chatter—is resumed. A girl with pomegranate cheeks is on my right, and at my left is Earl. The girl is saying something to me.

"Well, Mr. Kraus, how do you like it up here?"

"Oh, I think it is great," I whisper dreamily. "It is so—Bohemian."

The girl has creole eyes and I feast on them; but they are not magnetic enough to arrest the functioning of my other self—my subconscious self.

I can hear Earl's soft musical voice as he leans over and talks to the lady with the cossack hat, at his left.

"No, he isn't colored. Jewish—a friend of mine. What? No, I don't think so. Kraus is a poet, not an anthropologist."

"What is he doing up here, then?"

"He just came along with me, that's all."

"Humph, that is funny."

"What's funny?"

"This white man coming up here—I don't understand it."

"Oh, don't be silly, Daisy. I thought you always say you haven't any prejudice."

I am talking to the dark-eyed girl at my elbow. Of course, it is about the race question. Everyone seems to be talking about it these days. I ask her what are her views on that eternal bugaboo—social equality.

"Well, it is this way," she begins, knocking off her cigarette. "I am colored, and self-conscious. Very much so; I can not get over it. It is part of me. I believe it ought to be so that if I want to marry a Dutchman, I can. I am of age, and I think I know what is best for me. More than the ignorant mob out on the street. Yes, I believe in social equality—if by social equality you mean intermarriage, and that is what it means nowadays."

I don't know what sort of look has crept into my eyes, but it must be an alarming one.

"Understand me clearly!" she hastened to add, "By that I do not mean that I personally wish to marry a white man. Get that straight."

I am conscious of an enveloping silence. I drink the tea that is put before me and try to think up clever things to say. I can not explain it. It is sepulchral—the silence. Even the girl beside me is taken up with the string of Spanish beads around her neck. Occasionally I would glance over at the woman on Earl's right. She is toying with the Japanese ash tray on the table. But I am sure now and then she emits a grunt. Something ugh-ish. I am sure of it. I look around. On me a houseful of eyes is cast. I do not feel out of place. I rejoice in the reaction. I know why they are staring at me. I am white.

$\mathcal{V}$ignettes of the Dusk

It is lunch time. I am in the heart of America's financial seraglio. It is a lovely day. Spring. Oceans of richly clad people sweep by me. In my pockets I jingle coins of gold. Gold! I am tired of eating at Max's Busy Bee. The fellows who dine there are so—so—rough sometimes. Still it is the most democratic eating place I know. There is no class prejudice; no discrimination; newsboys, bootblacks, factory slaves, all eat at Max's.

Today I am "flush" and I think I ought to blow myself to a decent meal. My courage is bolstered up. Rich, I am extravagant today. I rub elbows with bankers and millionaires and comely office girls. Of seraphs and madrigals I dream—nut that I am. I look up at the sparkling gems of architecture and marvel at the beauty that is America. America!

I almost ran past it. There it is, the place with the swinging doors and the chocolate puffs in the show case. Myriads of Babbitts and elfin girls pour into it. Tremblingly I enter. It reminds me of a mediaeval palace. Mirrors, flowers, paintings, candelabra; waiters in gowns as white as

From *Opportunity* January 1924. Reprinted
by permission of the National Urban League.

alabaster; and at the table a row, two deep, of eager, bright faced youths and maidens.

I stand back in bewilderment. How efficient these waiters are! Don't they ever make mistakes? Don't they ever give wrong change? Don't they ever serve a frappe for a temptation, a soda for a sundae? Don't they ever—

The waiter's inquiring eyes are on mine. He has got round to me. I whisper my order to him.

"Oyster salad—and vanilla temptation."

I put both hands in my coat pockets and think of the beauty and romance to be found in this place. Up my sleeve I laugh at your intellectual immigrants who howl about the barrenness of America. To me it offers exhaustless possibilities. It opens up entirely new and unexpurgated editions to life. Yes, I say to myself, I must come back again. It is weirdly enchanting. The cuisine is so good. And the people here are such refined eaters! So unlike Max's, where everything is bolted down at a gulp!

Oh, why does he put himself to all that trouble? Couldn't he just hand it to me over there instead of having to come all the way round the counter to make sure that it gets into my hands? Couldn't he have saved himself all that trouble?

He is at my side. Stern and white-lipped he hands me a nice brown paper bag with dusky flowers on it. He holds it off with the tips of his fingers as if its contents were leprous.

"Careful," he warns farsightedly, "else you'll spill the temptation." I do not argue. Sepulchrally I pay the check and waltz out. It is the equivalent of being shooed out. And, listen folks, he was careful *not* to say, "No, we don't serve no colored here."

II

In 1918 he came to America. That means he is still a foreigner. He is not a citizen—yet! But he is going to be. It is going to be the Big Adventure of his life. But wait—

Sometimes he stops and thinks. He is a Negro. He is a foreign Negro. Every day he reads of lynchings in the South. He is besieged on all sides by vicious soul pricks. No, they'd say to him, you mustn't go South; you won't like it down there. In some places, like Texas, you can't stand up under the same roof with a white man unless you take off your hat. You would rebel against it. You, with your white man's point of view (don't you know, the white nurse woman who attends his wife once told him, as she cocked her red head on one side and shut one of her ugly cross eyes, "I think English Negroes are more like white people in their point of view, don't you think so? They're so fine—and not so race conscious)." You, they say to him, you with your white man's ways and outlook will not stand for it. They'd string you up on a tree! They'd. . . .

"But I must go," he screams back at them. "I must! I can't be an American unless I am able to go South! I've got to go."

He thinks of his friend Williams. Williams is a Jamaican. But he is thoro[ugh]ly, spiritually, euph[em]istically American. Some dusky folks, mistaking him for a native, so perfect is his philological assimilation— I am referring to those Afro-Africans who speak of West Indians as "monkey chasers"—come to him and say, "You know, Bill, dem monkey wimmin is de dummest—"

But Williams, who owns a lovely home in Jersey, and has a pretty wife, a jewel of one of the best colored families of Baltimore, is not a citizen. And he doesn't intend to be one. He has been here twenty years. "America is all right," he'd say, "but I ain't taking no chances!"

III

I am a listening post. I am anchored in the middle of life's gurgling stream. It is a stream that is anthropologically exotic. Up in the Negro belt.

I am at a chop house on Lenox Avenue. It is a rendezvous for Negro Bohemians. I am amazed at the conglomerateness of it. Quadroons, octoroons, gypsies, yellows, high and low browns, light and dark blacks, of all shades and colors of shades.

"Well, what do you think of this young Negro generation? Think they'll amount to anything?"

"Oh, they'll fizzle out like all the rest. Wind up as porters . . . elevator men . . . janitors. . . ."

Silence.

IV

I am thinking, thinking, thinking. Of white supremacy; of the Nordic Renaissance. . . .

And again I don the armor of the listening post.

Right of me is a Negro, a very black Negro clarionetist, who, as I take my seat, rises to go out. At the table from which he rose two other men sit. One is a mulatto; the other is fair, very fair, almost white. He of the golden hair and thin lips leans back in his chair and looks at the young man about to go out.

"Say," he whispered, "kin—kin ah come along?"

The other played with it. Slowly he took the tooth pick out of his mouth and wagged his head decisively.

"Nope," he said, "I can't take you along, old top. Where I'm going the folks don't like no yalla men."

$\mathcal{V}$

Out on the street. I whine at the whirl of dust and dirt the wind blasts up on me. I am slowly going down the avenue. In front of me is a jet black trollop. Her hair is bobbed. I snort at the bumps—barber's itch—I am forced to see on the back of her scraped neck. Ugh! Glass bottle!

I stop at Archie's. I always stop at Archie's on the way down. Out on the steaming boulevard he is, as usual. Myriads of men—please don't tell me they all work at night—talk to him about horses, horses, horses. Coming up the avenue is a woman, an anthropological meta-morphosis. . . .

"May God strike me dead if I ain't telling you the truth," Archie is trying to convince a skeptic of something. "Eight years, I tell you. After me for eight long years. But I didn't bother. And talk about pretty, she was a dream. Her father was one of the richest colored men in Virginia. And she had a lovely bungalow on the South Side. Oberlin graduate too. But I didn't marry her. And I didn't have anything against her. . . . She was so fine and thoughtful. Come any time at the house. I'll show you the little cuff links . . . things like that. . . . I didn't have anything against her. . . . Not a thing. Only thing she was too white. Her hair was a bit too much like old gold. . . . She was too white. . . ."

Coming up the avenue is the anthropological metamorphosis.

"Sure she ain't white, Archie?"

"Ah don't know. . . ."

"Seems lek she. . . ."

Goes the mystery by. Then. . . .

"Naw," Archie spits, "she ain't white. Can't you see her neck?"

$\mathcal{T}$he Voodoo's Revenge

At the edge of Faulke's River a fleet
of cayukas* lay at anchor. It was a murky slice of water front. Half Latin,
it was a rendezvous for those French creoles who had left the service
of the Americans to go into business for themselves as liquor dealers,
fishermen, coal burners, black artists, etc. On the side of it facing the
muddy rivulet with its coral islets and turtle shoals, were the usual cafes,
dance halls and fish markets. Behind these stretched a line of "Silver"
quarters—cabins of the black Antillian canal diggers.

One ran across in this part of the Silver City Negroes who spoke patois*—blacks and brunettes from St. Lucia and Trinidad and Martinique.
Fronting their quarters a road meandered, dusty on sunny days and a lake
of mud and slush on rainy ones, up to Monkey Hill.*

Along Faulke's River folk gathered each morning to buy up the
offerings of the fishermen and the pearl divers who had come in the night
before. In the group of traders one saw pretty Negresses from the isles
of the Caribbean who wore flame-colored skirts and East Indian ear-
rings and heavy silver bangles reaching up to their elbows. Some, those
of "higher caste," wore in their bosoms cameos and pearls and Birds of

From *Opportunity* July 1925. Reprinted by permission of the National Urban League.

Paradise feathers to ornament their already gorgeous head dress. In those days short skirts were foreign to the women of the tropics—and one saw long beautiful silk dresses, a faint echo of Louis Quinze,* trailing behind the dusky grand dames as they went from stall to stall and with bamboo baskets bought dolphins and pigeon peas and guinea birds. For hours, as the tropical sun beat down upon them, these lovely angels of Ethiopia would shop and dye their lips with the wine of luscious pomegranates and talk lightly of the things on sale. With them it was a Spring rite. They made a holiday out of it. And far into the morning cayukas full of coral and oranges and yam-pies would come swinging up out of the dark tremulous bowls of the lagoon beyond, to empty themselves upon the wharf while the *patois* men would stand by and fill their pipes, chin, and ofttimes steal away in soft bits of voodoo melody.

Zoomie maca le
Maca le la
Le a le a le

Zoomie tell me
Pape say kiss
'Am a' ready

Tell me mama say wahlo . . .

Zerry wuz a mambe
Zerry.
Wahlo, wahlo, wahlo.

Zamba le a le a le a
Zoke! Zoke! Zoke!

A queer lot these men. Huge, gigantic, black as night, each grew a mustache or a grizzly beard. In them one saw a transplantation of the ancient culture of Europe. In the oil Maiden Islands one saw big hairy black ship chandlers and fishing boat men who walked with the grace and majesty of university professors. And in these silent old witch-worshipping seamen on Faulke's River, unlike the voluble Maches and Spaniards who infested the crumbling wharves along Limon Bay, was a lingering strain of those heroic men who set out at the beginning of the Nineteenth Century to conquer in the name of France the tropic isles of the Caribbean.

Night in the tropics is an erotic affair. As it flung its mantle over the shining form of the lake the fishermen along it would sit on the bottoms of upturned cayukas and for hours dream of far off weird things. Dreaming; dreaming; dreaming. That is all they seemed to do. For it was difficult to penetrate the mind of a *patois* man. He spoke little. He preferred solitude. He preferred to smoke his cow-dung pipe for days in silence. But he never slept. The fire in his lustreless eyes never went out.

One of these *patois* men was a robust son of the soil who still went by the name of Nestor Villaine. Certainly it had been a comparatively easy thing for him to get in, jabber a few mouthfuls of broken French, and live as an *obeah* man.* Up in the hills he lived the life of a hermit, ate *bobo* fish* and iguanas and corn cakes and grew up as hardy and as hairy-chested as the oaks and mahogany he tore down to burn his coal. Away from the society of men and the endearments of women Nestor grew to be a stern son of the jungle. Hard, cold, relentless, he hated the sight of human beings.

Villaine plotted revenge!

II

Caught in the maelstrom of local politics Editor Villaine of the *Aspinwall* Voice drew a breath of righteous indignation as he was jostled into the *alcadia*.* Alongside him was a crouching bit of humanity—a short, brown-skinned stranger whose immaculate duck, white and tan shoes, jippi-jappa hat,* branded him an enemy; in all probability in the pay of the reactionary Ex-Governor Tejada. One of his arms was in a sling; a bit of plaster adorned his left temple. His nose was cut. Dark spots, of ink, soiled the *caballero's* otherwise white suit.

As if they were made by sharply pointed finger nails, gashes and bruises covered his copper-coloured face. His eyes threatened to close up. His lips hung unbeautifully. Not only an arm was in a sling, but tied about his head was a red neckerchief. Unlike his fistic antagonist he had on workmen's clothes. Ink stained his jacket. Dust and dirt disfigured his already ink-stained trousers. Indubitably Nestor was not at his best.

In walked the alcalde. He was a tall, finely built man. Former Deputy Salzedo was one of the handsomest men in the Republic. Friend and foe admitted that. It had an added significance, especially when one is brilliant and fearless and something of a radical. That was what he was.

He was the hope of the Liberal Party. He had been swept into office, a few weeks previous, on the crest of a mighty wave of rebellion. In the coastal provinces he was hailed as a Messiah, a man to lead the people out of the chaos brought on by the Tejadistas.

"*Orden!*"

The *tinterillos* came to a verbal halt. The *alcaldia* was full of them. They sat in the best wicker chairs. They buzzed around it like a nest of hungry bees. Out at the door Pablo, the black porter, who belonged pathologically to the leper asylum at Palo Seco, kept order with an *agente's** baton. Leaning up against the newly papered wall was the dean of the *tinterillos*, the celebrated Dr. Cecilio Rhodes, a West Indian Negro. As the alcalde entered, and malleted for order, Rhodes, dragging the tooth pick out of his mouth, yelled to his colleagues engulfed in the soft wicker chairs to "Rise, in respect to His Excellency, el Senor Alcalde!"

The *tinterillos* rose with one accord out of respect to His Excellency El Senor Alcalde.

Alcalde Salzedo gazed at the prisoners, Editor Villaine and the truculent *extranjero** with the white and tan shoes.

"Well, what is the trouble with you two?"

The *agente* testified. At high noon, as the labor train had emptied its freight and had started on its way back to the round house, he had been standing in front of the kiosk at the corner of Sixth and Bolivar Streets when a shrill cry attracted his attention. Seizing his baton he raced in the direction whence it had come. In the middle of the block, in the offices of the *Aspinwall Voice*, he found the prisoners wrestling and throwing rolling pins at each other. After a terrific struggle in which he lost a button off his coat and a bit of skin off the third finger of his left hand, he had succeeded in arresting the scoundrels and there they were. . . .

"Now, what have you got to say for yourself?" asked His Excellency as the *agente* retired.

Villaine bristled. Ah, to hear his master's voice! To be able to look into his mentor's dusky eyes and tell the story of his love and fidelity to him! To relate, by a striking tale of primordial lust, just how far he was willing to go for the Liberal Party! To do that! For years, as a fly-by-night pamphleteer, he had longed for an opportunity to show these native leaders, like Salzedo, just how loyal a "Chumbo"*—that is, a black from the English colonies—could be. For Nestor was a native of Anguilla who had come to the isthmus as a "contract laborer" to dig the canal. But he didn't want to do that; he had ideas, big, earth-quaking ideas. So when the *Magdalena*, the ship on which he had arrived, docked, he managed, as the laborers disembarked, to slip out of the line and secrete himself behind a bale of merchandise in front of the wharf. When the car in which the men were sardined began to pull out, he had raced across the railroad tracks and had joined the carnival of folk which swept leisurely up Front Street. Dusk found him safely ensconced in a Chinese lice-ridden rooming house on Bottle Alley.

But that was six years before.

"Nothing to say?" the alcalde inquired impatiently. He was annoyed at the glow in Villaine's dreamy black eyes.

"Ah," he breathed, "I was—way—this brute came in my office and without provocation at all began to abuse the Liberal Party, began to swear at Alcalde Salzedo—vilely—criminally! And when he did that I got red in the eyes, and I—well, I went after him, that's all!"

"And you?" inquired the alcalde, turning to the other.

"*Nada!*"

"All right then, sixty days, both of you."

Madre de Dios! Villaine staggered under the weight of the sentence. Sixty days—sixty days—

Naively, very naively, he went up to the desk, put his black ink-stained hands on it, and faced his gaoler.

"Surely," he smiled eagerly, "surely, you do not mean me?"

"Yes, you too. Both of you. Next."

The *tinterillos* began besieging the *alcalde* with their preposterous requests. Pablo with his baton hopped in and escorted the prisoners to the cuartel,* which was nearby.

Villaine was in a psychic stupor. It took a long time for it to sink into him. He couldn't understand it. It was a nightmare, a hideous dream. His head ached.

On a cold, wet slab he sat in the cuartel, staring at the crumbling ceiling. Why, he had been fighting Salzedo's battles! He fought for him! He was—get away you—rat! Yes, come to think of it he had been Salzedo's champion right along. The *Aspinwall Voice* was willingly and freely his. It boosted him. It came to be known as the Liberal Party's keenest weapon of satire.

Still . . . ah, the fleas in this place! Still Salzedo, on his magisterial throne, had sentenced him to sixty days in jail as if he were a common felon. His body was sore. It was full of cuts and bruises. Cuts and bruises that he had suffered while fighting his jailer's battles.

Revolution surged through him. And at night when the prisoners conspired to break through the walls of that terrible inquisition Nestor Villaine, the "Chumbo" *herido** would be plotting, plotting.

At Porto Bello, where he broke rocks, he was gruff and brooding. His fellow prisoners avoided him. The *guardias** chucked the food at him and had as little dealings with him as possible. Plainly Villaine had something on his mind.

III

One of the show places of the river front was a cafe with a brothel in the rear. Here the *patois* men drank goblets of anisette and vermouth and met their women. It was the prototype of Sablo's Baron Bolivar Street. But this nameless rendezvous also served a deadly purpose. It was here that the black artists met "their" cooks and servant girls who worked for the white Americans— folk of the "Golden City"—and gave them for a pittance tips on secret poisoning through vegetable alkaloids, etc. And here it was one dark still night Nestor agreed to meet a young St. Lucian by the name of Sambola.

As the clock struck twelve the boy flung aside the dingy curtain and stepped into the room. Except for Nestor, alone at a table with a glass of green liquor, it was deserted. Squeezing through a network of demijohns the boy came and sat at Nestor's table. Silently the man pushed the bottle over to him and pretending to take a puff at his pipe threw out a haze of smoke to hide the flames that had leapt into his eyes. Sambola poured out a drink and dashed it down his throat. Nestor lowered his eyes in assurance.

Yes, this boy was just the one for it. He came from a family that wallowed in *obeah*. His brother, who was a time-keeper on the Zone, which was a big job for a grammar-school boy to hold, had kept his job there all three years by virtue of it. His other brother, the one all of whose front teeth were capped with gold, steered clear of dagger-gemmed combs and senorita's vials simply because his old witch-stricken mother sat up nights and burned *obeah* for the dusky ladies with whom he consorted in *El Barrio Rojo*.

"Now, look a here," he dashed the pipe away, "I don't wan' no bunglin', *oui?*"

"Non," Sambola dared not blink, so potent was the power Nestor exerted over him.

"You must hide it safely in yo' pocket till the men begin fo' get sleepy— till it is late. Lissen out fo' de polise wissle fo' one o'clock. Pape is likely fo' go a bit early, you say? But that don't matter. Be sure you get it in *his*, though . . ."

Far into the night the older man talked to the boy. He talked to him with the petulance and the nervous gestures of an Oriental. But the thing was Nestor's life balm. For ten long years he had been cherishing it. And there it was—within his grasp!

"Here, take this, and don't lose it, *oui?*"

"Non!"

He took the green vial and tucked it safely in his bosom. Nestor gleamed at him fiendishly. Drink after drink he made the boy swallow. Thru the curtain of the night came the sound of fish splashing in the molten river. From atop the undulating *cordilleras** in the distance a lion howled.

About four o'clock in the morning Sambola slipped out.

Later in the day, as the dusky folk flocked to the waterfront to gobble up the oysters and cayukas of venison, among the things offered for sale was the big yellow cayuka of the trader Villaine.

IV

"Sambola, don't forget the Chess Club meets tonight. And I want you to run over to Calavaggio's and get some of that Jamaica rum he's got."

Mr. Newbold, the manager of the West Indian Telegraph Company, was a social climber. A mulatto, he was something of a mogul. In a small place like Aspinwall, it was easy to know and talk with the mayor and the governor and the agents of the steamship lines that plied to the city. Born in the Cayman Islands, he had been to Liverpool, Calais, Bremen. He was a cosmopolitan. In Aspinwall, where life is more precarious than it is elsewhere, white men found time to cultivate one another. On the native side Mr. Newbold was well liked. Alcalde Munoz and Governor Salzedo were great friends of his. And at the governor's reception he was one of the principal guests. Moreover, his wife, a dark brown woman from one of the islands, passed as a shawl-swept *senora*. And his idea of a chess club had originated with Mr. Newbold. A few men in the Republic played it and he was bent on popularizing the game. It was too good to limit to a straggling few.

In Sambola, the West Indian office boy, he had a faithful and obedient servant. Sambola was a good boy. Unlike the others Mr. Newbold had

had he never smoked or whistled or stayed out late at nights or read "Old Sleuth," "Dick Turpin" or "Dead Wood Dick."* He hadn't any imagination. That, Mr. Newbold felt, was good for him. He would sit, out there in the front office, and watch Mr. Newbold's collie lying on the hot sun-drenched pavement growl and snap viciously at the flies on his nose.

"You know, Sambola," said Mr. Newbold as the boy returned, "I want you to put on a white apron—like a regular waiter. I was thinking of that the other day. Serving drinks to such a distinguished assemblage in your working clothes looks a bit out of place, don't you think?" So that night Sambola had on a white apron to serve the liquers.

The chess club met upstairs in Padros' Bar, facing Slifer's Park. On Friday nights the park band did not play. In consequence the park was deserted—shrouded in darkness. It was a good night for chess.

Sambola got there first. He opened the door, turned on the gas, and arranged the table. The place was in ship shape for Mr. Newbold always saw to it that Sambola clean and tidy it up the day after each game. In one corner was an ice box. Opening it Sambola examined the array of liquers, and again closed it. A moment later Mr. Newbold arrived.

"Well, Sambola, how's tricks? Are all the bottles there?" He went to the icebox, poked a nose in, and took out a bottle of champagne. He took down a glass.

"Don't drink, eh Sambola?" he asked as he filled the glass and put it to his lips.

"No, sir."

"Not even champagne?"

"No, sir."

"That's a good boy."

A few minutes later Herr Pape, the agent of the Hamburg American Line, blond, grey-eyed, a pipe in his mouth, entered. Following him Sir Winfield Baxter, the agent of the Royal Mail Steam Packet Company, a flippant, youngish old man, a perpetual twinkle in his cat grey eyes; Vincent Childers, the British Vice-Consul, hoarse, hump-backed, anaemic, and dribbling at a brown paper cigarette. Lastly came the Governor and Mayor Munoz.

The years of triumph had heightened the charms of the populist idol. Salzedo wore the usual duck, the same long French shoes with the narrow instep and pointed toes, the same gold and brown peacock charm at his watch, the same fascinating light in his eyes.

"Well, gentlemen," said Mr. Newbold, "this is our club's first anniversary. Let's drink to its health."

After which, the game began. Herr Pape and Mr. Newbold, Governor Salzedo and Sir Winfield, Alcalde Munoz and Vice-Consul Childers.

Thus it was for hours. Between times the men were served sherry and ice, whiskey and soda, coca cola. Silently Sambola served the drinks, got a check signed, and stole softly back to his stool out on the porch to watch the shadows of barques and brigantines and big ocean liners tied to their piers. Below, in the dusky shadows, he saw, too, brown boys and girls spooning. And Sambola grew reminiscent. For down in the Silver City he also had a girl, a yellow beauty from one of the isles, A'Minta, who went with him to the *parque* on Sunday evenings. . . .

Hours he sprawled on the balcony, the vial clutched to his bosom. . . . Ah, Pape was going. He always left early.

"Good luck, gentlemen, I've got to run along. Big day before me tomorrow."

Another hour slipped by. The policeman downstairs blew a long owlish wail. Once, twice, thrice. Twelve o'clock. Somewhere on the roof Sambola heard the unmistakable snarl of a lust-bound boar cat. He dimly glimpsed a yacht in the bay.

One more drink he served. Ensued a long sleeping spell . . . a sleep in which he dreamt of a shark tugging at his gizzard and of being washed up on the ebony shores of Faulke's River.

"Sambola!"

Sir Winfield wanted his glass refilled. He hadn't had anything for an age. The others also wanted theirs refilled. Alert, on the job, a wonderful host, Mr. Newbold also saw it.

"Here, Sambola, fill up the glasses. Why, governor, yours is quite empty."

"Oh, let me see, I'll take vermouth."

Unemotional as a clam, Sambola went to the ice box and began pouring out the liquers. As if he had forgotten something he turned to make sure. No, no one was looking at him. They were deeply engrossed in the game. The boy took the vial out of his bosom and uncorked it. Odorless. Colorless. He put three tiny drops in the governor's anisette. It scarcely created a ripple.

$\mathcal{V}$

The next day the Republic was thrown into a paroxysm of grief over the strange death of Governor

Manual Salzedo. The physicians said it was due to heart failure. Others privately attributed it to a vendetta in El Barrio Rojo. Donna Teresa demanded an autopsy. But it did not reveal anything. The newspapers, in dealing with it, threw a cloak of still further mystery over it. They hinted at assault by the ousted Tejadistas. El Dario went so far as to dig up or fabricate a parallel in the Republic's bloody history.

But no one ever got to the bottom of it. Not even the enterprising reporters of the fictional press—not one of them ever thought of linking the governor's death with the finding a few days later of a Negro's shark bitten body fished up out of the black lagoon on Faulke's River.

Soon, like everything else, it died down. And if you asked any of the old residents about it they'd say, "Ah, that is one of the legends of this legendary country. Like the failure of the French."

Yet Sambola, as meek as before, continued to serve liquers on Friday evenings to the members of Mr. Newbold's Chess Club. Only sometimes a strange, smoky gleam would creep into his eyes. On nights when he'd go to that brothel on the banks of the river by the Silver City there were those who couldn't help but compare it with the cat-like light they had often seen in the eyes of the old grouchy trader, Nestor Villaine. As a matter of fact, folk ofttimes, for no reason that they could explain, referred to Sambola as Nestor Villaine.

PART II

THE MAKING OF A NEW NEGRO

Through his work at *Opportunity* and his studies at City College and Columbia University, Walrond became associated with the burgeoning New Negro Movement. His "New Negro" writings appear in a variety of periodicals and Alain Locke's anthology, *The New Negro*. The essays exemplify frequent themes in his work, including migration, racial pride, and an emphasis on literature for its aesthetic rather than propagandistic values. However, some changes are apparent, including his blistering attacks on Garvey (as well as other Black leaders) in "The New Negro Faces America" and "Imperator Africanus." This change is signaled by his decision in 1925 to write regularly under the name Eric Walrond (rather than Eric D. Walrond), perhaps showing his desire to distance himself from his earlier writings.

Although the Caribbean is still central to his writings, Walrond's work begins to focus more frequently on his urban experience, reflective of his own recent move to Manhattan. In "The Godless City," Walrond describes a city of his youth, the decadent city of Aspinwall (Colón), which in many ways, offers similar temptations to New York City, his new home. This emphasis on city living is also displayed in such works as the impressionistic "The Black City" and the tale of Harlem night-clubbing, "The Adventures of Kit Skyhead and Mistah Beauty," but it is particularly evident in "Miss Kenny's Marriage" and "City Love," two of his best short stories. The city in these pieces can be wildly exciting and hedonistic, "a city of assignation," but it ultimately leads to destruction.

Journalism

The New Negro Faces America

The negro is at the crossroads of American life. He is, probably more than any other group within our borders, the most vigorously "led." On the one hand is the old-style leadership of Booker T. Washington's successor, Major Robert Moton, Principal of Tuskegee, who believes, like Christ, in "turning the other cheek," and in a maximum of industrial efficiency. On the other hand is the leadership of W. E. B. Du Bois of the National Association for the Advancement of Colored People, whose idea of salvation is in adequate political representation. This is the organization which is sponsoring the Dyer Anti-Lynching bill.*

Towering head and shoulders above these two is Marcus Garvey, "Provisional President of Africa," and President General of the Universal Negro Improvement Association and African Committees League. This organization is otherwise known as the "Back to Africa" movement. It sprang into public notice a few years ago through the appealing oratory and historic abilities of its West Indian leader, Marcus Garvey. Garvey is a Jamaican, short, black, swaggering, muscularly built. As a printer and journalist in the West Indies he suffered from the injustices heaped upon

From *Current History* February 1923.

members of his race. He went to South America, Europe and Africa. While in London he met Duse Mahomed Ali, the Egyptian editor of The African Times and Orient Review, from whom, it is said, he got his idea of an "Africa for the Africans."

Early in 1915 Garvey came to the United States and with a nucleus of seven formed in a dingy Harlem hall bedroom the most-talked-of negro movement in modern times. Just from the war, thousands of negro ex-service men, bitter, morose, disillusioned, fell into it. Stories of negro officers being stripped of their medals and epaulets and Croix de Guerres by "crackers" in the South stimulated recruiting in Garvey's African army. They dumped their money into it. The movement grew beyond Garvey's fondest hopes.

Early this year Garvey made a trip to Atlanta, Ga., where he interviewed the Imperial Wizard of the Knights of the Ku Klux Klan to find out, he said, "just what the Klan's attitude toward the negro was." Knowing the history of Ku Klux activities in reconstruction days in the South, the bulk of the American negroes who had faith in him, even after the colossal failure of the Black Star Line, viewed this as the last tie that linked them to the "American Emperor."

Just at this point it is well to observe that the negroes of America do not want to go back to Africa. Though Africa, to the thinking ones, means something racial, if not spiritual, it takes the same place in the negro's "colonization" plans as Jerusalem in the Jew's, for instance. This return, however, was the salient feature of Garvey's propaganda. In August of this year, at the Third International Convention of Negroes held at Garvey's Liberty Hall, a delegation of four was appointed, headed by G. O. Marke, a West African lawyer and editor, to go to Geneva to present a petition to the League of Nations asking it to turn over Germany's former African colonies to the Universal Negro Improvement Association. The delegation went and returned, and in glowing rhetoric at a riotously primeval festival at Liberty Hall told of the "impression" it made on the League delegates. The sending of this delegation, like most of Garvey's acts, was for theatrical effect.

Garvey, however, is paying dearly for these preposterous mistakes. A reaction has set in. The crowds who once flocked to hear how he was going to redeem Africa have begun to dwindle. The negroes have lost faith in Garvey. Still, in a thoroughly dispassionate survey of negro progress, one cannot deny that the idea of "Africa for the Africans" means a great deal to negroes in America. Some of them feel that with a strong native Government flourishing on the shores of Africa, evils like lynching in Georgia and exclusion laws in Australia would be dispensed with. Others, and these are in the majority, cannot see beyond the shores of the Hudson. They haven't any international vision. They, for the most part, are negroes of the agricultural regions, the very backbone of the South. To them Africa is a dream—an unrealizable dream. In America, despite its "Jim-Crow" laws, they see something beautiful.

On the other hand, there is the foreign negro to be considered. Yearly a certain percentage of West Indians come to America. On the whole the West Indian is intelligent. He is an indefatigable student. When the epic of the negro in America is written, it will show the West Indian as the stokesman in the furnace of negro ideals. What he lacks in political consciousness he makes up in industrial productivity. He works hard, saves his money, sends his children to the best schools and colleges, and does a little original thinking of his own.

The rank and file of negroes are opposed to Garveyism; dissatisfied with the personal vituperation and morbid satire of Mr. Du Bois, and prone to discount Major Moton's Tuskegee as a monument of respectable reaction. Even before the death of Booker T. Washington, Dr. W. E. B. Du Bois, Harvard Ph.D., was looked upon by the negroes as an intellectual icon. But there is now a revolt against Du Bois. The new negro feels that Mr. Du Bois is too far above the masses to comprehend their desires and aspirations. His "Darkwater,"* they feel, is a beautiful book, but it reveals the soul of a man who is sorry and ashamed he is not white. He hates to be black. In his writings there is a stream of endless woe, the sorrow of a mulatto whose white blood hates and despises the black in him. Clearly the issue is pretty well known on the fundamentals of present-day negro leadership. Garvey is a megalomaniac. Du Bois, unlike either Washington or the poet [Paul Laurence] Dunbar, suffers from the "superiority complex."

What, then, is the outlook for the new negro? Despite the handicaps of inadequate leadership, he is making tremendous headway in industry, to say nothing of art and literature. From 1900–1920 the value of farm property owned by negro farmers of the South has rapidly increased. This is true with reference to the value of the live stock, poultry, and implements and machinery owned. The value of land and buildings increased from $69,636,420 in 1900 to $273,501,665 in 1910, or 293 per cent. The value of land and buildings owned by the negro farmers of the South in 1920 was $522,178,137, an increase for the ten years of $248,676,472, or 91 per cent. ***

According to the Negro Year Book for 1922 "negroes in South Carolina paid taxes on a property value of $53,901,018. In Virginia, negroes in 1921 owned 1,911,443 acres of land valued at $17,600,148."

It is estimated that the value of the property now owned by the negroes of the United States is over $1,500,000,000. The lands which they own amount to more than 22,000,000 acres, or more than 34,000 square miles, an area greater than that of the five New England States, New Hampshire, Vermont, Massachusetts, Connecticut and Rhode Island.

With this background of industrial prosperity what is the outlook for the negro? To give an adequate answer to this one must examine the negro's mental state. In the first place he is race-conscious. He does not want, like the American Indian, to be like the white man. He is coming to realize the great possibilities within himself, and his tendency is to develop those possibilities. He is looking toward a broader leadership. That which he has at present is either old-fashioned, unrepresentative of his spirit and desires, or stupid, corrupt, and hate-mad. Though there are thousands of college-bred negroes working as janitors and bricklayers and railroad porters, there are still more thousands in colleges and universities who are fitting themselves to become architects, engineers, chemists, manufacturers. The new negro, who does not want to go back to Africa, is fondly cherishing an ideal—and that is, that the time will come when America will look upon the negro not as a savage with an inferior mentality, but as a civilized man. The American negro of today believes intensely in America. At times, when the train is whirling him back to dearly loved ones "below the line," he is tempted to be bitter and morose and, perhaps, iconoclastic. But he is hoping and dreaming. He is pinning everything on the hope, illusion or not, that America will some day find its soul, forget the negro's black skin, and recognize him as one of the nation's most loyal sons and defenders.

The Negro Comes North

To understand the present migra-
tion of southern Negroes to the North, one must go back to the spring of
1919, when there was a great shortage of industrial labor in the North.
To alleviate the situation in Connecticut some eight hundred Negro
students were conscripted to man its tobacco industry, and in a short
time they had demonstrated their usefulness as skilled and unskilled
workers. With the rigorous limitations placed on foreign immigration,
these Negro workers were very welcome. Psychologically the effect,
not only upon the northern employer, but—and this is the key to the
situation—on the cotton-picking Negroes of the South, was electrical.

Statistics show that in a few months the increase of Negro migration
jumped from 850—the normal influx—to 12,000 in a single month.
Then the Chicago stock yards advertised for 50,000 Negro laborers.
Chartering the Illinois Central for transportation, the Negroes, dropping
hoe and shovel, hastily answered the call. That event marked the
real beginning of the 1916–1918 migration. It swept from Chicago to
Detroit, the colored population of which city was increased four hundred
percent. Tales of the glory of work and high wages to be obtained in the

From *The New Republic* July 18, 1923.

North drifted back to the Negroes in the South. For weeks the Chicago Defender, a Negro weekly, carried across the top of its front page in bold-face type the magic sign: "Come on up North. Why Stay Down South?" Colorful descriptions of rides in Pullmans, of an equal measure of economic opportunity, plus a kind of nebulous mob fear, literally precipitated an emotional upheaval in Dixieland.

Altogether in the 1916–1918 boom 450,000 Negroes came North, 200,000 of whom in all probability remained, although it is difficult to give actual statistics on the extent of the move. The government estimates that 150,000 Negroes have come North since November 30th; Negro investigators put the number at 240,260. The emigrants travel not individually, but in small unorganized groups, and their principal destinations seem to be Youngstown and Cleveland, Ohio; Philadelphia, Pennsylvania; Hartford, Waterbury and Bridgeport, Connecticut; and New York. It is significant to note that the newcomers are not just illiterate greenhorns, but Negroes mentally and financially above the average.

Racial factors, as much as economic motives, have been responsible for the tremendous migration of the Negro to the North, for the treatment which he has been receiving from the southern white man has been making it literally every hour more undesirable and impossible for him to remain in the South. In sections of the South, where the Negro has gained control of corporations, banks, insurance and real estate companies, which represent the group investment of Negroes to the amount of millions of dollars, lynchings and race riots and the reign of mob terror are so much in the air that it needs only slight persuasion for the Negro to pack up, sell out and move North.

But on coming North, new problems confront him. In the South he is liked as an individual and proscribed as a group. In the North the situation is reversed, while, in addition, there are certain civic, political and educational responsibilities which he must learn to shoulder. The encouragement of interracial cooperation is greatly needed. If the Negro is to supplant the white immigrant labor, he should be allowed to enjoy the benefits that labor unions extend to foreign white workingmen, for the Negro is, after all, a staple American product with the soul and genius of a workman.

The Negro should remember in coming to the North where he hopes to find equal opportunity for white and black alike, that which has been so ably stated by Mr. Phil H. Brown, Commissioner of Conciliation in the United States Department of Labor, who is himself a colored man. He says: "Negro labor is about to have its real day in court, an opportunity to vindicate itself and its industrial value to the country. The crisis is double-edged, for in the same degree that it benefits those who migrate it will help those who remain at home. But this labor must never lose sight of the fact that it is on trial, and its defence and liberty are left in its own hands."

$\mathcal{T}$he Black City

North of 125th Street and glowing at the foot of Spuyten Duyvil is the sweltering city of Harlem, the "Black Belt" of Greater New York. With Negroes residing on San Juan Hill, on the East Side, in Greenwich Village, Harlem, undoubtedly, is the seething spot of the darker races of the world. As Atlanta, Georgia, is the breeding spot of the American Negro; Chicago, the fulfillment of his industrial hopes; Washington, the intellectual capital of his world; so is Harlem, with its 185,000 beings, the melting pot of the darker races. Here one is able to distinguish the blending of prodigal sons and daughters of Africa and Polynesia and the sun-drenched shores of the Caribbean; of peasant folk from Georgia and Alabama and the marsh lands of Florida and Louisiana. Here is banker and statesman, editor and politician, poet and scholar, scientist and laborer. Here is a world of song and color and emotion. Of life and beauty and majestic somnolence.

It is a sociological *el dorado*. With its rise, its struggles, its beginnings; its loves, its hates, its visionings, its tossings on the crest of the storming white sea; its orgies, its gluttonies; its restraints, its passivities; its spiritual yearnings—it is beautiful. On its bosom is the omnipresent symbol of

From *The Messenger* January 1924.

oneness, of ethnologic oneness. Of solidarity! Hence its striving, its desperate striving, after a pigmentational purity, of distinctiveness of beauty. It is neither white nor black.

It is a city of dualities. Yonder, as the sun shoots its slanting rays across the doorstep of a realtor or banker or capitalist there is a noble son of Africa Redeemed on whose crown it shines. Well groomed, he is monocled or sprayed with a leaf of violet. By way of a boutonniere he sports a white or crimson aster—and in he goes. It is the beginning of his day as merchant or realtor or whatever he is. . . . Towards sunset, as his pale-faced prototype resigns himself to supper or home or cabaret or adoring wife or chorus girl he is seen, is this black son, this time in denim or gold-braided toga, on his way to that thing that puts bread in his and his wife's and his children's mouths, and steels that silver-like spot glowing at the bottom of him, so that day in and day out he doggedly goes on, striving, conquering, upbuilding.

It is the beginning of his day as a domestic.

II

It is a city of paradoxes. You go to the neighborhood theatre and there is a play of Negro life. It is sharp, true, poignant. In awe you open your mouth at the beauty, the majesty, the sheer Russian-like reality of it. Grateful, the house asks for the author, the creator, the playwright. He is dragged forward; there is an outburst of applause—emotion unleashed. Modestly bowing the young man is slowly enveloped in the descending shadows—and the crowd is no more.

Wonderful! You go home; on a roseate bed you sleep, dream, remember things. In the morning you get up. Slipping into a dressing robe you go down in answer to the postman's shrilling whistle. Out of eyes painted with mist you go and take the letter, take the letter from the postman. Wholly by accident you raise your eyes and find, find yourself looking at—the playwright!

It is a city of paradoxes. Along the avenue you are strolling. It is dusk. Harlem at dusk is exotic. Music. Song. Laughter. The street is full of people—dark, brown, crimson, pomegranate. Crystal clear is the light that shines in their eyes. It is different, is the light that shines in these black people's eyes. It is a light mirroring the emancipation of a people and still you feel that they are not quite emancipated. It is the light of an unregenerate.

As I say, you are walking along the avenue. There is a commotion. No, it is not really a commotion. Only a gathering together of folk. "Step this way, ladies and gentlemen . . . step this way. . . . There you are. . . . Now this Coofu medicine is compounded from the best African herbs . . ." East Fourteenth Street. Nassau Street. The Jewish ghetto. Glimpses of them whirl by you. Not of the Barnum herd, you are tempted to go on, to let the asses gourmandize it. Seized by a fit of reminiscence you pause. Over the heads of the mob you see, not the bushy black-haired head of the Hindu "fakir," the Ph.D. of Oxford and Cambridge (in reality the blatant son of the acacia soil of Constant Springs, Jamaica, still basking in the shadows of dialectical oppression); not the boomeranging Congo oil magnate; nor the Jew invader with his white, ivory white cheeks, hungry, Christ-like features, and flowing rabbinical beard. Instead you see a black man, of noble bearing, of intellectual poise, of undefiled English, a university man, selling at 900 per cent profit a beastly concoction that even white barbarians do not hesitate to gobble up.

And there is a reason, a mighty reason, for this, for the conversion, for the triumphs of this black charlatan; a reason that goes up into the very warp and woof of American life. Imagine it—think, think about it sometime.

III

It is a house of assignation, a white man's house of assignation, is this black city. It is voluptuously accessible to him. Before cabarets and restaurants, cabarets and restaurants that black folk cannot go into, he stops, draws up his limousine, takes his lady, bathed in shining silk, out; squeezes through the molting, unminding folk, tips the black pyramidal *major domo,* and skips up to the scarlet draped seraglio. Here is white morality, white bestiality, for the Negroes to murmur and shake their bronzing cauliflower heads at.

It is wise, is this black city.

*R*eview of
There Is Confusion
by Jessie Fauset

This novel is significant because it is the first work of fiction to come from the pen of a colored woman in these United States.* It is evidence that we can with assurance look forward in the near future to having our fiction dealing with life among the Negroes written by the Negroes themselves. And this is as it should be. Long the object of burlesque and pitiless satire, it is natural that the Negro in his upward plunge should want to strike back, to write out of his own rich and varied experience, not for the delectation of the whites, but for the edification and enjoyment of his own people.

The mushroom growth of magazines published by the Negroes and the fiction to be found in them, the serialization of stories of obscure colored authors in Negro newspapers, the establishment, even, of reputable Negro publishing houses—all point to this new, up and pushing spirit.

Having as its motif the futility that must not arrest the conquering progress of the Negroes, Miss Fauset's book, however, is not really "younger generation Negro" stuff. Toomer's insouciant "Cane" in this respect is miles beyond it. Indeed, it is a sort of bridge between the old and the new Negro generations. For the literature of these strident

From *The New Republic* July 9, 1924.

neophytes is of a shockingly esoteric nature—full of beauty and passion and blackly steering clear of the inferiority complex. Mediocre, a work of puny, painstaking labor, There is Confusion, is not meant for people who know anything about the Negro and his problems. It is aimed with unpardonable naïvete at the very young or the pertinently old.

Imperator Africanus

MARCUS GARVEY: MENACE OR PROMISE?

One of the effects of the World War was the quickening of racial consciousness among the negroes of the Western Hemisphere, the group to which, because of its industrial, economic, and intellectual solidarity, the bulk of the blacks of the world look for leadership and guidance. Fresh from the war, from the bloodstained fields of France and Mesopotamia, the black troops, bitter, broken, disillusioned, stormed at the gates of the whites—pleaded for a share of that liberty and democracy which they were led to believe were the things for which they had fought. And it was of course a futile knocking. Hardened by the experience of the conflict, the negroes, drunk, stung, poisoned by the narcotics of white imperialism, rose in all their might to create for themselves those spoils of war and peace which they knew they could not hope for from the ruling whites.

In Egypt and Palestine and other parts of the war area the black troops of the Western Hemisphere met other blacks—native Africans. It was the first mass contact of the negro from the Old and the New Worlds. Here something which the white war lords had not bargained on resulted. The negroes met and exchanged and compounded their views on the

From *The Independent* January 3, 1925.

whites, their civilization, and their masters. Here the policies of France and Britain and Belgium and the United States with regard to their black wards were put in the scales. And when the blacks rose from the resulting pyre of disillusionment a new light shone in their eyes—a new spirit, a burning ideal, to be men, to fight and conquer and actually wrest their heritage, their destiny from those who controlled it.

It was upon this ideal that the gospel of Marcus Garvey came into being. Garvey is a black native of one of a cluster of tropical isles ruled by Great Britain in the Caribbean. He is the head of an international movement of, he says, some 4,000,000 negroes. Known far and wide as the Garvey movement, its real name is the Universal Negro Improvement Association and African Communities League at 56 West 135th Street, New York. Its history is so inextricably bound up with the affairs of Marcus Garvey that to properly comprehend it and its racial significance one must need study the man's life and the forces that have governed it.

First, Garvey is of unmixed negro blood. On its surface this may not appear significant, but it is indispensable to any consideration of the man. Goaded on by the memory that the first slaves stolen from Africa were full-blooded negroes, Garvey and the gospel he preaches appeal particularly and not unexpectedly to the very black negro element. In the island of his birth, Jamaica, a land with as many color distinctions as there are eggs in a shad's roe, and all through his life, the fact that he was black was unerringly borne in upon him. Wherever he went, whether to Wolmer's, the college patronized by the upper-class mulattoes in Jamaica, or to Europe or Central America as student and journalist, he was continuously reminded that he was black and that it was futile for him to rise above the "hewer of wood and drawer of water."

In Jamaica, as elsewhere in the United Kingdom, England differentiates between the full bloods and the half bloods. In Garvey's Jamaica, the mulattoes are next in power to the whites. The blacks, who outnumber them three to one, have actually no voice politically or economically.

With such a background, no wonder Garvey, the "Moses of the Negroes,"—applying the law of compensation,—idealizes black. Coming into the emancipation of his spirit, it was inevitable. No wonder he talks glibly of a black state, a black empire, a black emperor. No wonder he is creating a black religion, a black deity, a black "Man of Sorrows." Who knows, he says, but that Jesus the Christ was not a black man? And, naturally, the hordes of black peasant folk flock to Garvey. They worship him. They feel that he is saying the things which they would utter were they articulate. They swarm to hear his fiery rhetoric. They pour their money into his coffers. They stand by him through thick and thin. They idolize him as if he were a black Demosthenes.*

In turn, quite in keeping again with the law of compensation, but undoubtedly overdoing it, Garvey creates a fairy dream world for them which spiritedly makes up for the beauty and grandeur that are lacking in their drab, unorderly lives. Aping the English royalty, he manufactures out of black peasants of the lower domestic class dukes and duchesses, princes and princesses. Shall not, he quotes from the Bible, princes come out of Egypt, and Ethiopia stretch forth her hands unto God? An old white-haired negro, a veteran agitator, is made Duke of Uganda. A faithful ambassador just returned from a mission to the black Republic of Liberia is made Knight Commander of the Distinguished Order of the Nile. Out of the multitude of black stableboys, cooks and bottle washers, scullions and jim-swingers, is fashioned the timber of the crack African Legionnaires. Out of sombre-faced maidens from the French and Dutch and English colonies along the Spanish Main he creates "Black Cross Nurses." A black singer with the sacred eyes of a madonna becomes the "African Virgin Mary."

All the glamour, all the technique of delusion, is employed to satisfy the craving for this other thing which is missing in the lives of these long-repressed peasant folk. Essentially a movement of the black proletariat, Garveyism owes its strength largely to jangling swords and flaming helmets, titles and congeries of gold braid.

Arriving in the United States on March 23, 1916, Garvey, with a nucleus of thirteen, started in a Harlem hall bedroom the New York branch of the U.N.I.A. Briefly, the goal of the U.N.I.A. is the redemption of Africa—a black application of the Zionist principles. Afraid, according to its founder, that "if the negro is not careful he will drink in all the poison of modern civilization and die from the effects of it" and hearing the great cry of "Jerusalem for the Jews—Ireland for the Irish—India for the Indians"—the U.N.I.A. believes that it is about time for the negroes to raise the cry of "Africa for the Africans," at home and abroad.

In the United States Garveyism runs counter to the ideals governing most of the negro uplift movements. Garvey's reluctance, for example, to declare himself on the Ku-Klux Klan, with whose whole program he is said to be in perfect accord; his opposition to the negro middle and professional classes (in August, 1922, he issued a manifesto advising his followers not to invest their money in negro corporate enterprises other than his own) are indicative of two things: Garvey's slant on the black *bourgeoisie* and the pessimism with which he views the outlook for the negro in a hostile white world.

To get his ideas abroad Garvey started a weekly newspaper, the *Negro World*. Doubtless, it is the most bitterly racial newspaper published by negroes. Leading off with a full-page "message" weekly by Garvey, the journal is published in three sections—in Spanish, French, and English. It goes to every part of the world where there are black people. Numberless have been the times when it has been suppressed or otherwise debarred by the British and French authorities from entering their native Negroid possessions. As it is, the *bourgeois* colored people of the United States are ashamed to be seen with it. They do not care for it. It is too upstandingly, too sensationally, racial.

Yet it is through this medium of violence that Garvey hopes to unite the black people of the world. How successful he is in doing this is reflected again and again in the unswerving allegiance to the ideals set up by him no matter what the machinations of the enemy may do to throw him into disrepute.

Soon after he got his organization going Garvey conceived the idea of founding a steamship line to ply between North, Central, and South America, the West Indies, and Africa. And the name with which he christened it is illustrative of the spirit of the whole Garvey movement. He called it the "Black Star Line." Why not? Did not the whites have their "White Star Line?" And from all parts of the world the blacks bought stock in it. It found fertile soil in their repressed consciousness.

Now Garvey, a bewitching orator, a roof-raising propagandist, when it comes to actual comprehension of the forces governing the world of trade and commerce, is a hopeless nincompoop. He said it was not necessary for him to be an experienced seaman nor need he have a technical knowledge of shipping to direct a steamship line. Unwilling to relinquish the actual control of it, he said he'd get people, black people with the brains and experience, to run it. And here again, undoubtedly, Garvey was unconsciously drawing on his Jamaica experience. For back in his Jamaica days there were black pilots and engineers and captains of merchant vessels which traded along the Main. Garvey, his imagination leaping to the contemplation of boundless continents, staked all, some two or three million subscribed by the black folk, on the fulfillment of this exotic dream.

All the world knows, the "Black Star Line" failed, and for a moment Garvey's star took a downward plunge. Incompetency, dishonesty, mismanagement, fraud—these contributed to it. In his eagerness to put the project over, Garvey was a promiscuous chooser of men. He was bombarded on all sides by charlatans. Bogus engineers, unskilled experts, sloop masters all clamored for position and opportunity, and Garvey, blind to the things of the earth, fell prey to them—saw in them spirits hungry to show to the whites the oceanic genius of the blacks.

It was at this point that the opposition to Garvey assumed menacing shape. To understand it one must go into the situation of the negro in the United States proper and the efforts that are being made to improve it. Constituting one tenth of the 100,000,000 people in our country, the negro is burned, lynched, segregated, and disfranchised, all on account of his color and abject condition. Ever since the Civil War there have been, of course, efforts by liberal-minded white people, principally from the North, to correct this unseemly treatment of the blacks. It was not until about twenty-five years ago, however, that the blacks began to develop leaders of their own. Of these, Booker T. Washington, the renowned seer of Tuskegee, was by far the greatest. Born a slave, Washington believed that the solution of the negro problem lay in educating the black masses along industrial and commercial lines. Tuskegee Institute, situated in the heart of the Bourbon South, and erected at a cost of $5,000,000, is a living testimonial to the wisdom of this ideal, where thousands of negro peasant boys and girls go annually for training in domestic and industrial arts.

Booker Washington prospered and soon had all the large philan-thropic interests in the country behind him. That was up to 1906. Along about this time there appeared in the United States a book called "The Souls of Black Folk," whose author was a colored man. In that book, which up to this day is read as a sort of *Magna Charta* of the American negro, there is a scathing denunciation of Booker Washington's theory of industrial education. Discarding it as old-fashioned, out of date, the author pleaded for the higher education of the negro, for a share for the black man not only in the industrial and commercial life of the land, but in the social and political and governmental as well.

This, of course, fell on the national ears with the crash of a bombshell. It meant that there had risen out of the bosom of the Black Belt a voice, daring, challenging, disturbing in its ring, and for a time (and ever since) the eyes of the nation were focused on the man uttering it. And that man was W. E. Burghardt DuBois, at the time an obscure professor of economics at Atlanta University, a negro school in Georgia, one of the most bitter of the antinegro States in the American Union. Ph.D. of

Harvard, DuBois is undoubtedly the most brilliant negro in the United States today. Poet, scholar, editor, and author, he is the man to whom the country turns with any question bearing on the intellectual life and progress of the negroes. Proud, haughty, an incurable snob, he is probably the most unfit man temperamentally for the craft of leadership.

Of French and Dutch descent, DuBois' reaction to the color problem is angrily emotional, baldly personal, amazingly hyperbolical. He has no sympathy for the black masses. He is incapable of comprehending their dreams and aspirations. He himself in his autobiography says that when he was a boy in Massachusetts he despised the poor mill workers from South Germany and annexed as his natural companions the rich and well to do. In short, DuBois, the aristocrat, the snob, is a poet, an intellectual. He sees things through the eyes of the spirit. Garvey and Booker Washington did not. Naturally, his racial experience is colored by the psychosis of the poet in rebellion with his environment. The accident of birth which made him a mulatto is the only thing that lends significance to what he says or does. Had he been born in a country like France he would still be the same violent, sensitive individual.

Ultimately, the attack by DuBois on Washington, the only negro of more than sectional stature who could at one and the same time be on terms of comparative placidity with both the North and the South, served to show up DuBois as good "timber" for leadership. A group of white and colored leaders then got together and founded what is now known as the National Association for the Advancement of Colored People, with a white woman, Mary White Ovington, chairman of the board, and Moorefield Storey, a distinguished white barrister of Massachusetts, president. Nominally and theoretically, Miss Ovington and Mr. Storey are at the head of it, but the brains, the guiding genius is DuBois.

Having as its *raison d'être* the granting to the United States negro of equal social, political, and economic rights, the National Association is essentially an American movement concerned with the affairs of the 12,000,000 American negroes. One of the things it is championing is a national anti-lynching law. It advises the negroes at election time how to vote. It seeks to put down glaring instances of racial injustice. It seeks to awaken the Christian conscience of the white man. It believes that the destiny of the negro is in America, and that the solution of the race problem lies in amalgamation.*

When Garvey fell into disfavor through the sensational failure of the "Black Star Line," the dogs of the opposition took the opportunity to nip at his heels. DuBois, the best blood in the native kennel, was set on him. Through the *Crisis*, the monthly magazine published by the National Association, DuBois started a campaign against Garvey. After bewailing the riot of waste and corruption (DuBois' association is supported by funds contributed by both white and colored people, whereas Garvey has refused financial aid from the whites, relying solely on the negro masses) incident to the collapse of the steamship company, DuBois agreed that the idea of African colonization was not new, and not impracticable, but that Garvey, an "illiterate foreigner," was not the man for it. Going further, DuBois said, however, that it was madness to try to persuade the American negro, practical and unimaginative as he is, to settle in Africa. Which, so far, is the only fundamental fallacy of Garveyism.

Numerous others, following in DuBois' footsteps, have duplicated this stand, and for the last two years Garvey has been defending himself against attacks. Eventually, through the efforts of his enemies, he was haled before the United States District Court in New York for using the mails to defraud and sentenced to five years in a Federal penitentiary.

Out on bail, Garvey, while DuBois asked for his repatriation, held his Fourth International Convention of Negroes in New York from August 1 to 31 to which came over 3,000 negroes from various parts of the globe. Undaunted, unswerved by the enemy's fire, by an uncanny turn of fate, Garvey, so far as the black masses are concerned, is still at the helm—steering the negro ship of state and doing it with the old characteristic fire and spirit. Forever hitting at the high spots of the old international negro problem, it is natural that he should excite the wrath of nationalist negroes like DuBois in America and Herbert George DeLisser* in Jamaica—men who put national above racial consciousness. Yet through some divine mystery, Garvey is the "Moses" of the black masses. Instead of diminishing, his power is growing daily. It is one of the anomalies of the complex racial problem of the age.

The Negro Literati

Of course it is pretty hard for anyone to live the creative life in the United States, but for the Negro I think it is doubly so. What right has a Negro, anyhow, to think of the creative life at all, much more aspire to it? Isn't he of a people who for countless generations have had to rely on others—preferably unsympathetic masters—for their thinking and dreaming and creating? Yet this very enforced affliction is destined, I believe within a comparatively brief period of time, to react to the enormous advantage of the blacks.

Aesthetically, the blacks have been restrained all their lives. They have been made to bear the brunt of civilization. Voiceless, tongue-tied by virtue of the shackles of thralldom placed upon them, they've yet been able to preserve an acute sensitiveness to color, beauty, emotion. Of such timber are an artistic people made.

Years they've been harvesting—storing up—moments; tears, sorrows, joys, laughter. Into the nugget chests of their hearts they've had to lock them until the time has been ripe to bring them out and jealously exhibit them to the world . . .

From *Brentano's Book Chat* March/April 1925.

And this race of which I speak is superbly romantic. In the entire world I can not imagine a people who've lived more, who've dared and died and suffered more, who've traveled and experienced more, who've sipped more of the wine of joy and tragedy, of comedy and despair—in short, who have by virtue of circumstance been made to slake their thirst at the very well springs that water the fields of art.

And think, too, especially here in the United States, of the astounding biologic composition of the Negroes. Haven't you ever been to Harlem, New York's black ghetto, on a Sunday afternoon and seen the gay throngs of folk parading along Seventh Avenue? There is nothing like it— this amazing metamorphosis . . . All the colors of the rainbow do not suffice to do them justice. It is like a human mardi gras: Yellow and gold and brown—of Latin and Dutch origin—Indians, creoles, jet blacks . . . What a heterogenous people!

And there is something about the life the Negro lives not only in the United States but everywhere that is immensely enthralling. Here he is a serf. Cotton picking is manna to him. Yonder at the wheel of a river boat—on the wharf staggering under the weight of a sugar hogshead. In rural life he is king. Up North he is a steel worker or a coal miner. Across the color line he may be "passing—" and here the limit to his acculturation is beyond us. He traverses the seven seas. He is everything from captain to cabin boy. Unhampered he is not always a trouper—a hobo; he belongs to the bourgeoisie; he stirs the liquors of millionaires. He is the roamer, the boulevardier of the universe.

You tell me where to find a white man—or eskimo—and I point you out a black. And there are places even now (I'm not thinking of Africa only) where he flourishes and where it would be suicidal for a white man to endeavor to penetrate.

What if an exotic beast like this were to become unchained artisti-cally?

As it is, it is futile to brush the question aside. For there is something in the Negro spirit—in the life the blacks live—that gives aproponess to the query. For to them life is one seething nightmare—one immeasurable dream. Intense as the dawn, it goes madly by them—illumining their spirits by the way—leaving them gay, colorful, conquerless.

Futilitarians all, nothing to them matters—money, power, position. Nothing.

What is to be done when such a people begin to write, to create? Already there is evidence in the jazz rhythms created by the American Negro of what is in store when the blacks roll up their sleeves and begin furiously to write and paint and model . . .

And the thing that is preventing the Negro from giving expression to the submerged emotions that are native to him is the fact that he is not yet quite free. That, I agree, will come in time. At present he is free politically and socially, but spritually he is still enslaved. He is unable to let himself go . . .

As a foreigner, I think I can understand the reason for this. Always conscious of the color problem the Negro writer in the United States is vigilantly censorious of anything in his work or expression which may put the black race in a disparaging light. Thinking of the prejudiced white who'd take up his book and contemptuously review it, he writes with that preconceived bias in mind. And of course when he begins to write about his own people he lies miserably. He doesn't paint pictures of people—of tantalizing black people—he knows. No. He dishes up yarns about aristocratic blacks who go to Harvard. He goes down to Wall Street and hires a skyscraper and puts a Negro bank president in it. He goes up the Adirondacks and buys an estate and puts a black seamstress upon it. He then takes a trip back south. There he takes a malicious delight in poking hot irons in the ribs of the "po' white trash." Every white man his hero meets is a "nigger hater." Every yellow girl is a virgin who's got a devil of a time fighting off the white, lustful pack. And if the story doesn't wind up with a lynching or a race riot it is bound to do so with bloodhounds on the scent of the daring black who'd had the guts to go get a gun and shoot up that horrid "cracker" town . . .

On occasions these Negro tales deal with what is known about town as "high society." And by God if there is a society that is more stilted, more snobbish, that is harder to break into, than the Negro society these tales depict, then I've yet to hear about it . . .

All this to me represents the attitude of the person who is obsessed by the inferiority complex. That is what I meant when I said the Negro writer is still enslaved spiritually . . .

But don't let me be too harsh in my judgments. There is orientating on these shores a group of Negro writers who are utterly shorn of this negative manner of looking at life. Calling names is always a precarious undertaking but I venture to say that the work of Jean Toomer, Countee P. Cullen, Zora Neale Hurston, Rudolph Fisher, Gwendolyn Bennett, Langston Hughes and Esther Popel* in its "flyest"* moments is notoriously devoid of this irritating taint.

Of the group Toomer is by far the strongest. "Cane," a collection of vignettes of Negro folk life in Washington, D.C. and Georgia was issued by Boni & Liveright two years ago. It didn't take particularly, and for a reason that would hold true to the major work of this esoteric school.

In the first place, these swashbuckling neophytes are not going in for Charity or Uplift work. They don't give two hurrahs in hell for the sort of writing that attempts to put the Negro on a lofty pedestal. In fact they don't think of the Negro as a distinct racial type at all. They only write about him because they know more about him than about anyone else. He is closer to them. He is part of them. As such they see him . . . And they are writing of the Negro multitude—not in a way of course that would bring them favorably under the eye of Mr. Lorimer* (God forbid!) but in such a style that people will stop and remark, "Why, I thought I knew Negroes, but if I am to credit this story here I guess I don't."

Fact is, these writers are exploiting the primitive expanses of Negro life. They don't care a rap about the virgins and the millionaires and the tin-pot Booker T's. They are interested in going into the lives of typical folks—people who don't have to wait till the pig knuckly parson says good-bye and goes out the gate before they can be themselves. Instead, they go in for lummox psychology. Along State Street, Chicago, Wiley Avenue, Pittsburgh or Seventh Avenue, New York, they are in quest of Emma Bovary. Either as high priest or saint or deacon of Big Mt. Zion Baptist Church or as bouncer incomparable of the low-downest honk-a-tonk on the avenue they expect any minute to run into Casanova. And Jurgen!* Why there is a black Jurgen on every street corner in Harlem! And that is the way it is.

A retreat, I call it, a retreat to Lhassa!*

In time I fervently believe that the literature of the United States will be colored to an amazing degree by the exploits of these gallant youngsters, and the way the cards read at present that time is not very far off.

Negro Folk-Song

REVIEW OF *THE NEGRO AND HIS SONGS* BY
HOWARD W. ODUM AND GUY B. JOHNSON

No amount of urbanization, of flight into environments "hostile" to the true essence of the Negro spirit, can deprive the Negro of his enormous capacity as a creator of music and folk song. Georgia, Alabama, Africa, or the West Indies, is conducive to expressions of intense tropic warmth and beauty, but in Philadelphia, Chicago or New York this spirit-thing which differentiates the Negro from the Eskimo, for example, again struggles to the surface, albeit colored, not unexpectedly, by the consequences of life in an impressionably mechanical civilization. Which is to say that no matter where he finds himself, there is color, warmth, fervor in the black man's soul, so that, if he is not swerved by temptations of a nebulous racial present, whatever he does has the distinct mark of raciality upon it.

So far the best index of the character of the Negro is his music and folk songs. And particularly the songs, for while the music is symbolical of determinant currents in his life, the songs actually and oft-times crudely dramatize them. To an onlooker emphasis is placed upon moods or heart-desires that are relatively trivial. Or, what a white arranger may take to be an "immoral" expression may simply be a restatement through song

From *The Saturday Review of Literature* July 11, 1925.

of a differing moral point of view. Slaving on wharf or cotton field, driven to an emotional wall by the strenuousness of toil or the anger of an irate white "boss," the Negro realizes solace in song. In church or at camp meeting the divine flame of Jesus or the blistering prospect of a descent into Hell, give rise to spasms of fervent lyrical outbursts. Gathered together these songs or bits of folk-utterance make marvellous material for the study of both the folk lorist and sociologist.

Significant moments in the race's history and progress occasion many of these songs. There are, for instance, endless songs picturing the epic flow of peasant blacks from the South to the North. Unsophisticated flat-dwellers in the crowded negro tenements in Detroit and Philadelphia sing of the cold, frosty nights and the general physical disabilities of their new, virgin environment. When Marcus Garvey's "Black Star Line" collapsed the urchin gods of the Harlem pavements came along and dramatized the calamity in lines of the utmost "point" and power. And if there is one version of the "West Indian Blues," there are at least two hundred.

Of course it is not only in racial crises that the Negro bursts into song. It goes deeper than that; his is a musical nature. He may make a song out of a pal "going West," but the regular, uneventful flow of life also is dream-stuff for his lyre. Even "around the house,"—bare, drab, though it may be—there is provision for the realization of this song-quest. A whole family might have its roster of songs. I know for one that the songs which I heard in childhood are intelligible to few outside of my immediate relations. In fact, I have an idea that if each Negro would sit down and write from memory the songs concocted by his progenitors, or those to which he was exposed in adolescence, there would result the most amazing body of lore conceivable.

As the work of Southern white men, this book is a decided achievement. Although a large portion of the songs are culled from meritorious texts there is an amount of new material, gathered from negro sources in Northern Mississippi, Northern Georgia, North Carolina, and Tennessee. In that portion of the book devoted to "social songs" the collection is of immense value. Here is rich, vital stuff—"Stagolee," "Honey, Take a One on Me," "Railroad Bill,"—exploits of a gay highwayman, a characteristic love melody, and the rovings of a race-track "rounder." In the work songs there is "The Grade Song."

Well I tole my captain my feet wus cold,
"Po' water on fire, let wheelers roll!"

Told my captain my han's wus cold
"God damn yo' hands, let the wheelers roll!"

The volume is marred slightly by an attitude, which I honestly believe is unconscious, to arrive at ethnic truths regarding the Negro which at times are pitifully absurd. The interpretations for the most part are academic and intrusive. Songs of subtlety and sophistication are held down to a precious minimum.

To me, however, the best thing about this book is that it richly illustrates the enormity of lore awaiting the energy and awakening of the negro scholar and folk lorist. For it is more or less common property in these United States today that if you really want to get to the heart and spirit of the black people you must do it through the medium of one of their own.

$\mathcal{T}$he Epic of a Mood

REVIEW OF *NIGGER HEAVEN* BY CARL VAN VECHTEN

"Nigger Heaven" is the epic of a mood. At the outset there is much in it to excite and erupt, be one black or white, for it abounds in objectivity and truth. A deeply subjective study, from an exotic Nordic viewpoint, of an ebony Paris, it yet has its moments of racial fidelity and abiding reality. Here, despite a deceptive prologue, is no low-lifed darkey cabaret tale; no plaintive Negro tragedy of flight into virgin Northern wastes. Here is no jazz pæan to the musty rodents of an Upper Fifth Avenue basement. Mr. Van Vechten's concern is of a soberer kind. With the mantle of a showman and the sagacity of a journalist he has anticipated the mob and enthusiastically explored the glimmering summits of High Harlem. There he found, shrouded and gay, a Negro dream-world enchanting in its bewilderments. Its complex vastness, its eternal varieties left him excited and chaotic. His sympathies, however, following a tradition begun in "The Blind Bow-Boy" and "The Tattooed Countess,"* took him above the "lower Negro depths" to an austere colored upper crust.

Going above One Hundred and Twenty-fifth Street, Mr. Van Vechten was careful to be armed. His coat was of sparkling mail; his passions

From *The Saturday Review of Literature* October 2, 1926.

studied, distilled. But Striver's Row* is the one flexible spot in the engaging chrysalis that is Harlem and yielded much in excess of Mr. Van Vechten's wildest dreams. Among its dark-skinned aristocracy he expected to find, presumably, evidences of "culture," the source of jazz, swaggering opulence, "instinctive" gayety; but hardly, I gather, heirlooms of a pale, dim ancestral past, mulatto aversion to black a dominant tribal spirit, snobbishness, delightful crudity, neuroses, intellectuality. For all these Mr. Van Vechten found, and more.

ᗡᗡ

From the viewpoint of style and fulness "Nigger Heaven" is Mr. Van Vechten's finest job. The plot, which is subordinated to a very serious inquiry into the social riddle of Harlem, hinges on the loves and literary aspirations of Byron Kasson, a young Negro college graduate who wants to write. Byron is strong-willed and phlegmatic. He is desirous of creativity, but at every turn is jostled and engaged by a rising feeling of racial inequity. In delving into Byron's motives though, I often find Mr. Van Vechten at sea. He leads us at the outset to believe that Byron is burdened with none of the reticences of social caste. But as soon as Byron's defeat and unsuccess are to be accounted for "he-treated-me-that-way-because-I-am-a-Negro" is dragged in. It did not occur to his creator that Byron might have been charged with that spirit of unreasoning revolt which is the portion of most immature creative beings the world over. If the element of time in the book was intended to be A. D. 1900, Byron's psychosis would have been plausible, but today it is notoriously untrue.

Almost as illogical as Byron's primitive behavior is the idea of his regard for Mary Love. In essence she would provide a fine study of a mulatto girl who is more white in spirit than black, but etched against a background of such scintillating colors she creates a mood of unsympathetic discord. ***

Hers is one of the eternal tragedies of the borderline. In Harlem (she is a librarian there) she is unable to adapt herself to the society the refuge the frontier affords, and is too dependent a personality to risk the adventure of "crossing."

How different is Lasca! Lasca is remorseless, impulsive, divine. ***

One day in Central Park she rescues Byron from one of his fits of despair and takes him to her apartment. The boy is ecstatic. Lasca is such an adorable creature. But Lasca is the eternal bee in the flower; her seductive passion is short-lived and her desire for Byron soon dies to ebony cinders.

With that the tragedy of Byron's inadequate loves comes to a climax, with sorrow and gloom drenching the way.

The reaction to "Nigger Heaven" will be varied and tremendous. Colored people, who for the most part object to its title, will outlaw the lush lingo and the decadent cabaret passages on the ground that a white man wrote them and that "they do not show the race at its best." On the other hand, the majority of white people will prefer the Creeper's* slinking cruises on the Avenue to the glowing glimpses of splendor among the dusky Harlem smart set.

In the last analysis, however, "Nigger Heaven" will be pointed to as a frontier work of an enduring order. As literature with a strong social bias it prepares the way for examination of the fruits of a cultural flowering among the Negroes which is now about to emerge.

And no colored man, adept as he might be at self-observation and non-identification, could have written it.

*F*rom Cotton, Cane, and Rice Fields

Up from their peaceful homelands in the South, more than two million negroes have come in the past decade to put their shoulders to the busy wheels of Northern industry. Whole communities—undertakers, conjurers, hoary deacons—have pulled up stakes and joined in the "gold rush" northward to an eight-hour day and fortune. Crooning, sad-eyed Negro sections have sprung up in Northern cities; Negroes, overalled in working hours, silk-shirted in leisure moments, have suddenly become an increasing population factor where once their presence was negligible. Up from peaceful tilling of the soil to the hectic life of mill and shop.

For ages the Negro has been the heir of an agrarian culture, until the intense "protective" feeling of the South has twisted the origin of this group heritage into meaning that the Negro is more adaptable to the irresponsible life of river and stream, farm and dock. Fortunately the war did much to challenge such a view. It gave a ruthless logic to expedient legislation designed to curb the influx of European immigration. In 1914 we permitted 1,218,480 foreign-born whites to enter; of this number 303,338 returned. But in 1918, out of a reduced quota of 110,618, some

From *The Independent* September 4, 1926.

94,585 left. The total residue for the year was therefore pruned down to 18,585 as against 900,000 for 1914. As a result, a policy of unsentimental selectivity was resolved upon to fill the gap in the skilled labor ranks.

And the untried depths of Negro plantation labor yawned. Telling of the glories of work and fortune "up North," white corporation labor agents flooded the teeming "black belts" of the South. The Negro press, too,—temperamentally a "yellow" one—collaborated with lurid recitals of occurrences ill-calculated to advance the chivalry or purity of the South. But the South's time-worn attitude toward its black inhabitants had been one of unceasing duration, and the labor pirates found in the Negro belt mines of undreamed ore. Richmond alone yielded one firm 3,700 Negro laborers at $20 a man.

The South, with proprietary concern, forthwith enacted measures to restrict the "depredations" of labor agents. With 500,000 blacks leaving the farm regions of Georgia and Alabama between 1916 and 1920 it developed unexpected symptoms of interracial love. But Georgia, the lynch-star State of the Union, lost $3,000,000 in farm crops the first year of the exodus, and experts figured that between 1921 and 1925 another half-million Negroes had left the South. Fragrant mammy tales rivaled luscious idylls of adoration for the suddenly energized blacks; but the "departing Abyssinians" were loath to accept the antediluvianism that the Southern whites "understood" and "knew best how to deal with" the Negro. It was evident, moreover, by the returning grapevine tales of Negro prosperity abroad that it would be progressively difficult to restore blacks reared in Louisiana, Virginia, the Carolinas, Georgia, Alabama, Mississippi, and Texas to their traditional but unprofitable association with cane, cotton, tobacco, lumber, and turpentine.

And what of the North's reaction to this influx? When it did not raise a temperature at the physical proximity of droves of Southern Negroes, it became acutely resentful. The stark reality of streams of sable-skinned *émigrés* pouring into its cities was the basis of much feeling and unrest. As share-cropping peon or victim of mob law, the Negro— languishing in some palmetto hedge—is apt to excite the Christian piety of the liberty-loving North. But the actual presence of thousands of black immigrants, clad in semitropical garb and burdened with a load of "primitive racial traits,"—"unsanitary," "irresponsible as a class,"— was a matter of vital concern. In one city, Johnstown, Pennsylvania, it led to a riot and the expulsion by mayoral edict of six thousand dusky newcomers. In Cartaret, New Jersey, objection took a unique turn: a prize-fight brawl which culminated in the burning of a Negro church and threats to mop up the Negro section. In Detroit, whose Negro population during the exodus increased 611 per cent, a mob, resenting the invasion by Negroes of a certain residential area, fired into the home of Dr. Ossian Sweet, a Negro physician. With retaliating shots the Negroes fired back, killing one and wounding two others. The result has been a murder case upon whose outcome the Negro's civil and moral status in the North depends.* Chicago, East St. Louis, Tulsa, Springfield, Illinois, and Washington have also invoked the law of the jungle with ensuing terror and bloodshed.

With the Negro population in the North doubled by the migration to 2,167,179—Dr. Work of Tuskegee* sets 1,139,505 as the total number of Negroes leaving since it started—the stock notions of racial inequality which herded the Negroes into personal service began to be questioned. ***

All in all, the shift from the simple rural life of the South to the roaring mechanized civilization of the North has resulted in some 371,229 Negroes entering industry.

It was a star, risen in the North, and the dusky wayfarers moved towards it. It was one of the startling social upheavals of modern times, and the gauging eyes of the nation looked questioningly on. All the grating superstitions concerning the Negro's inability to withstand the cold, his susceptibility to disease—tuberculosis, pneumonia, varicose veins, weak heart, poor eyesight—his record as a lazy, indolent worker were exhumed and bandied about. He was whimsical, unreliable, "a stone around the employer's neck." One employer in Springfield went so far as to say, "I imagine if you hired them haphazardly and got very many of them, they'd be hard to handle." Another declared, "We do not have Negro employees. We've had them as janitors and they were not satisfactory."

But Edgar E. Adams, vice president of the Cleveland Hardware Company, gives an illuminating picture in contrast. "Some of the best records for speed in our plant," he affirms, "are held by colored men and women." ***

We are told that the World War "threatened" civilization, but it also quickened its tempo. It did marvels for the subject races, the American Negro not excepted. One, indubitably, is witnessed by the Negro's venture in industry, a pretty "unfixed" one at this time. The prospect may not always seem to be the "best thing for the North," but the best Negro minds are most flexible on the point. The Negro coming North, though instinct with a certain ingenuousness—a being of poignant sorrows and dreads—aspires to a place in industry measured on a basis of equalized right. Patriotism certainly entered into the urge to migrate, and he is often confused and bewildered by the cries of "Wolf! Wolf!" incident to his presence here.

‌The Color of the Caribbean

Considering the physical limits of the region, there is hardly to be found elsewhere in the Atlantic a richer fusing of cultures than has been at work in the sunny coral isles of the West Indies. For ever since the immortal Genoese's sail westward* the beauty and hypnotic splendor of these islands have contrived to attract to them a most daring and romantic set of empire-builders.

To begin with, there was, forming a base for the intense compounding of cultures that was to follow the gory footprints of the Spaniard, the Carib, whose continuance in the heat and dung of the Honduras forests today is proof of the reckless bid for perpetuity made by this people; and the austere symbols of whose past, just about come to light, suggest a legacy of undisputed sovereign worth destined to remain unshadowed by neither obscurity nor unintelligibility. Second, there were the slaves the Spaniards brought from Africa to work their Antillean estates, and, incidentally, to edge the Caribs into the dungeons of the sea. Coming some two hundred years before the *Mayflower* set sail, the surly African captives were overawed to find themselves transmuted to a region fully as tropical as the rich green banks of their late West African lagoons. Thus they took lustily to their new coral-rimmed abode. In its glens and dewy vales they sought to inject the essence of their jealous tribal way of being—did obeisance to grotesque *obeah* gods, invested vine and leaf and herb with startling medicinal properties; spoke a *patois* which borrowed from the disciplined rhythm of the African tongues and the unguarded idiomatic speech of the Europeans.

Then the crimson pirate wars were ushered in. Smoke from the mouths of vomiting pirate cannon blew from seashore and castletop the jeweled bands of Caribbean sunlight. Amidst the storm of strife and unrest, the fates were quick to seize the chance to shuffle the Caribbean deck of cards. Half a dozen precious isles changed hands; changed from Spanish to English, Spanish to French to English, to French to English to Dutch, to English to Danish, and so on. Two of these isles, years later,—one the brightest jewel in the West Indian crown—groaning under the yoke of the Spaniard, rebelled, and, with the benignant help of the United States, tore themselves "free."

But there also took place another, but perhaps less unified type of warfare—the sporadic outbreaks of the blacks—which reflect some of the temper and some of the spirit imbedded in the native grain. All during and before the shedding of intolerable yokes and the swapping of continental allegiances the slaves on the plantations were growing unmanageably more and more restive. Uprisings flourished. From a parapet in Nevis a band of slaves, disdaining the fruits of British dominion, jumped headlong into the rock-strewn bay; in Jamaica the Maroons, under Cudjo,* were slashing away to a victory which they have not yet ceased to cherish; in Peru and St. Croix and Surinam there were revolts and diabolic massacres; and in the Isthmus province of New Granada, Juanillo el Gacho was cutting a blood-red path through the Spanish bulwarks to a Stone Throne. In fact, on one isle,* ruled by the French, the blacks rose and seized the reins of power. And for years there roamed over nearby isles bands of escaping slaves, engaging squads of bewildered pursuers or seeking asylum in caves and passes, and ultimately carving out for themselves a destiny and a way of life far from the vision or comprehension of the whites.

In time, after a few legitimate moves on the Caribbean checker-board, the islands succeeded to a romantic mercantile calm, and life in West Indian seaport and village, city and estate hill, took on a dusty, dreamy serenity.

The warring rudiments of West Indian society reflect the exotic quality of its civilization. Going to the islands, the visitor is at once struck by the great variety of racial types dominant there. It is easy, of course, to recognize at the bottom of the social order the Negro, who forms the mass of the population. He is the islands' arch laborer and the sullen master of its affluent soil. It is true that since 1833, the first burst of freedom in the West Indies, he has met the competitive elbow of Chinese and Hindu coolies, who have drifted in with the fitful tides of emigration; but the shock has been either too short-lived or negligible, for the Asiatics in the West Indies possess an inexplicable genius for drifting into the shopkeeping class. And the absentee landlords in Nice and Monte Carlo continue to rivet their eyes on the resilient back of the Negro for brawn to man their scows and lighters, brawn to hoe and plant, cut and suckle sugar cane. This class of whites is not the only one that has fastened itself like a leech to the buxom sinews of the blacks. The colonizing settlers, a breed slightly distinct from the absentee land owners and consisting of planters, soldiers, beachcombers and adventurers, were notoriously free of scruples when it came to playing Condescending Adam to some maiden's Nile-lit Eve. You may not need to be told, but these whites, from the standpoint of the Bourbon blades afloat in Virginia and Louisiana, were either a jaundiced or a susceptible lot. For while they mingled freely with the blacks they rarely denied the offspring of their democratic endeavors the legal emoluments of kinship.

As a result, the mulatto, on coming into the world, came, as it were, with the ready-made conceits of one who had been legislated by Providence out of the squatter class. He was an intermediate concoction by more than one right. In community matters he was accorded a place midway between black and white. He was taught to consider himself superior to the blacks, and if not as good, then nearly as good as the whites. In the beginning the distinction, which was not at all a racial one, was accepted by reasons of certain property or material inheritances, but as time went on and the motives dimmed it became confused, notably in Jamaica and St. Thomas, with gradations in pigment and gave to the blacks a uniformly lower status than the mulatto. As a consequence, a black man in these two islands, unless he is a merchant or a member of the educated class, is scornfully looked down upon; whereas, a mulatto, regardless of the number of the decimals in his I.Q., can pass muster anywhere. It may be pointed out, however, that long before the growth of anti-black sentiment among the near-whites there were full-blooded Negroes who had risen out of the "hoe and bill" class and who sported manors and monocles and Edinburgh sheep skins.

It is singular that the mulatto-black issue is only agitated in colonies where the Anglo-Saxon spirit predominates. In countries governed by the Latin attitude to life, no hue or cry is ever raised by either white or mestizo over the shade of a man's skin. In these none too plenteous regions, the European point of view with respect to "social equality" is faithfully transcribed. Here, however, color gives way to intense national affection. In Cuba or Santo Domingo a blue-eyed Swede or a sunburnt Syrian, as foreigners ignorant of *las costumbres del pais*,* enjoy at best an arbitrary emotional relation; but for a *paysano*, be he salmon-colored or ebony, there is no post or measure of patronage too richly coveted for him. Indeed, it is a desultory commonplace that from the time of the first Spaniard settlers men of Negro descent have filled enduring roles in the affairs of Latin America.

Contrary to legend, the Europeans who went out to the West Indies were a long-headed set of Crown Colonists. Take, for example, the case of the English, the shadow of whose imperialistic arm hangs darkly over this region. The English did not go, like their near-sighted cousins of a century and a half later, with bombast and "darky-hating" acts and epithets. They went instead with the one defined purpose of exploiting the mighty resources of the tropics. They brought capital—not enough, it is true, to stem the tide of labor that sweeps over the banana lagoons of Tela and Changuinola, but enough to keep the royal cat o' nine greased and snarling in the colonial sun—they brought industry and builded docks and railways and warehouses and sugar mills. In their stern, unostentatious wake they left order and peonage and custom houses and the incomparable British system of common school education. As a kind of *cazrip** to season the Caribbean "pepper pot"* the Spaniards, whose impress was firmest, also unloaded gifts—dignity and ceremony and poverty; the worship of beauty and the Catholic clergy. And from the French there were traces of poetry and urbanity and an ill-fated penal colony.*

In the light of such a vivid past, the question of art, culture and folk-lore in the West Indies is one of engaging fascination and promise. It is of such vast and virginal proportions, however, that it is only possible here to skip lightly around it.

If we concede that history precedes sociology and sociology pure art, it can hardly be said that the cultural cycle in the West Indies has even begun, any more than we can say that art in the United States is on the eve of a Hellenic outburst. We need not look very far for the reasons. In the first place, it must be borne in mind that each island, or set of islands, is a world apart, with often a jealous history to boot, which, though it may not be quite as "relevant" as fabled Ionia's,* may merit more than passing half-mention; also, that each island is inhabited by part-Negro and full-Negro peoples, imbued with a mixed African and Latin outlook on life, whose sociology has not even been dimly guessed at.

In legends, folk-lore and the primary essentials of a folk-literature, the islands abound. Rich in superstition, witchcraft and Anancy tales;* having in its cities and towns a social life quite as gay and abandoned as any to be met with in Venice or Milan; equipped with a climate that is designed to give color and ease to the pursuit of the creative life,—it is a bit disconcerting to find in the output of the native, with perhaps one or two ineffectual exceptions, none but the remotest idea of the intrinsic artistic worth of all this. Indeed, the poets and creative writers of the West Indies, who, it seems, are just beginning to get excited over the literary traditions of Europe and the British Isles, succeed usually in giving little more than a pretty continentalized version of the life of their exotic tropic heath.

But in this regard the islands are no more "behind the times" than were the United States before Washington Irving wrote.

On coming to the United States, the West Indian often finds himself out of patience with the attitude he meets here respecting the position of whites and Negroes. He is bewildered—that is, if he is not "clear" enough to pass as a Greek or Spaniard or Italian—at being shoved down certain blocks and alleys "among his own people." He is angry and amazed at the futility of seeking out certain types of employment for which he may be specially adapted. And about the cruelest injury that could be inflicted upon him is to ask him to submit to the notion that because he is black it is useless for him to aspire to be more than a trap drummer at Small's,* a Red Cap in the Pennsylvania Station, or a clerk in the Bowling Green Post Office.

Fiction

$\mathcal{M}$iss Kenny's Marriage

I

If you went into her shop and in a perfectly harmless way asked: "Is this Miss Kenny's Hair Parlor?" she would poke her coiffeured head at you and in a manner that you would not easily forget, reply: "Come in; this is Miss Kenny's *Beauty* Parlor."

There was a difference, you see, between a mere hair parlor and a beauty parlor. As she privately confided to a friend:

"I don't merely iron hair, girlie; I beautifies; and I am not a hairdresser at all, but a beauty culturist. There are so many two-cent hairdressers around Brooklyn, girlie, I want to strike out and be a pioneer and establish a regular trichological* institute. That is why you see me working off my fingertips on the scalps of all these servant girls.

"Of course," Miss Kenny would add, "they are only a part, a very small part, of my regular trade. I can mention among my customers Rev. Brown's wife, Mme. Downing, Miss Jackson of the Y.W., Dr. Jones' niece—"

Again, if you walked into her cobwebby parlor and asked her if she had any of Mme. Walker's* Hair Goods she would relax in a beautifully ingratiating smile, while her big wolfish eyes would widen in pity as she snapped:

From *The Smart Set* September 1923.

"You see, I have no need to carry Mme. Walker's goods; other hair-dressers have to carry mine. I can give you Mme. Kenny's Tar Hair Grower or Mme. Kenny's Glossine."

At the Antioch Baptist Church, where she worshipped, Miss Kenny's reputation as a coloratura soprano equaled if it did not threaten that of "the nightingale of the race."* Whenever anybody was getting up a pageant or a choir concert or anything in which Negro folk songs played a part Miss Kenny simply had to be in it, or it would not be "representative." Once an enterprising young acolyte from Jersey prepared a program and did not include Miss Kenny. The choir in question was to sing at the annual convention of the Christian Endeavor Societies. The day before it came off an anonymous letter appeared in the columns of the Negro press lambasting it as "inartistic, unmusical and not representative of Southern culture."

II

The sun shone down brightly on the old dilapidated building in Atlantic avenue. Yes, she had it there—in Atlantic avenue. If any of her high-toned friends rebuked her for it she would retort: "I tell you, honey, when I came to Brooklyn Atlantic avenue had a good reputation. It is only since these Jews and Italians and low-down black folks moved on it that it got such a bad name. Of course it is so hard to get a decent place to move to nowadays that I thought the best thing to do was to stay, even though my friends ridicule me for it."

As a matter of fact, Miss Kenny, true to form, told only a part, a very small part, of the truth. Secretly she feared that if she took her shingle down and sought quarters uptown or down in the Myrtle avenue section, she would lose her customers. Moreover, in spite of its bad plumbing and the fact that it was situated in the headquarters of a local Camorra,* she loved it a great deal and a few weeks before had actually begun negotiations for the purchase of the house. That was just like her. Friends who had made a study of her reported that it was a habit which she could not easily get rid of. Not that Miss Kenny was a four-flusher* in the ordinary sense of the word. Heavens, no! She simply delighted in beating around the bush and misleading folks as to her personal affairs.

Take the matter of money, for instance. She always made it a rule to say boisterously to a crowded room of patrons that she "never kept money in the house."

"It is so dangerous," she murmured, "with all these burglars and stick-up men tramping around, honey. Only this very forenoon a man—sure, a white man, girlie. I am sick of 'em coming round here. I don't know where he got it from, but I could smell it loud on his breath.* It was a good thing Mr. Daniels was in here at the time. He came in and asked me if I had any face powder, that he wanted to buy some. I told him he could get some on the corner at the druggist's, that I didn't carry any, so he left. These drunks come in so often, girlie, I've got to be careful, awful careful."

Only a part of the truth. For as regular as the clock ticked she made it a point before going to bed at night to tie up the day's earnings in an old black stocking and hide it safely in one of the trunks on which she slept. Not that she was a miser and loved the smell or jingle of gold. But she liked, whenever she went down to the bank, to deposit two or three hundred dollars at a time. She liked, as she delighted in saying, to "make a decent showing." Moreover, the teller at the bank was a nice blond youth who parted his hair straight down the middle. She liked to look at his boyish cheeks; they were so round and ruddy. And whenever she made a "decent showing" the teller would smile and show his pearl-white teeth and, metaphorically speaking, pat her on the back, muttering: "Go to it, Miss Kenny; go to it! You will soon reach the ten-thousand-dollar mark." Yes, Miss Kenny had money. Of course she could never admit it. She always made it a point to impress strangers (and friends alike) with her utter destitution.

Until far into the night Miss Kenny worked; God only knows how she stood it. Still she was up with the chickens in the morning. Usually a queue of patrons would be at the door waiting for her, as if she were a fortune-teller. One would be tempted to jump to all sorts of conclusions as to her magic power. But it was really her Tar Hair Grower that did it. Not since the time of the famous Mme. Walker had a preparation met with such overwhelming success. It went like wildfire. Girls and old women, spinsters and preachers' wives, scrubwomen and colored ladies of gentility, all raved over it. Decidedly it was a phenomenon. But when approached by a local ad man, Miss Kenny strenuously objected to what she called "immoral" advertising. The idea of being pulled down from her empyrean heights to the level of a cheap, everyday merchant caused her to shudder and grind her teeth as if she had the ague.

"Do doctors advertise?" she chirped. "Or only quacks? My customers advertise me. I haven't got to put out my wares thet a-way. If a customer is satisfied she will tell somebody else, and if that person wants her hair done she will remember and come to me. I ain't got to stoop to such low tricks. My trade is not the harum-scarum, get-when-the-getting-is-good kind. It is what you call 'recommended.' "

One other peculiarity of Miss Kenny was that she never transacted business outside her store. You see, she had very definite ideas about business, especially about how it was conducted by colored people.

"I tell you, girlie, we cullud folks are an unbusinesslike lot. Yesterday I went on down to Mr. Daniels, the printer, to get some th'ow-arounds. Now I wanted to sit right there and count 'em, but Miss Murray of King Solomon Lodge was in at the time, and I didn't want her to think I was cranky. You know what I mean. Well, I paid him for them, taking his word for it that they was 5,000 in the package. When I got home I counted 'em and found that the rascal had only given me 2,643 and a half torn one. Of course I rang him up and told him that, while I did not look at it as an out-and-out attempt to rob me, I would be glad if he would be more businesslike in the future and not tell me 2,643 and a torn one is 5,000. As if I couldn't count!"

Once an enterprising young salesman met her on the street and tried to sell her a set of the Encyclopædia Britannica. Miss Kenny stood still with an interested smile on her lips and allowed him in rapid-fire language to rattle off his story. When the young man got around to that part which said something about brass tacks and contracts and so much down and so much a month Miss Kenny thought it was time to step in. Drawing herself up to an imperial height, she inquired: "Is this the right time and place to see me?" and swept on.

She had another very interesting reason for refusing to do business anywhere but in her store. If there ever was a psychologist, Miss Kenny was one and she knew it. She felt confident of her ability to out-argue any man who came into her store; and, as it was always crowded, she rejoiced in the effect it had on her dumb, sheep-faced customers. They formed a sort of wall around her and she felt surer of herself whenever she was thus fortified.

And Miss Kenny hadn't any secrets. What she had to say she said right out, declaring in no uncertain terms that she hadn't anything to hide, and if anybody wanted to go back and say she said so and so, why they could. Of course this was the best guarantee Miss Kenny had for the non-repetition of what she said, and no one knew that better than she. Deep down in her heart she did not want everything she said repeated. Her tongue flew like a serpent's. Limitless in its scope, it lighted on this, that and a multitude of things. On Monday talk drifted around to what happened at church the day before. Sometimes it had to do with what the president of the men's guild had to say about married women who flirt. Or what Mrs. So-and-So wore, or the screech in somebody's voice. On Tuesday it edged around to the scandal of Undertaker Williams, whose newly wedded wife had mysteriously given birth to a baby. Wednesday and Thursday Miss Kenny always devoted to a discussion of her rivals. She liked to tell in her clever way of the almost universal use of her "grower" by the rest of the profession.

"Not that I care anything about them tearing off my labels and sticking on theirs," she snickered, "but they oughtn't to cry down my grower in public when they are using it in private themselves."

"But why don't you prosecute them, Miss Kenny?" volunteered a chorus. "Why don't you patent your grower so that they wouldn't get a chance to rob you?"

"Oh," she replied, with a dash of braggadocio, "I am not as mean and as low-down as all that. I want to see everybody live and make a living. There ain't none of the nigger in me, honey."

III

One day the visitors to Miss Kenny's parlor got the shock of their lives. True, it was not the first time she had received a telephone call, but such a call! As usual, the place was packed, packed from stem to stern. Three of her "girlies" actually succeeded in climbing into the old, scarlet upholstered barber's chair that constituted her chief item of furniture. On top of the medieval piano in the corner sat three long-faced patrons. The only two available chairs accommodated no less than five sweating Buddha-like persons. There was scarcely room for her iron-chained door to swing to. Just the same they sat, and awaited their turn, while behind the ox-marrow curtain the cackling voice of Miss Kenny was astonishingly flippant.

"Her and I went down to see it last week. Yes, yes, but I don't know about that. I'd rather—not. Can't you make it Sunday? Aren't you coming to breakfast Sunday morning? No? Ugh. Oh, I see. Well, I'll have to tell Antony—Yes, I got it all right. Very lovely of you. All right, I'm busy mahself—place's crowded. S'long."

Yes, Miss Kenny, like every lady of her time, had a lover. Of course she had a naïve way of saying she had been favorably regarded by a number of marriageable young men. Always speaking in platitudes, it was easy for her to bamboozle her customers as to her charm and beauty. But the fact of the matter was Miss Kenny hadn't any charm or beauty at all. Persons in the know would look at the tar tumbling down the temples of her bronze face and retreat in terror. That, one would imagine, was a highly ingenious thing from a business standpoint. But socially it did not work. It was a miserable failure. Other beauty culturists, when the day's work was over, discarded their wreaths of hair nets and took down their coiffures and tidied up to conform to flapper standards. But Miss Kenny, with all her brains, hadn't brains enough to give herself a thorough tonsorial overhauling. Take the matter of water, for instance. If she could have reconciled herself to a liberal use of it on, say, her upper parts, around the region of her neck and shoulders, there is no telling, with that tongue of hers, what would have been the scope of her marital potentialities, but Miss Kenny hated water—hated it like poison.

When she put down the receiver and came out of her niche of a bedroom her customers one and all gasped at the woman's magic transformation. Miss Kenny was lavender pink!

"I tell you what, girls," she spoke rapidly, "I've just had a hurried call from my legal adviser and he wants me to drop everything and come on down to the court right this minute. I am to testify in that curtain case I told you all about. Now I hate to do it, honest I do, for that is just what the white folks like to see us do. Two niggers squabbling in court over a pair of $40 curtains! But it is the only way you can learn our folks a lesson—how to do business in the proper way. You've got to drag 'em right out in the light and let the white folks see what rascals— Can you all come back tomorrow? I guess I am late already. He said he'd be—that is, that I must be down there by two."

After the last one had gone Miss Kenny heaved a sigh of relief as she fastened the chain on the door. One would have thought that she would be in an awful hurry to get on her things and get out, but all she did was to pack the gas range and the hair straightener and the vaseline vial safely in a box under the sink. Going into a soap-box larder on the wall she extracted a huge broiled chicken and began to singe it. Deftly she cut it up, seasoning it as she did so. She took a paper bag of flour from the washtub and emptied the greater portion of it into a yellow platter. On top of this she broke an egg, poured in water and started to mix. That done, she took a cupful of cocoa and poured it into a kettle on the fire. Meanwhile she opened a door in the side of her room leading to the hallway. Poking out her ferret face, Miss Kenny yelled "Antony!" Instantly a little Italian girl appeared.

"Run down to the corner and buy me a dime of lettuce, Antony. Hurry, honey."

Back in her smoke-filled room Miss Kenny laid the table. She flung the greasy curtain that separated the sittingroom from her passageway of a workroom on top of the pole, so as to be able to get the maximum of service out of her magnificent dining table. There was a bit of romance attached to that table. Over in Jersey—but this certainly is not the place for it. Miss Kenny went down to the bottom of her trunk and dug up the prettiest silver set you ever want to see. As she worked, her face grew blacker and blacker. Not only did the tar begin to trickle down the sides of it; even her neck became infected. Alarmed, Miss Kenny took her apron and made a big westward wipe. What she saw on the apron as she held it up before her eyes sent her scurrying in front of the mirror. Then began the beautification of Miss Kenny. First, she took the big steel brush on the mantel and gave the bushel of horse hair on her head a vicious stay-as-you-are-put. Next she took a wet towel and lathered her face good and plenty. Yes, she went down in her trunk and forked up a cake of honest-to-goodness soap. Not cold cream—soap. After a speedy rub or two on her neck she ducked under the curtain that led to her sleeping quarters. When she came out again she wore an immaculate apron—one so high at the top that it covered up her oil-glittering neck. It had a challenging effect. Only one thing got lost in the shuffle—the perpetual shine on Miss Kenny's face. It now looked as if it had been banished by an edict from On High. Miss Kenny had a liberal dab of powder on her nose.

IV

About five minutes later Miss Kenny heard someone knocking at the door. Going to it as fast as her feet could carry her she curtsied as she ushered in Counsellor Elias Ramsey.

Miss Kenny was a woman of about forty-eight. The Counselor was just turning twenty-five. What prompted a man of his age and standing to pay homage to a woman who could be his mother, and a hairdresser besides, is not our purpose to disclose. Suffice to say Mr. Ramsey was a young man born and bred in Brooklyn. Haughty and dictatorial, it was easy to see that he came from Brooklyn. No, he had not studied at the University of Berlin, nor had he in any way come under the influence of Germans. Germans, after all, are awfully nice people, and Mr. Ramsey was not only human, but a dull, unemotional person. In him one got an edifying glimpse of the Negro placed in a community where there is a minority of colored folk. All his life had been spent among white people and, being what he was, uppity, ignorant, arrogant, he felt that he was not only the equal of the best of white men, but superior to a whole lot of them. But even Napoleon stoops to conquer, and the mere fact that he had condescended to dine with the hairdresser was proof of Mr. Ramsey's stooping to conquer. For, don't forget, Mr. Ramsey belonged to one of the oldest families of color in Brooklyn. He was bound hard and fast to the rule not to commingle with aliens, outsiders—that is, anybody who could not trace his ancestors back to the Battle of Long Island.* And Miss Kenny had been in Brooklyn only three years.

"I thought I'd be able to get you a nice pork chop," said Miss Kenny as they started to eat, "but I chased all over the block and couldn't get a single one. This chicken is not as tender as I thought it was."

As a rule, Mr. Ramsey allowed Miss Kenny to do all the talking. It was an arrangement that she, like most of her sex, delighted in. Lawyers have such an enormous lot to think about. She liked to sit and reel off tales of her own creation for his amusement and edification. While Mr. Ramsey, being a Brooklynite, kept his eyes open and his mouth shut. It is significant to note, however, that whenever he spoke it was in a dry, legal-like fashion with very little animation. To him it was the same as dining out with a client, but Miss Kenny interpreted every word, every glance, every touch of the hand as a bit of well-directed flattery and giggled over it. Contrasting her with the cold, austere hair-ironer, one is obliged to reflect damningly on the iconoclasm of love. Yes, he had Miss Kenny completely in his power, and if you chanced to look at him you would have wondered how he managed to do it. There was not anything presupposing about the man. He had thin, sandy hair, a weak yellow complexion, and eyes that always looked past you. But Miss Kenny, it must be explained, paid no attention to such trifles. He was a man. That settled it. And she was man-mad. One of her life's ambitions was to marry and settle down. So when Mr. Ramsey asked her to become his wife one is consummately at a loss to adequately picture the emotions and heart-beats of Miss Kenny.

"Oh, Elias," she cried, "if you only knew how happy I am. At last my prayers are answered. Now I shall be able to take my place in society, to go out and not wash hair all my life. The wife of a prominent lawyer! It is big enough to swell my head."

"But—" It was the restraining voice of her legal adviser—"as I told you the other day, Catherine, I've got a long way to go yet. I've just started out, and it takes time to get established."

"As if I didn't know," she reproached, climbing up into his lap, "as if I'd let you bear all the burden of our love. Elias, I love you so blamed much I am willing to bury myself in this rotten old hole the rest of my life, so long as I know I'm helping you. And don't think I haven't been saving my money, sweetie. Here, I'll run and show you."

She got down and with a girlish swing disappeared behind the curtain. As she returned, in her joyful mood, she failed to note the look in her legal adviser's eyes.

"Look," she said, "this is what it is to date."

Mr. Ramsey looked. What he saw fairly brought the blood to his face, but he was a lawyer, an emotionless lawyer, and from Brooklyn. Nine thousand five hundred and eighty-six dollars!

"And that does not include yesterday's nor today's receipts," broke in Miss Kenny. "Yesterday alone I made $34. Fancy my working until one and two o'clock in the morning doing heads! Nor has this anything to do with the money I am paying on the house. Let me see, I think there is only a first mortgage of $1,200 left. I don't think I have done so bad for three years."

Evidently these mundane things had no place in Mr. Ramsey's universe. As he spoke she glimpsed in his eyes the dreamily idealistic light which had attracted her from the beginning.

"That is very well, Catherine. It is frugal and commendable. It is the quality a man admires in a woman. But you see I had in mind getting a job nights as an elevator operator or porter. It really doesn't matter what I do, so long as I get the money. Or perhaps I could pick up my trombone again—only that would be kind of out of place just now. I could not very well get away with that and practice, too. I know what I'll do, I'll get a porter's job out on Long Island somewhere at night so as to earn money enough to support both of us."

Miss Kenny was horrified at the determination she saw in his eyes. A lawyer working nights as a porter? Unthinkable! That was the very thing she wanted the men of the race to get away from!

"Why, Elias, who ever put such a crazy idea into your head? Do you think I'd allow you to sacrifice your wonderful future doing work of that kind? My dear, that is the least of our worries. With this shop going I alone can clean up $100 a week. No, dearie, get the idea out of your head. Get it out entirely. What is mine is as good as yours."

"Just as you wish," sighed Mr. Ramsey wearily. "Only I don't want to impose on you in any way."

"Oh, my darling boy, I can understand how you must feel. I can! I can. But, sweetie, I want you to love and trust and confide in me. Only that and everything will come out all right. Don't think for a moment that I am trying to be the man. I am not! I don't believe in all this talk about woman's suffrage noways. Woman's place is in the home and she ought to stay there. Don't for a moment think of being obligated in any way. When two people love each other they are as good as one in flesh and blood; in everything, in fact."

"Well," sighed Mr. Ramsey again, "I am glad you look at the thing in the right light. I certainly—"

"Don't say it, honey," interjected Miss Kenny, planting a wet kiss on his lips, "don't utter a single word. Don't I understand thoroughly? Trust me, honey, lay your head on my bosom and stop mourning. I am too experienced not to know any better."

V

Up to the eve of her wedding Miss Kenny worked. All that day a stream of frenzied folk poured into the tar-smelling establishment to bid her Godspeed. It is at such times that one's popularity is tested. While Miss Kenny was not in any sense a member of the olive-skinned aristocracy of Brooklyn, there was evidence abundant to testify to the esteem in which she was held by, as she pertly expressed it, "gangs and gangs of folks." Presents of all descriptions were received that afternoon, and Miss Kenny, while presiding over a turbulently unruly head, rolled out thanks and appreciations to her affectionate friends. Even Mme. Kennedy, a rival hairdresser, thought she would send the tar queen bride a lovely bunch of geraniums.

Miss Kenny was so impressed that she ordered one of her "girlies" to sit right down and scribble the lady a grateful note of acknowledgment. She was too busy, she explained, to stop and wash her hands just to write a short note. The girl, not stopping to investigate Miss Kenny's chirographic* ability, wrote it, and read it to her, after which it was despatched to Miss Kennedy. Out of the morass of gifts she received Miss Kenny cherished one more than all the others. It was the charming lavallière* sent her by the Willing Workers Club of the Antioch Baptist Church.

The day broke calm and beautiful as Miss Kenny prepared for the event of her life. To assist her in her trousseau Miss Kenny had a friend, Mrs. Williams, from across the street. The knowledge of Miss Kenny's forthcoming marriage had penetrated every home on Atlantic avenue.

As the hour drew near a curious mob gathered in front of the now gorgeously decorated store. The fact that Miss Kenny elected to marry in her dingy workshop did not seem to bother anyone. Fortunately, the hour was fixed toward sundown, so as to enable her attendant, Mrs. Bryan, who did housework in Flatbush, to get there in time. Mr. Ramsey was accompanied by a colleague of his, a Mr. Blake. The wedding was a simple one. Nothing exciting or unduly dramatic took place. The bride and groom were both there, as arranged, and there was no third party to bolt in at the last moment to claim either. The bridal supper was served on Miss Kenny's magnificent table, the pastor presiding in the upholstered barber's chair. Everyone had a good time. At midnight the couple departed for Atlantic City, where, the local colored weekly informed the public a few days later, they spent an enjoyable five-day honeymoon. During her absence Miss Kenny left Mrs. Bryan in charge, who, because she did not happen to be Miss Kenny, only served to spirit away the regular inflow of trade. They were content to wait, pouted the beauty lovers, until Miss Kenny returned from her honeymoon.

Yes, Miss Kenny got back safely. Her small black squirrel eyes sparkled as she told them about the wonderful time she had had. Once more on her throne, she ruled in the old queenly way.

"Chile, I never knowed what love was until I got married. All the time I felt it was a feeling you could shake off at will, like hunger or thirst. But, girlie, it is a tremendous thing. Tremendous! Takes hold of you by the collar and says, 'Here, you are in my clutches for the balance of your life. So look out now!' Just like that."

Suddenly the telephone rang.

"Oh, Elias," sobbed Miss Kenny, "do come on up at once. I must see you this very minute. My head starts to ache me as if it will never stop. Try, honey, and break away. I am dying to be in your arms again."

Yes, Miss Kenny was happily married. And if anyone out in the street dropped a remark about her still "doing heads" her blatant defense was, "That is just like us cullud folks. I tell you, girlie, I am not like a lot of these new niggers you see floating around here. A few hundred dollars don't frighten me. Only we used-to-nothing cullud folks lose our heads and stick out our chests at sight of a few red pennies.

"Tell 'em I'll stop working when I've got a million dollars in the bank, so that I won't have to go to anybody and ask them to lend me some."

So there she was, as homely in her philosophy as of old, with a primitive pride, bigoted, lovable, and as happy as any bride need be.

VI

There came a time, however, when fate blew harsh and stormy winds to Miss Kenny's gates. It was about three months after her ecstatic wedding. The counsellor, it seemed, had succeeded in getting her to daub the old shack with a coat of chocolate brown paint. It stood out from the rest of the chaff along the block. Bit by bit the tale leaked out. How true it was no one had been able to say, as Miss Kenny was naturally reticent, and it would take a wrecking crane to hoist anything out of her. But it had to come out, and one evening, throwing a dark shawl over her shoulders, Miss Kenny made her way to the house of her friend, Mrs. Bryan, in Downing Street. As she rang the bell and was let in, Mrs. Bryan gasped as she saw the big black rings around Miss Kenny's eyes. Tar or no tar, it was clear that Miss Kenny had been weeping—weeping her soul out. "O, Teresa, Teresa, what must I do? My God, to think that my marriage is a failure!"

"Tell me, Miss Kenny, what is ailing you? You are delirious!"

"No, I ain't Mrs. Bryan, I ain't delirious. I'm perfectly normal. Oh, my God, what is to 'come of me? All my savings gone, just gone like a-thet! It was about three nights ago—yes, Wednesday night. I had a terrible headache and was lying crossways on the bed. Elias had just come in from work and after having his supper was sitting outside, smoking. My head ached so I asked him to go and get me the cologne. Oh, Mrs. Bryan, I hate to say it. It galls me. Yes, he went to the chiffonier, and brought me the bottle with the cologne. I asked him to wet a towel with some and put it on my forehead. That is the last thing I knew. All I remember is seeing him hovering around me, with the wet towel in his hand. And the room seemed to be suffocated with chloroform or something, but I thought it was the cologne and fell asleep. This morning I went down to the bank and I was surprised to learn that my account was overdrawn. Can you imagine it? Over nine thousand dollars was taken out. Of course I laughed and told the teller that he must have made a mistake, but he said no, and went to the drawer and brought out a cashed cheque and showed it to me. It was my signature all right. There was no denying that."

"But who was it made out to?" screamed Mrs. Bryan, "who got the money?"

"Elias, chile, Elias Ramsey," sobbed Miss Kenny, "I wonder where I can find him."

The Godless City*

In the night the U.S.S. *Manodnock* glowed like a bronze pebble on the tropic sea; slowly, slowly—like a cop on the beat—kept vigil; guarded the gateway to the canal. All round, the water—oily, greasy, marrow-like—lapped up against the side of the huge slate-colored monitor-type body. Yonder, not thirty miles away, the city of Aspinwall slept—lay wrapped in doleful slumber.

On the berth deck, the Negro cooks and firemen in their B.V.D.'s, their black bodies shining like bits of sculptured bronze, avidly strove to soften the perils of restlessness—of being down there in latitude nearly nine, and "a millyun miles from nowhar." It was a terribly hot night. Beads of sweat rolled down their black, black faces. Lying in their hammocks, they sang and swore and smoked, as two crap-shooters on the deck—like an angry cat and dog—flew at each other's throats.

"*Born in Alabama*
Raised in Tennessee
Ef you don't like mah peaches
Don't shake mah tree. . . ."

From *Success Magazine* January 1924.

"Hmm!"

"Let 'em roll dey, big boy! Let 'em roll!"

"Two bits he don't five again."

"Hmm!"

"Two bits he don't five again."

"Hmm!"

"Dispose of him dice!"

"Five!"

"Dispose of him dice!"

"Hmm!"

"Come five! Five!"

"Roll 'em out dey, big boy. Roll 'em out!"

In his cabin, Captain Wingate—lily in a flower-bed of silver, roses, orchids, pennants, electric fans—looked up as Ezekiel Yates, last of that tribe of black vikings, the Maroons of Jamaica, put a demi-tasse of cognac in front of him. As usual, Ezekiel, the only man aboard who could recite you "by heart" the Songs of Solomon, was dark and solemn and grotesquely ghoulish. Black as the ace of spades, in a white sailor suit, the edge of his trousers' bottoms rolled up to his hairy calves—bare of foot, bald of head, his big heavy lips clamped down like a mummy's—"Zeek" was not at all a happy soul from which to seek solace.

Half clad, lying on the picture-strewn couch, Captain Wingate swallowed the cognac and gazed at a picture on the wall—a picture of a young girl in a tennis jacket with a racquet in her hand. Near the picture, a port opened out on the night—the black tropical night. Through it Captain Wingate, who had been lying there gazing at his daughter's picture, thought he saw the shadow of a star rise and burst and fall. He looked again. Again the star—a rain of stars—crimsoned the sky.

"Zeek!" Captain Wingate cried, getting up and going to the port. "What is that out there—a celebration?"

"No," Zeek said slowly, "it ain't no celebration."

Across the ocean a wall of ebony rose to the sky. There, like a streak of gold, a sky rocket illumined it.

"For God's sake, Zeek—don't stand there like a mummy! Open your mouth! Speak! What is it?"

Still Ezekiel, humming a song he used to sing when he was a Jamaica "Bedwardite,"* went about the chores of the cabin, seemingly unmindful of the Captain's voice.

Snatching a pair of eye-glasses, the Captain rushed on deck and gazed towards Aspinwall on the skyline—and the mysterious crimsoning of the clouds. Behind him, like a blooming apparition, Ezekiel's naked feet pattered up to him.

"Aspinwall—wiped out again—that's what it means. 'Bout time. In 1894—that was first. Again in 1906. And now—it's time."

Turning, Captain Wingate stared into the Negro's gargoyle-like face. The terrible whiteness of his great big eyes in the black, black night caused the officer to shudder.

Again the Maroon started to go back in to the cabin as unconcerned as the strangeness of his words was cryptic. Exasperated at the Negro's weird communication, Captain Wingate, frowning sharply, arrested him with the sternness of his voice.

"What nonsense are you talking?"

"It's down in the Big Book—way back in Preston's days.* God's doings, that's what it is. Every ten or twelve years the city's got to be cleaned— wiped out—destroyed. A plague—a fire—something. God's work. Back in 1894 I got caught in it—lost everything I had. Then it burned to cinders—burned like a lake of white lime. Not a thing was left. Just acres of smoking ashes—ashes of flesh—ashes of bone—ashes of wood. White—all white! 'Z got to be clean."

In the still night all that was heard was the dipping of the bow—and of a sudden Captain Wingate's barking sardonic laugh.

"That's all right, Zeek. Those were in the old days before Uncle Sam got here. Now things are different."

Buttoning up his coat, his face stern and set and carved out of granite, Captain Wingate strode briskly up on to the flying bridge. Lieut. Cornwall, the officer of the deck, already had a pair of binoculars focused upon the sky rockets—Aspinwall's S. O. S.—pinking the sky.

"Order all hands to their stations!" Captain Wingate thundered. "Fire Ashore! Assemble the crew! Ring the chief engineer—full speed ahead—under forced draft! Open her up! All she's got!"

In five minutes the *Manodnock* was alive with bustling men, some— those from the engine room—black in the face, assembling hose and hatchets and fire fighting apparatus.

Up on the bridge, Captain Wingate ground his teeth at the terrible import of the message—a city begging for succor—a city Gomorrah-like in its paganism—crying—howling to the gods to spare it—to send it mercy!

It was pay-day in Aspinwall, and the town was celebrating. Down Cash Street there meandered a river of creole cafés. In them, as the night cast her wings over the lust-ridden inter-ocean city, the crust of the Black Art idolators were in the habit of gathering.

They were chiefly Negroes from St. Lucia and Martinique, who cut roses and dug graves and planted anemones up at the cemetery at Monkey Hill. Dark as tar, dumb as beasts, they took with them various pieces of primitive musical instruments—flutes, *gobies*, banjos, goatdrums, *steel*, harmoniums. Far into the tropical night they would sip liquors and dance—quadrilles and lancers and calidonias. Some of them went to the heart of Africa for their music: a spoon scratched on the surface of a grater furnishing the required melody. It produced a swishing chin-chilla rhythm, and, played only as the French Negro colonials know how, it was as good as a battery of violins at the Red Raven.

Far into the night, these believers in the magic of *obeah* would sit and chant old voodoo songs and dream and sip Maube* and anisette. Along the narrow streets there was a string of dark—always densely dark—shops, where fried fish, *callaloo*, and *fungee* were sold; where lozenges and sling* and plums and jam and jelly and myriad tropical preserves could be had. About the place, on old logs and rocks and tin cans, sat the *patois* man and his pipe-smoking spouse; while the little black children ran across the streets—played, shouted, and ofttimes were slapped to bed.

Oh, for the legends of Lower Cash Street! One familiar legend handed down from generation to generation by both *obeah*-loving and *obeah*-hating, had to do with a certain Monsieur Baptiste, of Castries, the Island of St. Lucia, British West Indies. Baptiste was a tall, stalwart, fierce-looking black, said to be the royal descendent of a war-like tribe which once flourished on the banks of the Zambesi. He was the chief of the *obeah* idolators in the West Indies. As such, it was his duty to administer the rites of his unholy cult. According to the legends afloat, in the early days of the construction of the Panama Canal, Baptiste one night held a secret session of the hoodlum order in one of the dense mango groves of Castries. At the session it transpired that Chief Hoodlum Baptiste had received a red-hot summons from his master "On High" which ordered him to make a sacrifice and make it at once! A cup of blood! Several days later a Negress, one of the town's water carriers, missed her little curly-haired boy. And at the next midnight caucus of the *obeah* men, Baptiste, solemn, his eyes bulging out of their sockets, plucked the boy's heart out of his bosom; a hand, with a white cup in it (so the legend ran), was there ready to receive it!

These were the stories that whetted the pallets of the black folk who sang and crooned slave songs on the goat-bottomed chairs* which adorned nightly the piazza. Some of the men were fishermen: big black strapping fellows, whose faces in the dim kerosene light shone like polished bits of ebony. Others were too old or too decrepit to do anything but sit on the goat-bottomed chairs, and with a palm leaf fan brush the flies off the cocoanut cakes, the perishing mangoes, and other odoriferous things they peddled.

One of the most cherished tales of this decaying decade in the history of Boca Grande related to the French engineers who failed to build the Canal. Some had it that a young dusky beauty from Martinique had been the consort of one of the French officers. She was a hot, passionate, tempestuous creature. Jilted by the Frenchman, she withered bit by bit. In a few weeks she was as dry and as passionless as a prairie flower. Her body became thin. Her hair whitened. She lost her rhythmic motion when walking.

This girl kept a Maubé shop on Bottle Alley. Maubé is a French colonial pop similar to the "ginger beer"* of the Negroes of the Guianas. After years of chemical experimenting, the girl concocted an "abortive" mixture which she threw into the emerald waters of Limon Bay. As she did it, she took an oath that the French would never build the Canal!

Others of doubtful origin ended the same way, but substituted Delessep's* name for the anonymous engineer's.

In this particular section of Aspinwall, ghosts and legends and scarecrows were the order of the night. It was voodoo-stricken. It smacked of witches and hobgoblins. The very calm somberness of it was uncanny. Walking down the street, one was likely to pass unmolested. The French colonial in Aspinwall was a creature who appealed to one's spirit, to one's emotions.

Of late, Lower Cash had taken on a missionary flavor. Six blocks up, of course, was as untamable as the jungle. It glittered. Landaus* drew up in front of the cantines and beautifully lighted restaurants. Cabaret singers danced and sang before the greedy eyes of applauding conquistadores. One place was particularly enchanting. It was the notorious Red Raven. Ask any sailor on any transatlantic liner plying to South America, and he will name you off-hand the girls who entertained there. They came from France, Sweden, Germany, Cuba, Costa Rica, West India. It was hoisted on a roof of evergreen leaves. Argentine Tango, merengue, "shimmy shawabbie,"* the "passion glide"—it was the most cosmopolitan café in the district.

On "G" Street, a block away, shrouded in perpetual semi-darkness, flourished the less well-to-do places. Here the Bush Negroes of Paramaribo* and the "Big Tree" men of Jamaica* predominated. Here the standard on which a man's prowess was judged was on a higher plane.

Here one-armed men and Chinese lottery ticket vendors and Japanese candy-makers grew. Work other than the knuckle-dusting kind was unknown. Only the men who stabbed without spilling blood, shot without being heard, danced on a dime—these, only, survived. Only the men who went to dances—and, single-handed, broke them up—defied the police and stayed out of jail; only the men who wore the best suits, consorted with none but the wealthiest, never got picked up for *bagos*—only these artists of the road could populate "G" Street.

It was a humming hell. In the day if you passed by it, you would have seen a set of bars, and shops with high windows—the shutters of which were always carefully down. The sidewalk was always scrupulously clean. One or two stray chairs would be seen knocking around the front, left in haste most likely by madame as she shuffled at sunrise into Fat Hing's to get herself a steaming omelette.

Down in the bowels of Lower Cash Street, however, stalked the living cancer. Chinamen with leprous ulcers on their skins; sloppy streets; dirt, vice, filth, disease; lice, fleas, *chiggers*.* It was a hell on earth.

And over this shimmering volcano of gluttony and licentiousness (to make matters worse), hovered the mystic spell of Black Art. In the little shops and eating-places and syrup-boiling holes, one saw bottles and flasks and demijohns of rum and falernum* and anisette. High up to the ceiling, the casks were piled. Jars of tamarind,* fruits, vegetables and meats made up the rest of the picture. How in the name of Providence they managed to sleep! But it did not matter. They didn't care anything about sleep. On Cash Street nobody slept. High noon saw Spanish girls, with their toes barely stuck in rose-colored slippers, sipping liquor in the saloons or whiling away the hours at the Red Raven. The folk on Lower Cash Street got their morals from those higher up—from those who visited the Red Raven!

On these pay-days, the "Gatun Lambs"* over-ran the district. McClintic Marshall, at that time, was in his heydey at the construction works at Gatun. Thousands of Negroes from the isles of the Caribbean worked as laborers on it. They were unused to high wages, and the lapsful of gold they drew at the end of each month disturbed their otherwise reliable mental equilibrium.

*III**

On the night of this fatal pay-day, a little dried-up man by the name of Carlos Del Campo elected to go down into the gutters of lower Cash Street. Up to that time no one had ever heard of Carlos Del Campo. He, however, kept a private school on Third Street where he taught French and English and the classics to the sons and daughters of the wealthy Chinese merchants of the city. He was the typical Spanish *maestro*. In Pizarro's time he would have been a monk. Something of an ascetic, he had a rabbinical countenance. He resembled the quiet rancheros seen on the misty hills of La Garta. He orated with a distinct effort. There was no timbre in his voice. In his throat was a nauseating gurgling sound.

The night Carlos Del Campo elected to got to Boca Grande—this very night of which we are speaking—was typical. Leaving the riotous splendor and magic glitter of the Red Raven, he made his way to the dregs, to the scum of the earth, to the heathenish folk who worshipped grotesque gods and wallowed in unbelievable squalor. With a book in his hand, Del Campo stopped in the middle of Lower Cash Street and took off his hat. Hair long as a horse's mane flowed down his sallow face. The moon seemed to focus its rays on the palm of his crown. At first no one paid any attention to him. He kept talking—slowly, pleadingly, like a Catholic priest.

"*Dios*, bring understanding to these people! Cleanse them of their woeful sin! Send another Deliverer in the shape of a storm or a fire or a hurricane—"

"*Bruja*! Witch! Witch!"

This man who dared invade the sacred confines of their homes, was actually invoking the gods against them!

Rough hands laid hold of the *maestro*. Rough hands put out his torch, grabbed at the tail of his coat, almost pushed him into the slimy gutter. Some of the *patois* men, unable to comprehend what it was all about, stood by, neutral. Others dropped their pipes and ran into their dimly lighted shops and began to burn candles. Others started to jig and dance and scrape the surface of graters with forks and spoons. But the fanatic's voice would not still. Some took it as a huge joke. Others jibed at him. On the whole, he had aroused their savage superstitions.

Lakes of fire now flooded Del Campo's eyes. They began to start out of their sockets. He pointed a trembling finger at them.

"You mark my word: a curse, a plague, a cyclone is going to sweep you all off the face of the earth! Vice and crime and immorality must go from these shores! The shadow of virtue and peace must rest on the bosom of this beautiful land of ours. Look at this street! Afire with lust and crime and venality. Bacchus is a saint in comparison to this! This old happy country—oh, for the Panama, the old Panama of pre-revolutionary days, the Panama of my youth!"

It was ludicrous. It sounded so funny. He got no farther. A police officer, gripping a baton, stepped up.

"Permit!" he exploded, seizing Del Campo by the collar. "Where is your permit?"

"Permit?" asked the *maestro* incredulously. "What permit?"

"To speak here. Permit!" Hot-headed, as were most of the native police, the officer tightened his hold on Del Campo, shouting: "Come on then—to the station house!"

"For *what*? What have I done?" Del Campo asked meekly.

"Shut up, before I break your damned head! Come on!"

Del Campo's eyes blazed angrily. He was a small man, much smaller than the officer; but as a law-abiding citizen he was not going to be brow-beaten out of his rights.

"I demand an explanation," he said, shaking the rough hand off his shoulder. "I am not going to be arrested—"

"Kaw! Kaw!" from somewhere in the crowd.

"You resist? Then take that—and that—and that—*vagamundo!*"

The staff's contact with Del Campo's skull was terrific. Women on the street fainted as the blood squirted—poured as if tapped from a cask. They were nearing the Red Raven. Out of it fluttered gaudily clad women and drunken men.

"*Da! le!* Give it to him! *Da! le!*"

It was music to the policeman's ears. It was the native battle cry. Sailors—again it is well to bring in the testimony of sailors—on transatlantic liners plying to the republics of the South, probably more than any other foreign group: know what it means. Some of them have left their lives in the hands of these unfeeling *agentes*. Once in the clouds, it was useless to put up a defense. It meant that the pack was howling at your heels.

"*Da! le! Da! le! En el coco-bolo,* chico!*"

Unmercifully the brigand let poor old bleeding Del Campo have it in the skull. His lips bled. His eyes were beginning to close.

"*Vamonos! Al cuartel!*"

Dragged and kicked and cuffed, he was the victim of a jeering mob which escorted him to the jail. Some men, on less provocation, had had their skulls cracked in a more artistic way. But this officer was a crude youngster. He had had it in for the first one that came along. The other night, at a dance on "G" Street, he had met with a serious accident. He had been dressed in plain clothes, and the mob forgot that he was an *agente* and did not seem to pay him the compliments that were due him. One-armed Walter, a Barbadian Negro, had sent him howling and moaning on the floor with a savage kick. It was several hours before he had come to.

Now poor defenseless Del Campo was paying for it.

In the station-house, the lieutenant at the desk, without taking record of the case, ordered Del Campo incarcerated—as if he were a common felon. He was put in a cell where an old white-haired hag was on her knees praying to the devil. In one corner a half-naked Negress glared fiendishly at him. In another, sitting in a pool of bloody water, was a young girl who had dared, at a *danson** in Cash Street, to resist an officer's attentions. Huddled, in the interior, on cots and on the cold cement, were crooks and murderers and vagabonds caught in the *agente's* dragnet. Some sang; others prayed; most of them stared asphyxiatedly at the newcomer. One other soul sent flying down the corridors of hell! That was how it seemed to most of them.

ℛ

Meanwhile, down rushed the Gatun Lambs. Special trains emptied thousands and thousands of their hurly-burly selves on the finely-wrought carpet of *El Barrio Rojo*. Earlier, a set of games—cricket, "rounders," baseball—was staged. Triumphant and inflamed with the passions and desires of wild primitive men, they stampeded into Cash Street. Rum, whiskey, anisette—casks and casks of the flowing scarlet— were uncorked that night. For the restaurants and cantines and brothels it was one of the richest harvests in years.

Who, on this side of Paradise, does not remember that memorable night in March, 1915? The night was beautiful—as only are nights of the tropics. Silver and ebony melted into it and spread their witchery over the sea. Stars raced across the dome of the clouds in careless glee. It was a hot night. Little zephyrs came struggling up awkwardly from the surface of Limon Bay. Most of the women, especially those who were dancing to the strains of the creole music, were dark, tropical cacti; others, women from the North, wore long trailing transparent gowns of soft clinging material. Roses, flowers of every description, were stuck in their black, in their golden, hair. Perfume took the place of air. One breathed it. Color, gorgeous color, was everywhere. Silver was temporarily taboo. Gold became the standard. It beat the extravagances of the yearly carnival. No one ever saw so much gold, so many pretty women, so many goblets of sparkling wine.

Upstairs, in the black shadows, men swarmed and plotted. Midnight was drowned by wild primordial shouts. Still the sky flung its spangled mantle over the city. There came a time when the phantasmagoria wearied: the music, the dancing, the singing, the caressing. It lost its youthful fire. The *Barrio* was lost in drunken slumber. Ancient Greece had nothing on *El Barrio Rojo* that night.

IV

Through the blackness the *Manod-nock*, Captain Courtland Wingate on the flying bridge, steamed to the rescue—at full speed mounted the waves superbly, like a swimming garfish.* Land was still a good way off. On the water's surface flashed sharks and mullets and *baracoudas*. Daring flying fish fluttered on the deck as the warship dug her bow into the ocean. Steadily she cut through the fortifications of the night; shot past the breakwater; dropped anchor. A life boat was lowered. By this time the bay was alive with honking tugs; with launches hurrying also to the rescue. It was still dark. To the sky rose clouds of oily black smoke.

Aspinwall was afire!

Men from the warship raced ashore. They skipped across the railroad tracks on Front Street. They crossed over to Bolivar. Early as it was, the city was awake. Figures in night-robes gathered on the verandas. Those whose backs were to the conflagration shouted to the excited and paroquet-prattling folk opposite, who gazed, entranced, at the scarlet sky—shouted to ask what it was all about.

"*Fuego! Fuego! En Boca Grande!*"

It was in the days before Panama knew anything of modern fire fighting. Of course it had a Corps of Bomberos,* made up of the sons of the rich: the smart set—light-faced youths who looked fine in scarlet flannel shirts and immaculate white trousers. But actual fire fighting is a strenuous business; and the word "strenuous" had not yet pierced the enervated consciousness of the young men of Panama.

In the night, either to awaken and warn sleeping residents or because of their sheer sense of helplessness, the police ran and shook their batons, blowing their whistles frantically. The crew from the *Manodnock*, led by Captain Wingate, like a set of Viking Kings trudged up Bolivar Street. In front of them, ten blocks away, rose mountains of roaring flames. Bursting and cracking and sweeping everything before it. Petroleum!

Cool as cucumbers the sailors went as far as the heat would permit and manipulated the nearest hydrant. There were only about fifty of them; but if there were fifty cool-headed men in the Republic on that tragic March morn, it was those fifty.

The *spiggoties** shouted and fumed and howled stupid orders. They spouted tons of water on a bank building at least a mile from the onrushing flames. The police blew their whistles and clubbed right and left.

"Ah, Sablo! Sablo's Bar! My God!"

On rushed the fire. A block away—no, half a block—it menaced Sablo's Bar. *Madre De Dios!* In it, piled high to the ceiling, were hundreds of casks of wine and rum and vermouth. Not a soul dared touch it. Eating up the very sand thrown at it by the men from the *Manodnock*, the fire licked the shingles of Sablo's Bar. It roared. A wind sprang up. Its pace accelerated. Half of the roof was gone. Back—back—to the crossing at Fifth Street the humidity sent the mob. Crackling, roaring, the fire enveloped Sablo's Bar. It zoomed like a mountain of burning tar. Into the black screen of smoke that covered the heavens, shots, like sky rockets, burst and dropped on nearby houses. Explosion after explosion rocked the earth as the fire hit Sablo's demijohns of liquor. Fowls screeched, pigs squealed—only to simmer down to a tragic monotonous silence.

In Fifth Street, just above the jail, crowds flowed into the Catholic Church. One spot of holy ground! Its spire in the night looked to the frenzied refugees like a light house to a storm-tossed ship. Away down in the bowels of *El Barrio Rojo*, girls remembered it—thought of fleeing to it. But already it was too late. Solemnly its bells began to chime. In front of it thousands of folk, not caught in the entangling net of *El Barrio Rojo*, fell on their knees and asked God for mercy.

The conquest of Sablo gave the fire a new lease on life. It spread to Bottle Alley and Cash Street. It cracked and roared and bristled as it sent volumes of smoke puffing to the heavens. Viewing it from the "Zone," the American border, one saw a city go up in flames and crumble like a hay stack. On the commissary pasture one looked across on the smoking desert which was once *El Barrio Rojo*. Nothing remained.

V

Towards dawn, the ships entering the harbor saw, on the crest of the sharply whitening clouds, a spot of rosy pinkness. It blossomed in a jiffy into something more. It colored the amphitheater of clouds. They saw, etched on the heavenly canvas, outlines of lambs and sheep and shepherds whose white curly heads reminded them of the North—of home—of cauliflowers.

How beautiful it looked!

But on shore a wail went up. The last fire had consumed that same part of the city but ten years ago. History was repeating itself. Lower Cash Street was a graveyard of ruins. Slowly the embers died down. Among refugees wailing and moaning on the lawn one saw but few scarlet folk. Not a single one of the revelers had survived. Mostly women and weeping children with beds and mattresses and other household goods.

On the other side of the city, Broadway, it was the same way. Crowds of mothers crying over lost loved ones—but not an echo of the neurotic life of *El Barrio Rojo*. That was completely wiped out!

Some of the wiseacres of police headquarters said it had originated upstairs at the Red Raven. A Spanish girl, on her way to greet a Mexican *enamorado*, had met an old discarded sweetheart on the stairs. Words followed. The Mexican, blind with rage, drew a knife, and the girl ran in flight. As he was about to tear the heart out of the girl, she threw a kerosene lamp at him. Instantly the place was aflame. But the Mexican, unmoved by the girl's piercing cries, refused to open the door. He died holding the knob.

As Captain Wingate staggered into his cabin, at noon that day—wet, black, drunk with fatigue—Ezekiel, the Negro cabin boy, was there, cleaning up the ashes—as cool and as prophetic as if nothing had happened.

The Adventures of Kit Skyhead and Mistah Beauty

AN ALL-NEGRO EVENING IN THE COLOURED CABARETS OF NEW YORK

"When mah feet gits cold," shivered Kit Skyhead, "I'm a cage o' apes."* Mr. Kit Skyhead proceeded to slip on his fur-lined gloves. A January night wind howled through the inky crescent.

"Yes, sah," corroborated his friend Mistah Beauty, "if you don't need dem gloves tonight you'll surely need 'em befo' tomorrow mornin'."

Following which Kit and Mistah Beauty decided to go to a cabaret.

"How 'bout a real big time, Kit? You know me. . . ."

"Jus' as you say, brother, only I don't want to disembarras nobody's pocket-book. I ain't so dumb 'at Ah don't know what it's all about. . . ."

"Oh, that's a bare skimshun," Mistah Beauty explained, "why, if I'm goin' to show you any kind o' time, I might as well show you a good one. . . ."

With no further ado Kit and Mistah Beauty cut through the frosty night up to the brilliantly illumined façade of the "Cotton Club"*

"Who's dat nigger all dressed up like Mrs. Astor's horse?" Kit inquired, puckering up his none too copper-wiry lips at the pompous anterior of the Negro door man.

"Hello, Doc," hailed the white gloved dignitary.

"Hello there, Jacmel, how is everything?"

"Everything is kopasettee* and the goose is quanking LOW!" That being the case, Kit and Mistah Beauty, after the mystic ritual of transferring a billete of high dimensions to the snowy paw of Jacmel, ascended the richly carpeted stairs to the jangling throne of Bandannaland.*

An eely streak popped out of the hazy mist and placed an embargo on their coats and things. Clinking of brass coat checks. . . .

As if by the delusion of a cinematograph* they found themselves in the obsequious clutches of the usher. Into a high, airy room, the roof of which lay pendant with the moss of leafy adornment, they were whirled. Dark. Lightning shadows. A squared circle. Tables set about the bamboo horizon. Ferns, wild, viny luxuriance—impedimenta of illusion—cling affectionately to the shrubbery poles. Whites galore at tables banked on the edge of the golden arena. Black, so far as the guests were concerned, at consequential premium. . . .

Seated at the right, near the Negro orchestra, Kit and Mistah Beauty took on the colour of their smoky milieu.

And on swept the dance. Swift as the pelting rain, the dusky revue, the clang of song and dance, of beauty and colour, whirl madly by— yellow girls, tightless, supple, deep-coloured, aflame, their eyes affluent of emotion, laugh—dance—sing—comedians crack jokes; figures glide on floor of marble, floor of gold.

"Dawggone," cried Kit, "if this ain't the cat's kanittans."

Silent, Mistah Beauty looked at Kit, at the empty bottles on the table. . . .

"You know onething," Kit observed, "there ain't another nigger in this place, but you and me and the waiters. . . ."

Mistah Beauty looked indifferently about.

"Not a jigaboo, but a whole lot o' ofay* gals. This is Mr. Eddy's place or I don't know what it is all about. Come on, Mistah Beauty. . . ."

ℛoosting at the Bamville Nest*

Later, at the Bamville-Nest on one of the side streets Kit and Mistah Beauty showed up. Rendezvous of the Negro big timers. High society folks. . . .

Here you've got to be a member of the "club" to be admitted. Insisting, to the clerk's placid acquiescence, that Mistah Beauty was Al Brown and Kit, Tiger Flowers,* and that they got their mail at No. 1 East River, they, with a buck apiece, joined. . . .

"Kind o' dickty* here, ain't it?" observed Kit, as the head waiter seated them. "Whole lot o' yella wimmin. . . . bunch o' blue* boys. . . ." Diagonally across from the jazz band the waiter anchored them. . . .

"Ladies and mah friends. . . ."

The Negro proprietor essays things. A girl, Bobby Something,* is dancing . . . Bobby's tights glow. Silk and old rose. Knees unbent, Bobby is going after a guilder* tossed her on the shimmering floor. Doing an unexaggerated shimmy, Bobby is the berries . . . posterial portions ahoy . . . there, going after that guilder.

Around them there is a welter of bronze folk. High yellows, medium browns, low blacks. Boys the colour of chocolate pudding, hair black and sleek; tall, slender youths, a bored, brother-there-ain't-a-doggone-thing-you-can-tell-me look in their eyes. Night hawks. Big timers. Niggers with "plenty money." Race horse touts. Bolita men. California jacks. Two storey guys.*

Women, the shimmer of pearls, slippers of gold, the yellow ombre, tell you what it is all about. High lifers, laughing, agreeable, hilarious folks.

Here to this cabaret come the black stars of the city's revues . . . Florence Mills and Johnny Hudgins and Sandy Burns and Johnny Dunn* . . . to sing and dance and sup and say hello to the folks. Here every man is a sheik and every girl is willing to go fifty-fifty with you on a proposition. Here it is the hotly dressed mamma or the alluringly sleek-haired papa— especially if he is dark brown and given to blue shirts, à la Prince of Wales, and diamond stick pins . . . that is the order of the night.

On the hazy horizon a white glow now and then bobs up, but not often. . . .

"Nigger," Mistah Beauty growled to Kit, "you talk the hinges off a brass monkey. Keep still!" Mistah Beauty was looking 'em over.

And a wounded light crept into Mr. Skyhead's eyes.

Pressed about them girls, sitting on their daddy's knees, drank gin, swopped yarns, dragged 'em down, and otherwise cut up. . . .

"Why, Mr. Beauty, why so pensive and consolinary?"

"Ain't he gramminary, though?" cried an ink-toed mamma* at Kit's side.

"Don't make Percy intoxicated, but give him a drink all the same."

"This is evidence of my sociability, boys. Trusting that the hinges of friendship may never grow rusty."

"Glass o' water, waiter, this liquor tastes like cake, how 'bout it, Percy?"

"Naw!" answered that midshipman, "I don't nevah build a fire and then put it out."

"Oh, man, you can't tell me nothin' 'bout Atlantic City. I used to pitch 'em around there. If anybody amounts to anything in Atlantic City I know what it is all about. . . ."

"You know Al Bush?"

"Course I know Al Bush. He's blacker'n I am. He is a big black nigger."

"That nigger? He ain't wo'th a quarter. . . ."

"Didn't I beat my wife up? I beat the hell out o' her. Didn't I catch her going with another nigger?"

III

Dawn in the region of One Hundred Thirty Fifth Street and Fifth Avenue is a sinister spectacle. A waste of echoes. A land of shadowy notes.

Yet, around the corner, the cellars are stark, clamorous, honkingly mad . . . ragtime is resuscitated; the boom-booming is fierce; folk nature is shrieking. . . .

> The American woman eats her chicken and rice
> And thinks she's eatin' somethin'
> But she ain't eat nuthin' till she tries
> Some monkey hips and dumplin'.

Here, at Sonny Decent's, the "openest" cabaret in Harlem, you've got to be part of the underworld pattern to fit in. Here folk lie prostrate. Insouciance. Here everybody knows what it is all about. Here the proprietor to all the world is familiarly Sonny. All Sonny asks of his heterogeneous patrons is that they be nice. They may fight and cut each other's throats, but boys, for God's sake, be nice!

Here, too, the family feeling runs high. It is a sort of laboratory for song and dance. Here it is that most of the jazz steps you see on Broadway, whether by Ann Pennington* or Florence Mills, are first tried out. Here songs like

176

Hickalah patickalah my black hen
She lays eggs foh gentlemen
Sometimes nine, sometimes ten
Hickalah patickalah my black hen

spring into being. Here "good 'art mek crab wit' out no back." Here King
Ja Ja, the Persian cat, is perched on the saxophone. Here the drummer
is a poet. Here Kit and Mistah Beauty eventually drifted. . . .

"Fo' cryin' out loud," cried Kit.

As if it were hewn out of a tree trunk, is this low, bare, naif cellar.
Unpainted and unadorned. A rough creaking floor, the boards ready
to flip through. A primitive coal stove. An incessant boom-booming,
tom-tom-ing. . . . Africa undraped!

Near the stove Kit and Mistah Beauty took seats. Hordes of blue people. Blue girls stunning in tomato reds . . . one of them, a dainty brown
elf, wearing a dress of rich henna with a basket weave. Hats to match. Cup
hats. Blinker-effect. High yellows, of the Spanish type, exhilarating in
peacock blue. Girls, dainty, sombre, cynical-eyed, passion-mouthed. . . .

"Why, at this rate," observed Mistah Beauty, "there won't be a single
dish washer no where in New York no time befo' four o'clock next
week. . . ."

Out of the contracting mass Mistah Beauty recognized Spoof Moses,
Four Eye Shadow, the prizefighter; Tunnah Kasha, Mr. Burt'n, Bread and
Cheese, Erasmus B. Black, Polanque, Woomsie Nurse, Miguel Covarru-
bias, Trick Skazmore, Bo Diddle, Eric Walrond, Jim Ar'try, West Henry,
Mary Stafford, Dolly May, Rachael Spilvens, Camilia Doo Right. . . .*

"Ain't you a West Indian?" someone asked Kit.

"Who, me? A West Indian? Brother, you ain't lookin' for trouble is
ya? I've had mo' fights on account o' dat dan fo' anything else in the
world. I look like any monkey man?"

"Everybody love my baby but my baby don't love nobody but me."

"Dat," observed the inquiring lady, primly, "are psychology from away
back."

"You ought to go to church, Trick, you. . . ."

"Nigger, you're a policeman and I'm a gambler. What you want me
to go to church fo'? Go yo' self."

"Dat nigger kin blew de hell out a dat horn, can't he, Mistah Beauty?"

"She needs her ashes hawled, that's what's the matter with that
wench."

"I'm gwine chalk yo' legs. . . ."

"Ain't you gwine nevah git yo' tongue split?"

"I had 'er doggin' round me fo' three whole weeks."

"When I get to the do' nigger wuz busy as a grave digger. . . ."

"Come on, Kit, let's be goin'. . . ."

"Dat's what yo' call runnin' wid blinkers on. A dyam new naygur comin' down de havenue wid a bran' new pair o' shoes on, each toe a stranger to de udder. . . ."

"Where's your check, Kit?"

"I just want to burn a nigger, dat's all. . . ."

"I'll knock yo' brains out, and argu wid you afta'. . . ."

"Gahr! Police! Murdah!"

"One oh five," breathed Kit, "dat's me. And ah, don't mean maybe."

City Love

From a gulf in the dark low sea of
rooftops there came mounting skyward the fiery reflexes of some gaudy
Convention Night on Lenox Avenue. With the fate of a sinning angel
the eye went *carombolling* 'cross the fizzing of a street lamp, caught the
rickety vision of a bus, topheavy with a lot of fat, fanning Jews, tottering
by on the cloudy August asphalt; flitted from the moon-shingled edges
of elm and oak, onward, finally settling on the dark murmuring folk
enlivening the park's green dusk rim.

"Quit that, honey!" warned the girl, softly. "I's skeert o' dirt, baby,
don't you do that." She steered the lad's menacing hand out the way.

"No tellin' wheh some o' dat grabble might go," continued Nicey,
making a pirate's cross bones of her legs.

A silence, dramatic to St. Louis, ensued. He was hurt, put out,
ashamed of himself at Nicey's gently unanswerable rebuke.

He risked a pair of greedy, sun-red eyes round at her, and his courage
took fresh impetus. "I know a place," he bristled suddenly with convic-
tion, and Nicey's head turned involuntarily. "An' here Ah wuz—" he
chuckled self-condemningly. "Come on, le's chance it."

From *The American Caravan*, Alfred Kreymborg
and others, eds. (New York: Macaulay, 1927).

"A nice place?" Nicey asked, quietly, not wishing to seem eager.

"Ah mean!" breathed Primus with deep-felt ardor.

"Yo' talk like yo' know it, like yo' done bin they orready," was what she was on the verge of saying, but large immediate interests possessed her, and she said instead, half-coyly, "No kiddin' now!"

"Honest," he said, getting up, "I ain't foolin'. I ain't green as I look. I bin there—"

"Oh yeah?" risked Nicey with surgical placidity.

"I mean," he stammered, admitting the error, but she checked the ripening flow of advances, and stood up. "That'll do," she said sagely, and walked, hips swinging, on down the hill in front of him.

He kept a little ways behind, feeling insecure and moody at his silly measure of self-puffing.

A flower coursed by, and she caught it, pressing the white dewy petals to her mouth. Dissatisfied, she flung it in a curdle of nettles. "Ah likes flowers dat got pa'fune," she said, "dis one ain't got a bit o' smell."

As they sped out on the flaky stone flight of steps leading toward St. Nicholas, clots of lovers, in twos and more than twos, leaned against the bowing foliage, forcing the dicks, bronze and pale-faced ones, to take refuge upon their fobs and palms behind the dark viny hedge.

A big muddy touring car filled with a lot of drinking Bolita Negroes skidded recklessly by into the gulch to One Hundred Thirty-Fifth Street. Pebbly dust bombarded the lids of Nicey's and Primus' eyes.

" . . . fur to go, baby?"

"Thutty fo'th . . . not fur . . . come . . . look out . . . you'll get run ovah, too."

A shanty, lodged beside an aerial railway track, with switches and cross ties, hovered dark and low above the street. A mob of Negroes passing underneath it hurried on as the trains rushed by, the lusty pressure chipping dust and rust off the girders.

Cars lurched in and out of side streets, assuming and unloading cargoes of vari-hued browns and blacks of conflicting shades of ebony splendor.

"How much furrer we got to go, honey," cried Nicey, dusty, eager, ill-at-ease.

"Not fur, honey, here we's at—"

They stopt before a brown stone dwelling. In the thickening night-light they glimpsed a fat butter-yellow Negress lolling in a rocker on the stoop and fanning herself with the long end of her apron.

There they stood, naked of pleats and tucks, frills and laces . . . orphans.

"Go on down t' the basement," the woman directed, with a wave of her heavy hand.

"You'd better wait here, Nicey," Primus said, with a show of manly vigor. Skipping to the basement the smells of a Negro cook shop came somersaulting at him. His senses were placid beside the sickening essences of corn and pork and candied yams.

The man who shared in this riotous obscenity was spotted by a kerosene torch swaying from a hook nailed in the wall. He was bald and tall and huge and spade black. He wore a shirt and flabby blue jeans and braces. Under such a low ceiling his fading oak skull threatened to violate the plumbing. In such a tiny passageway he seemed with his thick rotund figure to be as squat as an inflated bull frog.

He turned, at the shadow absorbing a length of the trembling light, and there was hair on both sides of his broad black face. He looked into Primus' eyes and a mist of mutuality sprang between them.

"Wha' yo' wife at?" he muttered in a whining Southern voice.

"I'll call 'er—"

"No, yo' don't hav' to call her," he assured him. "She outside?"

"Yeah."

"That's orright."

"Any bags?" he plied further, eyeing St. Louis closely. "Wha' yo' bags at? Outside, too? Don't le' 'em stay dere. Bring 'em on down in yah."

"Bags?" cried Primus, quickly, "I ain't got no bags. Wha' kind o' bags?" He hung on eagerly for the rest.

"Ain't yo' know," the man said, with that faculty for understatement which seems to be the pride of Negroes of the late plantation class, "that yo can't register at no hotel without bags? Go git yo'self a armful o' bags!"

He fled, breathless, to the girl on the pavement.

"Well!" Nicey said, both hands on her spreading hips.

He was excited and hurt, and he stuttered. "They—he—won't take us like this. I mean—we got to git weself some bags—bags—bags—"

Nicey sighed, a plaintive sigh of relief—a sigh that was a monumental perplexity to him. "Don't look at me like that!" he swore, angry at his ineffectuality. "I did my darndest to git 'im to take us, but he won't do it. Says it's 'gainst the law."

"What yo' gwine do now?" she cut in, distrustful of self-defenses.

"Git me a bag, that's all! Ain't nothin' else to do. C'm awn!"

2

In the resistless languor of the sum-
mer evening the Negroes wandered restively over the tar-daubed roofs,
squatted negligeed on shelterless window sills, carried on connubial
pantomimic chatter across the circumscribed courts, swarmed, six to
a square inch, upon curb and step, blasphemously jesting.

"I'll run," he said, pausing before the portals of a greasy tower of flats.
"You wait here, baby, I ain' gwine b' long."

And he cut a slanting passage through the mob, leaped up half a dozen
crumbling steps, through a long narrow corridor, ending, blowing, before
a knob on the sixth floor.

He rattled a key in the lock, and entered. A strip of oilcloth, dimly
silvery in the shadowy interior, flashed at him. He put the strip behind
him, flicked on the lights, and stared in Son Son's big starry eyes. The
child was the browning purple of star apple and was gorgeously animated.
He was strapped in a ram-upholstered chair cocked against the window
opening out upon a canyon of street. He jiggled at Primus a plumed
African Knight of a doll.

The doll, profuse with bells and spangled half-discs, tinkled annoy-
ingly. "Less noise, sah!" shouted Primus, descending on all fours and
industriously examining the debris piled under the davenport which
separated the cluttered room in two. Dimples of satanic delight bright-
ened the child's face. He jiggled his toy, wagged his legs, carolling. He
puffed his cheeks and booed, scattering mouth-mist about.

"Ain't I tell you to less noise, yo' lil' water mout'* imp yo'," cried
St. Louis, flying up, seizing and confiscating the tasseled ebony knight
and slapping the kid's dusk-down wrists. "Ain't I tell yo' not to botha'
yo' pappy when 'e come 'ome, to less yo' noise?" The youngster's sudden
recourse to imperturbability annoyed him. "Yo' ain't gwine cry no? Well,
tek dat, an' dat, an' dat! Cry, Uh say, Cry! Yo' won't open yo' mout', no,
yo' won't buss loose, yo'—"

A pair of claws fell viciously on Primus' back, and, combined with
the soaring quality of Tiny's voice, served to wheel him aboutface with
a swift downing jolt.

He had forgotten, alas! to push the bath room door when he came in.

"Look yah, man, wha' de hell yo' tink yo' his, hennyhow? Yo' tink yo'
dey down in de Back Swamp whey yo' come from, wha' dem don' know
nutton but fi'* beat up people? Hey, dis yah sinting yo' Ah see 'tan' up
yah, 'im tink 'im his back in Lucy a prog bout fi' yampies an' hunions in de
picknee* head. Come tumpin' de po' picknee roun' like him hone him!"

A fit of conquering rage narrowed and hardened and glistened Tiny's small, tight, mole-flecked face.

From the piano she flew to Son Son's side. The child was bashful, and in a dazed, defensive mood. "Hit dis yah picknee a next* time 'n see if me don' cahl a policeman fi' yo' hay. Hey, yo' na'h ashame' o' yo'self, no, fi' come down pon' a puny liggle picknee like dis 'n a show arf yo' strengt'? Why yo' didn't knock de man de oddah day when 'im bruk 'im wheel barrow 'cross yo' neck back 'pon de wharf? Why yo' didn't ram yo' hook in 'im gizzard, yo' dutty old cowrd yo', yo' can't fight yo' match, but yo' must wait till yo' get 'ome an' tek it out pon' me po' boy picknee."

He was on his knees, ransacking the amassing litter.

"Yo' a prowl 'bout now," Tiny went on, hugging Son Son to her bosom, "like a cock sparrow, but go 'long. Me na'h say nutton to yo', me jes' ah wait till de cole weddah come roun' again. An', boy, me will see yo' faht blue hice* fuss befor' yo' get anyt'ing from me to shub in yo' stinkin' guts! The day yo' say yo' got de back ache, an de foot ache, an' de turrah ache, don't le' me hear yo' wit' me name 'pon yo' mout', yo' hear? Fo' if yo' tink yo' gwine get me fo' go out fi' scrub me finger nail dem white fi' cram bittle* down a neygah man troat like yo', yo is lie! Yo' bes' mek up yo' mine now it warm 'n get yo'self a helevator job fo' when de winter come. Fo' so 'elp me Gawd me will see yo' in holy hell fuss befo' yo' a see me trudge hup an' down dem yah stair' like I is any whore fi' do as yo' dam well please."

"Oh, woman," he chuckled, unconcernedly, "tun yo'self out o' me way, yo' smell bad." He banged the door after him, a frayed valise under his arm.

3

He espied her, not leaning toward the frog-ringed moon rising out the river, against the red-spotted rods barricading the way to the cellar, where he had left her; but standing facing him, a speck in the dusk, on the opposing piazza, in an arrow of shadow in the court. He crossed the street, and was inside the marbled sink.

Nicey detached herself from the wall and waved a red, exacting mouth before his tense, sweating face. "Got any idea o' de time," she asked, impatiently.

He had taken a virgin pride in the valise, and was wrestling with it. "Le' me see—" He yanked out the coruscant* disc, and Nicey's calm was star-cut. "Ten nine," he said, looking full and composed at her. It broke him up to be there facing her with the lamplight, stealing past her clouded face, giving an added lustre to the curves and brackets of her body.

"Well," she cried, aroused, "I'll be jail housed! You mean to tell me you had me waitin' down here fo' you fo' nearly a hour, yo' lanky suck egg son of a bitch!" She swung herself free of his grovelling embraces.

"Oh, Nicey," he begged, running after her, "don't go, sweet, I got de bag—"

"An' now yo' got it," she turned, interrogatively, "Wha' yo' expect to do with it?"

"Tek it on back there!" he avowed in one of his recurrent moments of self-assertiveness.

"Like hell we do!" she swore, "I'm gwine home."

"Oh, don't go, Nicey," he cried, swinishly, "I know a place. Don't let's go home after all the trouble we bin to."

"Aw, hell, boy, yo' give me a pain in the hip. Yo' know a place me eye! Where is this place at?"

"Come awn, I'll show yah! Don't be skeert, I know what I'm talkin' 'bout—"

"Like hell you do."

" . . . it ain't the same one we bin to orready."

"Fur?" she perked up, with returning curiosity.

"Oh, no, jes' roun' de corner, I'll show yo'. Yo' tink it's fur? It ain't fur." His lurid efforts at self-assertion were taking a strange weight with her.

And so they peddled on. The dust, the city's dissoluteness, the sensory pursuits, gave a rigorous continuity to themselves, and to their needs, sent them burning against the sinister sovereignty of Upper Fifth Avenue.

Here there was a cluster of figures aloft. "Come on up," cried the man, "look out, lady, fo' dat ole runnin' hoss. Little Bits, ain't I tell you not to leave yo' things knockin' 'bout like dat? Come 'n tek 'em in miss . . . look out, mistah, get up there, Mignon, an' let the gemman pass."

As a sort of imposed ritual the woman remarked, with a friendly frown suggestive of a discovery of startling import, "Ain't it hot tonight?"

"Ain't it though?" returned Nicey, flopping grandly by.

"This way, folks," cried the man, showing them to the parlor.

Passing the opulent hangings, sinking ankle deep in the rugs, Nicey was moved to observe, "Gee, I'd like to sleep in a swell place like this."

As the female of the occasion she was led to the reddest plush couch in the room. Outside by the coat rack the two men stopt.

Primus' head bared, he was dabbing for the sweat sizzling in the rim of his hat. He put the valise down and went through his pockets for the money.

A princely urbanity governed the man. He edged the light behind him and scanned the most vagrant impulses lurking in Primus' eyes.

"Why don't you people come right?" he scolded in fatherly fashion. "Yo' don't come right," he insisted, trusting to the fleetness of the young's man's mind.

Of the two listening there was no doubt that Nicey's ears were cocked nearer the big man's voice.

"Now take the lady," he went on, with disarming felicity, "Why—why don't she wear a hat?"

With the feet of a deer, the girl shot out the parlor, sped past St. Louis, through the vestibule and out into the Harlem night.

"I keep on tellin' 'em they won't come right," he said, as Primus trotted, valise in hand, down the stairs. "Don't they know that folks don't ... avel that-a-way?"

As she was about to merge in with the dusk saturating Lenox Avenue, he caught up with her.

"Jee, you're an unlucky bastard!"

"I'm sorry, Nicey."

"I never heard o' anybody with your kind o' luck. Yo' must o' spit on a hot brick or somethin'."

"I'd give anything to prove to you, Nicey, that I ain't nobody's simp."

"You're a long time provin' it, big boy."

"Oh, honey, giv' me time!"

"Say, big fellah, go to the judge, don't come to me. I can't giv' yo' any mo' time."

"I'd do anything—"

"Go stick yo' head in a sewer then."

"Let's go back, sweet, come, let's."

"Go back where?"

"I mean—with a hat. I'll go git yo' a hat."

"Christ, what next, buyin' me a hat. All I got to do is stick roun' you long enough an' you'll be buyin' me a teddy aftah awhile."

At a Hebrew hat shop on the Avenue they stopt and when they came out again Nicey was none the worse for a prim little bonnet with bluebells galloping wildly over it.

Crowds of high-hitting Negroes, stevedores from the North River docks—Cubans prattling in sugar lofts on the Brooklyn water front— discarding overalls and gas masks and cargo hooks—revelling in canes and stickpins and cravats—strutting light browns and high blacks— overswept the Avenue. And the emotion of being part of one vast questing whole quickened the hunger in Nicey's and Primus' breasts.

Waddling down the long moldy corridor, he let the girl go on ahead of him. The man was behind him, carrying the candle and jingling keys, ready to exact the casuallest ounce of tribute. "Don't forget," he said, "that if you want hot water in the morning, it'll be fifty cents extra."

PART III

Tropic Death (Boni & Liveright, 1926) represents the culmination of Walrond's creative genius. With few exceptions, each of the ten stories is skillfully crafted, and taken together, the collection remains one of the finest achievements by a Black short story writer. The stories—largely set in Panama and Barbados—are linked not only by the grisly deaths that occur in each of them, but by Walrond's masterly use of dialect and his employment of folk culture, enabling him vividly to portray Caribbean life. He particularly captures the complexity of Caribbean culture, most palpably manifested by an ongoing Creole/colonial tension. Despite the harshness of the environment and the pervasive legacy of colonialism, the stories ultimately celebrate the resilience of Caribbean folk.

*D*rought

I

The whistle blew for eleven o'clock. Throats parched, grim, sun-crazed blacks cutting stone on the white burning hillside dropped with a clang the hot, dust-powdered drills and flew up over the rugged edges of the horizon to descent into a dry, waterless gut. Hunger—pricks at stomachs inured to brackish coffee and cassava pone*—pressed on folk, joyful as rabbits in a grassy ravine, wrenching themselves free of the lure of the white earth. Helter-skelter dark, brilliant, black faces of West Indian peasants moved along, in pain—the stiff tails of blue denim coats, the hobble of chigger-cracked heels, the rhythm of a stride . . . dissipating into the sun-stuffed void the radiant forces of the incline.

The broad road—a boon to constables moping through the dusk or on hot, bright mornings plowing up the thick, adhesive marl on some seasonal chore, was distinguished by a black, animate dot upon it.

It was Coggins Rum. On the way down he had stopped for a tot— zigaboo word for tin cup—of water by the rock engine. The driver, a buckra* johnny—English white—sat on the waste box scooping with a fork handle the meat out of a young water cocoanut. An old straw hat,

First published in *The New Age* (London) October 1925.

black, and its rim saggy by virtue of the moisture of sweating sun-fingers, served as a calabash for a ball of "cookoo"*—corn meal, okras and butter stewed—roundly poised in its crown. By the buckra's side, a black girl stood, her lips pursed in an indifferent frown, paralyzed in the intense heat.

Passing by them Coggins' bare feet kicked up a cloud of the white marl dust and the girl shouted, "Mistah Rum, you gwine play de guitah tee nite, no?" Visions of Coggins—the sky a vivid crimson or blackly star-gemmed—on the stone step picking the guitar, picking it "with all his hand. . . ."

Promptly Coggins answered, "Come down and dance de fango fo' Coggins Rum and he are play for you."

> Bajan girl don't wash 'ar skin
> Till de rain come down. . . .

Grumblings. Pitch-black, to the "washed-out" buckra she was more than a bringer of victuals. The buckra's girl. It wasn't Sepia, Georgia, but a backwoods village in Barbadoes. "Didn't you bring me no molasses to pour in the rain-water?" the buckra asked, and the girl, sucking in her mouth, brought an ungovernable eye back to him.

Upon which Coggins, swallowing a hint, kept on his journey—noon-day pilgrimage—through the hot creeping marl.

Scorching—yet Coggins gayly sang:

> O! you come with yo' cakes
> Wit' yo' cakes an' yo' drinks
> Ev'y collection boy ovah deah!—
> An' we go to wah—
> We shall carry de name,
> Bajan boys for—evah!

"It are funny," mused Coggins, clearing his throat, "Massa Braffit an dat chiggah-foot gal. . . ."

He stopped and picked up a fern and pressed the back of it to his shiny ebon cheek. It left a white ferny imprint. Grown up, according to the ethics of the gap,* Coggins was yet to it a "queer saht o' man," given to the picking of a guitar, and to cogitations, on the step after dark—indulging in an avowed juvenility.

Drunk with the fury of the sun Coggins carelessly swinging along cast an eye behind him—more of the boys from the quarry—overalled, shoeless, caps whose peaks wiggled on red, sun-red eyes . . . the eyes of the black sunburnt folk.

He always cast an eye behind him before he turned off the broad road into the gap.

Flaring up in the sun were the bright new shingles on the Dutch-style cottage of some Antigua folk. Away in a clump of hibiscus was a mansion, the color of bilgy water, owned by two English dowager maidens. In the gap rockstones shot up—obstacles for donkey carts to wrestle over at dusk. Rain-worms and flies gathered in muddy water platoons beside them.

"Yo' dam vagabond yo'!"

Coggins cursed his big toe. His big toe was blind. Helpless thing . . . a blind big toe in broad daylight on a West Indian road gap.

He paused, and gathered up the blind member. "Isn't this a hell of a case fo' yo', sah?" A curve of flesh began to peel from it. Pree-pree-pree. As if it were frying. Frying flesh. The nail jerked out of place, hot, bright blood began to stream from it. Around the spot white marl dust clung in grainy cakes. Now, red, new blood squirted—spread over the whole toe—and the dust became crimson.

Gently easing the toe back to the ground, Coggins avoided the grass sticking up in the road and slowly picked his way to the cabin.

"I stump me toe," he announced, "I stump me toe . . . woy . . . woy."

"Go bring yo' pappy a tot o' water . . . Ada . . . quick."

Dusky brown Sissie took the gored member in her lap and began to wipe the blood from it.

"Pappy stump he toe."

"Dem rocks in de gap . . ."

"Mine ain't got better yet, needer . . ."

"Hurry up, boy, and bring de lotion."

"Bring me de scissors, an' tek yo' fingers out o' yo' mout' like yo' is starved out! Hey, yo', sah!"

" . . . speakin' to you. Big boy lik' yo' suckin' yo' fingers. . . ."

Zip! Onion-colored slip of skin fluttered to the floor. Rattah Grinah, the half-dead dog, cold dribbling from his glassy blue eyes on to his freckled nose, moved inanimately towards it. Fox terrier . . . shaggy . . . bony . . . scarcely able to walk.

"Where is dat Beryl?" Coggins asked, sitting on the floor with one leg over the other, and pouring the salt water over the crimsoning wadding.

"Outside, sah."

"Beryl!"

"Wha' yo' dey?"

"Wha' yo' doin' outside?"

"Answer me, girl!"

" . . . Hey, yo' miss, answer yo' pappy!"

"Hard-ears* girl! She been eatin' any mo' marl, Sissie?"

"She, Ada?"

"Sho', gal eatin' marl all de haftahnoon. . . ."

Pet, sugar—no more terms of endearment for Beryl. Impatient, Coggins, his big toe stuck up cautiously in the air,—inciting Rattah to indolent curiosity—moved past Sissie, past Ada, past Rufus, to the rear of the cabin.

II

Yesterday, at noon . . . a roasting sun smote Coggins. Liquid . . . fluid . . . drought. Solder. Heat and juice of fruit . . . juice of roasting *cashews.**

It whelmed Coggins. The dry season was at its height. Praying to the Lord to send rain, black peons gathered on the rumps of breadfruit* or cherry trees in abject supplication.

Crawling along the road to the gap, Coggins gasped at the consequences of the sun's wretched fury. There, where canes spread over with their dark rich foliage into the dust-laden road, the village dogs, hunting for eggs to suck, fowls to kill, paused amidst the yellow stalks of cork-dry canes to pant, or drop, exhausted, sun-smitten.

The sun had robbed the land of its juice, squeezed it dry. Star apples, sugar apples,* husks, transparent on the dry sleepy trees. Savagely prowling through the orchards blackbirds stopped at nothing. . . . Turtle doves rifled the pods of green peas and purple beans and even the indigestible Brazilian *bonavis.** Potato vines, yellow as the leaves of autumn, severed from their roots by the pressure of the sun, stood on the ground, the wind's eager prey. Undug, stemless—peanuts, carrots—seeking balm, relief, the caress of a passing wind, shot dead unlustered eyes up through sun-etched cracks in the hard, brittle soil. The sugar corn went to the birds. Ripening prematurely, breadfruits fell swiftly on the hard naked earth, half ripe, good only for fritters. . . . Fell in spatters . . . and the hungry dogs, elbowing the children, lapped up the yellow-mellow fruit.

His sight impaired by the livid sun, Coggins turned hungry eyes to the soil. Empty corn stalks . . . blackbirds at work. . . .

Along the water course, bushy palms shading it, frogs gasped for air, their white breasts like fowls, soft and palpitating. The water in the drains sopped up, they sprang at flies, mosquitoes . . . wrangled over a mite.

It was a dizzy spectacle and the black peons were praying to God to send rain. Coggins drew back. . . .

Asking God to send rain . . . why? Where was the rain? Barreled up there in the clouds? Odd! Invariably, when the ponds and drains and rivers dried up they sank on their knees asking God to pour the water out of the sky. . . . Odd . . . water in the sky. . . .

The sun! It wrung toll of the earth. It had its effect on Coggins. It made the black stone cutter's face blacker. Strong tropic suns make black skins blacker. . . .

At the quarry it became whiter and the color of dark things generally grew darker. Similarly, with white ones—it gave them a whiter hue. Coggins and the quarry. Coggins and the marl. Coggins and the marl road.

Beryl in the marl road. Six years old; possessing a one-piece frock, no hat, no shoes.

Brown Beryl . . . the only one of the Rum children who wasn't black as sin. Strange . . . Yellow Beryl. It happens that way sometimes. Both Coggins and Sissie were unrelievably black. Still Beryl came a shade lighter. "Dat am nuttin'," Sissie had replied to Coggins' intimately naïve query, "is yo' drunk dat yo' can't fomembah me sistah-in-law what had a white picknee fo' 'ar naygeh man? Yo' don't fomembah, no?" Light-skinned Beryl. . . .

It happens that way sometimes.

Victim of the sun—a bright spot under its singeing mask—Beryl hesitated at Coggins' approach. Her little brown hands flew behind her back.

"Eatin' marl again," Coggins admonished, "eatin' marl again, you little vagabon'!"

Only the day before he had had to chastise her for sifting the stone dust and eating it.

"You're too hard ears," Coggins shouted, slapping her hands, "you're too hard ears."

Coggins turned into the gap for home, dragging her by the hand. He was too angry to speak . . . too agitated.

Avoiding the jagged rocks in the gap, Beryl, her little body lost in the crocus bag frock jutting her skinny shoulders, began to cry. A gulping sensation came to Coggins when he saw Beryl crying. When Beryl cried, he felt like crying, too. . . .

But he sternly heaped invective upon her. "Marl'll make yo' sick . . . tie up yo' guts, too. Tie up yo' guts like green guavas. Don't eat it, yo' hear, don't eat no mo' marl. . . ."

No sooner had they reached home than Sissie began. "Eatin' marl again, like yo' is starved out," she landed a clout on Beryl's uncombed head. "Go under de bed an' lay down befo' I crack yo' cocoanut. . . ."

Running a house on a dry-rot herring bone, a pint of stale, yellowless corn meal, a few spuds, yet proud, thumping the children around for eating scraps, for eating food cooked by hands other than hers . . . Sissie. . . .

"Don't talk to de child like dat, Sissie."

"Oh, go 'long you, always tryin' to prevent me from beatin' them. When she get sick who gwine tend she? Me or you? Man, go 'bout yo' business."

Beryl crawled meekly under the bed. Ada, a bigger girl—fourteen and "ownwayish"—shot a look of composed neutrality at Rufus—a sulky, cry-cry, suck-finger boy nearing twenty—Big Head Rufus.

"Serve she right," Rufus murmured.

"Nobody ain't gwine beat me with a hairbrush. I know dat." One leg on top of the other, Ada, down on the floor, grew impatient at Sissie's languor in preparing the food. . . .

Coggins came in at eleven to dinner. Ada and Rufus did likewise. The rest of the day they spent killing birds with stones fired from slingshots; climbing neighbors' trees in search of birds' nests; going to the old French ruins to dig out, with the puny aid of Rattah Grinah, a stray mongoose or to rob of its prize some canary-catching cat; digging holes in the rocky gap or on the brink of drains and stuffing them with paper and gun-powder stolen from the Rum canister and lighting it with a match. Dynamiting! Picking up hollow pieces of iron pipe, scratching a hole on top of them, towards one end, and ramming them with more gunpowder and stones and brown paper, and with a pyramid of gunpowder moistened with spit for a squib, leveling them at snipes or sparrows. Touch bams.

"Well, Sissie, what yo' got fo' eat to-day?"

"Cookoo, what yo' think Ah are have?"

"Lawd, mo' o' dat corn mash. Mo' o' dat prison-gruel. People would t'ink a man is a horse!" . . . a restless crossing of scaly, marl-white legs in the corner.

"Any salt fish?"

"Wha' Ah is to get it from?"

"Herrin'?"

"You t'ink I muss be pick up money. Wha' you expect mah to get it from, wit' butter an' lard so dear, an' sugar four cents a pound. Yo' must be expect me to steal."

"Well, I ain't mean no harm. . . ."

"Hey, this man muss be crazy. You forget I ain't workin' ni, yo' forget dat I can't even get water to drink, much mo' grow onions or green peas. Look outside. Look in the yard. Look at the parsley vines."

Formerly things grew under the window or near the tamarind trees, fed by the used water or the swill, yams, potatoes, lettuce. . . .

Going to the door, Coggins paused. A "forty-leg" was working its way into the craw of the last of the Rum hens. "Lahd 'a' massie. . . ." Leaping to the rescue, Coggins slit the hen's craw—undigested corn spilled out—and ground the surfeited centipede underfoot.

"Now we got to eat this," and he strung the bleeding hen up on a nail by the side of the door, out of poor Rattah Grinah's blinking reach. . . .

Unrestrained rejoicing on the floor.

Coggins ate. It was hot—hot food. It fused life into his body. It rammed the dust which had gathered in his throat at the quarry so far down into his stomach that he was unaware of its presence. And to eat food that had butter on it was a luxury. Coggins sucked up every grain of it.

"Hey, Ada."

"Rufus, tek this."

"Where is dat Miss Beryl?"

"Under de bed, m'm."

"Beryl. . . ."

"Yassum. . . ."

Unweeping, Beryl, barely saving her skull, shot up from underneath the bed. Over Ada's obstreperous toes, over Rufus' by the side of Coggins, she had to pass to get the proffered dish.

"Take it quick!"

Saying not a word, Beryl took it and, sliding down beside it, deposited it upon the floor beside Coggins.

"You mustn't eat any more marl, yo' hear?" he turned to her. "It will make yo' belly hard."

"Yes . . . pappy."

Throwing eyes up at him—white, shiny, appealing—Beryl guided the food into her mouth. The hand that did the act was still white with the dust of the marl. All up along the elbow. Even around her little mouth the white, telltale marks remained.

Drying the bowl of the last bit of grease, Coggins was completely absorbed in his task. He could hear Sissie scraping the iron pot and trying to fling from the spoon the stiff, over-cooked corn meal which had stuck to it. Scraping the pan of its very bottom, Ada and Rufus fought like two mad dogs.

"You, Miss Ada, yo' better don't bore a hole in dat pan, gimme heah!"

"But, Mahmie, I ain't finish."

Picking at her food, Beryl, the dainty one, ate sparingly. . . .

Once a day the Rums ate. At dusk, curve of crimson gold in the sensuous tropic sky, they had tea. English to a degree, it was a rite absurdly regal. Pauperized native blacks clung to the utmost vestiges of the Crown. Too, it was more than a notion for a black cane hole digger to face the turmoil of a hoe or fork or "bill"*—zigaboo word for cutlass—on a bare cup of molasses coffee.

III

"Lahd 'a' massie. . . ."

"Wha' a mattah, Coggins?"

"Say something, no!"

"Massie, come hay, an' see de gal picknee."

" . . . open yo' mout' no, what's a mattah?"

Coggins flew to the rainwater keg. Knocked the swizzle stick—relic of Sissie's pop manufactures—behind it, tilting over the empty keg.

"Get up, Beryl, get up, wha' a mattah, sick?"

"Lif' she up, pappy."

"Yo' move out o' de way, Mistah Rufus, befo'. . . ."

"Don't, Sissie, don't lick she!"

"Gal playin' sick! Gal only playin' sick, dat what de mattah wit' she. Gal only playin' sick. Get up, yo' miss!"

"God—don't, Sissie, leave she alone."

"Go back, every dam one o' yo', all yo' gwine get in de way."

Beryl, little naked brown legs apart, was flat upon the hard, bare earth. The dog, perhaps, or the echo of some fugitive wind had blown up her little crocus bag dress. It lay like a cocoanut flap-jack on her stomach. . . .

"Bring she inside, Coggins, wait I gwine fix de bed."

Mahogany bed . . . West Indian peasants sporting a mahogany bed; canopied with a dusty grimy slice of cheesecloth. . . .

Coggins stood up by the lamp on the wall, looking on at Sissie prying up Beryl's eyelids.

"Open yo' eyes . . . open yo' eyes . . . betcha the little vagabon' is playin' sick."

Indolently Coggins stirred. A fist shot up—then down. "Move, Sissie, befo' Ah hit yo'." The woman dodged.

"Always wantin' fo' hit me fo' nuttin', like I is any picknee."

" . . . anybody hear this woman would think. . . ."

"I ain't gwine stand for it, yes, I ain't gwine. . . ."

"Shut up, yo' old hard-hearted wretch! Shut up befo' I tump yo' down!" . . . Swept aside, one arm in a parrying attitude . . . backing, backing toward the larder over the lamp. . . .

Coggins peered back at the unbreathing child. A shade of compassion stole over Sissie. "Put dis to 'er nose, Coggins, and see what'll happen." Assafetida,* bits of red cloth. . . .

Last year Rufus, the sickliest of the lot, had had the measles and the parish doctor had ordered her to tie a red piece of flannel around his neck. . . .

She stuffed the red flannel into Coggins' hand. "Try dat," she said, and stepped back.

Brow wrinkled in cogitation, Coggins—space cleared for action—denuded the child. "How it ah rise! How 'er belly a go up in de year!"

Bright wood; bright mahogany wood, expertly shellacked and laid out in the sun to dry, not unlike it. Beryl's stomach, a light brown tint, grew bit by bit shiny. It rose; round and bright, higher and higher. They had never seen one so none of them thought of wind filling balloons. Beryl's stomach resembled a wind-filling balloon.

Then—

"She too hard ears," Sissie declared, "she won't lissen to she pappy, she too hard ears."

❧

Dusk came. Country folk, tired, soggy, sleepy, staggering in from "town"—depressed by the market quotations on Bantam cocks—hollowed howdy-do to Coggins, on the stone step, waiting.

Rufus and Ada strangely forgot to go down to the hydrant to bathe their feet. It had been a passion with Coggins. "Nasty feet breed disease," he had said, "you Mistah Rufus, wash yo' foots befo' yo' go to sleep. An' yo', too, Miss Ada, I'm speaking to yo', gal, yo' hear me? Tak' yo' mout' off o' go 'head,* befo' Ah box it off. . . ."

197

Inwardly glad of the escape, Ada and Rufus sat, not by Coggins out on the stone step, but down below the cabin, on the edge of a stone overlooking an empty pond, pitching rocks at the frogs and crickets screaming in the early dusk.

The freckled-face old buckra physician paused before the light and held up something to it. . . .

"Marl . . . marl . . . dust. . . ."

It came to Coggins in swirls. Autopsy. Noise comes in swirls. Pounding, pounding—dry Indian corn pounding. Ginger. Ginger being pounded in a mortar with a bright, new pestle. Pound, pound. And. Sawing. Butcher shop. Cow foot is sawed that way. Stew—or tough hard steak. Then the drilling—drilling—drilling to a stone cutter's ears! Ox grizzle. Drilling into ox grizzle. . . .

"Too bad, Coggins," the doctor said, "too bad, to lose yo' dawtah. . . ."

In a haze it came to Coggins. Inertia swept over him. He saw the old duffer climb into his buggy, tug at the reins of his sickly old nag and slowly drive down the rocky gap and disappear into the night.

Inside, Sissie, curious, held things up to the light. "Come," she said to Coggins, "and see what 'im take out a' ar. Come an' see de marl. . . ."

And Coggins slowly answered, "Sissie—if yo' know what is good fo' yo'self, you bes' leave dem stones alone."

$\mathcal{T}$he Yellow One

I

Once catching a glimpse of her, they swooped down like a brood of starving hawks. But it was the girl's first vision of the sea, and the superstitions of a Honduras peasant heritage tightened her grip on the old rusty canister she was dragging with a frantic effort on to the *Urubamba's* gangplank.

"Le' me help yo', dahtah," said one.

"Go 'way, man, yo' too farrad*—'way!"

"'Im did got de fastiness* fi' try fi' jump ahead o' me again, but mahn if yo' t'ink yo' gwine duh me outa a meal yo' is a dam pitty liar!"

"Wha' yo' ah try fi' do, leggo!"* cried the girl, slapping the nearest one. But the shock of her words was enough to paralyze them.

They were a harum scarum lot, hucksters, ex-cable divers and thugs of the coast, barefooted, brown-faced, raggedly—drifting from every cave and creek of the Spanish Main.

They withdrew, shocked, uncertain of their ears, staring at her; at her whom the peons of the lagoon idealized as *la madurita:* the yellow one.

Sensing the hostility, but unable to fathom it, she felt guilty of some untoward act, and guardedly lowered her eyes.

Flushed and hot, she seized the canister by the handle and started resuming the journey. It was heavy. More energy was required to move it than she had bargained on.

In the dilemma rescuing footsteps were heard coming down the gangplank. She was glad to admit she was stumped, and stood back, confronted by one of the crew. He was tall, some six feet and over, and a mestizo like herself. Latin blood bubbled in his veins, and it served at once to establish a ready means of communication between them.

"I'll take it," he said, quietly, "you go aboard—"

"Oh, many thanks," she said, "and do be careful, I've got the baby bottle in there and I wouldn't like to break it." All this in Spanish, a tongue spontaneously springing up between them.

She struggled up the gangplank, dodging a sling drooping tipsily on to the wharf. "Where are the passengers for Kingston station?" she asked.

"Yonder!" he pointed, speeding past her. Amongst a contortion of machinery, cargo, nets and hatch panels he deposited the trunk.

Gazing at his hardy hulk, two emotions seared her. She wanted to be grateful but he wasn't the sort of person she could offer a tip to. And he would readily see through her telling him that Alfred was down the dock changing the money.

But he warmed to her rescue. "Oh, that's all right," he said, quite illogically, "stay here till they close the hatch, then if I am not around, somebody will help you put it where you want it."

Noises beat upon her. Vendors of tropical fruits cluttered the wharf, kept up sensuous cries; stir and clamor and screams rose from every corner of the ship. Men swerved about her, the dock hands, the crew, digging cargo off the pier and spinning it into the yawning hatch.

"Wha' ah lot o' dem," she observed, "an' dem so black and ugly. R—r—!" Her words had the anti-native quality of her Jamaica spouse's, Alfred St. Xavier Mendez.

The hatch swelled, the bos'n* closed it, and the siege commenced. "If Ah did got any sense Ah would Ah wait till dem clean way de rope befo' me mek de sailor boy put down de trunk. Howsomevah, de Lawd will provide, an' all me got fi' do is put me trus' in Him till Halfred come."

With startling alacrity, her prayers were answered, for there suddenly appeared a thin moon-faced decker, a coal-black fellow with a red greasy scarf around his neck, his teeth giddy with an ague he had caught in Puerta Tela and which was destined never to leave him. He seized the trunk by one end and helped her hoist it on the hatch. When he had finished, he didn't wait for her trepid words of thanks but flew to the ship's rail, convulsively shaking.

She grew restive. "Wha' dat Halfred, dey, eh," she cried, "wha' a man can pacify time dough, eh?"

The stream of amassing deckers overran the *Urubamba's* decks. The din of parts being slugged to rights buzzed. An oily strip of canvas screened the hatch. Deckers clamorously crept underneath it.

The sea lay torpid, sizzling. Blue rust flaked off the ship's sides shone upon it. It dazzled you. It was difficult to divine its true color. Sometimes it was so blue it blinded you. Another time it would turn with the cannon roar of the sun, red. Nor was it the red of fire or of youth, of roses or of red tulips. But a sullen, grizzled red. The red of a North Sea rover's icicled beard; the red of a red-headed woman's hair, the red of a red-hot oven. It gave to the water engulfing the ship a dark, copper-colored hue. It left on it jeweled crusts.

A bow-legged old Maroon, with a trunk on his head, explored the deck, smoking a gawky clay pipe of some fiery Jamaica bush and wailing, "Scout bway, scout bway, wha' yo' dey? De old man ah look fa' yo'." The trunk was beardy and fuzzy with the lashes of much-used rope. It was rapidly dusking, and a woman and an amazing brood of children came on. One pulled, screaming, at her skirt, one was astride a hip, another, an unclothed one, tugged enthusiastically at a full, ripened breast. A hoary old black man, in a long black coat, who had taken the Word, no doubt, to the yellow "heathen" of the fever-hot lagoon, shoeless, his hard white crash pants* rolled up above his hairy, veiny calves, with a lone yellow pineapple as his sole earthly reward.

A tar-black Jamaica sister, in a gown of some noisy West Indian silk, her face entirely removed by the shadowy girth of a leghorn hat,* waltzed grandly up on the deck. The edge of her skirt in one hand, after the manner of the ladies at Wimbledon, in the other a fluttering macaw, she was twittering, "Hawfissah,* hawfissah, wear is de hawfissah, he?" Among the battering hordes there were less brusque folk; a native girl— a flower, a brown flower—was alone, rejecting the opulent offer of a bunk, quietly vowing to pass two nights of sleepful concern until she got to Santiago. And two Costa Rica maidens, white, dainty, resentful and uncommunicative.

He came swaggering at last. La Madurita said, "Wha' yo' been, Halfred, all dis lang time, no?"

"Cho,* it wuz de man dem down dey," he replied, "dem keep me back." He gave her the sleeping child, and slipped down to doze on the narrow hatch.

In a mood of selfless bluster he was returning to Kingston. He adored Jamaica. He would go on sprees of work and daring, to the jungles of

Changuinola or the Cut at Culebra,* but such flights, whether for a
duration of one or ten years, were uplifted mainly by the traditional
deprivations of Hindu coolies or Polish immigrants—sunless, joyless.
Similarly up in Cabello; work, sleep, work; day in and day out for six
forest-hewing years. And on Sabbaths a Kentucky evangelist, a red-
headed hypochondriac, the murky hue of a British buckra from the beat
of the tropic sun, tearfully urged the blacks to embrace the teachings of
the Lord Jesus Christ before the wrath of Satan engulfed them. Then,
one day, on a tramp to Salamanca, a fancy struck him. It stung, was
unexpected. He was unused to the sensations it set going. It related
to a vision—something he had surreptitiously encountered. Behind a
planter's hut he had seen it. He was slowly walking along the street,
shaded by a row of plum trees, and there she was, gloriously unaware of
him, bathing her feet in ample view of the sky. She was lovely to behold.
Her skin was the ripe red gold of the Honduras half-breed. It sent the
blood streaming to his head. He paused and wiped the sweat from his
face. He looked at her, calculating. Five—six—seven-fifty. Yes, that'd
do. With seven hundred and fifty pounds, he'd dazzle the foxy folk of
Kingston with the mellow *Spanish* beauty of her.

In due time, and by ample means, he had been able to bring round
the girl's hitherto *chumbo*-hating folk.

"Him mus' be hungry," she said, gazing intently at the baby's face.

"Cho'," replied Alfred, "leave de picknee alone, le' de gal picknee
sleep." He rolled over, face downwards, and folded his arms under his
chin. He wore a dirty khaki shirt, made in the States, dark green corduroy
pants and big yellow shoes which he seldom took off.

Upright on the trunk, the woman rocked the baby and nursed it. By
this time the hatch was overcrowded with deckers.

Down on the dock, oxen were yoked behind wagons of crated bananas.
Gnawing on plugs of hard black tobacco and firing reels of spit to every
side of them, New Orleans "crackers" swearingly cursed the leisurely
lack of native labor. Scaly ragamuffins darted after boxes of stale cheese
and crates of sun-sopped iced apples* that were dumped in the sea.

II

The dawning sunlight pricked the
tarpaulin and fell upon the woman's tired, sleep-sapped face. Enamel
clanged and crashed. A sickly, sour-sweet odor pervaded the hatch. The

sea was calm, gulls scuttled low, seizing and ecstatically devouring some reckless, sky-drunk sprat.*

"Go, no, Halfred," cried the woman, the baby in her arms, "an' beg de backra man fi' giv' yo' a can o' hot water fi' mek de baby tea.* Go no?"

He rolled over lazily; his loggish yellow bulk, solid, dispirited. "Cho', de man dem no ha' no hot water, giv' she a lemon, no, she na'h cry." He tossed back again, his chin on his arms, gazing at the glorious procession of the sun.

"Even de man dem, ovah yondah," she cried, gesticulating, "a hold a kangfarance fi' get some hot water. Why yo' don't get up an' go, no man? Me can't handastan' yo', sah."

A conspiration, a pandemonium threatened—the deckers.

"How de bleedy hell dem heckspeck a man fi' trabble tree days an' tree whole a nights beout giv' him any hot watah fi' mek even a can o' tea is somet'ing de hagent at Kingston gwine hav' fi' pint out to me w'en de boat dey lan'—"

"Hey, mistah hawfissah, yo' got any hot watah?"

"Hot watah, mistah?"

"Me will giv' yo' a half pint o' red rum if yo' giv' me a quatty* wut' o' hot watah."

"Come, no, man, go get de watah, no?"

"Ripe apples mek me t'row up!?"

"Green tamarin' mek me tummack sick!"

"Sahft banana mek me fainty!"

"Fish sweetie giv' me de dysentery."

Craving luscious Havana nights the ship's scullions hid in refuse cans or in grub for the Chinks hot water which they peddled to the miserable deckers.

"Get up, no Halfred, an' go buy some o' de watah," the girl cried, "de baby a cry."

Of late he didn't answer her any more. And it was useless to depend upon him. Frantic at the baby's pawing of the clotted air, at the cold dribbling from its twisted mouth, which turned down a trifle at the ends like Alfred's, she began conjecturing on the use to which a decker could put a cup of the precious liquid. Into it one might pour a gill* of goat's milk—a Cuban señora, a decker of several voyages, had fortified herself with a bucket of it—or melt a sprig of peppermint or a lump of clove or a root of ginger. So many tropical things one could do with a cup of hot water.

The child took on the color of its sweltering environs. It refused to be pacified by sugared words. It was hungry and it wished to eat, to feel coursing down its throat something warm and delicious. It kicked out of its mother's hand the toy engine she locomotioned before it. It cried, it ripped with its naked toes a hole in her blouse. It kept up an irrepressible racket.

The child's agony drove her to reckless alternatives. "If you don't go, then I'll go, yo' lazy t'ing," she said, depositing the baby beside him and disappearing down the galley corridor.

Her bare earth-red feet slid on the hot, sizzling deck. The heat came roaring at her. It swirled, enveloping her. It was a dingy corridor and there were pigmy paneled doors every inch along it. It wasn't clear to her whither she was bound; the vaporing heat dizzied things. But the scent of stewing meat and vegetables lured her on. It sent her scudding in and out of barrels of cold storage, mounds of ash debris of an exotic kind. It shot her into dark twining circles of men, talking. They either paused or grew lecherous at her approach. Some of the doors to the crew's quarters were open and as she passed white men'd stick out their heads and call, pull, tug at her. Grimy, ash-stained faces; leprous, flesh-crazed hands. Onward she fled, into the roaring, fuming galley.

Heat. Hearths aglow. Stoves aglow. Dishes clattering. Engines, donkey-engines,* wheezing. Bright-faced and flame-haired Swedes and Bristol cockneys cursing. Half-nude figures of bronze and crimson shouting, spearing, mending the noisy fire. The wet, clean, brick-colored deck danced to the rhythm of the ship. Darky waiters—white shirt bosoms—black bow ties—black, braided uniforms—spat entire menus at the blond cooks.

"Slap it on dey, Dutch, don't starve de man."

"Hey, Hubigon, tightenin' up on any mo' hoss flesh to-day?"

"Come on fellahs, let's go—"

"There's my boy Porto Rico again Hubigon, Ah tell yo' he is a sheik, tryin' to git nex' to dat hot yallah mama."

On entering she had turned, agonized and confused, to a lone yellow figure by the port hole.

"Oh, it's you," she exclaimed, and smiled wanly.

He was sourly sweeping dishes, forks, egg-stained things into a mossy wooden basket which he hoisted and dropped into a cesspool of puttering water.

He paused, blinking uncomprehendingly.

"You," she was catching at mementoes, "you remember—you helped me—my trunk—"

"Oh, yes, I remember," he said slowly. He was a Cuban, mix-blooded, soft-haired, and to him, as she stood there, a bare, primitive soul, her beauty and her sex seemed to be in utmost contrast to his mechanical surroundings.

"Can you," she said, in that half-hesitant way of hers, "can you give me some hot watah fo' my baby?"

He was briefly attired; overalls, a dirty, pink singlet.* His reddish yellow face, chest and neck shone with the grease and sweat. His face was buttered with it.

"Sure," he replied, seizing an empty date can on the ledge of the port hole and filling it. "Be careful," he cautioned, handing it back to her.

She took it and their eyes meeting, fell.

She started to go, but a burning touch of his hand possessed her.

"Wait," he said, "I almost forgot something." From beneath the machine he exhumed an old moist gold dust box. Inside it he had pummeled, by some ornate instinct, odds and ends—echoes of the breakfast table. He gave the box to her, saying, "If any one should ask you where you got it, just say Jota Arosemena gave it to you."

"Hey, Porto Rico, wha' the hell yo' git dat stuff at, hotting stuff fo' decks?"

Both of them turned, and the Cuban paled at the jaunty mug of the cook's Negro mate.

"You speak to me?" he said, ice cool.

Hate shone on the black boy's face. "Yo' heard me!" he growled. "Yo' ain't cock-eyed." Ugly, grim, black, his face wore an uneasy leer. He was squat and bleary-eyed.

A son of the Florida Gulf, he hated "Porto Rico" for reasons planted deep in the Latin's past. He envied him the gentle texture of his hair. On mornings in the galley where they both did their toilet he would poke fun at the Cuban's meticulous care in parting it. "Yo' ain't gwine sho'," Hubigon'd growl. "Yo' don't have to dress up like no lady's man." And Jota, failing to comprehend the point of view, would question, "What's the matter with you, mang, you mek too much noise, mang." Hubigon despised him because he was yellow-skinned; one night in Havana he had spied him and the chef cook, a nifty freckle-faced Carolina "cracker" for whom the cook's mate had no earthly use, and the baker's assistant, a New Orleans creole,—although the Negro waiters aboard were sure he was a "yallah" nigger—drinking *anee* in a high-hat café on the prado which barred jet-black American Negroes. He loathed the Latin for his good looks and once at a port on the Buenaventura River they had gone ashore and met two native girls. One was white, her lips pure as the petals of a water lily; the other was a flaming mulatto. That night, on the steps of an adobe hut, a great, low moon in the sky, both forgot the presence of the cook's mate and pledged tear-stained love to Jota. "An' me standin' right by him, doin' a fadeaway." He envied Jota his Cuban nationality for over and over again he had observed that the Latin was the nearest thing to a white man the *ofay* men aboard had yet met. They'd play cards with him—something they never did with the Negro crew—they'd gang with him in foreign ports, they'd listen in a "natural" sort of way to all the bosh he had to say.

Now all the mate's pent-up wrath came foaming to the front.

He came up, the girl having tarried, a cocky, chesty air about him. He made deft, telling jabs at the vapors enmeshing him. "Yo' can't do that," he said, indicating the victuals, "like hell yo' kin! Who de hell yo' t'ink yo' is anyhow? Yo' ain't bettah'n nobody else. Put it back, big boy, befo' Ah starts whisperin' to de man. Wha' yo' t'ink yo' is at, anyhow, in Porto Rico, where yo' come fum at? Com' handin' out poke chops an' cawn muffins, like yo' is any steward. Yo' cain't do dat, ole man."

It slowly entered the other's brain—all this edgy, snappy, darky talk. But the essence of it was aggressively reflected in the mate's behavior. Hubigon made slow measured steps forward, and the men came flocking to the corner.

"Go to it, Silver King, step on his corns."

"Stick him with a ice pick!"

"Easy fellahs, the steward's comin'."

All of them suddenly fell away. The steward, initiating some fruit baron into the mysteries of the galley, came through, giving them time to speed back to their posts unobserved. The tension subsided, and Jota once more fed the hardware to the dish machine.

As she flew through the corridor all sorts of faces, white ones, black ones, brown ones, leered sensually at her. Like tongues of flames, hands sped after her. Her steps quickened, her heart beat faster and faster till she left behind her the droning of the galley, and safely ascending the hatch, felt on her face the soft, cool breezes of the Caribbean ocean.

Alfred was sitting up, the unpacified baby in his arms.

"'Im cry all de time yo' went 'way," he said, "wha' yo' t'ink is de mattah wit' 'im, he? Yo' t'ink him tummack a hut 'im?"

"Him is hungry, dat is wha' is de mattah wit' 'im! Move, man! 'Fo Ah knock yo', yah! Giv' me 'im, an' get outa me way! Yo' is only a dyam noosant!"

"Well, what is de mattah, now?" he cried in unfeigned surprise.

"Stid o' gwine fo' de watah yo'self yo' tan' back yah an' giv' hawdahs an' worryin' wha' is de mattah wit' de picknee."

"Cho, keep quiet, woman, an' le' me lie down." Satisfied, he rolled back on the hatch, fatuously staring at the sun sweeping the tropic blue sea.

"T'un ovah, Halfred, an' lif' yo' big able self awf de baby, yo' Ah crush 'im to debt," she said, awake at last. The baby was awake and ravenous before dawn and refused to be quieted by the witty protestations of the Jamaica laborers scrubbing down the deck. But it was only after the sun, stealing a passage through a crack in the canvas, had warmed a spot on the girl's mouth, that she was constrained to respond to his zestful rantings. "Hey, yo' heah de picknee ah bawl all de time an' yo' won't even tek heed—move yah man!" She thrust the sleeping leg aside and drawing the child to her, stuck a breast in his mouth.

The boat had encountered a sultry sea, and was dipping badly. Water flooded her decks. Getting wet, dozing deckers crawled higher on top of each other. The sea was blue as indigo and white reels of foam swirled past as the ship dove ahead.

It was a disgusting spectacle. There was the sea, drumming on the tinsel sides of the ship, and on top of the terror thus resulting rose a wretched wail from the hatch, "Watah! Hot Watah!"

The galley was the Bastille. Questioning none, the Yellow One, giving the baby to Alfred rushed to the door, and flung herself through it. Once in the corridor, the energy of a dynamo possessed her. Heated mist drenched her. She slid on grimy, sticky deck.

He was hanging up the rag on a brace of iron over the port hole. His jaws were firm, grim, together.

The rest of the galley was a foetic blur to her.

He swung around, and his restless eyes met her. He was for the moment paralyzed. His eyes bore into hers. He itched to toss at her words, words, words! He wanted to say, "Oh, why couldn't you stay away—ashore—down there—at the end of the world—anywhere but on this ship."

"Some water," she said with that gentle half-hesitant smile of hers, "can I get some hot water for my little baby?" And she extended the skillet.

He took it to the sink, his eyes still on hers. The water rained into it like bullets and he brought it to her.

But a sound polluted the lovely quiet.

"Hey, Porto Rico, snap into it! Dis ain't no time to git foolin' wit' no monkey jane.* Get a move on dey, fellah, an' fill dis pail full o' water."

He was sober, afar, as he swept a pale, tortured face at Hubigon. As if it were the song of a lark, he swung back to the girl, murmuring, "Ah, but you didn't tell me," he said, "you didn't tell me what the baby is, a boy or girl?" For answer, the girl's eyes widened in terror at something slowly forming behind him.

But it was not without a shadow, and Jota swiftly ducked. The mallet went galloping under the machine. He rose and faced the cook's mate. But Hubigon was not near enough to objectify the jab, sent as fast as the fangs of a striking snake, and Jota fell, cursing, to the hushed cries of the woman. For secretly easing over to the fireplace Hubigon had taken advantage of the opening to grasp a spear and as the other was about to rise brought it thundering down on the tip of his left shoulder. It sent him thudding to the deck in a pool of claret. The cook's mate, his red, red tongue licking his mouth after the manner of a collie in from a strenuous run, pounced on the emaciated figure in the corner, and kicked and kicked it murderously. He kicked him in the head, in the mouth, in the ribs. When he struggled to rise, he sent him back to the floor, dizzy from short, telling jabs with the tip of his boot.

Pale, impassive, the men were prone to take sides. Unconsciously forming a ring, the line was kept taut. Sometimes it surged; once an Atlanta mulatto had to wrest a fiery spear from Foot Works, Hubigon's side kick, and thrust it back in its place. "Keep outa this, if you don't want to get your goddam head mashed in," he said. A woman, a crystal panel in the gray, ugly pattern, tore, fought, had to be kept sane by raw, meaty hands.

Gasping, Hubigon stood by, his eyes shining at the other's languid effort to rise. "Stan' back, fellahs, an' don't interfere. Let 'im come!" With one shoulder jaunty and a jaw risen, claret-drenched, redolent of the stench and grime of Hubigon's boot, parts of it clinging to him, the Cuban rose. A cruel scowl was on his face.

The crowd stood back, and there was sufficient room for them. Hubigon was ripping off his shirt, and licking his red, bleeding lips. He circled the ring like a snarling jungle beast. "Hol' at fuh me, Foot Works, I'm gwine sho' dis monkey wheh he get off at." He was dancing round, jabbing, tapping at ghosts, awaiting the other's beastly pleasure.

As one cowed he came, his jaw swollen. Then with the vigor of a maniac he straightened, facing the mate. He shot out his left. It had the wings of a dart and juggled the mate on the chin. Hubigon's ears tingled distantly. For the particle of a second he was groggy, and the Cuban moored in with the right, flush on the chin. Down the cook's mate went. Leaping like a tiger cat, Jota was upon him, burying his claws in the other's bared, palpitating throat. His eyes gleamed like a tiger cat's. He held him by the throat and squeezed him till his tongue came out. He racked him till the blood seeped through his ears. Then, in a frenzy of frustration, he lifted him up, and pounded with his head on the bared deck. He pounded till the shirt on his back split into ribbons.

"Jesus, take him awf o' him—he's white orready."

"Now, boys, this won't do," cried the baker, a family man. "Come."

And some half dozen of them, running counter to the traditions of the coast, ventured to slug them apart. It was a gruesome job, and Hubigon, once freed, his head and chest smeared with blood, black, was ready to peg at a lancing La Barrie snake.*

In the scuffle the woman collapsed, fell under the feet of the milling crew.

"Here," some one cried, "take hold o' her, Butch, she's your kind— she's a decker—hatch four—call the doctor somebody, will ya?"

They took her on a stretcher to the surgeon's room.

The sun had leaped ahead. A sizzling luminosity drenched the sea. Aft* the deckers were singing hosannas to Jesus and preparing to walk the gorgeous earth.

Only Alfred St. Xavier Mendez was standing with the baby in his arms, now on its third hunger-nap, gazing with a bewildered look at the deserted door to the gallery. "Me wondah wha' mek she 'tan' so lang," he whispered anxiously.

Imperceptibly shedding their drapery of mist, there rose above the prow of the *Urubamba* the dead blue hills of Jamaica.

The Wharf Rats

Among the motley crew recruited
to dig the Panama Canal were artisans from the four ends of the earth.
Down in the Cut drifted hordes of Italians, Greeks, Chinese, Negroes—
a hardy, sun-defying set of white, black and yellow men. But the bulk of
the actual brawn for the work was supplied by the dusky peons of those
coral isles in the Caribbean ruled by Britain, France and Holland.

At the Atlantic end of the Canal the blacks were herded in boxcar
huts buried in the jungles of "Silver City"; in the murky tenements
perilously poised on the narrow banks of Faulke's River; in the low,
smelting cabins of Coco Té. The "Silver Quarters" harbored the inky
ones, their wives and pickaninnies.

As it grew dark, the hewers at the Ditch, exhausted, half-asleep, naked
but for wormy singlets, would hum queer creole tunes, play on guitar or
piccolo, and jig to the rhythm of the *coombia*.* It was a *brujerial* chant,
for *obeah*, a heritage of the French colonial, honeycombed the life of
the Negro laboring camps. Over smoking pots, on black, death-black
nights legends of the bloodiest were recited till they became the essence
of a sort of Negro Koran. One refuted them at the price of one's breath.
And to question the verity of the *obeah*, to dismiss or reject it as the

ungodly rite of some lurid, crack-brained Islander was to be an accursed pale-face, dog of a white. And the *obeah* man, in a fury of rage, would throw a machete at the heretic's head or— worse—burn on his doorstep at night a pyre of Maubé bark or green Ganja weed.

On the banks of a river beyond Cristobal, Coco Té sheltered a colony of Negroes enslaved to the *obeah*. Near a roundhouse, daubed with smoke and coal ash, a river serenely flowed away and into the guava region, at the eastern tip of Monkey Hill. Across the bay from it was a sand bank—a rising out of the sea—where ships stopt for coal.

In the first of the six chinky cabins making up the family quarters of Coco Té lived a stout, pot-bellied St. Lucian, black as the coal hills he mended, by the name of Jean Baptiste. Like a host of the native St. Lucian emigrants, Jean Baptiste forgot where the French in him ended and the English began. His speech was the petulant *patois* of the unlettered French black. Still, whenever he lapsed into His Majesty's English, it was with a thick Barbadian bias.

A coal passer at the Dry Dock, Jean Baptiste was a man of intense piety. After work, by the glow of a red, setting sun, he would discard his crusted overalls, get in starched *crocus bag*, aping the Yankee foreman on the other side of the track in the "Gold Quarters," and loll on his coffee-vined porch. There, dozing in a bamboo rocker, Celestin, his second wife, a becomingly stout brown beauty from Martinique, chanted gospel hymns to him.

Three sturdy sons Jean Baptiste's first wife had borne him—Philip, the eldest, a good-looking black fellow; Ernest, shifty, cunning; and Sandel, aged eight. Another boy, said to be wayward and something of a ne'er-do-well, was sometimes spoken of. But Baptiste, a proud, disdainful man, never once referred to him in the presence of his children. No vagabond son of his could eat from his table or sit at his feet unless he went to "meeting." In brief, Jean Baptiste was a religious man. It was a thrust at the omnipresent *obeah*. He went to "meeting." He made the boys go, too. All hands went, not to the Catholic Church, where Celestin secretly worshiped, but to the English Plymouth Brethren in the Spanish city of Colon.

Stalking about like a ghost in Jean Baptiste's household was a girl, a black ominous Trinidad girl. Had Jean Baptiste been a man given to curiosity about the nature of women, he would have viewed skeptically Maffi's adoption by Celestin. But Jean Baptiste was a man of lofty unconcern, and so Maffi remained there, shadowy, obdurate.

And Maffi was such a hardworking *patois* girl. From the break of day she'd be at the sink, brightening the tinware. It was she who did the chores which Madame congenitally shirked. And towards sundown, when the labor trains had emptied, it was she who scoured the beach for cockles for Jean Baptiste's epicurean palate.

And as night fell, Maffi, a long, black figure, would disappear in the dark to dream on top of a canoe hauled up on the mooning beach. An eternity Maffi'd sprawl there, gazing at the frosting of the stars and the glitter of the black sea.

A cabin away lived a family of Tortola mulattoes by the name of Boyce. The father was also a man who piously went to "meeting"— gaunt and hollow-cheeked. The eldest boy, Esau, had been a journeyman tailor for ten years; the girl next him, Ora, was plump, dark, freckled; others came—a string of ulcered girls* until finally a pretty, opaque one, Maura.

Of the Bantu tribe Maura would have been a person to turn and stare at. Crossing the line into Cristobal or Colon—a city of rarefied gayety—she was often mistaken for a native *señorita* or an urbanized Cholo* Indian girl. Her skin was the reddish yellow of old gold and in her eyes there lurked the glint of mother-of-pearl. Her hair, long as a jungle elf's was jettish, untethered. And her teeth were whiter than the full-blooded black Philip's.

Maura was brought up, like the children of Jean Baptiste, in the Plymouth Brethren. But the Plymouth Brethren was a harsh faith to bring hemmed-in peasant children up in, and Maura, besides, was of a gentle romantic nature. Going to the Yankee commissary at the bottom of Eleventh and Front Streets, she usually wore a leghorn hat. With flowers bedecking it, she'd look in it older, much older than she really was. Which was an impression quite flattering to her. For Maura, unknown to Philip, was in love—in love with San Tie, a Chinese half-breed, son of a wealthy canteen proprietor in Colon. But San Tie liked to go fishing and deer hunting up the Monkey Hill lagoon, and the object of his occasional visits to Coco Té was the eldest son of Jean Baptiste. And thus it was through Philip that Maura kept in touch with the young Chinese Maroon.

One afternoon Maura, at her wit's end, flew to the shed roof to Jean Baptiste's kitchen.

"Maffi," she cried, the words smoky on her lips, "Maffi, when Philip come in to-night tell 'im I want fo' see 'im particular, yes?"

"*Sacre gache!*" All de time Philip, Philip!" growled the Trinidad girl, as Maura, in heartaching preoccupation, sped towards the lawn. "Why she no le' 'im alone, yes?" And with a spatter she flecked the hunk of lard on Jean Baptiste's stewing okras.

As the others filed up front after dinner that evening Maffi said to Philip, pointing to the cabin across the way, "She—she want fo' see yo'."

Instantly Philip's eyes widened. Ah, he had good news for Maura! San Tie, after an absence of six days, was coming to Coco Té Saturday to hunt on the lagoon. And he'd relish the joy that'd flood Maura's face as she glimpsed the idol of her heart, the hero of her dreams! And Philip, a true son of Jean Baptiste, loved to see others happy, ecstatic.

But Maffi's curious rumination checked him. "All de time, Maura, Maura, me can't understand it, yes. But no mind, me go stop it, *oui*, me go stop it, so help me—"

He crept up to her, gently holding her by the shoulders.

"Le' me go, *sacre!*" She shook off his hands bitterly. "Le' me go—yo' go to yo' Maura." And she fled the room, locking the door behind her.

Philip sighed. He was a generous, good-natured sort. But it was silly to try to enlighten Maffi. It wasn't any use. He could as well have spoken to the tattered torsos the lazy waves puffed up on the shores of Coco Té.

II

"Philip, come on, a ship is in—let's go." Ernest, the wharf rat, seized him by the arm.

"Come," he said, "let's go before it's too late. I want to get some money, yes."

Dashing out of the house the two boys made for the wharf. It was dusk. Already the Hindus in the bachelor quarters were mixing their rotie* and the Negroes in their singlets were smoking and cooling off. Night was rapidly approaching. Sunset, an iridescent bit of molten gold, was enriching the stream with its last faint radiance.

The boys stole across the lawn and made their way to the pier.

"Careful," cried Philip, as Ernest slid between a prong of oyster-crusted piles to a raft below, "careful, these shells cut wussah'n a knife."

On the raft the boys untied a rowboat they kept stowed away under the dock, got into it and pushed off. The liner still had two hours to dock. Tourists crowded its decks. Veering away from the barnacled piles the boys eased out into the churning ocean.

It was dusk. Night would soon be upon them. Philip took the oars while Ernest stripped down to loin cloth.

"Come, Philip, let me paddle—" Ernest took the oars. Afar on the dusky sea a whistle echoed. It was the pilot's signal to the captain of port. The ship would soon dock.

The passengers on deck glimpsed the boys. It piqued their curiosity to see two black boys in a boat amid stream.

"All right, mistah," cried Ernest, "a penny, mistah."

He sprang at the guilder as it twisted and turned through a streak of silver dust to the bottom of the sea. Only the tips of his crimson toes—a sherbet-like foam—and up he came with the coin between his teeth.

Deep sea gamin,* Philip off yonder, his mouth noisy with coppers, gargled, "This way, sah, as far as yo' like, mistah."

An old red-bearded Scot, in spats and mufti, presumably a lover of the exotic in sport, held aloft a sovereign. A sovereign! Already red, and sore by virtue of the leaps and plunges in the briny swirl, Philip's eyes bulged at its yellow gleam.

"Ovah yah, sah—"

Off in a whirlpool the man tossed it. And like a garfish Philip took after it, a falling arrow in the stream. His body, once in the water, tore ahead. For a spell the crowd on the ship held its breath. "Where is he?" "Where is the nigger swimmer gone to?" Even Ernest, driven to the boat by the race for such an ornate prize, cold, shivering, his teeth chattering—even he watched with trembling and anxiety. But Ernest's concern was of a deeper kind. For there, where Philip had leaped, was Deathpool—a spawning place for sharks, for baracoudas!

But Philip rose—a brief gurgling sputter—a ripple on the sea—and the Negro's crinkled head was above the water.

"Hey!" shouted Ernest, "there, Philip! Down!"

And down Philip plunged. One—two—minutes. God, how long they seemed! And Ernest anxiously waited. But the bubble on the water boiled, kept on boiling—a sign that life still lasted! It comforted Ernest.

Suddenly Philip, panting, spitting, pawing, dashed through the water like a streak of lightning.

"Shark!" cried a voice aboard ship, "Shark! There he is, a great big one! Run, boy! Run for your life!"

From the edge of the boat Philip saw the monster as twice, thrice it circled the boat. Several times the shark made a dash for it endeavoring to strike it with its murderous tail.

The boys quickly made off. But the shark still followed the boat. It was a pale green monster. In the glittering dusk it seemed black to Philip. Fattened on the swill of the abattoir* nearby and the beef tossed from the decks of countless ships in port it had become used to the taste of flesh and the smell of blood.

"Yo' know, Ernest," said Philip, as he made the boat fast to a raft, "one time I thought he wuz rubbin' 'gainst me belly. He wuz such a big able one. But it wuz wuth it, Ernie, it wuz wuth it—"

In his palm there was a flicker of gold. Ernest emptied his loin cloth and together they counted the money, dressed, and trudged back to the cabin.

On the lawn Philip met Maura. Ernest tipped his cap, left his brother, and went into the house. As he entered Maffi, pretending to be scouring a pan, was flushed and mute as a statue. And Ernest, starved, went in the dining room and for a long time stayed there. Unable to bear it any longer, Maffi sang out, "Ernest, whey Philip dey?"

"Outside—some whey—ah talk to Maura—"

"Yo' sure yo' no lie, Ernest?" she asked, suspended.

"Yes, up cose, I jes' lef' 'im 'tandin' out dey—why?"

"Nutton—"

He suspected nothing. He went on eating while Maffi tiptoed to the shed roof. Yes, confound it, there he was, near the stand-pipe,* talking to Maura!

"Go stop *ee, oui*," she hissed impishly. "Go 'top ee, yes."

III

Low, shadowy, the sky painted Maura's face bronze. The sea, noisy, enraged, sent a blob of wind about her black, wavy hair. And with her back to the sea, her hair blew loosely about her face.

"D'ye think, d'ye think he really likes me, Philip?"

"I'm positive he do, Maura," vowed the youth.

And an ageing faith shone in Maura's eyes. No longer was she a silly, insipid girl. Something holy, reverent had touched her. And in so doing it could not fail to leave an impress of beauty. It was worshipful. And it mellowed, ripened her.

Weeks she had waited for word of San Tie. And the springs of Maura's life took on a noble ecstasy. Late at night, after the others had retired, she'd sit up in bed, dreaming. Sometimes they were dreams of envy. For Mama began to look with eyes of comparison upon the happiness of the Italian wife of the boss riveter at the Dry Dock—the lady on the other side of the railroad tracks in the "Gold Quarters" for whom she sewed—who got a fresh baby every year and who danced in a world of silks and satins. Yes, Maura had dreams, love dreams of San Tie, the flashy half-breed, son of a Chinese beer seller and a Jamaica Maroon, who had swept her off her feet by a playful wink of the eye.

"Tell me, Philip, does he work? or does he play the lottery—what does he do, tell me!"

"I dunno," Philip replied with mock lassitude, "I dunno myself—"

"But it doesn't matter, Philip. I don't want to be nosy, see? I'm simply curious about everything that concerns him, see?"

Ah, but Philip wished to cherish Maura, to shield her, be kind to her. And so he lied to her. He did not tell her he had first met San Tie behind the counter of his father's saloon in the Colon tenderloin, for he would have had to tell, besides, why he, Philip, had gone there. And that would have led him, a youth of meager guile, to Celestin Baptiste's mulish regard for anisette which he procured her. He dared not tell her, well-meaning fellow that he was, what San Tie, a fiery comet in the night life of the district, had said to him the day before. "She sick in de head, yes," he had said. "Ah, me no dat saht o' man—don't she no bettah, egh, Philip?" But Philip desired to be kindly, and hid it from Maura.

"What is it to-day?" she cogitated, aloud, "Tuesday. You say he's comin' fo' hunt Saturday, Philip? Wednesday—four more days. I can wait. I can wait. I'd wait a million years fo' 'im, Philip."

But Saturday came and Maura, very properly, was shy as a duck. Other girls, like Hilda Long, a Jamaica brunette, the flower of a bawdy cabin up by the abattoir, would have been less genteel. Hilda would have caught San Tie by the lapels of his coat and in no time would have got him told.

But Maura was lowly, trepid, shy. To her he was a dream—a luxury to be distantly enjoyed. He was not to be touched. And she'd wait till he decided to come to her. And there was no fear, either, of his failing to come. Philip had seen to that. Had not he been the intermediary between them? And all Maura needed now was to sit back, and wait till San Tie came to her.

And besides, who knows, brooded Maura, San Tie might be a bashful fellow.

But when, after an exciting hunt, the Chinese mulatto returned from the lagoon, nodded stiffly to her, said good-by to Philip and kept on to the scarlet city, Maura was frantic.

"Maffi," she said, "tell Philip to come here quick—"

It was the same as touching a match to the *patois* girl's dynamite. "Yo' mek me sick," she said. "Go call he yo'self, yo' ole hag, yo' ole fire hag* yo.'" But Maura, flighty in despair, had gone on past the lawn.

"Ah go stop *ee, oui*," she muttered diabolically, "Ah go stop it, yes. This very night."

Soon as she got through lathering the dishes she tidied up and came out on the front porch.

It was a humid dusk, and the glowering sky sent a species of fly—bloody as a tick—buzzing about Jean Baptiste's porch. There he sat, rotund, and sleepy-eyed, rocking and languidly brushing the darting imps away.

"Wha' yo' gwine, Maffi?" asked Celestin Baptiste, fearing to wake the old man.

"Ovah to de Jahn Chinaman shop, mum," answered Maffi unheeding.

"Fi' what?"

"Fi' buy some wash blue, mum."

And she kept on down the road past the Hindu kiosk to the Negro mess house.

IV

"Oh, Philip," cried Maura, "I am so unhappy. Didn't he ask about me at all? Didn't he say he'd like to visit me—didn't he giv' yo' any message fo' me, Philip?"

The boy toyed with a blade of grass. His eyes were downcast. Sighing heavily he at last spoke. "No, Maura, he didn't ask about you."

"What, he didn't ask about me? Philip? I don't believe it! Oh, my God!"

She clung to Philip, mutely; her face, her breath coming warm and fast.

"I wish to God I'd never seen either of you," cried Philip.

"Ah, but wasn't he your friend, Philip? Didn't yo' tell me that?" And the boy bowed his head sadly.

"Answer me!" she screamed, shaking him. "Weren't you his friend?"

"Yes, Maura—"

"But you lied to me Philip, you lied to me! You took messages from me—you brought back—lies!" Two *pearls*, large as pigeon's eggs, shone in Maura's burnished face.

"To think," she cried in a hollow sepulchral voice, "that I dreamed about a ghost, a man who didn't exist. Oh, God, why should I suffer like this? Why was I ever born? What did I do, what did my people do, to deserve such misery as this?"

She rose, leaving Philip with his head buried in his hands. She went into the night, tearing her hair, scratching her face, raving.

"Oh, how happy I was! I was a happy girl! I was so young and I had such merry dreams! And I wanted so little! I was carefree—"

Down to the shore of the sea she staggered, the wind behind her, the night obscuring her.

"Maura!" cried Philip, running after her. "Maura! come back!"

Great sheaves of clouds buried the moon, and the wind bearing up from the sea bowed the cypress and palm lining the beach.

"Maura—Maura—"

He bumped into some one, a girl, black, part of the dense pattern of the tropical night.

"Maffi," cried Philip, "have you seen Maura down yondah?"

The girl quietly stared at him. Had Philip lost his mind?

"Talk, no!" he cried, exasperated.

And his quick tones sharpened Maffi's vocal anger. Thrusting him aside, she thundered, "Think I'm she keeper! Go'n look fo' she yo'self. I is not she keeper! Le' me pass, move!"

Towards the end of the track he found Maura, heartrendingly weeping.

"Oh, don't cry, Maura! Never mind, Maura!"

He helped her to her feet, took her to the stand-pipe on the lawn, bathed her temples and sat soothingly, uninterruptingly, beside her.

V

At daybreak the next morning Ernest rose and woke Philip.

He yawned, put on the loin cloth, seized a "cracked licker" skillet* and stole cautiously out of the house. Of late Jean Baptiste had put his foot down on his sons' copper-diving proclivities. And he kept at the head of his bed a greased cat-o-nine-tails which he would use on Philip himself if the occasion warranted.

"Come on, Philip, let's go—"

Yawning and scratching Philip followed. The grass on the lawn was bright and icy with the dew. On the railroad tracks the six o'clock labor trains were coupling. A rosy mist flooded the dawn. Out in the stream the tug *Exotic* snorted in a heavy fog.

On the wharf Philip led the way to the rafters below.

218

"Look out fo' that *crapeau*,* Ernest, don't step on him, he'll spit on you."

The frog splashed into the water. Prickle-backed crabs and oysters and myriad other shells spawned on the rotting piles. The boys paddled the boat. Out in the dawn ahead of them the tug puffed a path through the foggy mist. The water was chilly. Mist glistened on top of it. Far out, beyond the buoys, Philip encountered a placid, untroubled sea. The liner, a German tourist boat, was loaded to the bridge. The water was as still as a lake of ice.

"All right, Ernest, let's hurry—"

Philip drew in the oars. The *Kron Prinz Wilhelm* came near. Huddled in thick European coats, the passengers viewed from their lofty estate the spectacle of two naked Negro boys peeping up at them from a wiggly *bateau*.*

"Penny, mistah, penny, mistah!"

Somebody dropped a quarter. Ernest, like a shot, flew after it. Half a foot down he caught it as it twisted and turned in the gleaming sea. Vivified by the icy dip, Ernest was a raving wolf and the folk aboard dealt a lavish hand.

"Ovah, yah, mistah," cried Philip, "ovah, yah."

For a Dutch guilder Philip gave an exhibition of "cork." Under something of a ledge on the side of the boat he had stuck a piece of cork. Now, after his and Ernest's mouths were full of coins, he could afford to be extravagant and treat the Europeans to a game of West Indian "cork."

Roughly ramming the cork down in the water, Philip, after the fifteenth ram or so, let it go, and flew back, upwards, having thus "lost" it. It was Ernest's turn now, as a sort of end-man, to scramble forward to the spot where Philip had dug it down and "find" it; the first one to do so, having the prerogative, which he jealously guarded, of raining on the other a series of thundering leg blows. As boys in the West Indies Philip and Ernest had played it. Of a Sunday the Negro fishermen on the Barbadoes coast made a pagan rite of it. Many a Bluetown dandy got his spine cracked in a game of "cork."

With a passive interest the passengers viewed the proceedings. In a game of "cork," the cork after a succession of "rammings" is likely to drift many feet away whence it was first "lost." One had to be an expert, quick, alert, to spy and promptly seize it as it popped up on the rolling waves. Once Ernest got it and endeavored to make much of the possession. But Philip, besides being two feet taller than he, was slippery as an eel, and Ernest, despite all the artful ingenuity at his command, was able to do no more than ineffectively beat the water about him. Again and again he tried, but to no purpose.

Becoming reckless, he let the cork drift too far away from him and Philip seized it.

He twirled it in the air like a crap shooter, and dug deep down in the water with it, "lost" it, then leaped back, briskly waiting for it to rise.

About them the water, due to the ramming and beating, grew restive. Billows sprang up; soaring, swelling waves sent the skiff nearer the shore. Anxiously Philip and Ernest watched for the cork to make its ascent.

It was all a bit vague to the whites on the deck, and an amused chuckle floated down to the boys.

And still the cork failed to come up.

"I'll go after it," said Philip at last, "I'll go and fetch it." And, from the edge of the boat he leaped, his body long and resplendent in the rising tropic sun.

It was a suction sea, and down in it Philip plunged. And it was lazy, too, and willful—the water. Ebony-black, it tugged and mocked. Old brass staves—junk dumped there by the retiring French—thick, yawping mud, barrel hoops, tons of obsolete brass, a wealth of slimy steel faced him. Did a "rammed" cork ever go that deep?

And the water, stirring, rising, drew a haze over Philip's eyes. Had a cuttlefish, an octopus, a nest of eels been routed? It seemed so to Philip, blindly diving, pawing. And the sea, the tide—touching the roots of Deathpool—tugged and tugged. His gathering hands stuck in mud. Iron staves bruised his shins. It was black down there. Impenetrable.

Suddenly, like a flash of lightning, a vision blew across Philip's brow. It was a soaring shark's belly. Drunk on the nectar of the deep, it soared above Philip—rolling, tumbling, rolling. It had followed the boy's scent with the accuracy of a diver's rope.

Scrambling to the surface, Philip struck out for the boat. But the sea, the depths of it wrested out of an æon's slumber, had sent it a mile from his diving point. And now, as his strength ebbed, a shark was at his heels.

"Shark! Shark!" was the cry that went up from the ship.

Hewing a lane through the hostile sea Philip forgot the cunning of the doddering beast and swam noisier than he needed to. Faster grew his strokes. His line was a straight, dead one. Fancy strokes and dives—giraffe leaps . . . he summoned into play. He shot out recklessly. One time he suddenly paused—and floated for a stretch. Another time he swam on his back, gazing at the chalky sky. He dived for whole lengths.

But the shark, a bloaty, stone-colored mankiller, took a shorter cut. Circumnavigating the swimmer it bore down upon him with the speed of a hurricane. Within adequate reach it turned, showed its gleaming belly, seizing its prey.

A fiendish gargle—the gnashing of bones—as the sea once more closed its jaws on Philip.

Some one aboard ship screamed. Women fainted. There was talk of a gun. Ernest, an oar upraised, capsized the boat as he tried to inflict a blow on the coursing, chop-licking maneater.

And again the fish turned. It scraped the waters with its deadly fins.

At Coco Té, at the fledging of the dawn, Maffi, polishing the tinware, hummed an *obeah* melody

> Trinidad is a damn fine place
> But *obeah* down dey. . . .

Peace had come to her at last.

The Palm Porch

I

Below, a rock engine was crushing stone, shooting up rivers of steam and signaling the frontier's rebirth. Opposite, there was proof, a noisy, swaggering sort of proof, of the gradual death and destruction of the frontier post. Black men behind wheelbarrows slowly ascended a rising made of spliced boards and emptied the sand rock into the maw of a mixing machine. More black men, a peg down, behind wheelbarrows, formed a line which caught the mortar pouring into the rear organ of the omnivorous monster.

"All, all gone," cried Miss Buckner, and the girls at her side shuddered. All quietly felt the sterile menace of it. There, facing its misery, tears came to Miss Buckner's eyes and a jeweled, half-white hand, lifted gently to give a paltry vision of the immensity of it.

"All of that," she sighed, "all of that was swamp—when I came to the Isthmus. All." A gang of "taw"-pitching* boys, sons of the dusky folk seeping up from Caribbean isles, who had first painted Hudson Alley and "G" Street a dense black, and were now spreading up to the Point— swarmed to a spot in the road which the stone crusher had been especially

An earlier version was published in *The New Negro*, Alain Locke, ed. (Albert & Charles Boni, 1925)

cruel to, and drew a marble ring. Contemptibly pointing to them, Miss Buckner observed, "a year ago that would have been impossible. I can't understand what the world is coming to." Gazing at one another the girls were not tempted to speak, but were a bit bewildered, at this show of grossness on their mother's part. And anyway, it was noon, and they wanted to go to sleep.

But a light, flashed on a virgin past, burst on Miss Buckner, and she became reminiscent. . . .

ω

Dark dense thicket; water paving it. Deer, lions, tigers bounding through it. Centuries, perhaps, of such pure, free rule. Then some khaki-clad, red-faced and scrawny-necked whites deserted the Zone and brought saws to the roots of palmetto, spears to the bush cats and jaguars, lysol to the mosquitoes and flies and tar to the burning timber-swamp. A wild racing to meet the Chagres* and explore the high reaches of the Panama jungle. After the torch, ashes and ghosts—bare, black stalks, pegless stumps, flakes of charred leaves and half-burnt tree trunks. Down by a stream watering a village of black French colonials, dredges began to work. More of the Zone pests, rubber-booted ones, tugged out huge iron pipes and safely laid them on the gutty bosom of the swamp. Congeries of them. Then one windy night the dredges began a moaning noise. It was the sea groaning and vomiting. Through the throat of the pipes it rattled, and spat stones—gold and emerald and amethyst. All sorts of juice the sea upheaved. It dug deep down, too, far into the recesses of its sprawling cosmos. Back to a pre-geologic age it delved, and brought up things.

Down by the mouth of a creole stream the dredges worked. Black in the golden mist, black on the lagoon.

With the aftermath there came a dazzling array of corals and jewels— jewels of the griping sea. Magically the sun hardened and whitened it. Sandwhite. Brown. Golden. Dross surged up; guava stumps, pine stumps, earth-burned sprats, river stakes. But the crab shell—sea crabs, pink and crimson—the sharks' teeth, blue, and black, and purple ones—the pearls, and glimmering stones—shone brightly.

Upon the lake of jeweled earth dusk swept a mantle of hazy blue.

II

"W'en yo' fadah wake up in de maw-nin' time wid 'im marinah stiff out in front o' him—"

"Mek fun," said Miss Buckner, rising regally, "an' be a dam set o' fools all yo' life." She buried the butt in a Mexican urn, and strode by Anesta sprawling half-robed on the matted floor. "Move, gal, an' le' me go out dey an' show dis black sow how we want 'ar fi' stew de gunga peas* an' fowl."

"Oh, me don't wan' fi' go to no pahty," yawned Hyacinth, fingering the pages of a boudoir textbook, left her one evening by an Italian sea captain, "me too tiad, sah."

"An' me can't see how de hell me gwine mek up to any man if me got fi' fling in him face a old blue shif' me did got las' week. W'en is Scipio gwine bring me dat shawl him pramise fi' giv' me?"

"Me no fond ha-tall o' any 'Panish man," cried Anesta, "an' me don't see how me can—"

Miss Buckner swung around, struck. "Yo' t'ink so, he, his dat wha' yo' t'ink? Well, yo' bes' mek up unna* mind—all o' unna! Well, wha' a bunch o' lazy ongrateful bitches de whole carload of unna is, dough he?

Suddenly she broke off, anger seaming her brow, "Unna don't know me his hindebted to him, no? Unna don't know dat hif hit wasn't farrim a lot o' t'ings wah' go awn up yah, would be street property long ago—an' some o' we yo' see spo'tin' roun' yah would be some way else, an' diffrant altogaddah."

"Ah know not me."

"Ah know Oi ain't owe nobody nothin'—"

"Yo' think yo' don't! But don't fool yourselves, children, there is more to make the mare go than you think—I see that now."

She busied herself gathering up glasses, flouncing off to the pantry.

The Palm Porch was not a canteen, it was a house. But it was a house of lavish self-containment. It was split up in rooms, following a style of architecture which was the flair of the Isthmian realtors, and each room opened out on the porch. Each had, too, an armor of leafy laces; shining dust and scarlet. Each had its wine and decanters, music and song.

On the squalid world of Colon it was privileged to gaze with hauteur, for Miss Buckner, the owner of the Palm Porch, was a lady of poise, charm and caution. Up around the ribs of the porch she had put a strip of canvas cloth. It shut out eyes effectively. Glancing up, one saw boxes of rosebush and flower vines, but beyond that—nothing. The porch's green paint, the opulent flower pots and growing plants helped to plaster on it the illusion of the tropical jungle.

There clung to Miss Buckner an idea of sober reality. Her hips were full, her hands long, hairy, unfeminine, her breasts dangling. She was fully seven feet tall and had a small, round head. Her hair was close to it—black, curly. Courageously she had bobbed and parted it at a time when it was unseasonable to do so, and yet retain a semblance of respect among the Victorian dames of the Spanish tropics.

Urged on by the ruthless spirit which was a very firm part of her, Miss Buckner was not altogether unaware of the capers she was cutting amid the few beings she actually touched. Among the motley blacks and browns and yellows on the Isthmus, there would be talk—but how was it to drift back to her? Via Zuline? Shame! "Who me? Me talk grossip wit' any sahvant gyrl, if yo' t'ink so yo' lie!" But the lack of an elfin figure and the possession of a frizzly head of hair, was more than made up for by Miss Buckner's gift of *manners*.

"Gahd, wha' she did got it, he?" folk asked; but neither London, nor Paris, nor Vienna answered. Indeed, Miss Buckner, a lady of sixty, would have been *wordless* at the idea of having to go beyond the dickty rim of Jamaica in quest of *manners*. It was absurd to think so. This drop to the Isthmus was Miss Buckner's first gallop across the sea.

And so, like sap to a rubber tree, Miss Buckner's manner clung to her. Upon those of her sex she had slight cause to ply it, for at the Palm Porch few of them were allowed. Traditionally, it was a man's house. When Miss Buckner, beneath a brilliant lorgnette,* was gracious enough to look at a man, she looked, sternly, unsmilingly down at him. When of a Sabbath, her hair in oily frills, wearing a silken shawl of cream and red, a dab of vermilion on her mouth, she swept regally down Bolivar Street on the way to the market, maided by the indolent Zuline, she had half of the city gaping at the animal wonder of her. Brief-worded, cool-headed, by a stabbing thrust or a petulant gesture, she'd confound any fish seller, any dealer in yampi or Lucy yam,* cocoanut milk or red peas—and pass quietly on, untouched by the briny babel.

In fact, from Colon to Cocoa Grove the pale-faced folk who drank sumptuously in the bowl of life churned by her considered Miss Buckner a woman to tip one's hat to—regal rite—a woman of taste and culture. Machinists at Balboa, engineers at Miraflores, sun-burned sea folk gladly testified to that fact. All had words of beauty for the ardor of Miss Buckner's salon.

Of course one gathered from the words which came like blazing meteors out of her mouth that Miss Buckner would have liked to be white; but, alas! she was only a mulatto. No one had ever heard of her before she and her five daughters moved into the Palm Porch. It was to be expected, the world being what it is, that words of murmured treason would drift abroad. A wine merchant, Raymond de la Croix, and a Jamaica horse breeder, Walter de Paz, vowed that they had seen her at an old seaman's bar on Matches Lane serving ale and ofttimes more poetic things than ale to young blond-headed Britons who would especially go there. But De Paz and De la Croix were men of frustrated idealism, and their words, to Miss Buckner at least, brutal though they were, were swept aside as expressions of useless chatter. Whether she was the result of a union of white and black, French and Spanish, English and Maroon—no one knew. Of an equally mystical heritage were her daughters, creatures of a rich and shining beauty. Of their father the less said the better. And in the absence of data tongues began to wag. Norwegian bos'n. Jamaica lover—Island triumph. Crazy Kingston nights. To the lovely young ladies in question it was a subject to be religiously highhatted and tabooed. The prudent Miss Buckner, who had a burning contempt for statistics, was a trifle hazy about the whole thing.

One of the girls, white as a white woman, eyes blue as a Viking maid's, had eloped, at sixteen, to Miss Buckner's eternal disgust, with a shiny-armed black who had at one time been sent to the Island jail for the proletarian crime of prædial larceny.* The neighbors swore it had been love at first sight. But it irked and maddened Miss Buckner. "It a dam pity shame," she had cried, dabbing a cologned handkerchief to her nose, "it a dam pity shame."

Another girl, the eldest of the lot (Miss Buckner had had seven in all), had, O! ages before, given birth to a pretty, gray-eyed baby boy, when she was but seventeen and—again to Miss Buckner's disgust—had later taken up with a willing young mulatto, a Christian in the Moravian Church. He was an able young man, strong and honest, and wore shoes, but Miss Buckner almost went mad—groaned at the pain her daughters caused her. "Oh, me Gahd," she had wept, "Oh, me Gahd, dem ah send me to de dawgs—dem ah send me to de dawgs." He was but a clerk in the cold storage; sixty dollars a month—wages of an accursed silver employee. Silver is nigger; nigger is silver. Nigger-silver. Why, roared Miss Buckner, stockings could not be bought with that, much more take care of a woman accustomed to "foxy clothes an' such" and a dazzling baby boy. Silver employee! Blah! Why couldn't he be a "Gold" one? Gold is white; white is gold. Gold-white! "Gold," and get $125 a month, like "de fella nex' tarrim, he? Why, him had to be black, an' get little pay, an' tek way me gal picknee from me? Now, hanswah me dat!" Nor did he get coal and fuel free, besides. He had to dig down and pay extra for them. He was not, alas! white. Which hurt, left Miss Buckner cold; caused her nights of sleepless despair. Wretch! "To t'ink a handsam gal like dat would-ah tek up wi' a dam black neygah man like him, he, w'en she could a stay wit' me 'n do bettah." But few knew the secret of Miss Buckner's sorrow, few sensed the deep tragedy of her.

And so to dam the flood of tears, Miss Buckner and the remaining ones of her flamingo brood, had drawn up at the Palm Porch. All day, the sun burning a flame through the torrid heavens, they would be postured on the porch. Virgin to the sun's gentle caresses, with the plants and flowers keeping the heat at bay, they'd be there. Slippers dangled on the tips of restive toes. Purple-lined kimonos falling away gave access to blushing, dimpled bodies. Great fine tresses of hair, the color of night, gave shadows to the revelations, gave structure.

III

"Come, Zuline,—hurry—it's getting late." The porch was vacant, dusk had fallen, and Miss Buckner wore an evening gown of white taffeta, fashioned in the Victorian epoch. It was tight and stiff and created a rustle, and there was a black bandeau pasted on to her skull.

Sullenly the girl came, and gathered up the debris. "Sweep up dis ash, an cayh dis slip in Goldy's room, de careless t'ing," said Miss Buckner.

She went to one of the dusk-flooded rooms and seized a studded dagger which she stuck among the watches and brooches which shone on her bosom. She patted it, made sure it was safely a part of the glittering pattern, and ordered the night on.

"Get up, girls," she shouted, invading room after room, "it is late, get up!"

"Hello, Sailor Mack. Hit any home runs to-day!"

"An' you, you Kentucky millionaire—how many ships came through the locks to-day?"

"Bullocks—did you say?"

"Fie!"

"Oh, Mistah Council," she said, "how do you do?" Young Briton, red-faced, red-eyed, red-haired. Yellow-teethed, dribble-lipped, swobble-mouthed, bat-eared.

He kissed the proffered hand, and bowed low. He was gallant, and half-drunk. "Where's my girl, Anesta," he said, "by God, she is the sweetest woman, black or white—on the whole goddamned—"

"Sh, be quiet, son, come," and Miss Buckner led him to a chair among a group of men.

Constantly, Miss Buckner's hand kept fluttering to the diamond-headed pin stuck in her bosom.

Chaos prevailed, but Miss Buckner was quite sober. All about there were broken vases, overturned flower-pots, flowers, women's shoes. All the men were prostrate, the women exultant.

As midnight approached, the doorbell suddenly rang. And Miss Buckner rose, cautioning serenity. "All right, boys, let's have less noise—the captain's comin'."

In Anesta's lap there was an eruption, a young Vice-Consul staggered up—shaking her off, ready to face the coming of the visitor.

"Sit down, Baldy," she implored, "come back here to me—"

"Skipper, eh? Who is he? Wha' ya hell tub is he on?" He was tall and his body rocked menacingly.

"Put that goddam lime juicer to bed, somebody, will ya?"

"Yo' gawd dam American—why—"

Anesta rose, flying to him. "Now, Tommy," she said, patting his cheek, "that isn't nice."

"Let the bleddy bastard go to—"

But apparently an omnipotent being had invaded the porch, and a deep-throated voice barked sweetly down it, "Anesta, darling, take Baldy inside, and come here!"

"But, mother—"

"Do as you are told, darling, and don't waste any more time."

"No, Gawd blarst yo'—nobody will slip off these pants of mine. Lemme go!"

"Be a gentleman, sweet, and behave."

"What a hell of a ruction it are, eh?"

"Help me wit' 'im, Hyacinth—"

Ungallantly yielding, he permitted the girl to force him along on her arm. He stepped in the crown of Mr. Thingamerry's hat.[*] Only yesterday he had put on a gleaming white suit. Done by the Occupation, the starch on the edges of it made it dagger sharp. Now it was a sight; ugly drink stains darkened it. Booze, perspiration, tobacco weeds moistened it. His shirt, once stiff, was black and wrinkled. His tie, his collar, and trousers awry. His fire-red hair was wet and bushy and rumpled. Black curses fell from his mouth. But six months in the tropics and the nights and the girls at the Palm Porch had overpowered him. Held him tight. Sent from Liverpool to the British Consulate at Colon, he had fallen for the languor of the seacoast, he had been seized by the magic glow of the Palm Porch.

Seeing the Captain, Miss Buckner was as bright-eyed as a débutante. Instinctively her hands fled to her beaming bosom, but now the impulse was guided by a soberer circumstance.

The Captain was smiling. "Well, good lady," he said, "I see you are as charming and as nervous as usual. I hope you have good news for me to-day." He bowed very low, and kissed the jeweled hand.

"Oh, dear Captain," exclaimed Miss Buckner, touched by the Spaniard's gentility, "of course I have!" And she went on, "My renowned friend, it is so splendid of you to come. We have been looking forward to seeing you every minute—really. Was I not, Anesta, dear?" She turned, but the girl was nowhere in sight. "Anesta? Anesta, my dear? Where are you?"

It was a risky job, wading through the lanes of wine-fat men. As she and the Captain sped along, she was careful to let him see that she admired his golden epaulets, and the lofty contemptible way he'd step over the drunken Britons, but she in her own unobtrusive way was hurling to one side every one that came in contact with her.

"Christ was your color. Christ was olive—Jesus Christ was a man of olive—"

"Won't you wait a moment, Captain—I'll go and get Anesta." And she left him.

About him tossed the lime-juicers, the "crackers"—wine-crazed, woman-crazed. He turned in disgust, and drew out an open-worked handkerchief, blowing his nose contemptuously. He was a handsome man. He was dusky, sun-browned, vain. He gloried in a razor slash he had caught on his right cheek in a brawl over a German slut in a District canteen. It served to intensify the glow women fancied in him. When he laughed it would turn pale, stark pale, when he was angry, it oozed red, blood-red.

Miss Buckner returned like a whirlwind, blowing and applying a Japanese fan to her bosom.

In replacing it, a crimson drop had fallen among the gathering of emeralds and pearls, but it was nothing for her to be self-conscious about.

Very gladly she drew close to him, smiling. "Now, you hot-blooded Latin," she said, the pearls on the upper row of her teeth shining brighter than ever, "you must never give up the chase! The Bible says 'Him that is exalted' . . . the gods will never be kind to you if you don't have patience. . . . No use . . . you won't understand . . . the Bible. Come!"

Pointing to the human wreckage through which they had swept, she turned, "In dear old Kingston, Captain, none of this sort of thing ever occurred! None! And you can imagine how profusely it constrains me!"

"Anesta, where are you, my dear? Here's the Captain—waiting."

Out of a room bursting with the pallor of night the girl came. Her grace and beauty, the tumult of color reddening her, excited the Captain.

Curtseying, she paused at the door, one hand at her throat, the other held out to him.

It was butter in the Captain's mouth, and Miss Buckner, at the door, viewing the end of a very strategic quest, felt happy. The Captain, after all, was such a naughty boy!

The following day the *policia* came and got Tommy's body. Over the blood-black hump a sheet was flung. It dabbed up the claret. The natives tilted their chins unconcernedly at it.

Firm in the Captain's graces Miss Buckner was too busy to be excited by the spectacle. In fact, Miss Buckner, while Zuline sewed a button on her suède shoes, was endeavoring to determine whether she'd have chocolate soufflé or maidenhair custard for luncheon that afternoon.

The Black Pin

"Wha' dah Alfie got in 'e han'?"

"It ent nutton," spoke up Din, "yo' is ah 'larmer, dah is wha' yo' is."

"Orright den," replied Mirrie, "oi muss be blin'."

"Like dah is anything de worl' don' know orready."

"Wha' yo' got dey, boy?" murmured April, bent over the washtub, soap suds frosting on her veiny brown arms. She caught up the bulk of her starch-crusted patchwork frock and dried her hands in it.

"Oi tell yo' de boy got somet'ing," Mirrie said, "yo' is such a ownway somebody yo' can't even hear yo' ears ringin'."

"Hey, it muss be a cockroach."

"Or a forty-leg—"

"It ent!"

"Look out deah, boy, yo' gwine stump yo' toe. Bam—tell yo' so! Go help 'e up, Mirrie."

" . . . won't stay whe' yo' belong, ni? Why yo' got to be runnin' 'bout de gap like yo' ent got nobody? Like yo' is some sheep who' ent got no muddah or no faddah. Come yah, wha' yo' got in yo' han'? Lemmah see it!"

"Woy, woy, it nearly jook* mah fingah!"

"Um is a black pin!" exclaimed Mirrie in terror.

"Wha' yo' get dis pin from, boy?" asked April, paling and pausing, then venomously seizing it.

"*Obeah!*"

"Heaven help mah!"

"Who giv' yo' dis pin, boy?" April insisted. Her brows were wrinkled; she exposed the pin to the sun.

"Open yo' mout', boy," she said, "whe' yo' get dis pin?"

"Miss Diggs giv' it to me, mum," murmured Alfie slowly, afraidly.

"Zink Diggs?"

"Yassum."

"Whelp!"

"Giv' yo' dis pin? Wha' fo'? Wha' she giv' yo' a pin fo'? Hey, boy, tek um back to she."

"Sen' he back wit' um!"

"Wha' she mean, yes?"

"Yo' too stupid," shouted Mirrie, assuming an air of worldly wisdom not wholly unsuited to her. "She is wukkin' *obeah* fo' yo', dat is wha' is de mattah."

"De bad-minded wretch!" cried April. "Hey, wha' Ah do she, ni? Did Ah tek wey she man? Did Ah break she sugar stick?* Did Ah call she teef? Did Ah steal she guamazelli plum* f'om she? Hey, Ah can't understan' it, yes. Wha' she wan' fo' giv' me a black pin, fo'?"

April held the ghastly symbol against the ripe Barbados sun. Moving in the shadow of the spreading *dounz** she stared at it long and hard. Dark April, a lanky, slipshod woman in a half-dry print skirt and old, sprawling, ratty shoes, stood up, amazed at the lurid import. "Ah wondah why she sen' me dis," she pondered, bewildered.

At her side one of the girls shuffled, cracking the dark, crisp dirt under her feet. "Yo' too stupid," she said. "Little as I is I know wha' um mean."

In something of a trance April went to the shed-roof. Cooing pigeons and doves swarmed upon it. Beaten by the rain, dung spattered upon it, ran white and dark blue. Under the shingled edges of the roof bats took refuge. White-spotted canaries sang to the lovely robins poised on the bowing limbs of the *dounz*.

" . . . let she alone, sha', g'way."

"Eatin' de po' dog bittle."

"It ent."

"It is."

"Yo' chirrun, behav' unna-self!" April turned, an angry look flooding her dusky face. "Oi gwine beat all yo', yes."

Devil-symbol, *obeah*-symbol—a black pin. "Gwine stick um yah." She bored it into a sunless, rainless spot in the side of the shed-roof. "All yo' ent gwine tetch dis pin, unna understan'? Unna heah wha' Oi say? Nobody ent gwine tetch dis pin! If anybody tetch it, they bess get ready fo' tetch me. Oi tell unna dah f'um now."

"Oi know Oi ent gwine got nutton fo' do wit' it."

"Nor me."

"Nor me needah."

"Da, da, unna bess not, for' Oi'll wash unna behind de fuss one wha' do."

II

Blue cassava—unfit for cakes—about to be grated and pressed for its starch; withering twigs; half-ripe turnips, *bolonjays** a languid flush of green and purple, a graveler—a watery, cork-light potato endwardly dangling; a greedy sow, tugging at a stake, a crusty, squib-smoked "touch bam"—hand-magic, earth-magic, magic of the sun, magic of the moon, magic of the flowing Barbadian gap.

Soft, round, ash-gray, dark violet, purple peas—peas Alfie and Ona and Din and Mirrie ate raw; grown by her own nimble, prolific hands.

Only—the soft quiet of Goddard's Village, Demerara (Mud-Head Land)* to Barbadoes . . . on a barque, owned by a West Indian "speckah-latah"—dealer in sweet and Irish spuds—aboard ship, ashore, January to December, wearing thick British tweed, baggy, hairy, scratchy and hot. On the zigaboo's boat April had taken flight. Soft nights; nights of ebony richness; of godless splendor. On the shining waters—blue, frosty, restful—a vision of Jesus walked.

An' crown-un-un Him Lahd av ahl
An' crown-un-un Him Lahd av ahl
An' crown-un-un Him Lahd av ahl
An' Crown Him!
Crown Him!
Lahd!
Av!
Ahl!

The bow of the ship jammed against a brilliant Barbadian sunset, April, a pique shawl swathing her aching body, saw a wiggling *queriman** resist being dragged up on the smooth, spotless deck. Kingfish, sprat, flying fish—sprang, fought, grew enraged at the proximity of sea-less earth. On a half-dry mattress the children slept . . . sucked on sour plums. . . . One more sunset, and the noisy, dusty music of Bridgetown.

All for the remote joys of a gap in Goddard's Village, and of a rosier one: sending the children to school and to St. Stephen's Chapel.

Accomplishing it had been a tear-drenching ordeal.

Up above the brace of stone, up above Waterford's, beyond The Turning, up a dazzling white dusty road, sugar canes on either side of it, an old ox cart driver at Locust Hall had had an empty shack crumbling slowly on the side of the slanting grass hill. Under the rigid hammering of the sun, with a strip of swamp land below—shy of lady canes, with a rich ornate green—the green of fat juicy canes—the shack was slowly perishing. On hot days centipedes, and scorpions, and white mice, and mongooses prowled possessively through it. On wet ones raining winds dumped on the roof flowers, tree-drips, soggy leaves.

Thirteen sovereigns the man had asked, and she had given him seven. Parts of the house, visibly the beams and foundations, of oak, fell to dust at the touch of the husky black movers, men used to the muscle-straining task of loading ox carts with hefts of loose sugar cane. Husky black movers moaning:

Jam Belly, Quakah Belly,*
Swell like a cocoa,
Tee hey, tee hey—
Sally bring grass in yah!

Untouched by the noise, and the heat, and swarming of cane dust, a centipede ran up one of the men's legs. Bawling. Scratching. Portions of the gabling roof lifted on to the dray sagged and dragged all the way to Goddard's Village. From Locust Hall it scraped the ground. Behind it, April, and Alfie and Mirrie and Ona and Din—sagged through the heavy oceans of stone dust.

Of the star apples and *dounz* sunset carved a framework of purple mist. Etched, flung upon the sky. On a stone step Bay Rum, a worker in marl, twanged a guitar; beyond the dingy cabin the ragged edges of an old mortar house were imprisoned against the glowing sky. In the imminent dusk cane arrows swung to and fro, on some peasant farmer's hedge. A donkey cart, wagged in and wagged on, down to the eternity of the gap.

April explored the waterholes along the gap for stones to prop her house on. Some had to be cut, shaved, made small. Hoisting it, smoothing the floor—was a man's job. Plenty of stones, dug up, stolen, at night or early dawn, from obscure vacant spots in the village, to be used in myriad ways. That done, the hammering began. At Locust Hall it must have been a magnet for rusty nails. It took more muscle than was at the command of a woman to swing them out of their sockets. Often an adamant one sent April reeling against the breadfruit tree. Did she have to take them out, at all? Yes. No old nails in her house for her. Wall pockets,* too, had to be put in. The lamp, a brilliant one, was crowned with a violet dome.

III

Down through the spine of the lane was a watercourse. Fish—blue, gold, crimson—whirled languidly in it. And from the watercourse sounds came. Busy buttering the soft part that was not exposed to the sun, of the banana leaf into which she was to spread the cornmeal and spice and molasses and then tightly fold to make the conkee,* April was quick to hear it. The kids squabbling again.

She put down the platter and made for the watercourse. Zenona, the nanny goat, scampered away at her rustling approach.

"Alfie, wha' is it?" she cried, running up.

"He hit my Crump," said Zink Diggs, bivouacked on the fringe of the land, a switch twirling in her hand.

"It ent!" the boy retorted, crying.

"Who tell he fo' hit my Crump?"

"He han' too fast."

"Are dat so?" said April, boiling with rage. "Hey, a big neygah uman like yo' hit a little boy like dis. Yo' ort to be ashamed o' yo' dutty self." She clasped the boy against her knees. He was slyly eying, through a shiny mist, Crump's mother with the rod in her hand.

"Evah sence yo' bin in dis gap yo' been pickin' 'pon me. Why yo' don' le' me an' me chirrun alone, ni?'"

"Well, why yo' don't tell dem not to extafay* wit' mine, den, no? Tell dem de little watahmout' runts, not to come on my hedge-row an' pick an' mo' o' my tam'rin's. Oi'll set poison fo' dem, too. Why yo' don't feed dem? Why yo' don't giv dem a good stiff ball o' cookoo so dat dey won't hav' to teef my tamarin's? Pack o' starved-out runts!"

"Who is any starved-out runt?"

"Yo'! Who yo' t'ink Oi is talkin' to, but yo'?"

"Yo' nasty t'ing yo'!"

"Yo' murrah!"

"Bad-minded wretch!"

"Call me all de bad-minded wretch yo' like but Oi betcha yo' don't hit mah!"

"Oi don't hav' to low-rate myself fi' suit any field han' neygah uman like yo'."

"Hey," laughed Zink Diggs, her arms akimbo, "hey, anybody hear she talkin' would 'a' t'ink she is the Queen of England!"

"Come, Alfie, le' we go an' leave de wretch!"

IV

At serene peace with the Lord, April was sent one dusk, the reddish tints of a Barbadian twilight spreading a lovely fervor over the land, into a spasm of alarm.

"Hey, Miss Emptage—"

A high-pitched neighbor's voice rose above the music of the wind humming over the cane piece.

"Wha'm is, negh?"

"Zink Diggs tek up yo' goat."

"Pig!"

"Go' quick befo' she chop awf she head."

"Run, mahmie—"

Chasing through the corn April went to the end of the boundary line, just in time to see Zink Diggs tethering the goat. She was singing and an air of joyous conquest was about her.

"Giv' me my goat," said April.

"Come an' tek she," said the other, pointing the reins at her. "Come an' tek she, ni, if yo' t'ink yo' is de uman Oi is dam well sure yo' ent."

"Always jookin' yo' han' in yo' matty* saucepan," cried April.

"Wha' dah yo' say?" she cried, bewildered.

"Gypsy t'ing!"

"Wha' dah yo' say!" she cried, enraged. "Why yo' don't talk plain so dat a body can understan' yo'? Why yo' ha' fi' fall back 'pon dah gibberish unna tahlk dey whe' unna come from."

"Giv' me my goat," said April, "dat is ahl ah ax yo'."

"Dey she is," repeated Zink Diggs, pointing to Zenona. "Go tek she, ni!" But the goat was safely on Zink Diggs' ground.

April made a step to cross it.

"If yo' put a foot 'pon my sorrel* I'll brek um fo' yo'," she murmured, vengefully.

"How much yo' wan' fo' de goat?" asked April at last.

"A shillin', an' yo' bettah be bleddy well quick 'bout it befo' ah carry de starved-out t'ing 'ome and mek currie outa she."

"Teefin' vagybon' yo'," said April, water seeping into her eyes.

"Call me all de bad name yo' lik', but yo' ent gwine get dis goat back to-night till yo' fork up dat shillin'. Dey'll have to jump ovah my grave befo' dey'll get yo' hungry goat fuss."

She turned to one of the children. "Go in de lardah, Mirrie, an' reach up 'pon de ledge an' bring de* dah shillin' Bay Rum giv' me yestiddy fo' de eggs." She sighed, for it was her last one.

The child sped through the bush—spindling legs leaving the brown earth—and in a jiffy was back with the piece of silver bright in her dirt-black palm.

"Hey," said April, taking it and leaning over the ripening sorrel, "hey, tek yo' old shillin' an' giv' me my goat."

Zink Diggs grew hysterical at her approach. "Don't come near mah," she said, her eyes rolling wildly. "Stan' whey yo' dey an' put de shillin' 'pon de groun'! Don't come near muh! An' tek yo' ole hungry goat along."

April took the goat and dropped the shilling on the ground.

"Yo' t'ink Oi gwine tek anyt'ing out o' yo' nasty hand'?" she said. "Yo' put um 'pon de ground." But before she picked it up she went in her bosom and drew out a little salt sack. She sprinkled two or three pinches of it on the coin before she picked it up.

ॐ

The sun came out again. The crops bristled, the birds were singing. Triangles of birds, blackbirds and peewits, swarmed to the fragrant fruit, gave music to the wind. Hummingbirds—doctor birds—buzzed at the mouths of alluring red flowers.

April, a calico bag swung around her waist, picking the pigeon peas planted on the hedge facing Zink Diggs' land, sang hosannahs to the Lord. . . .

An' Crown-un-un Him Lahd av ahl

As she went along husking them, shelling the peas, she was soon
aware of some one burrowing in the nearby hedge, and whistling

> Donkey wahn wahtah, hole 'im Joe
> Donkey wahn wahtah, hole 'im Joe
> Hole 'im Joe, hole 'im Joe,
> Hole 'im Joe, don't let 'im go—
> Donkey wahn de wahtah, hole 'im Joe.

She readily recognized Zink Diggs, but hardly, the words that followed.

"Good mawnin', Miss Emptage."

Being a child of the Lord, April answered, "Good mawnin.'" She
continued singing a Sankey hymn,* and shelling the peas.

"You're not a quarrelsome uman," she heard Zink Diggs say, "but
you're dam side mo' determined than I am!"

But she went on, not turning her head, singing the Sankey hymn.

V

It was spring; spring in Barbadoes.
For the dogs—evil omen. Grippe. Sickness. Across the flowing acreage
the brindle pup took a post near the goat. Nearby Alfie, Mirrie, Ona
and Din were twittering. "Come, doggie; come, doggie—" and giving
the poor wretch parsley.

"Go back an' put de pot on de fiah," April shouted to Mirrie as she
strode through the cornpatch. "Go back an' boil de pigeon peas."

"Oi wan' fi come, too."

"Go down de stan' pipe an' get a bucket o' water an' mek yo' oven,
den."

They left her, and she went madly down to the end of her ground.
On the rim of her land she met Zink Diggs. "Wha' yo' doin' 'pon my
ground'?" she said. "Yo' muss be mek a mistake, uman, yo' ent survey yo'
ground right."

"Yo' t'ink so?" the other cried. "Now look yah, Miss Emptage, yo' bin'
lookin' fo' trouble evah sence yo' move in dis gap, yo'—yes, yo'—an'
yo' dam well know dat when yo' wuz plantin' dem peas an' corn yo' wuz
trespassin' 'pon my groun'. Uman, yo' mus' be outa yo' senses."

With a rope of banana trash to tie up her skirt—up so high that her
naked legs gleamed above the tops of her English patent leather boots

which the Doctor had ordered her to wear as a cure for "big foot"*—Zink strode swiftly through the patch, dragging up by their roots, cane, corn, peas, okra—April's plantings.

"Move outa my way, uman, befo' Oi tek his gravellah an' ram it down yo' belly! Don' mek me lose me head dis mawnin' yeh, Oi don' wan' fo' spend de res' o' my days in de lock-up fo' killing nobody."

No rock engine, smoothing a mountain road, no scythe, let loose on a field of ripened wheat, no herd of black cane cutters exposed to a crop, no saw, buzzing and zimming, could have outdone Zink Diggs' slaying and thrashing and beheading every bit of growing green. Flat, bare, she left it. April was afraid to open her mouth. She stood by, dumbfounded, one hand at her throat.

Gleaming in triumph, Zink gathered her bill and graveller and paused before she went. "Look at she dough," she said, "she look like Jonah when de whale puke he up!" And she flounced through the orchard, singing *Hole 'im Joe.*

ॐ

"Ona, come yah, quick!"
"Yo' always boddering me, why yo' don't—"
"Come, yah, gal—gal, Oi call yo'!"
"Wha' do yo', ni?"
"Me wan' fi' show yo' somet'ing, gal."
"Wah'm is, ni?"
"De black pin is ketchin' de house afiah."
"Gahd! Go tell mahmie—"
"Wha' she is?"
"Roun' by de shed-roof."
"Mirrie, come yah, an' see wha' Din do! Ketch de house afiah!"
"It ent me! It is de black pin burnin'—"

Down by the back of the breadfruit tree Alfie and Mirrie were sitting close to each other—very close. They hated to be diverted by such silly inquisitiveness. Calm, unexcited, Mirrie was prodding the boy to do something to her. She had put it down on a matchbox, in edgy, scrawly letters—one word—but it refused to stir Alfie's sluggish desire. The scent of something ripe and rich and edible—something to be tasted with the lore of the tropics deep in one's blood—something bare and big and immortal as the moon—compelling something—began to fill the air about the little boy. He secretly felt it surging in Mirrie, and something beat a tattoo in his temples. Upon him a certain mirage fell—sure, unerring.

"Wha' yo' two doin' heah?" shouted Din, coming up. "Hey, Oi gwine tell mah mahmie 'pon yo' two."

"Wha' yo' gwine tell she? Yo' mouthah!"

"Dat—"

"Mout' run jess lik' sick neygah behine."

"Dat what? Wha' yo' ketch me doin', yo' liad t'ing yo'? I ent doin' nutton. I was just showin' Alfie—"

"Mirrie!"

"Comin', mum!"

His tongue thick, heavy, Alfie rose. "Yo' girl chirrun, if unna don't behave unna self, Oi gwine tell unna mahmie 'pon unna, too. Wha' all yo' makin' all dis noise fo'?"

"De pin ketch de house afiah."

"Wha' pin?"

"Fomembah de black pin Zink Diggs giv' Alfie fo' he mahmie?"

"Hey, yes."

"Gal, shut up yo' mout', yo' too stupid, how kin a pin ketch de house afiah?"

"Wha' is dah smoke, den?"

"Run an' tell mahmie, quick."

Ona, Din, Alfie, Mirrie—the last one, dusting, aggrieved, thwarted—galloped past the shed roof round to the kitchen.

"Mahmie."

"Quick, de black pin is ketchin' de house afiah."

"Gyrl, yo're crazy."

Swiftly drying her hands, she sped around to the shed roof. A gust of smoke darted, on the crest of a wind, from the place where the deadly missile had been imprisoned.

Surely, it was burning—the black pin had fired the shed roof! Out April tugged it. Once more she held it trembling in the sun. A smoking black pin. Some demon chemical, some liquid, some fire-juice, had been soaked into it originally. *Obeah* juice. "But Oi gwine sick de Lord 'pon yo'," vowed April, tossing it upon a mound of fowl dung and wormy provisions scraped together in the yard, and set a bonfire to it all. The fire swallowed it up and the wind sent a balloon of gray-white smoke puffs streaming over Zink Diggs' hedge.

∾

It had speed, and energy, and a holy vitality—the smoke; for it kept on till it got to Zink Diggs' house and then it burst puffing into it. It had hot, red, bitter chemicals, the smoke of the pin, and Zink Diggs' reaction to them was instantaneous. The smoke blew by, taking life—animal, plant. The dog dropped, the leaves of tea bush she had picked and had on the kitchen table, withered suddenly. It left her petrified by the stove, the white clay pipe ghastly in her mouth. Even her eyes were left sprawling open, staring at the cat, likewise dead, by the smoking coal pot.

The Vampire Bat

He was one of the island's few plan-
tation owners and a solid pillar of the Crown. He had gone forth at
the King's trumpet call to buck the Boer's* hairy anger. But at last the
guerilla warrior had become a glorious ghost and the jaunty buckras were
trekking back to Barbadoes.

Flying into a breastwork of foam, the English torpedo boat had
suddenly stopped, wedged in a sargasso reef a dozen miles from the
Caribbean sea. After landing at a remote corner on the jungle coast,
Bellon was forced to make the trip, a twelve mile affair, on drays and
mule carts over the brown, hoof-caked road to Mount Tabor.

But Mount Tabor, once a star on a pinnacle of wooded earth, was lost
to old Sharon Prout's Boer-fighting son.

Wrecked in the storm which swept the island the very week Bellon
had embarked for South Africa—it was a garden of lustrous desolation.
Weedy growth overspread it. The lichened caverns below the stoke hole,
once giving berth to hills of cane husk—fodder for the zooming fire—
fertilized beds of purple beans. A stable, housing a mare and landau,
stood on the old mill's bank. Rows of *taches*—troughs into which the
cane's juice was boiled and brewed through a succession of stages until

it became a quarry of loaf sugar—frothed green on the rich, muggy land. One was a pond. Frogs and green water lilies floated on it. Another, filled to the maw, gave fathomless earth to breadfruit.

The old shaggy mare, a relic of the refining era at Mount Tabor, plodded through the dead, thick marl. Wearing a cork hat and a cricketer's white flannel shirt, open at the throat, Bellon drew near the woods to Airy Hill.

He trotted down a slanting road in to Locust Hall. A mulatto cane cutter, poxy progenitor of twenty-one husky mule-driving sons, stood under the raised portcullis,* talking to a woman. Pulling at a murky clay pipe he was slyly coaxing her to a spot in the cane piece. His juice-moist bill, bright as a piece of steel, shone in the fern-cluttered gut. Blacks on sluggish bat-eared asses mounted the hill mouthing hymns to drive away the evil spirits.

Father, O Father
. . . past the fading rays of night
Awake! awake!

Game-vending squatters streamed down from Flat Rock, cocks gleaming on trays which saddled their heads. From the shining hills the estate's night hands meandered in, pecking at greasy skillets. Corn meal flecked the snowy marl.

Reminiscently Bellon ruffled the horse's mane. "You old war horse, you." Once, long before the storm, the blacks at Arise, one of the old man's estates—a stark, neurotic lot—had burned and pilfered the old sugar mill, while the buckras were confabbing on the seashore of Hastings. Rayside, then but a frisky colt, smelling a rat, had make a wild dash for the city—neighing the tidings to the buckras.

Now it fell to the young heir to be returning to Waterford, the last of the old man's estates, on the back of the heroic old mare.

It was ten o'clock at night and he had yet fourteen miles to go.

A lone moon-swept cabin or a smoker's pipe light, blazing in the canes, occasionally broke the drab expanse of night. The road trickled on, deepening into a gully. There rose above it rocky hedges, seeding flower and fruit. Swaying in the wind, the cane brake grew denser, darker. The marl lost its prickly edge and buried the animal's hoofs in soft, gray flour. Laboriously she loped through it.

The road gently lifted. It perceptibly dazzled the myopic beast. The marl returned. It blazed white, and shone. The earth about it seemed bare and flat and the cane brakes thinner. And the moon hung lower. A rickety donkey cart suddenly came jogging down the hill. A creole woman, atop an ass, trotted by. The wind soared to a higher, sturdier level. It blew like breezes on the gay Caribbean sea. Had it been noon, or dusk, blackbirds would have speckled the corn fields or sped low above the reeling canes. But the moon ribbed the night and gave the canes, tottering on the high flat earth, a crystal cloaking.

Now the road faltered, steadied, and as the road slanted, the marl thickened until it became flour dust again. The cottages at The Turning hove into view.

"At last," the captain cried, and the lanky mare quickened at the proximity of feed. Her reins fell on her back, limp with sweat.

Opposite a Negro baker shop Bellon dismounted, hitched the animal to a guava tree, and knocked upon the door.

"Who dat?" shouted a voice from within.

"Captain Prout," he replied, and the door swung to.

Squat and stout, Mother Cragwell, a Ba'bajan creole—mixture of white and Negro—admitted him, and shuffled back behind the counter, eying the visitor. She had been kneading dough, the counter was lathered with it, and her hands were scaly with shreds of flour.

"Mas' Prout," the old woman exclaimed, "wha' yo' a do down yah dis time o' night? Yo' na'h go home no?"

"Why, yes, Mother Cragwell," replied the officer jovially, "can't a law-abiding colonist walk the King's highway after dark?"

"De King's highways," the old woman sarcastically muttered, "Wha' dey care 'bout any King?"

Fixing her brownish red eyes on the buckra, she looked puzzled, skeptical.

"Why, is that the sort of welcome you give a returning soldier, Mother Cragwell?" he inquired, flattered by the old woman's characteristically racial concern.

She shook her head, ruefully bestirring herself. "Han' me dat bucket dey," she said. "How much yo' want?"

"Oh, fill it," he said, fetching the pail, "the road is beginning to tell on the old wretch."

"'Bout time," murmured Miss Cragwell, who'd been a fixture at The Turning for over thirty years.

She half-filled the pail with molasses, burst a bag of flour into it and began mixing the mash with a ladle.

"Well, I suppose this is her last trip to Waterford—she's entitled to a pension for the rest of her life, the horny old nag."

He took the mare the foaming mash and returned to be confronted by a cup of chocolate, a knot of burnt cane and a tasty banana tart. Among bill-twirlers, mule cart drivers, and cork-hatted overseers and estate owners, Mother Cragwell's "drops" and sweet bread, turnovers and cassava pone, were famous to the farthest ends of the Ba'bajan compass.

He cordially sat down to the mulatto's informal hospitality. "I knew," he observed, "that I'd have to wait till I reached The Turning before I could prove I was back in the colony." He took a relishing sip and the old creole's glare fell.

"Mas' Prout," she said, "yo' bes' don't go down de gully to-night, yo' hear?"

"Why, what's happening in the gully, Mother Cragwell?" he smiled, splitting the sugar cane. "Is the man in the canes prowling about? Or do you think the duppies* will be haunting Rayside's tracks?"

But the young Briton's banter chilled the old mulattress. "If yo' know what is good fo' yo'self, yo' bes' hear wha' Oi tell yo'," was all she said.

"H'm! this tastes like good old West Indian rum!" he cried, taking another fig of the cane. "Did you burn it yourself, Mother Cragwell?"

"Who, me? No, bo," she retorted, looking up. "Dah cane yo' got dey come from down de road."

"What, did they have a fire there recently?"

"Yes, bo. Las' night. The fire hags ketch it fire las' night."

"The who?"

"Hey," the old woman drawled, shocked at the young man's density. "Hey, look at his boy, ni. Yo' don't fomembah wha' a fire hag is, no? An' he say he gwine down de gully to-night."

Bellon burst into a fit of ridiculing laughter. "Why, shame upon you, Mother Cragwell!"

"Ent yo' got piece o' de ve'y cane in yo' mout', suckin'?" she cried, fazed, hurt.

"Tommyrot! Some jealous squatter fired the brake, that's all."

"Yo' believe dat?" challenged the old lady, "Orright den, go 'long, bo. All yo' buckras t'ink unna know mo' dan we neygahs. Go 'long down de gully 'bout yo' business, bo."

He rose, handed her a shilling and started for the door.

Suddenly a whinny from the mare—a wild scream in the night— startled him.

"Who dat?" shouted Mother Cragwell, seizing an old cricket bat and going towards the door.

"Oh, me Gard, me Gard, me Gard—"

The door was slapped open and a Negro woman, draped in white, shaking a black parasol and a hand bag, entered. She was shivering and white-eyed and breathless.

"Calm yo'self, girl, an' stop wringin' yo' hands. Yo' gwine poke out a body eye wit' dat parasol yo' flo'ish dey."

"Oh, Miss Cragwell, Miss Cragwell—"

"Hey, sit down, Lizzie. It is Lizzie Coates. Wha' yo' doin' up yah dis time o' night, girl?"

"Oh, de man in de canes, de man in de canes—"

"Wha' he do to yo'?"

"Oh, de man in de canes, de man in—"

"Stop cryin' yo' big able goat 'n let a body see what's de mattah wit' yo'," frowned Miss Cragwell; she turned to Bellon. "Go behind de counter," she said, "an' like a good boy hand me de candle grease yo' see dey 'pon me chest o' draws."

"Oh, nutton ain't do me—he ain't do me nutton."

"Hey, yo' hear ris alarmer, ni," drawled Mother Cragwell, her lower lip hanging. "Wha' yo' mekin' all dis noise fo' den?"

A look of revulsion shone on Bellon's face as he returned. "God, she's black!"

"Oh, Mother Cragwell," the woman pleaded, dropping into a seat, "le' me tell yo'—"

Every word she uttered was punctuated with jabs of the inevitable parasol. "The light fool me," she said. "It war so light I bin taught it wuz morning."

"Yo' mean to say a big able woman like yo' ain't got a clock in yo' house?"

With difficulty the buckra kept back an oath of amused disgust.

"The light fool me, Ah tell yo'—"

"Yo' got a watch, Mas' Prout, wha' time it are?" asked Mother Cragwell.

He shifted his body to the other side. "Quarter to twelve," he said.

"Hey, it ent even twelve o'clock yet," breathed the black sweating woman, "an' here I wuz startin' fo' walk to St. Georges. I musta wuz drunk, an', gal, jess as I tu'n de corner—"

"Wha' corner?"

"Codrington Corner. By the wall. You know—down dey—"

"Ah'm."

"Who should I see standin' up 'gainst dey but a man."

"Lahd, tek me!"

"A man, gal, a man!" She fanned her black eagle face, the sweat brilliant on it.

"Wuz he alone?"

"Yes, ni."

"An' nobody wuz 'pon de road?"

"Not a blind soul gwine up or comin' down! An' me by meself mekin' fo' Waterford Bottom!"

"Gal, wha' yo' a do? Try fo' be a buckra?" And she cast an accusing eye at the white man.

A slow chuckle escaped Bellon as he tapped on his leggings with a black sage switch.

"Soul,* I wuz so frighten I couldn't swallow good. I nearly choke, yes. But anyway I had my trus' in de Lord—

"Fust I taught it wuz a duppy—one o' de mans in de canes come back fo' haunt de po' neygah."

"Dey do dat," agreed Mother Cragwell, irrelevantly.

"Well, soul, when I mek de gap fo' tu'n into de gulley somet'ing tell me fo' change me umbrella from my lef' han' into my right an' my bag from my right into my lef'."

"Whe' wuz de man all dis time?"

"I put he out o' me taughts, girl. I wuzn't t'inkin' 'bout he. I had my mind 'pon de Lord an' de goodness o' His wuks—"

"Wha' a foolish ole goat yo' is! Why, girl, I su'prize at you! Wha', you ain't know any bettah? Wha' de man in de canes got fo' do wit' de Lawd? He don't care nutton' 'bout he!"

"Well, anyway, when I got down in de gulley it wuz so quiet yo' could heah de mongoose runnin' in de canes. It wuz so dahk yo' couldn't see yo' own hand."

"Hey . . ."

"Den I mek out anudder man comin' down de road . . ."

"Me po' Lizzie."

"Down de road. He wuz lightin' he pipe an' walkin' fast."

"Did he see yo'?"

"No, I don't t'ink he see me, but I could see he, dough, an' just ez I get up to he, I move one side fo' let he pass. An' soul just ez I got out o' he way, he bump right into somebody walkin' behind me!"

"Gard!"

"De man behine me wuz followin' me, gal, dah's wha' it wuz. Followin' me all dis time an' dere I wuz wouldn't knowin' it!"

"Yo' lucky, yes."

"Gal, I'm lucky fo' true! Soul, he bump into de man so ha'd de man even bu'n he mout' wit' de matches."

"An' wha' he do, buss he mout'?"

"De man comin' down de hill ax he pardin, but, soul, yo' should o' hear how he cuss he! 'Why yo' don't look where yo' gwine,' he shout out, 'yo' t'ink yo' own de road, no?'"

"An' wha' de man say to he?"

"Oh, de man only ax he pardin, an' went 'long 'bout he business."

"Why didn't he look whey he wuz goin'—"

"Shucks, he wuz so bent 'pon wha' he wuz gwine do he couldn't hav' eyes fo' nobody but me! An' de man humbug he object, dat's all. But wait, le' me tell yo'. Dah happen down in de gully. An' I went long, ent eben t'inkin' 'bout no man—"

"Ah tell all you' Seven Day 'Ventists unna is a pack o' nanny goats—"

"When all uva suggen somebody from behind put two long greasy arms roun' me neck, like he wan' fo' hug me!"

"De Lord hav' mercy!"

"Gal, I wuz so frighten I tek me umbrella an' I jerk it back ovah my lef' shoulder so ha'd de muscles still a hu't me!"

"Go 'way!"

"Jook! Straight in he eye—"

"Murdah!"

"Deed I did! Wha' business he ha' puttin' he ole nasty claws roun' me!"

"An' what he do, ni?"

"Gal, he le' me go so fas' yo' would' 'a' t'ink de lightnin' strike he! An' I wuz so frighten I tu'n roun' ready fo' hollow fo' blue murder, but de Lord was wit' me an' He protect me. Fo' girl, he wen' runnin' in de gutter, pickin' up stones an' shying* them at me."

"De wutliss whelp—"

"But girl, like I wuz heah, he was firin' dem ovah yondah! 'Yo' brute,' he say, 'yo' whelp, yo' wan' to jook out my eye, no! Yo' wan' to mek me blind, no!' An' all de time he was peltin' an' peltin' de rock stones at somebody a mile f'um fo'm me!"

"Yo' musta jook he in he eye—"

"Chile, if it wuzn't fo' dis umbrella I wouldn't know where I'd be by now. It's de Lord's own staff o' life."

With a piercing chuckle the buckra walked to the door. "Well," he drawled, "I guess I'd better be going. It's getting late."

Abruptly Mother Cragwell rose and went to him. "Yo' still gwine down de gully, son?" she begged, half-tearfully.

"Oh, don't be sentimental, Mother Cragwell," he said, with good-humor. "I'll manage somehow."

"Orright, bo," she shrugged, helplessly. "I can't say any mo' to yo'," and he went forth, loftily.

The mare took the road at a jog and a trot, till the huts grew dim, the canes and the hedges bushy. The moon was buried in a lake of blue mist and the marl ate into the animal's hoofs.

The Negro woman's tale excited a magic concern in the buckra.

There was a road opposite the baker shop which led through a disman-tled estate, providing a short cut to Waterford. But Bellon remembered that it led over a steep gulley range—a tunnel a mile deep—a rattling river when it rained or stormed—now a rocky cave harboring wild dogs and lame mules, tusky boars and other, mystic finds.

He evaded it—the old Negress' tale ringing in his ears.

Somber, ruthless—the marl. The mare pawed and sieved it, stones soared topwards.

The moon burned the mist. It burned it away, leaving but a white crest of flame fire.

Suddenly, over the earth of gentle winds and sugar canes, balls of crimson fire plagued the sky! Fire hags at night—St. Lucia sluts, *obeah*-ridden, shedding their skins and waltzing forth at night as sheep and goats, on errands of fiery vengeance. Sometimes, on returning, at the end of the eventful night, they would find their skins salted—by the enemy—and, unable to ease back into them, the wretches would inquire, "Skin, skin yo' no know me?" And for the balance of their thwarted lives they'd go about, half-slave, half-free, muttering: "Skin, yo' no know me, Skin yo' no know me?"

A bright-spirited party of Negro farm folk wrestling up the hill on basket-laden mules, came into view.

"Howdy, Massa."

"God bless yo', Massa."

"Gwine town, Massa?"

"Be ca'ful—de fire hag dem a prowl 'bout yah, Massa."

He pulled up the horse, puzzled at the spreading of the squirting fire.

"God—fire hags—surely the niggers can't be right."

He turned ashen, the reins in his hands tight, the horse pawing and pegging the marl understandingly.

The balls of fire subsided, but he was deep in the marl gully and unable to trace the origin of the pink hazes bursting on the sky's crest. The wind, however, was a pure carrier of smell, and the tainted odor of burnt cane filled the road.

"Wonder whose canes they're burning—"

Burning cane—the sky reflecting the distant glow—casks of rum boiling to waste at the will of some illiterate field hand!

He shouted to the animal.

"Giddup, horse!"

His head went swirling—the temptation to relapse conquered—barbaric *obeah* images filled his buckra consciousness.

Sugar canes burning—men in the canes—fire hags—nigger corpses—Perspiration salted Bellon's brow.

Nigger corpses—nigger corpses—

And a legend, rooted deep in the tropic earth, passed pell-mell before him.

ॐ

It concerned a river, a river red as burning copper and peopled by barques and brigantines, manned by blacks wedded to the *obeah*.

Once, the master of a vessel, taking a cargo of dry cocoanuts to a mulatto merchant on the other side of the coast, cheated; a few English crowns were at stake. But the trader was a high-priest of the *obeah*, and was silently aware of it. Forthwith he proceeded to invoke the magic of the *obeah* against the vessel.

At late dusk the returning vessel hoisted anchor. The festival rites, incident to her voyage, had drawn to the wharf, selling mango and grape, the mulatto courtesans of the river town. And the crew rained on them silver and gold, and bartered till the sun went down.

Upon reaching the vessel's deck the crew—the wine of lust red on their lips—grew noisy and gay at the sinking of the river sun. From below they brought a cask of rum, part of the cheated trader's store, and drank of it. With a calabash they dipped and wallowed in it, finding it sweeter than falernum.

Stars bedecked the night and a torch was lit. The vessel rocked on, falling in with the trade winds.

The rum was a siren, it led one on. The cask was deep, immense, but the liquor shrank till the huskiest of the Islanders had to be pummeled to lean over into it and dip the liquid out. With a score of itching throats there was a limit to the cask's largess, and the bottom was early plumbed.

When they got to it, however, it was to find a rum soaked Negro corpse doubled up in the bottom!

The horse came to a dead, rigid stop. It was death dark and they had just entered the heart of the marl gully.

He was already fidgety, and grew urgent. "Come on, Rayside," he shouted, "giddup." But the mare shook, stamped, shuddered.

He stroked her mane, but a strange strong-headedness took hold of her. She flung her ears forward.

Bellon dismounted, and the mare's inelegant tail switched her bony flanks. He coaxed and patted her, but all she did was jerk her head the more.

Resorting to a flashlight, Bellon clicked it at her feet.

As the glare hit the marl, he recoiled, as one struck, at the spectacle it revealed—a little Negro baby sleeping in the marl!

"God, what's next!"—

Hesitatingly he approached, discerning that it lived, and moved.

For a spell he gazed at it, half-afraid. But for a diaper of green leaves it was nude. Then it occurred to him to pick it up.

Instantly the child reacted to its contact with human warmth and snuggled to Bellon's bosom. He smoothed its soft, bronze skin and the waif, with hands flagrantly like a bird's claws, burrowed closer to him.

With the child held close the buckra started for the horse, but—like a shot—Rayside bolted!

"Steady, mare!" Bellon growled, quietly reining her back in, "Easy, horse!"

One ear pasted flat on her mane, she stood impatiently still while he reached for the chamois blanket and swaddled the Negro baby in it.

Only then was he able to remount her.

Another of the colony's lurking evils, the desertion—often the murder of illegitimate Negro babes.

O God—another of the island's depraved nigger curses!

All the way up the hill Rayside reared and trotted, kicked and pranced, keeping to the edge of the marl road.

And the Negro waif's bird-like claws dug deeper into the buckra's shirt bosom.

He rode up the hill's moon-white crest until the shadow of Waterford fell upon him. He was tired, his brain fagged, his legs sore, his nerves on edge.

On the brink of a rocky hill extending beyond the estate stood a buckra overseer's cabin. Here Bellon's journey ended. He stabled the mare in the shed, glad to be rid of her. "Why, you don't even give me a chance to be temperamental—"

He took the Negro child in the cabin, angry at the physical proximity of it. "If any one had told me three weeks ago that after dodging Boer-shot I'd next be mothering a deserted nigger ragamuffin at two o'clock in the morning on a West Indian country road, I'd certainly have called him a God damned liar!"

He found a spot on the floor and brusquely cushioned the burden in it.

He was edgy, unstrung; he could not sleep. He tossed, half-awake, tortured by the night's fairy-like happenings.

As a boy at Arise the old man'd tell of fresh-born Negro babes dropped in eely wells in remote parts of the plantation jungle or wrapped in crocus bags and left in the canes for some ferocious sow to gnaw or rout.

Rapacious Negro ghosts—"men in the canes"—ha! ha! preying upon the fears of the uncivilized blacks.

Fire hags! St. Lucia mulatto sluts—changing their skins—turning to goats—sheep—prowling—going forth—

And weirdly interchangeable—Black Negro babes and vampire bats!

All night the fussy mare, with glassy eyes glued on the buckra hut, refused to touch corn or oats—stamping, kicking, growing uneasy.

The glory of the morning sun neared the cane hills. It burned past the mare's shed, leaving the animal still nervously gazing out it.

Inside the hut there sprawled the dead body of Bellon Prout. With a perforation pecked in its forehead, it was utterly white and bloodless.

On the ground the chamois blanket was curiously empty.

Coming up the hill the mulatto *obeah* girl who tidied the overseer's hut felt deeply exultant. For she was strangely conscious of the fact— by the crystal glow of the sun, perhaps—that a vampire bat, with its blood-sucking passion, had passed there in the night.

*T*ropic Death

I

The little boy was overwhelmed at being suddenly projected into a world of such fluid activity. He was standing on the old bale and cask strewn quay at Bridgetown watching a police launch carry a load of Negro country folk out to a British packet smoking blackly in the bay.

He was a dainty little boy, about eight years of age. He wore a white stiff jumper jacket, the starch on it so hard and shiny it was ready to squeak; shiny blue velvet pants, very tight and very short—a little above his carefully oiled knees; a brownish green bow tie, bright as a cluster of dewy crotons; an Eton collar, an English sailor hat, with an elastic band so tight it threatened to dig a gutter in the lad's bright brown cheeks.

He was alone and strangely aware of the life bubbling around Nelson's Square. Under the statue masses of country blacks had come, drinking in the slow draughts of wind struggling up from the sea. City urchins, who thrived on pilfering sewers or ridding the streets of cow dung which they marketed as manure; beggars, black street corner fixtures, their bodies limp and juicy with the scourge of elephantiasis; cork-legged wayfarers, straw hats on their bowed crinkly heads; one-legged old black women vending cane juice and hot sauce.

It was noon and they had come, like camels to an oasis, to guzzle Maube or rummage the bags of coppers, untie their headkerchiefs, arrange their toilet and sprawl, snore, till the sun spent its crystal wrath and dropped behind the dark hulk of the sugar refineries to the western tip of the sky. Then it was their custom to pack up and sally forth, on the singing jaunt to the country.

Scores of ragged black boys, Gerald's size and over, filled the Square, half-covered by the dust, snoring. Old boys, young boys, big boys, little boys; boys who'd stolen on the wharves at sundown and bored big holes in the wet sacks of brown sugar; boys who'd defied the cops, and the sun, and the foaming mules, or the ungodly long whip of the driver, and skimmed on to tin cups the thick brackish froth the heat had sent fomenting up through the cracks in the molasses casks; boys who'd been sent to the Island jail for firing touch bams at birds lost in the bewildering city or for flipping pea-loaded popguns at the black, cork-hatted police.

Melting target for the roaring sun, the boy turned and gazed at the sea. It was angry, tumultuous. To the left of him there rose the cobwebbed arch of a bridge. Under it the water lay dark and gleaming. Against its opaque sides there were scows, barges, oil tankers. Zutting motor boats, water policemen, brought commotion to the sea. Far out, where the sun kissed it, the sea shone like a sheet of blazing zinc.

Creeping to the edge of the quay, he peeped over and saw a school of black boys splashing in the water. They were diving for coppers flung by black tourists on the side lines. They slept on the Congo-slippery rafts holding up the city, and would, for a ha'penny, dart after parasols or kites—that is, if the kites happened to be made of hard glazy "B'bados kite papah"—lost on the rolling bronze sea.

"Come, Gerald, eat this."

He turned and there was his mother. His big bright eyes widened for her. And a lump rose in his throat. He wanted to hug, kiss her. With the heat of his mouth he wanted to brush away her tears, abolish her sorrow. He wanted, too, to breathe the lovely, holy beauty of her.

"Come, son, tek yo' fingah outa yo' mout', quick, de launch will be yah any minute now."

He took the lozenge, the sun making it soft and sticky.

"Don't yo' want some ginger beer, son?"

"Oh, mama, look!"

The launch had come up, and one of the sailor-cops, a husky, black fellow, was making it fast.

"Orright lady, yo' is de nex'—come ahlong."

With much agitation she got in the boat. She had to hang on to her bag, to Gerald, and she was not prepared to get the ends of her slip wet. The men seized him, and she stepped down, barely escaping a carelessly dangling oar.

Bewildered, they clung to each other. "All right, son?" she said. But he was too unspeakingly concerned over the concurrent miracles of sea and sky.

Leaping through the sea, the boat would drown them in a shower of spray every time it came up, and Gerald was repeatedly tempted to put his hand in the water. "Keep yo' hands inside, sah," she cried, "shark will get you, too."

He remained aware of only foam and water, and the boat's spit and sputter, and the warmth of Sarah's bosom. Away back, on the brown and gold of the horizon, he saw speeding into nothingness the scows and warehouses and the low lofts of Bridgetown. Now, the sea rose—higher, higher; zooming, zooming; bluer, darker—the sky, dizzier, dizzier; and in the heavens war was brewing—until the shroud of mist ahead parted and there rose on the crest of the sky the shining blue packet!

II

Sunday came. The sun baptized the sea. O tireless, sleepless sun! It burned and kissed things. It baked the ship into a loose, disjointed state. Only the brave hoarse breezes at dusk prevented it from leaving her so. It refused to keep things glued. It fried sores and baked bunions, browned and blackened faces, reddened and blistered eyes. It lured to the breast of the sea sleepy sharks ready to pounce upon prey.

Falling night buried the sun's wreckage. To the deckers below it brought the Bishop of the West Indies, a wordy, free-jointed man. He was a fat, bull-necked Scot with a tuft of red grizzly hair sticking up on his head and the low heavy jowl of a bulldog. He wore a black shiny robe which fell to the tips of his broad shiny black shoes. An obedient man, he had deserted the salon on the upper deck—deserted red-faced Britons in cork hats and crash on a jaunt to the iron mines of Peru—to take the Word of the Lord Jesus Christ to the black deckers below.

He very piously resisted grime and filth. On one occasion to avoid stepping on a woman's sleeping arm, he was obliged to duck under a hammock. It swayed gently and the man in it was one of those rare specimens—a close-mouthed, introspective Savanilla trader. As he shot up from beneath it, the Bishop was just in time to have splashed on the breast of his shining robe a mouthful of the trader's ill-timed spit. For half a second he blinked, and heated words died on his lips. But seeing the Colombian unaware of the impiety, he gruffly scrambled onward, brushing his coat.

Edging between a carpenter's awl and a bag of peas and yams, something ripped a hole in the Bishop's coat. He was sweating and crimson. His collar was too high and too tight. Stepping over a basin of vomit, he barely escaped mashing a baby. He was uncertain that he had not done so, and he swiftly returned and without saying a word gave the sea-sick mother half a florin.*

He clapped a fatherly hand on Gerald's head, and the boy looked up at him with wondering bright eyes. Sarah Bright was sitting on the trunk skinning a tangerine.

"Your little boy?" smiled the Bishop, "smart-looking little chap, isn't he?" It was a relief to come upon them.

"Tu'n roun' yo' face, sah," she said, "an' lemme brush de sugah awf yo' mout'—" Assiduously she tidied him.

It was dark, and the ship was rolling unsettlingly. A kerosene torch spun a star-glow on the Bishop's pale tense face. He was about to address them. He was buried amongst a cargo of potatoes and the litter of the deckers. His was a sober impulse. On all sides the Dutch of Curaçao, the Latins of the Pass, the Africans of Jamaica, and the Irish of Barbadoes—spat, rocked, dozed, crooned.

In a fetid mist odors rose. Sordid; tainted; poised like a sinister vapor over the narrow expanse of deck. And with a passionate calm, the Bishop, clasping the Book of Books, faced them.

"O Lord, our God," he trembled, "O everlasting Father, again it is our privilege to come to Thee, asking Thy blessing and Thy mercy. Great God and Father! Thou knowest all things, Thou knowest the hearts of all men, and especially the hearts of these, Thy children! O Sacred Jehovah! purify their wretched souls—give unto them the strength of Thy wisdom and the glory of Thy power! Lead them, O Blessed Father, unto the pathway of righteousness that they may shine in the glory of Thy goodness! Help them, O! Divine Father! to see the light that shineth in the hearts of all men—we ask Thee Thy blessings in Thy son, Christ Jesus' name, Amen!"

III

Fish, lured onto the glimmering ends of loaded lines, raged in fruitless fury; tore, snarled gutturally, for release; bloodied patches of the hard blue sea; left crescents of gills on green and silvery hooks. Some, big and fat as young oxen, raved for miles on the shining blue sea, snapping and snarling acrobatically. For a stretch of days, the *Wellington* left behind a scarlet trail.

∾

He was back in Black Rock; a dinky backward village; the gap rocky and grassy, the roads dusty and green-splashed; the marl, in the dry season, whirling blindly at you; the sickly fowls dying of the pip and the yaws;* the dogs, a row-rowing, impotent lot; the crops of dry peas and cassava and tannias and eddoes,* robbed, before they could feel the pulse of the sun, of their gum or juice; the goats, bred on some jealous tenant's cane shoots, or guided some silken black night down a planter's gully—and then only able to give a little bit of milk; the rain, a whimsical rarity. And then the joys, for a boy of eight—a dew-sprayed, toe-searching tramp at sunrise for "touched" fruit dropped in the night by the epicurean bats, almonds, mangoes, golden apples; dreaming of the day when the cocoanut tree planted at a particularly fecund part of the ground would grow big enough to bear fruit; waiting, in the flush of sowing time, for a cart loaded to the brim to roll rhythmically over the jarring stones and spill a potato or a yam. After silence had again settled over the gap, he'd furtively dash out on the road and seize it and roast it feverishly on a waiting fire; he'd pluck an ear of corn out of the heap his mother'd bring up from the patch to send to town, and roast it, and stuff it hot as it was in his tiny pants pocket and then suffer excruciating rheumatic pains in his leg days afterwards.

Usually on a hike to Bridgetown Sarah would stop at the Oxleys' on Westbury Road. Charlie Oxley was a half-brother of hers. Once he had the smallpox and the corrugations never left him. He was broad and full-bellied and no matter how hot it was he wore severe black serge. He was a potato broker, and a man of religious intelligence.

He had, by as many wives, two girls—and they were as lovely as fine spun silk. But Suttle Street, a pagan's retreat, was hardly a place for them so they were sent to Codrington to absorb the somber sanctity of the Moravian Mission. Now there came to crown the quiet manor on Westbury Road, another mistress, a pretty one, herself a mother of two crimson blown girls, *the quintessence of a spring mating*. They were a divine puzzle to Oxley. It was queer that their fathers, both firemen on a Bristol tramp, now blissfully ensconced in the heart of the Indian Ocean, had forgotten to return to tickle and fondle their pure white faces. . . .

It had happened in a peculiar way. And all through a silly love of song. Why did she ever encourage such a feeling? The legend of it was fast taking its place beside the parish's scandals of incest. Sea songs; songs sailor-men sang; ballads of the engine room and the stokehole; ditties fashioned out of the crusted sweat of firemen. Ah, it went beyond the lure of the moment. Bowing to it, she'd go, the lovely whelp, to wharf and deck when sunset was spreading a russet mist over the dusky delta of Barbadoes and give herself up to the beauty of song. Greedily songs go to the heart; go to the heart of women. It was bad enough being maid at a grog shop on a bawdy street and the upsquirt of a thundering Scot and an African maiden, but it was worse when the love of songs of the deep, led one at dusk, at dark, to descending stairs to stokeholes or to radiant night-walks on the spotless fringe of Hastings.

Mosquito one
Mosquito two
Mosquito jump in de ole man shoe.

At last, song-scorning, no more a slinger of ale, she had crawled, losing none of the primal passion she had formerly dazzled him with, over to Oxley's—to fatten on a succession of gorgeous nights of deep-sea singing and unquestionable sailoring.

Meditating on the joys attendant to the experience of seeing the Oxleys there came to little Gerald's mind the vision of soup. Rockhard crabs, tight-fisted dumplings, little red peppers, Cayenne peppers, used all to be in it. Sometimes there would be seasoning it *hossah* or *corass*[*] and parsley and white eddoes. And when they left, Mr. Oxley always gave Sarah a bag of potatoes to take home; but she was a lady and proud and it pained her to take it home on her head; but one of the neighbors, who had a donkey cart which came to town each day, would stop by and get it for her.

One forenoon when the sun was firing the hills of Black Rock, she had hurriedly decided to visit the Oxleys. To every one, down to the idiot Lynchee King, he of the maw worm,[*] it was clear that something was tugging at Sarah Bright's throat.

To Gerald it was a quickening ordeal. All along the gap they went; up St. Stephen's Road—the birds brilliant-plumaged in the ripening cornfields—past the Gothic exterior of the Chapel to a steep decline where the hilly road was crowned by the falling leaves of a giant evergreen tree whose roots spread to every point of the compass. Up the road, the sun bright as a scimitar, the inexorable dust-marl heavy on them; past cow pens and meadows; past shops and cottages where folk inquisitively spied at them through half-shut jalousies. Then past the Mad House and Wolmer Lodge, a branch of the Plymouth Brethren, where Sarah "broke bread" and Gerald slept; up to Eagle Hall Corner and onward down to the roaring city. On the way he'd lift his piteous eyes to her sobbing face and implore, "Don't cry, mama, don't cry, God will provide for us."

At the Oxleys' the tension slackened. It was easing to be there. They had a big, pretty house, plenty to eat, and the girls were lovely as the flowers whose fragrance was a dewy delight to the boy.

Again it was some sort of soup, fish soup, and the sensation of a hearty meal helped considerably to dissipate Gerald's concern over the things agitating his mother.

After dinner he and the girls, Vi and Rupertia, slid to the floor to play. A Bible was their toy. On their lips the letters of the word *contents* made a lascivious jingle. *Charlie open 'nen's t'ing ent 'nen's ting sweet.* Caught in their own impishness, they clapped their hands over their mouths, shutting off the laughter, and rocked against each other in riotous glee.

"Hey, Sarah, duh ought to lock he up, yes. Hey, you would 'a' t'ink a man wid fi' chirrun would ha' a bit o' conscience. W'en yo' say yo' hear from 'e las'?"

"June—le' mah see," snuffled Mrs. Bright, diving in her hand bag, "yes—it is June. June will be eight months sense Oi las' hear from 'e."

"An' yo' mean fo' tell muh," cried Mr. Oxley, his incredible eyes big and white, "dat dah neygah man ent ha' de graciousness in 'e 'art fuh sen' yo' a ha'penny fuh de chirrun awl dis time?"

"No, Charlie."

"Gord! Dah man muss be got de heart uv a brute!"

"He must be fuhget we, Charlie."

"Wuh, moy Gord, yo' don't even fuhget ah doig yo' fling a bone to, much mo' a big fambaly like yo' got dey. Fuhget yo'?"

"He must be," wept Mrs. Bright, swallowing hard, but Gerald was too impassioned himself to rise or let the girls share his sorrow.

"But wha' yo' gwine do, ni, Sarah? Wha' yuh gwine do? Yo' an' all dese chirrun yo' get dey, ni?"

"Oi ent stop fuh t'ink, Charlie, to tell yo' de troot. But de Lord will provide Charlie, Oi is get my truss in Him."

"But wha' kin de Lord do fo' yo' now yo' doan heah fum dat woofless vargybin?"

"Ev'yt'ing wuks togeddah fuh dem dat truss in de Lorrd. Oi'll manage somehow. Oi'll scratch meself togeddah. De lil' bit o' money Oi get fum de house an' de piece o' lan' will jus' buy me an' Gerald ticket. Now all Oi is axin' yo' fo' do is put up de show money. Oi ent wan' no mo'. Dah is anuff. An' as de Lord is in heaven Oi'll pos' it back tuh yo' when the boat land at Colon."

"An' wuh yo' gwine do wit' de chirrun, ni, Sarah? Wuh you gwine do wit' dum?"

"Oi got Rosa fuh look aftah dem fo' me, bo. Yo' know Peony is wid she evah sense de holliduhs, an' she don't even wan' fuh come way, de ownway t'ing. But, yo' know, Charlie, Oi can't blame de chirrun, ni. Um ent nutton home fuh duh. Rosa is berry well satified fi' hav' she, aldo me can't say she ah happy riddance. No, not at all. Well, an de uddah gyrls, it gwine be ha'd 'pon dem, but Rosa house on Coloden Road is big enough fee tek cyah ah all uh dem, an' Mistah Foyrd only come home once a mont'. Rosa so lonesome, an' she so like de picknee dem. She will tek cyah uh dem fuh muh till Oi sen' back fuh dem. An' Oi only takin' Gerald wit' muh, po' fellah."

"Oi gotto go," she went on, in a hollow, dejected voice, "an' see wha' de mattah wit' Lucian. Oi can' go 'long tyin' mi guts no mo'. Oi too tired."

"Hey, but dah is a beast uv a man fuh yo', ni!" muttered Oxley in incredible outrage.

"Yo' know, sometimes Oi t'ink he muss be sick—"

"Sick?" he flew up, like a hen striking at a mongoose. "Dah man sick? Gyrl, hush up yuh mout'! Dah man sick? He ent sick no 'way! If he was sick doan yuh tink de nurse in de horspitral can write a letter even fuh a shillin' fuh he? Gyrl, go talk sense, ni! Dah man ent sick. He is jess a wufless stinkin' good fuh nutton vargybin' who ent learn fuh tek cyah uh he fambaly, dah is wuh he is! Oi tell yuh 'bout dese fancy mud-head men! Ent a blind one o' dem any blasted good! A pack o' rum-drinkin', skirt-chasin' scoundrels—dah's wuh duh is! Dey ort tuh lock he up, dey ort tuh get he 'n roast he behind fuh he—"

"Charlie!"

"Wha' Oi doin'? Ent um is de troot, ent um?"

"Oi ent gwine giv' up hope, Charlie, Oi still got my truss in de Lord."

"Yuh is ah bettah uman dan Oi is ah man, Oi know."

"If um is de will uh de Lord fuh me tuh suffer like dis, Oi is willin'. Didn't Christ die on Calvary's Cross tuh save yuh an' me an' Lucian—"

"Who, dat vargybun', don't put 'e 'long side o' me, Oi ent wan' none o' 'e nasty self fi' tetch me."

Some one intruded upon them. Sarah wiped away a tear. It was difficult to be there, denuding herself before that woman and her saucy girl children.

She came in, one of the girls at her side. "Hexcuse me, Charlie, but wuh yo' say, le' dem go?"

"Go weh?" he roared suddenly looking up.

"*To de fungshan*, no?" she replied, scornful of his brilliant memory.

"Chu," he said, turning back to Sarah, and staring at her searchingly, "All de time sochalizin', sochalizin'." He swiveled back round. "Ah say no! Yo' heah? No! Dem a stay in de house!"

"But it no a gineral saht o' shindig," she pleaded, "it a Miss Coaltrass dawtah what a hav' it."

"Ah don' giv' a dam pity hell who dawtah a hav' it—dem n'ah go!"

"But Charlie—don't!"

"Me don't mean fi' insult yo', Sarah, wit' me nasty tongue, but yo' mus' excuse me. But dese pahties dem 'nuf fi' mek Christ hesell bre'k loose."

"But me don't tink it are much—"

"Dem n'ah go—dat a sure t'ing! Could as well put it in yo' pipe an' smoke it! Saht'n fact! Dem tek up wit' too much gwine out orready. Wha' ah mo', dat Miss Persha, dem low-neck dress she ah wear, dem gwine giv' ar cold, too, yo' mahk an fi'-mee wud."*

"Wha' time it hav' let out, Persha."

"Early, mam."

"Oh, le' de picknee dem go, Charlie, yo' too a'd on de gal chile dem."

"Dat's juss why me don't wan' dem fo' go. Awl yo' go out o' dis house at all howahs o' de night time, like unna is any umans, disregardin' whatevah awdahs dere is. Look at dat Miss Persha, she bin gwine out eve'y night dis week. Wha' she a go so? Wha' she a fine place fi' go so? But no mind; wait till me catch she, yo' wait."

"Dat a fac', Charlie, me hagree wit' yo' dey, me gwine put my foot down once an' far-all 'pon dem trampoosin's."*

"Well, let de rascals dem go dis time."

IV

One day Gerald stole out on the deck. The sun was broiling hot. His mother was with him.

"Mama," he said, "let's go roun' de uddah side."

"Wha' fuh, sonny?"

"Ah wan' fuh go out dere at the Portugee shop an' buy a ball o' cookoo an' a piece o' salt fish. My mout' ain't got a bit o' taste."

"Yo' can't do that, son, there ain't any shops in the sea," she said, smiling weakly at him, "Come, let's go back—I don't feel so good."

Then it suddenly happened. They were below, it was dark, quiet, noiseless. Even the engines had stopped. Boom! it came. It sounded like the roar of a cannon. It shook the ship. Glass jingled. Things fell. Gerald's energetic mind flew hurriedly back to Black Rock. Often there would be sun and rain—all at once. The gap folk had become so used to it that they said it was the "devil and his wife fighting."

Until now lazy and half-asleep, the deckers rose, scrambling up on the above deck. Their baggage was going with them.

Gerald turned to his mother, busy combing her hair. She said, "Come, Gerald, put on yo' Sunday hat, son, yo' at Colon."

But he was skeptical. He stole upstairs and was an eager witness to the ship's surrender. The *Wellington*, a princess of the sea, had given in to the greater force of the earth. Soberly and serenely she had done so.

𝒱

"Well, Sarah, who's this?"

"The last one, Gerald."

"He grow big, yes."

"Skipper don't even know he own son."

"Suck fingah buay."

"Shut up, Saboogles!"

"Fairf!"

"Come heah, son, don't cry—come 'n say howdee to yo' pappy."

"Tek yo' fingah outa yo' mout', sah."

"Say, something, no, Gerald—"

"Howdee!"

"Say howdee pappy."

"Howdee pappy."

"Oi don't know wha' mattah wit' dis' boy, ni. Comin' on de boat he was—"

"Come an' kiss me, sah."

He flinched at the suggestion. But there was no escape and he had to put up his face to receive the wet, disgusting kiss.

"Like yo' ent glad to see yo' pappy," he heard his mother say, and was ferocious at her, "an' bin talkin' an' exquirin' 'bout what yo' look like, Lucian, evah sense we lef' B'bados."

He slunk back, shuddering at the touch of the man, and took a good look at him. He was crouched before a machine. He was fairer than Sarah—she was black, he a yellowish brown. He was soft, yet not fat, but he gave one the appearance of being weak and flabby. He was biting thread. Gold-rimmed brown glasses barely shaded eyes circulating in two seamy bloodshot pools. His hairy arms rested soft and heavy on the machine. He was bald, and his mouth was large and sensuous. It was a roaming mouth. His hands were of putty. Every time he swallowed, or raised his head, a rum goggle* as modest as a turkey gobbler's would slide up and down.

The place was noisy and vulgar. It smelt of brandy and Jamaica rum, but tuxedos and crash tunics were sewed there for the dandy *bomberos* of the Republic. Far into the night it kept twenty men on the job, but it was an idler's and a lazy man's joint. Customers like the judge, a proud, blue-eyed Spaniard, would stop by on their way home at night—but it was a hang-out and an assignation spot for *cabrons** and barefooted black mares.

"Go an' pick up dah cotton reel fuh mah," Bright said to him, "an' put dis empty bottle behind the counter—"

It was here that Gerald was to take on the color of life.

VI

"*Mama, a las siete!*"

It was seven o'clock. Anger, noise, confusion—a cock's lofty crowing. Opening his eyes, he stood quietly, deciding. In a tall bare room, he had been warmed in the night first by one adult body, then, an eternity later, by another. Now he was free of the sense of both.

A sun, immortal, barbaric as any reigning over Black Rock, shot hazes of purple light on the evening's litter scattered about.

"*Mama, a las siete!*"

Ah, he was not now on the ship. Nor was he at the tailor shop. This must be—home.

He sat up in bed, gazing at the enormity of things in the room. "Oh, Mama—" he cried, but no answer came. He jumped off the bed and dragged on his boots. He dressed and made for the door. He was struck once more by the glow of the bright Panama sun. The room opened out on a porch, not very wide, and there was no awning to cool it.

"*Mama, a las siete!*"

Down by the stairs a half-sick, half-clothed little child was crying. Standing above him was a lank, black, cruel-faced woman, brewing a cup of hot milk. As soon as the milk was shifted from one cup to the other, she would turn and stamp at the little boy on the floor.

"Where am I to get it from?" she screamed at him, "shut up, I say—shut up—before I cuff you—what do I care if you haven't eaten for two days—your stomach burning you—well go to sleep—you been already—well go again—sleep, sleep—it will do you good—it will make you forget you ever had a belly.

"Think I pick up smoked sausage? I've got to buy it. And what have I got to buy it with? Filth! May the heavens consume you! Shut up, I say! Who cares whether it is seven o'clock—or eight o'clock—or nine o'clock? Let me be! The baby's got to eat, and you'd better begone, you're too noisy. Seven o'clock! Sing it to the birds, sing it to the canary, sing it to the winds. Winds can wake up the dead. Go try—bawl it to the winds! But I've got my own song, I've got my own tune. I don't want to hear you, shut up, I say."

All this in a tongue musical to Gerald, but the cries of the little boy and the pox on his face and sores making a batter of his toes unforgettably moved him.

At the cesspool he espied a girl. Her back was to him. She was of mixed blood, of assafetida brown, and had once had the smallpox. She was shouting at the top of her voice to the Chinaman downstairs to "giv' me wattah, yo' dam China-mang, you giv' me de wattah."

It took a long time for it to treacle upstairs. The water struggling up at last, she proceeded to bathe Madame's canary. To supervise the rite, Madame came herself—adding to the Cholo girl's swift parrot-like chatter words just as swift and as parrot-like.

Madame was a beauty. Wife of a Colombia rum merchant, she was fat and rosy and white. "Me white," she'd say to the West Indian lodgers in her tenement, "you no see fo' my skin?" The plate of her jeweled bosom soared high. Encountering it, one's first impulse would be not to lay one's head on it, but to cling, climb, sit safely and plumply on it. Her flat, wrinkled face had been smothered in some starch-like powder. She was white, as whites on the Isthmus went, but the flour or powder which she dabbed so thick on her face sometimes failed to accomplish its task. At intervals the wind or the latitudinous heat dissipated splotches of the starchy pallor, and Madame's neck, or the rim of Madame's mouth, or the balloons under Madame's eyes—would expose a skin as yellow as the breasts of the Cholo girl.

Mistress of the tenement, and using a row of six of its one-rooms, Madame's love of jewels rose to a fetish. Her suite was full of jewelry. Her opulent person was ablaze with them. Her bright, thick black hair was prickly with hairpins of silver, hairpins of gold. She wallowed in colors, too. Some of the pins were blue, some red, others green. Her fat, squat arms were loaded with bangles. Her gaping stomach shimmered in a sea of rich white silk. Walking, it rolled, and dazzled, and shimmered.

Waltzing by Madame and the Cholo girl, there sallied out of the kitchen a woman. She was a mulatto. She was carrying a smoking dish of stewed peas and her head was held high in the clouds. Squat as Madame, she, too, was mad about jewelry. Her arms were creased with bracelets. And no jewel-ankled Hindu maiden had finer nuggets of gold flung about her neck. Her clogged feet sent buxom out at you a belly bursting with a fat, mellow tumor.

She came clogging straight at Gerald, and smiled. One of the one-room flats on that side of the porch belonged to her, but on spying him she swept past it.

"Run down to the John Chinaman's like a good little boy and bring me a loaf of French bread and a tin of sardine—"

"Come, wash yo' face and drink yo' tea, Gerald, befo' it get cold," cried a voice.

"Orright, mama, ah comin'," and he ran away, uncertain of the escape, leaving the St. Thomas virgin with the *peso* in her hand, stumped.

ow

Fired by the beauty of the marbles and the speed of the tops—gigs— he'd go on secret escapades to the alley below and spin gigs and pitch taws with the boys who'd gather there. He had to be careful of the *pacos.*[*] He had to be careful of the boys he played with. Some of them used bad words; some had fly-dotted sores on their legs. A city of sores. Some of them had boils around their mouths. Some were pirates—they made bloody raids on the marbles.

One day he was alone spinning his gig. It was a particularly rhythmical one. It was pretty, too—for he had dabbed a bit of washblue on top of it so that it looked beautiful when it was spinning.

Suddenly a gang of boys came up, Spanish boys. One of them, seeing his top, circling and spinning, measured it; then winding his up, drew back and hauled away. The velocity released made a singing sound.

Gerald stood back, awed. The top descended on the head of his with astounding accuracy and smashed it into a thousand pieces. The boys laughed, and wandered on.

At marbles some of the boys would cheat, and say, "if you don't like it, then lump it! *Chumbo!* Perro!"* Some of them'd seize his taw or the marbles he had put up and walk away, daring him to follow. In the presence of all this, he'd draw back, far back, brooding. . . .

Sea on top of sea, the Empire mourned the loss of a sovereign; and to the ends of the earth, there sped the glory of the coronation.*

Below Gerald's porch there spread a row of lecherous huts. Down in them seethed hosts of French and English blacks. Low and wide, up around them rose the faces and flanks of tenements high as the one Gerald lived in. Circling these one-room cabins there was a strip of pavement, half of which was shared by the drains and gutters. But from the porch, Gerald was unable to see the strip of pavement, for the tops of these huts were of wide galvanize, which sent the rain a foot or two beyond the slanting rim.

But it wasn't raining, the sun was shining, and it was the day of the Queen's coronation. On that galvanized roof the sun bristled. Flaky, white—the roof burned, sizzled. The sun burned it green, then yellow, then red; then blue, bluish white, then brownish green, and yellowish red. It was a fluid, lustrous sun. It created a Garden of the roof. It recaptured the essence of that first jungle scene. Upward, on one of the roof's hills spread the leaves of banyan tree.* Fruit—mellow, hanging, tempting—peeped from between the foliage of coffee and mango and pear. Sunsets blazed forth from beyond the river or the yellowing rice hills on some fertile roof.

All day, the day of the coronation, Gerald stood on the porch, peering down on the burning roof. It dazzled him, for up from it came sounds; sounds of music and dancing. Sounds of half-drunk creoles screaming, "*Sotie, sotie!*" Flutes and "steel" and hand-patting drums; fast, panting music, breathless, exotic rhythm; girls, with only a slip on, wild as larks, speeding out of this room, into that one. All day, the day of the coronation, the music lasted, the dancing lasted, the feeling mounted.

A slippery alley connected Bottle Alley and Bolivar Street. Through it Gerald tiptoed, surreptitiously, to see the *bomberos* on parade. He stood at the edge of the curb, gazing up the street at the clang and clash of red flannel shirts, white pants, brass helmets and polished black leggings. Behind him was a canteen and it was filled to its swinging half-sized doors with black upholders of the Crown. Gazing under a half-door he could see hosts of trousered legs vaguely familiar to him.

The coronation rags of the bar were a dark, somber kind. Dark green leaves, black-green leaves—wreaths and wreaths of them.

"Come on, Dina, an' behav' yo'self. Yo' ain't gwine wine* no mo' fi' suit any big teet' Bajan."

"Who is a big teet' Bajan?"

"Who yo' tink 's talkin' to? I didn't know yo' wuz hard a hearing."

"Bet yo' ah lick yo' down, if yo' go long talkin' like dat?"

"Say dah again, ni, betcha yo' don't say dah again."

"Look at dese two, ni. Wuh, Bright, yo' ort to be shame o' yo'self, man, fightin' ovah a chiggah foot gal."

"Who yo' callin' chiggah-foot? Me?"

"Oi ent talkin' to you, soul."

"Ah buss yo' head open fuh yo', yes, yo' go on playin' wit' my Trinidad uman! See dah stick in de corner—"

"Butt 'e! Butt 'e down!* Don't lick 'e wit' de stick! Butt 'e down!"

"Wuh 'bout it?"

"Wuh 'bout it? Wait an' see!"

"Look out, Lucian, befo' he chop open yo' head."

"Oh mi Gahd!"

"H'm! Yo' beast! Yo' whelp! Leave my uman alone."

A figure, washed in blood, fell backwards through the half-door on to the refuse-littered pavement.

ᘯ

All night Sarah sat up, imploring the Lord to have mercy upon them, and beseeching Bright to mend his reckless ways. His head bandaged up, he lay on the bed, a ghastly figure, the pain crushing the fire out of his eyes.

"Yo' ort to tek dis as a warnin'," she said, "an' steady yo'self." And he only moaned in pain.

All night Gerald was restless, bruised by his mother's sorrow, and unable to rid himself of the hideous nightmares surrounding it.

In the morning the lodgers grew restive.

"Yo' heah all dah ruction las' night, Maria, like dey wuz bringing up a dead man up de stairs?"

"Oi taught dey was gwine break down de house—"

"No," flounced Maria, "no ask-ee fuh me, me no no."

"But ent yo' hear um, Miss Collymore? Ni?"

"No harm meant, soul—"

"Didn't you, Mrs. Bright?"

"Yes, I heard it."

"Wha'm wuz, ni? Yo' know?" All eyes were turned upon her. But she calmly responded, "It was my husband. He went to a ball given by the tailors and he must have had too much ice cream—"

"Yes?" some one tittered.

"Fuh true?"

"Yo' see, evah since he wuz home he liked to eat ice cream, but it don't agree wit' him—"

"Yo' don't say."

"No, it don't agree wit' he, an' he nose run blood like a stan'pipe run water. An' dey put 'e out 'pon the verandah fuh hol' 'e head back, and he fell asleep an' de moon shine 'pon 'e all night—"

"Oi had a boy who got de moon in he face, dah way, heself."

"Well, you know den. As I wuz—he sit dey all night wit' de moon shinin' in 'e face, wit' he head cocked back, an' when dey fomembah an' come out an' look at 'e dey fine 'e had one eye shut up, an' instead o' stoppin' de blood de moon only start it running wussah."

"Hey, we can't 'elp yo' wid 'e, ni, Miss Bright?"

"No, soul, Oi jess takin' dis fish tea* fuh 'e. Dey say it is good fo' wash 'e eye wid. Dey say it will ca'y way de redness an' de soreness."

"G'long, soul, an' do yo' bes' fuh get 'e bettah."

Taking broth to him, she murmured, "Ain't yo' shame o' yo'self to hav' me bring yo' something to eat—"

"Oh, God, uman, don't torture me," he cried, tossing in misery and pain.

"Don't torture yo', ni, Oi mus' love yo'—is dah wha' yo' wan' me fuh do?"

"Oh, God, lemme 'lone," he cried, raving like a bull, "lemme bones rest in peace, ni?"

"Yo' scamp yo'! Yo' heart ort to prick yo' till yo' las' dyin' day fuh all yo' do to me an' my po' chirrun—"

"Oh, how many times I gwine heah de same old story?"

"Old? It will never be old! As long as I've got breath in my body—as long as I is got my boy child to shield from de worle—from de filth and disease of this rotten, depraved place—as long as I got my fo' gal chirrun in B'bados in somebody else han'—um can't be a old story!"

"Giv' me de t'ing, no," he cried, tired and exhausted, "if yo' gwine giv' me, an' le' me head res' in peace. Yo' don't know how bad it is hurtin' me now."

The day he was ready to go back to the shop, she said to him, "Tek heed, Lucian, yo' heah, yo' bes' tek heed, an' men' yo' ways—"

"O Jesus! jess because yo' been tendin' to me when I wuz sick, yo' tink yo' gwine tell me wha' to do, ni, but yo' lie, uman, yo' lie!" and he sped downstairs, swanking,* one eye red and flashing.

To the pirates and urchin gods of Bottle Alley, Gerald was the bait that lured a swarm of felt-hatted *pacos* who kept the alley under sleepless surveillance. It was risky to loiter, play marbles, spin gigs—and there wasn't enough to keep Gerald occupied upstairs. So he hit upon the notion of going at dusk to his father's shop. There he'd gather rum bottles and cotton reels, open up the backyard and inveigle the Judge's son to come down and play shells—and shut his ears to the men's vile banter. . . .

One day, after the men had gone, he saw his father take a glass bowl from a shelf far back in the shop and put it on his machine. He was drawn to it, for, squirming about in the weed and moss, was a congeries of little black reptiles.

"Papa, wha' is dese, ni?"

"Leave them, sir!" his father shouted, "an' get away from there!"

He drew back, afraid. The place was silent. He watched his father furtively. His face was clouded, agitated, aflame. He tore off his coat, peeled back his shirt sleeve, and revealed a red, sore arm. He squeezed it, the while gritting his teeth. He moved over to the bowl, wincing in pain. Gerald was stricken dumb. Up to the bowl his father crept, taking one of the shiny, slimy reptiles and planting it on the red sore, to feast there. Uncomprehending Gerald patiently waited.

Later he was in bed, half-asleep, listening to the storm. A hurricane of words passed by—hot, carnal words. The fury subsided, and there ensued a sober sympathetic calm.

"Lucian, darling," he heard his mother say, "wha' yo' doin' fuh de arm, ni?"

"Oh, Oi is orright."

"Yo' bin to de doctor, man?"

"No."

"An' you mean to tell me yo' gwine sit down an' not do nutton fuh dah han'* yo' got dey. Hey, man, yo' know wuh is good fo' yo'self?"

"Oh, Oi put a leech on it teeday. Dah ort to draw out all de bad blood."

As the nights advanced, the heat became more and more severe. It was useless to try to sleep. Body smells, body vapors, the room's need of oxygen—grew tense, exacting.

"Yo' know, Sarah, dis t'ing is really hurtin' me; why um is worse dan Oi taught um wuz. Um is stickin' me jess like a needle."

"H'm, tell yo' so—tell yo' yo' won't men' yo' ways."

"O Christ," he roared, "why yo' don't say yo' glad an' done?"

At Sixth and Hudson Alley there was a branch of the Plymouth Brethren, and Sarah suddenly went about the business of securing "acceptance" there. Now, so far as running it went, the shop was out of Bright's hands. He was ill, and had to stay at home. One of the men, Baldy, a mulatto Antiguan, took hold of things.

By way of the Sixth Street Mission, his mother rooted religion into his soul. Every night he was marched off to meeting. There, he'd meet the dredge-digging, Zone-building, Lord-loving peasants of the West Indies on sore knees of atonement asking the Lord to bring salvation to their perfidious souls. In the isles of their origin they were the tillers of the soil—the ones to nurture cane, and water sorrel, stew cocoanuts and mix Maube—now theirs was a less elemental, more ephemeral set of chores. Hill and vale, valley and stream gave way to wharf and drydock, dredge and machine shop. Among the women the transfiguration was less brilliant. Dull. The "drops" and cakes and foods and pops vended to the serfs and squatters on insular estates found a husky-throated market at the ends of the pay car lines.

Thursday night was prayer meeting. Religiously Sarah and Gerald went. All the brothers and the sisters took a deep and vital interest in him. They'd bring him sweets, and coppers, and stare long at him, their eyes wet, and soft. They came, a drove of them, to the house, all dressed in black, which set the neighbors talking.

He was not a child of the Lord, he did not believe in the Scriptures, but it did not serve to rob them of their sense of charity. So they came to see, and give words of courage to the family of the sick man. They'd read passages of the Bible to him, and marvel at the priceless wonders of Christ Jesus. And then one day he said to her, "Sarah, I think I ort to go to the horspitral—I can't see—my eyes is painin' me so bad. Oi wondah wha' is de mattah wit' dem."

"Didn't de medicine de doctah giv' yo' do yo' any good, Lucian?"

"Oh, that bitter t'ing? Good wha'! Oi feel like Oi could cut off this bleddy old han'—"

"It still hurtin' yo, Lucian?"

"Cuttin' me like a knife."

After they came and got him, Gerald began to feel things ever so much more keenly. His vision, too, grew less dim. But a pallor fell on things. In the morning he went to the cesspool to whistle to the canary while the Cholo girl washed it. But as he approached she fled in terror screaming "No, no, don't touch—go 'way—yo' no good—no clean—me no like yo' no mo'." The little boy, the seven o'clock one, refused to let him come near him. "No, no," he also cried, "me mama no like—" None of the old gang, who'd been willing to elude or defy the *pacos* and foregather down in the alley came any more. And he didn't go to the shop, either. It was so dark and silent over there. Only Baldy looked on—all the other men, one by one, had gone to other places to work. Dust grew high, thick. Spiders spun webs on the very frame of the door.

But he went oftener to the Sixth Street Mission, he and Sarah. The folks there weren't fickle—firm, solid, lasting. His mother had become one of them. He was one of them now. He'd go on Thursday evenings to prayer meetings. The evenings were long and hot. He would go to sleep in the midst of some drowsy exhaustless prayer. All would be silent. Hours of silence to God. Then they'd rise, slowly, back-crackingly, and he'd be left kneeling, snoring. He would be immune to pinches, nudges, murmurs. They'd be useless, he would be fast asleep. His mother'd pinch him, quietly, but he'd be as stiff as a log till the service was over.

All in black—veil, hat, gloves, shoes, dress.

At Sixth and Bolivar they took one of those modest subdued coaches, not adorned by any wig-powdered Jamaican Pretty Socks, and bade the driver take them to the city hospital.

The sun dealt the city some stern body blows. The piazzas were strewn with folk. Bees and flies and fleas sang and buzzed and added to the city's noise and squalor. Swinging onto rafts hoisted high on porches parokeets and parrots screeched and chattered incessantly. In cages set in the shades of windows bright-feathered and trill-voiced birds languished half-sleepily. Down on the piazza among the old women and the children the Duque ticket sellers and the sore-footed heathens, there were monkeys. Tied to poles greasy and black with banana grime they were lathering their faces with spit. Slowly they ascended the head of the street, the chapel of the Christ Church, felt a bit of the onrushing sea wind, and made the drive. The sea wind beat against them. It was cool and refreshing. At last they were at the hospital.

A high box, square, gauze-encased and white with a dim black object in it was set at the end of a back porch—wide, long, screened, isolated. Facing it was a planted plot, gardened by Asiatics, seen through the dusty screen. Near the sloping end of the porch the rosebush was withering; mocking the bitter fury of the sun the sunflowers were slightly bowing. Accustoming one's eyes to the dead reach of things beyond the screen one saw a terra cotta sky and lank, parched trees with reddish brown foliage. One saw, sizzling, at the mouths of dying flowers, blue-winged humming birds—

An eternity had passed since the doctor had brought them there, and all the sorrow and anguish inside her rushed to Sarah Bright's eyes.

"Yo' mus' pray fuh me, Sarah," were the words that came to her from the box square.

"Yes, Lucian," she said, concurring in their finality.

He emitted a groan, and she patted Gerald's face, forcing the child to look away.

"An' wuh duh say, Lucian," she asked, with piety and anxiety, "wuh duh say, ni?"

Their eyes were fastened on the fixed intensity of the sun, but their ears were attuned to the tiniest rustle of the glazed sheets, and the restless figure under them. Then he said, "Ah'm in a bad way, gyrl."

She took out a little white handkerchief and dried first Gerald's mouth and nose, then her own glistening eyes.

He groaned, and was restive again, "De doctah say no use—de oil ent no good."

"No?" there was a quiet suspense in her voice.

"No bloomin' good!" he flung, unearthing some of the old asperity.

"Don't, Lucian," she entreated, "fomembah Jesus."

"Oh, God, dis han'!" he groaned, tossing fiercely.

He ruffled the sheets, and a lizard, a big lanky bark-hued one, slid down the trunk of the cocoanut tree, after some gawkier prey.

"An' dey ent try nutton else," she said, again exhuming the handkerchief.

"Oh, dese Yankees don't cyah wuh de do to yo'—dey don't cyah. Duh wouldn't even giv' yo' a drop o' hot wattah, if yo' ask me. No, dey ent try nutton else."

"Hush, don't cry, Gerald," she said, hunting for a piece of Chinese candy, "yo' mustn't cry, son."

"An' wuh dey gwine do, Lucian," she said, reluctantly risking the query.

"Put me 'way—Palo Seco—dah's de colony."

"Don't cry, son, never min', mamma will tek care o' Gerald—oh, my son, you'll break my heart."

" 'E love 'e pappy, ent 'e?" he smiled, then turned his moistening eyes to the black wall behind him.

"Well," she said, her eyes clear and dry, "the Lord wuks His wonders in a mysterious way. What's to be, will be."

He, too, was weeping; but she held on, driving the mirage to the winds.

"Yo' kin come to see muh, Sarah," he said, "dey allow yo' one visit a year—yo' mus' come, yo' hear?"

"Yes, Lucian, I'll come."

"An' yo' mustn't call me bad, yo' heah?" he pleaded, the water in his eyes, like a young culprit.

"God forbid, dear—be quiet now. Come, Gerald, time fi' go, son." She adjusted his hat, and a bell started ringing.

"An' yo' mus' tek good cyah o' yo'self, heah Sarah, an' don't le' nobody tek exvantage o' yo', yo' heah, dis is a bad country—"

"Yes, Lucian."

PART IV

BRITISH PERSPECTIVES

$\mathcal{A}$lthough the quantity of Walrond's publications declined markedly after his arrival in Europe, his stories and articles did appear sporadically over twenty years. After settling in London in 1932, he became actively involved in its Black community, as characterized by his reconciliation with Garvey. Many of his essays at that time, particularly his essays for Garvey's *Black Man*, dealt with the condition of Blacks in England. His stories, on the other hand, tended to focus on his early life in the Caribbean, which remained the dominant influence in his life. In "Consulate" and "Morning in Colon," for example, he demonstrates that he has not lost his ability to portray the everyday language and culture of West Indian life with vigor. Appropriately, the latest piece published here, "Poor Great," one of only a few stories Walrond set in British Guiana, returns to his homeland.

Journalism

White Man, What Now?

As a West Indian Negro, I was reared on the belief that England was the one country where the black man was sure of getting a square deal. A square deal from white folk has always seemed so important to us black folk. Our position in the West Indies, in virtue of the ideas instilled into us by our English education, has been one of extreme self-esteem. We were made to believe that in none of the other colonies were the blacks treated as nicely as we were.

We developed an excessive regard for the English. We looked upon them as the most virtuous of the colonizing races. It was to us a source of pride and conceit to be attached to England. We became even a bit truculent about it.

We took on as much of English civilization as lay in our power. In one island, Barbadoes—a British colony since 1605—the natives drifted so far away from the African ideal as to be considered even more English than are the English themselves! Our love of England and our wholehearted acceptance of English life and customs, at the expense of everything African, blinded us to many things. It has even made us seem a trifle absurd and ridiculous in the eyes of our neighbours. But the

From *The Spectator* April 5, 1935. Reproduced with kind permission of *The Spectator*.

absurdity of our position—an ostrich-like one—was not revealed to us until we began to travel. . . .

I remember as a small boy going to Panama. In Panama, where thousands of British West Indians had settled, I got my first taste of prejudice—prejudice on the grounds of my British nationality!

The natives were a mongrelized race of Latins with a strong feeling of antipathy toward British Negroes. But their hatred of us, curiously enough, had been engendered by our love of England.

Since the abortive efforts of the French in the '80's to dig the Panama Canal, emigrants from the British West Indies had settled in large numbers on the Isthmus. They kept sternly aloof. This, to the sensitive and explosive Latins, was regarded as a slight. It was interpreted as an affront to *las costumbres del pais*. Reprisals took the shape of epithets such as *chombos negros* and occasional armed incursions into the West Indian colony.

From Panama I went to Hayti, the Negro republic torn from France early in the nineteenth century by the rebellious slaves under the Negro general, Toussaint L'Ouverture. In Hayti I somehow imagined that I would be taken at my face value as a black man. This notion was soon dispelled the moment I entered Port-au-Prince, by the violent prejudices I encountered there against all foreign Negroes, but particularly Negroes from the British West Indies.

Instead of taking flight, I stayed on, fascinated by the beauty of the country and the curious mentality of the people. I found that the Haytians, a proud and long-memoried, but vain and self-conscious folk, bore a grudge against the English. This grudge was loosely extended to Britain's black wards in the Caribbean area. Personally, I was regarded with mixed suspicion and scorn. In the refined sarcasm of the country I was a *vieux anglais:** someone on whom to take revenge for the reports about cannibalism, insanitation, witchcraft and political instability spread by Froude,* Spenser St. John *et al.*

In the northern part of Hayti I crossed the frontier into Santo Domingo. It was as if I was again in Panama. A Spanish country with a hybrid mixture of Indians, Negroes and Gallegos.* Only the terms of endearment, the epithets slyly hurled at me, were not the same. I suddenly found that instead of a Chombo I was called a Cocolo. I scratched my head, mystified.

At last, venturing down to the sugar-cane delta of San Pedro de Macoris, I found the revealing clue. Cocolo, a rabid term of dislike, was a corruption of the word Tortola, the name of a nearby British isle, whence came thousands of Negroes annually to work in the sugar mills and cane fields of Santo Domingo.

I went on to New York. I settled in the Harlem Negro quarter. I found the community fairly evenly dominated by Southern Negroes and West Indian emigrants. A wide cleavage existed between the two groups. The West Indian with his Scottish, Irish or Devonshire accent, was to the native Black who has still retained a measure of his African folk-culture, uproariously funny. He was joked at on street corners, burlesqued on the stage and discriminated against in business and social life. His pride in his British heritage and lack of racial consciousness were contemptuously put down to "airs."

The white man in America, strangely, does not consider the West Indian a "nigger." He is to him a "foreigner."

Now, on coming to England, West Indians invariably do so somewhat in the spirit of chickens coming home to roost. We possess the undying certainty that in England we shall be on the equivalent of native soil. Trained to believe "there is nothing in race," and that there is no difference between ourselves and white folk, we expect to be treated on that basis. We do not suspect the existence of a Colour Bar. And so thorough has been our British upbringing that if, in the event, we did find a Colour Bar, we would consider it "bad form" openly to admit its existence.

The Negro in London

Viewing the "Mother Country" with an adoring eye, the Negro in the British overseas colonies is obviously at the mercy of the rainbow. He sees England through a romantic and illusive veil. What he so affectionately imagines he sees does not always "square" with the facts.

This deception, common to the virgin gaze of African and West Indian alike, is partly a case of "distance lends enchantment," partly a by-product of the black man's extraordinary loyalty to the Crown.

On coming to England the first impression the black man gets is that of utter loneliness. He is not greeted with a friendly eye as in France nor looked upon with disdain or kindly benevolence as in America; the reaction to him is one of cold indifference. The Negro is made to feel as some species of exotic humanity from another planet, and this despite the 50,000,000 negroes in the British Empire.

It takes a Negro longer actively to enter into the corporate life of England than it does in France or America—two countries whose treatment of the Negro can compare favourably with that of England.

From *The Black Man* Late March 1936.

In the British Isles, despite so little one hears about it, there is a peculiar Negro problem. Large colonies of Negroes exist at Cardiff, Liverpool, Tyneside and London. For the most part the majority of the Negroes are discharged seamen. They are a polyglot mixture from the farthest corners of the Empire. Most of these men have settled in England with the idea of seeking a wider social and economic opportunity. Most of them sooner or later marry English wives. In communities where there has been a great deal of inter-mixing the feeling among the whites is one of subtle antagonism. Although there is no universal segregation of blacks in residential areas, Negroes are not permitted in certain districts. The colour bar manifests itself in other ways as well.

In the case of the Negroes isolated in the distressed areas of the North of England, the colour bar is probably severest. Most of these are seamen by profession and are constantly on the look-out for a chance to ship to sea; but owing to the depression in the shipyards the number of white unemployed seamen is considerable. This results in a keen competition for jobs—a competition which is sometimes marked by racial clashes. Moreover, the coloured seamen are for the most part unorganised, owing to the inability to unite in a common cause and ignore the facts of their diverse origin. They therefore find themselves at an acute disadvantage with their white competitors, who are not only well organised but are frequently given the preference of jobs.

Few of these men are ever successful in leaving the class of seamen. No opportunity is given them to enter in other trades or in industry. Many of them are married to respectable English women and are bringing up a rapidly growing number of half-caste children.

With the economic barriers set up against them, there is nothing left for them to do but fall back on the dole or eke out a miserable existence in some shady precarious undertaking.

Unlike the position in the north, the problem of the Negro in London is much more complex and varied.

In the East End, where there is a large colony of seafaring men, the conditions of the Tyneside area are reproduced with close fidelity. It is after one has left the West India docks that the problem in London becomes enmeshed in a maze of bewildering subtleties and paradoxes.

There is no clean-cut definition of the Negro's position. So far as accommodation is concerned, the policy of individuality—or the legend that a man's home is his castle—is extended to both hotels and lodging houses. A Negro coming to London may secure a suite at the Park Lane Hotel, although Mr. Robeson has been barred from the Savoy, and the Mills Brothers were refused admission to forty hotels. Some landladies manifest a touching sympathy towards Negro lodgers, but others prefer not to have them. A Negro entering a Bond Street shop or a bank in the City may occasion a derisive sneer, or on the other hand, subterranean currents of sympathy. The black man never knows just how the Englishman is going to take him. Though the feeling of Empire is strongly present in the average Englishman he frequently displays an abysmal ignorance of the coloured races within the Empire. He does not pretend to distinguish amongst them; he lumps them all together, and is invariably astonished to find them in command of the English language.

The Negroes who come to London to study at any of the big Universities experience little or no prejudice, but are subtly discouraged from settling in England upon the completion of their courses. In consequence, the number of Negro professional men residing in England is negligible.

The educated Negro who is neither a doctor or lawyer is of necessity "a bird of passage." With the clerk and artisan there are no openings for him. If he wishes to remain in England by the sweat of his brow he has to create something for himself. Many of these men, side by side with compatriots from the dives of Soho and the East End docks, occasionally find employment as "extras" in the big film studios outside London. This is well paying but erratic and unreliable work. Possibly the best recognised outlet for Negro talent in London is in the theatre and on the variety stage. From the days of Ira Aldridge, the great Shakespearian actor of the middle of the nineteenth century, the English have always been quick to recognise the genius of the Negro artist. This is a field in which the American, over and against the competition of Africans and West Indians, excels. This fact is illustrated by the enduring place which artistes like Florence Mills, Paul Robeson, John Payne, Leslie Hutchinson* and Louis Armstrong have made for themselves in the hearts of the English people.

Not only have film, stage and variety artists of colour secured from time to time a warm welcome in England, but musicians and poets as well. The popularity of Coleridge Taylor's* music remains undiminished. The personal visits and lyrical beauty in the works of Paul Lawrence Dunbar and Countee Cullen—two Negro poets separated by a span of nearly thirty years—shall always have a warm place in the secret heart of the English.

It is indeed a paradox that London, the capital of the largest Negro Empire in the world—the cradle of English liberty, justice and fair-play— the city to which Frederick Douglass fled as a fugitive from slavery—

should be so extremely inexpert in the matter of interracial relations. But in this respect London may be easily compared with New York twenty years before the big migration which resulted in the establishment of Harlem.

The Negro before the World

The world in which the Negro lives is a chaotic one. It becomes day by day even more chaotic and complex. Merely to attain a measure of stability in it requires a cunning only sparingly given to the oppressed. But no ostrich with his head buried in the sand can be expected to acquire that cunning.

Too long has the Negro been behaving like that African bird. Too long has he had his head buried in the sand. If he aspires to rise and move on to a high destiny, and not be just a helpless pawn in the game of Power Politics, he may have to alter his whole outlook on the world he lives in. He can not afford to be a stick-in-the-mud. He may even have to revise his scale of values. He must be resilient and adaptable, and not be a romantic,—out of step with the rhythm of the times. As with anyone who has his ear to the ground, he must bow to the eternal and dynamic forces of evolution and change. He can not escape the inevitable, if he is going to face up to the problems that assail him on all sides.

Far removed from either the Pre-war, or the immediate Post-war era, is the world that he lives in. The contrast is underlined not so much by

From The Black Man March 1938.

the element of time as by the force of events: from the great awakening after the war and the astronomical strides that followed, to the misery and uncertainty into which the world was plunged by the economic crisis.

Until the war the sentiment of racial unity was foreign to the concept of the Negro masses. In Africa, the heritage of the black man was the source of intense rivalry among the colonial powers. (It was this rivalry which set the world aflame in 1914.) His life, since the white man first set foot on his shores, was one long vigil against rapacity and greed. He was forced to take up arms in self-defense. A plague of "partition wars" beset him. He was mown down by shot and shell. The tragedy which has just ended in the eclipse of Abyssinia as a sovereign Negro state had only begun.

His lands taken away from him, he became a squatter and a quasi-serf. He was disarmed and de-tribalized. Off the fertile hilltops of the East he was swept to make way for white settlers. He was no longer master in his own house, but a "boy" to soldier, missionary, trader. Until he acquires some of the magic of the white man—in science, industry and in the art of forging new weapons of war—the combat between them can only be a fatally unequal one.

Yet, side by side with his enforced humility, the black man—dreaming away in the African sun—has kept the spirit of independence alive. Who knows but that at a time not far distant the war-clouds over Europe may darken into night? When, and if, that time ever comes (no one doubts but that it will mean the collapse of the capitalist system in Europe) the white man's rule over Africa will be at an end.

Outside the Dark Continent the black man found himself in shackles on alien soil. He was sold like cattle in the slave markets of the New World. For three hundred years he winced under the slave-driver's lash. If he showed a spark of resentment at the way he was treated he was tortured, mutilated and often put to death. Such measures of cruelty and repression were sanctioned by the law of the land. His lot was no better than that of oxen and sheep—with which he ranked in the white man's scale of property values.

When, after the reading of the Emancipation Acts,* "freedom" was revealed in all its emptiness, the powers that be contrived by their system of economy to re-enslave the Negro. As a slave his value to his owner was chiefly as a source of free labour. He was yoked to a system that was set up with but one aim in view: to enrich and confer power upon a small governing class in the community. After "freedom" dawned the status of the ex-slave underwent a change, but the economic system in which he had grown up did not. The men wielding the whip-lash—the sugar barons and the cotton kings, the factory owners and the absentee landlords—were just as greedy for profits as before. What was more, they were not going to let a little thing like the abolition of the blacks thwart them in their desire to perpetuate themselves and their class in power. By exercising a monopoly on capital, by having the means of production under their control, they were able to exploit the black man, thrown penniless on a hostile world, just as easily as when he was a chattel slave.

His labour, the commodity on which they had grown rich, and the ex-slave's only asset, was paid for at starvation rates. He was ill-fed and ill-housed. The result of years of bodily and mental enslavement began to reflect itself. His self-confidence, already nearly extinct, sank even lower. He began to look upon the white man (whom his ancestors in Africa had regarded as a blight upon the earth) as if he were a god. He was adjured to think of himself as an inferior being—without a past or a future, a heritage or a destiny—ordained by God to occupy the lowest rung of the human ladder. And to escape from the blind alley up which he was being pressed the black man, instead of opposing the system that oppressed him, set out, curiously, to build his hopes and ideals around it. Nothing could be more cowardly, futile, or child-like.

If the Negro is to be free he must rid himself of whatever illusions he may still have about the social and economic system that has grown up under capitalism and imperialism. A system that fattens off the labouring masses—black, yellow and white—and that enriches the privileged few is one which he can never be reconciled to. Until and unless he takes up a firm stand against it, there can be no salvation for him: none of the things which he prizes in life,—a higher scale of living, the end of race and class hatred, the hegemony of the Negro over Africa—will ever be realized.

On England

When I first came to England I
stayed with a family in a London suburb, not far from the Crystal Palace.
An Indian medical student, a retired civil engineer and I were the only
"paying guests" in the house. A Tory of the deepest dye, the engineer
struck me at the time as being a kind of museum-piece. He was one of
those dyspeptic chauvinists who, in the normal course of events, winds
up in a big job in the colonies. An obsession that he had was to foist
upon the Government a plan to change the North Sea into the British
Sea, as a gesture to the men who had died at Jutland!* But to out-Herod
Herod, to swallow hook, line and sinker all the Pukka Sahib nonsense
of the British Raj seemed to be the Indian's peculiar failing.

One day at dinner I was asked to sum up the thing which had struck me
most about England. "The love and worship of tradition," I replied. My
host, a Cambridge man, who secretly indulged a taste for Wild Western
tales, took that as a compliment, which was not at all my intention.
But later on I was able to square accounts, I believe, by asking for a
definition of a gentleman. After a long and puzzled silence I was told

From *The Black Man* July 1938.

that "Anybody who is well-dressed is a gentleman." "A gentleman," spoke up the engineer, "is one who is not intentionally rude."

In short, any person of gentle birth, any unborn candidate for the playing fields of Eton,* any suave, gilt-edged rascal may be a gentleman. He may be a jewel thief, a blackmailer or one who lives by his wits, and yet be one.

This definition, which is fairly common in Britain, is consistent with the class basis of English society. It has nothing to do with morality in the abstract. No bloke of a Cockney, however decent or upright, may aspire to that lofty estate. Purity of mind or heart is not enough.—If he manages by sheer merit to emerge from the ruck and carve out a career for himself say, in diplomacy, like the Chargé d'Affaires who went out to China after the shooting of the Ambassador by the Japanese, he is looked upon at best as a curiosity. Not to be a gentleman is to be a cad or, a "member of the lower classes."

"Gentleman" is nothing but a catch-word; but a catch-word that serves a deadly purpose. It is used to bolster up the social and economic division between the upper and lower classes. It puts a premium on the well-born and serves notice on the under-dog that the line which separates him from his "superiors" is an ineradicable one.

The word has no end of affinities. Two of them whose powers of distortion are difficult to excel are "liberty" and "democracy." More crimes are committed in their name than one would care to enumerate. But it is characteristic of the English, in their hypocrisy and love of deception, loudly to proclaim the existence of that which does not exist or which they do all in their power to suppress.

Some of the things which they point to with unfailing pride is the love of law and order that prevails in the land and the liberty which the subject, like the press, enjoys. But so far as one can see the subject has not, like the French of all classes, an innate respect for law, order and discipline which springs from a wide sense of social responsibility; he is merely bowed down with fear of the heavy hand of the law. The press, too, suffers from the same finicky fear. If it is not muzzled by the severity of the libel laws, it is subtly regimented by the powers that be. But in spite of the ubiquitous flag-waving of the Tory Die-Hards the negation of liberty is not a passing phenomenon but a historic condition against which men like Byron and Shelley tilted with all their poetic fervour. ***

But the grim pretence of liberty can only be matched by the farce of "democracy." According to its apologists the British Empire is a democracy, in contrast with the countries governed by one or another form of dictatorship. Let us examine the truth of that statement.

The Empire is an unwieldy, complex amalgam. At the centre is the monarchy and at the top is the Crown—"the link of Empire."

The monarchy is not absolute—it has not been so since the days of Charles I*—but it is at once constitutional and bourgeois. The king cannot act without the consent of Parliament. All power resides in that body, which is in itself an incarnation of the "democratic" spirit of the Empire.

It is an elected body with a strong middle-class bias. It sits in Westminster on a mandate from the voters of Britain. Were the Empire restricted to the area of the British Isles the term "democracy" in relation to it would not be a meaningless one. It would accurately describe it. But the Empire is not confined to the British Isles; it sprawls over vast territories halfway round the globe and includes among its citizens millions of black, brown and yellow men, women and children in Africa, India, the Far and Near East and the Caribbean area. But these millions of citizens have no voice in the government of the Empire. There is no one at Whitehall or Westminster to plead their case. If as workers they find themselves in conflict with the sugar interests of Jamaica or the oil field owners of Trinidad, there is nothing they can do but submit to the repressive acts of the Colonial Office. They are a crushed, unorganized and completely voiceless mass. Unlike the coloured natives of the French Colonies, who send their own men to represent them in the Chamber of Deputies in Paris, they are utterly at the mercy of a system which even refuses to give them a hearing. Under such conditions can anybody seriously call England a democracy?

Review of Twelve Million Black Voices by Richard Wright

Inevitably Mr. Wright's new book,[*] 'a folk history of the Negro in the United States,' invites comparison with a pioneer in the field, W. E. B. Du Bois' *Souls of Black Folk*; but whereas Dr. Du Bois, a product of Harvard and Heidelberg, approached the subject of Negro oppression from the point of view of the aspirations of the Talented Tenth—the emerging Negro intelligentsia of half a century ago—Mr. Wright, writing as a poet and a novelist with an eye for 'that which is qualitative and abiding in Negro experience', bases himself upon the broad masses.

He writes of the Negro's way of life in Africa before the slave trade began, of the horrors of the Middle Passage and of the long night of slavery. When freedom dawned in 1865, after the Civil War, there were some 4,000,000 blacks 'stranded and bewildered' upon the soil which they had tilled under compulsion for two and a half centuries. As if to test the worth of the Emancipation Proclamation 'thousands of us tramped from place to place for the sheer sake of moving, looking, wondering, landless upon the land'. But the overwhelming mass of the ex-slaves, eager to keep together in family units, remained on the tobacco, cane,

From *Life and Letters* November 1948.

rice, and cotton plantations to form a new relationship with their former masters.

Himself the son of a share-cropper, Mr. Wright who, in *Black Boy*, has given a blistering account of his childhood and youth in Jackson, Mississippi, has known at first hand the pattern of the new bondage: 'full of the fear of the Lords of the Land, bowing and grinning when we meet white faces, toiling from sun to sun, living in unpainted wooden shacks that sit casually and insecurely upon the red clay'—deprived of the franchise, lynched, exposed to mob violence, subject to a poll-tax, segregation, and the thousand and one manifestations of Jim Crow.

Between 1890 and 1920 over 2,000,000 Negroes packed up and left the South. North of the Ohio River the Negro migrants met *indifference*, silent hostility, a colour line in industry and the trade unions. 'Restrictive covenants' (the device by which property owners keep Negroes out of certain residential areas) hemmed them in. Race riots often flared up. . . .

In 1937 Mr. Wright's first book, *Uncle Tom's Children*, appeared. A collection of four short novels, it was awarded a national prize for the best book written by an employee of the Federal Writers Project of the Works Progress Administration under the New Deal. The high promise shown in *Uncle Tom's Children* was fulfilled three years later with the appearance of *Native Son*. The story of Bigger Thomas, the 'hero type of cowardly bully', the Negro boy who only began to live as he was about to die, not only placed Mr. Wright in the forefront of that tough, resilient and highly race-conscious school of Negro novelists thrown up in America during the depression. Something else had happened. Negro literature—with its traditions stretching back to Francis Williams, a free Negro in Jamaica who early in the eighteenth century, went to Cambridge as the protégée of an English duke, owned slaves, and wrote in Latin the much-quoted *Ode Ethiopissa**—had with the power and brilliance of Mr. Wright's performance miraculously come of age. And now, with *Twelve Million Black Voices*, Mr. Wright has again demonstrated that it has indeed done so.

Fiction

*I*nciting to Riot

Neither the mestizo lad, face clouded beneath a palm leaf hat, nor the one-eyed Basque grocer, Juan Poveda, turned a hair. The boy was engrossed in a dazzling new toy. He was juggling with a bolero—spinning in the air the leashed, vari-hued ball, tunnelled half-way to the core, and then trying to settle the revolving spherical shape upon the polished end of a wooden stump. More often than not he failed.

Son of a Culebra peon and eight years old, the boy trailed in behind the two negresses. He was the first served. The act was characteristic of a mental bias which the grocer possessed regarding the merits and "rights of priority" of non-Latin blacks and mestizos, respectively. For the boy was a Panameno—already he seemed to possess all the exuberant self-esteem of the Panama mongrel which so warmed the cockles of Juan Poveda's heart—while the women were only *chombos*—"savages" from the British West Indies.

The distinction in itself was sufficiently explicit. It was, more directly, the result of Juan Poveda's persistent effort to even up the score. It

From *The Evening Standard* (London) July 26, 1934.
Reprinted with permission.

was due to his blind, ungovernable way of showing that he had not ceased, though the occasion was fast dimming, to brood over the loss of his eye.

"Five cents worth of salted cod," cried the boy.

"Like a body ain't got nutton else fo' do but stan' yah," cried Miss Fashion.

She was large, black and barefooted. Gold and silver bangles jingled on her huge chocolate-coloured arms. Her headkerchief of red, green, and yellow was like a clump of gaudy autumn crotons. She wore a peony-coloured shawl and a white calico skirt, gathered up from just beneath the hips by a girdle of banana shags.

"My Joey," cried Mrs. Piggott, "will be home tereckly the whistle blow fo' knock-off."

A small wizened creature with a squeaky voice and a mottled nutmeg hue, Mrs. Piggott, like Miss Fashion, shared with an ebony *comado** a one-room flat in a box car lying on a shunting in the Culebra foothills. She was newly shod and wore a deep-crowned straw hat. Her dress of spotless white drill was stiffly starched.

"Shut up!" snarled Poveda, glaring.

Delving in a crate beneath the counter, the grocer extracted the codfish, spread it across the redwood slab, and cut off a thick slice. He weighed and wrapped it up and shoved the parcel before the boy.

"Dime of spuds."

Fastening the bolero in his belt as he would a redskin's scalp, the boy seized up the parcel and began unfolding it. "Then when he carry it home to he murrer," murmured Miss Fashion, "he'll swear to Gawd the dog snatch it out o' he hand."

"Lil' forced-ripe brat!"*

Poveda weighed out two pounds of Irish potatoes and poured them in a sack which the boy extended to him.

"Hurry up an' give me a chopine* o' black-eyed peas," cried Miss Fashion, "me is next."

"Yo' don't got no black puddin' an' souse,* me?" cried a squeaky voice.

The boy paid the bill and strolled out.

Sweeping the coins in the cash drawer, Poveda proceeded to measure out two pints of the speckled grain.

"Pound o' corn' pork," added Miss Fashion.

Mrs. Piggott's inquiries might be ignored, but she was determined not to be silenced by the grocer's predilection to curry favour. "The las' souse I got heah," she said, "was so hard it musta come from the sow gran'murrer. Hard no rock stone. The bone was so hard, chile, an' de seasonin' taste so wishy washy, an' de cucumber water wuz so sour, ah must needs tell yo', Mistah Poveda, dat it berry nearly aggle me stomach."

With a preoccupied air Juan Poveda fetched up from the pork barrel a slab of meat and laid it before Miss Fashion.

"That's too fat," cried that elegant lady, turning up her lips, "don't give me that, man. Ain't yo' got no lean?"

Poveda held the leg high up before her gaze. The fast encrusting brine twinkled on it like silver spangles. "Yo' don't like fat," cried Poveda in astonishment, "but every people like fat."

"No," sulked Miss Fashion, "yo' bes' lemme have de salt beef. When de pork fat so, it stan' 'pon me stomach an' giv' me de krolick."

Poveda slipped the leg of corned pork back into the cask of brine.

"An' tree cents worth o' yucca."

"Yo' tek," cried Poveda, wrapping up the corned beef, "when yo' go out." He nodded toward a medley of fruits and vegetables lying beside the door.

"How much is the yucca?" asked Miss Fashion, counting out her coppers.

"Two fo tree cents."

"Lahd, yo' dear wid yo' tings though, eh?"

Packing her purchases carefully in her basket, she turned and moved away from the counter.

"Come now, Mistah Poveda," cried Mrs. Piggott, "lemme get out o' yah. My Joey gwine soon come home now. Gimme a gill o' ripe plantains."

There was a big bunch of plantains hanging overhead. Poveda reached up and twisted off two ripe, deeply-dyed ones. As he started to wrap them up, he turned and glimpsed Miss Fashion lifting from the vegetable heap something which she had neither asked nor paid for.

"*Trampo!*"* cried Poveda, running from behind the counter.

Mrs. Piggott turned and observed, scandalised: "Hey, look 'pon she though, teefin' the man red pepper."

" 'Clare to Heaven," vowed Miss Fashion, lamely. "A body can't even tek up a pepper fo' look 'pon it beout all yo' tink me gwine teef it."

Poveda's swarthy face turned purple with fulsome rage.

"To look 'pon dis yah man," continued Miss Fashion, "yo' would a tink me gwine run 'way wid him dutty ole red pepper. The man go on so like me nebber see a lil' ole red pepper in me life befo'." With an affected air of injured pride and exalted self-righteousness, Miss Fashion scornfully tossed the incriminating object back upon the vegetable heap and, throwing up her chin, strutted out.

"*Tramposa!*" cried Poveda, gazing after her.

"Some people can teef an' got so much mout' besides," ruminated Mrs. Piggott.

Bending down over the pyramid of yams, eddoes and cassavas, Poveda shuffled the basket containing the peppers, thyme, okras and watercress; tore a russet leaf off a cluster of sapodillas,* then, growling savagely, returned to the counter. He was entirely unprepared for the tirade which greeted him:

"Look yah, Mistah Poveda, wha' dis yo' giv' me? Me ax yo' fo' ripe plantains, yes, but yo' don't oblige fo' giv' me nutton as sawf as dis. Ain't yo' got no harder ones? Pick them from up top yonder," she cried, pointing to a cluster of green ones nearer the stem. "Why man, these is sawf as pap." She sank her fingers in them to convince him of their softness.

Poveda stood petrified. Suddenly he seized the plantains and flung them upon the vegetable heap. "Go!" he spluttered in a violent rage. "*Allez . . . allez . . . rut!** You savvy?" he leered at her angrily, his one blueish grey eye aflame. "You shameless *chombos,* you *sacré negras* jamaicans, me no like you! Go to the Chinaman next door—he please you! Don't come again my store."

Alarmed at the grocer's sudden explosive manner, the negress turned and swiftly walked out the door.

II

If Pelota y Gracios had not been a *contre-maitre** in Egypt, Juan Poveda would never have had the pluck to leave Oracq and a job in a blacksmith's shop to join the French in Panama. A chubby weasel of a man with rosy cheeks, a walrus moustache and mocking blue eyes, Pelota y Gracios was the richest peasant in Oracq. He was held on a pedestal by the peasants in the small Pyrenees village as a model deserving of emulation.

The path which Pelota y Gracios had trodden to fame and fortune lay paved with the bottomless mud and silting sands of the Nile delta. As an overseer at Lake Timsah during the excavating of the Suez Canal, Pelota y Gracios had had supervision of a gang of Arab *fellahs.** He early got on to the ways of overseers and was not slow in mastering the art of padding the payroll. When, after an absence of five years, Pelota y Gracios returned to Oracq he was wealthy enough to buy up half the farming properties in the valley and the big seignorial mansion on the ramparts.

One day Pelota y Gracios met Juan Poveda in the street and quietly said to him:

"Juan, my boy, take my advice and go to Panama."

"Panama?" cried the blacksmith's apprentice.

"Yes, Panama," declared the crafty *contre-maitre*. Then drawing Juan by the lapel of his blue velvet jacket, Pelota y Gracios added: "The same syndicate I worked for in Egypt is now in Panama, cutting a canal there. This is the chance of a lifetime, Juan. It's idiotic to be frittering away your life in a place like Oracq earning wages no Arab *fellah* would spit on, in a blacksmith's shop. Get out and try your luck in Panama."

"Panama!" cried Juan Poveda, dreamily, "Panama. . . ."

Dusk deepened into night.

With a splash the propellers started vibrating and the steamer again got under way. The lights of Cartagena, growing steadily dimmer, flickered along the invisible shore.

Lying in a hammock on the poop deck, Juan Poveda experienced a twinge of joy. Only one more night at sea and then Colon, gateway to the Promised Land! It was a far cry now from Oracq, slumbering at the feet of a Pyrenees altitude.

He was riding on the voluptuous bosom of the Sea of Darkness! He was nearing, at last, the *chantiers** of Panama!

Landing at Colon, Juan Poveda was given the rank of *contre-maitre* and sent with a batch of Jamaica negroes and Chinese coolies to a settlement on the Cruces River. Tons of cement and a quantity of high-powered machinery were to be brought in, the jungle cleared and a reservoir built. It was all part of a vast engineering project to harness the Chagres and its numerous tributaries.

One day in a dispute with one of the negroes a scuffle ensued and the big muscular *contre-maitre* was seized by the back of the neck and butted into unconsciousness. One eye shut up instantly, never to open again. Juan Poveda was taken to the clinic on Buccaneer Hill and the eye was removed. He wore a piece of crêpe, like a blinker, over the hollow and from then onward hated the very sight of a West Indian negro.

He gave up the Cruces job and settled down in San Felipe, a pueblo outside Panama City, as a vendor of celery, white cheese and strips of meat dried in the sun. Still a good Oracq peasant as regards frugality—still a disciple of Pelota y Gracios—Juan Poveda, at the end of two years, was ready to join the mad rush to Culebra, the centre of the canal excavations, and set up as a retail grocer.

III

A negro labourer entered the shop.

"Poveda," he said, "gimme a pound o' corn meal."

The grocer scooped up a ladle of the bright yellow dust, poured it out upon a sheet of brown paper and wrapped it up.

"A dime o' okras," cried the man.

"Take," gestured Poveda, "yonder—when you go out."

"Got any lard oil?"

"Yes, how much you want?"

Producing an empty olive oil bottle, the negro answered: "Oh, fill it half full."

"Anything else?" asked Poveda.

"Tree cents worth o' fat pork."

Poveda's forearm sank in the adjacent cask of brine. He drew up a leg of pork and spread it upon the redwood slab. He sliced off a large portion, stuck it upon a piece of paper and placed it in the scales. Just then the negro intervened.

"Wait there, Mistah Poveda," he said, "lemme see dat piece o' meat yo' got there."

Poveda tossed it over at him: whereupon the negro examined it as might a veterinary surgeon the tick-infested flank of a pedigree cow.

"Why, man, this pork is nothin' but fat," drawled the labourer, "it ain't got a bit o' lean. Ain't you got no mo' lean? Go look in the barrel yonder an' see if yo' can't find a piece with a little bit mo' lean 'pon it fo' me."

With a snarl and a volcanic burst of rage, Poveda leaped upon the counter and kicked the negro full in the chest. Reeling across the room, the negro fell at the foot of the pyramid of fruits and vegetables, lying in a half-dazed condition.

"You *sacré negros jamaicanos!*" cried Poveda, striding with a machete toward the fallen man. "Don't any o' you cross my doorway again! Stay out! *Chombos negros!*"

Slowly the labourer rose to his feet. Red as a beet and puffing furiously, Poveda stood above him with the machete twirled high in the air.

"Is fight yo' want, fight?" cried the negro. "Tell me, is fight yo' want fight?"

"Aw, what you want?" growled Juan Poveda, uncertainly.

"Knock me, no," teased the negro, advancing to meet the machete. "See me here—why don't yo' knock me?"

Poveda wavered. He was seized by a strange indecision. Somehow the negro's unexpected bravado disarmed him.

The tension slackened and the labourer stepped out calmly from beneath the menacing machete. "Wait!" he said, shaking a finger under Juan Poveda's nose. "You wait till I come back and see if yo' ain't gwine have to buss open my head wit' yo' machete."

He turned and slowly walked out the shop.

Plagued by the rising suspicion that the negro in some way had triumphed in the fray, Poveda returned behind the counter in a black, angry mood.

A shrill warning cry—someone shouting his name—roused the grocer. Rushing to the door, Juan Poveda went out upon the veranda and stood gazing across the ravine. On the edge of the railway embankment stood Coloradillo, a squat Napacundi albino, employed as a *vigilante* in the native constabulary.

"The Jamaicans!" cried Coloradillo, breathlessly, "they are coming to attack you! A hundred of them—"

Poveda fled to the dark interior of the shop. He took down from a shelf a long carbine and rammed it full of shells. In case of attack he had certain decisive factors on his side. A person entering the shop by the veranda was like a spot upon a disc, a silhouette against the sky. With a gun at his elbow he would always have the better of the invader.

Someone was crossing the plank lying across the swampy ravine from the edge of the railway embankment to the veranda. An impression of swagger was conveyed by the person's long free strides.

Above the sound of the approaching footsteps Juan Poveda also heard the murmurings of a mob. The blacks were talking: saying how—if and when they caught him—they were going to mince his meat.

Suddenly the doorway darkened.

"See me here now," cried the negro, "why don't yo' knock me now?"

Juan Poveda, crouching beside an oil drum, resolved to take the negro at his word. Quickly bringing the carbine to his shoulder, he fired. The negro fell bleeding like a stuck pig.

The shot quickened the mob's advance. Poveda crept deeper in the shop. Another negro, flying to the side of the fallen man, darted within Poveda's range and the carbine again blazed forth.

Poveda flicked out the smoking shell and again cocked the carbine. But no more blacks advanced to satisfy the grocer's avenging passion.

Above the confusion of flaming tongues and the wheeling movement of the mob, Poveda recognised the voice of the chief of the Culebra *chantier*:

"If you men don't get back to your barracks, I'll set the Federal cavalry on you, too."

Poveda heaved a deep sigh. His ears tingled with the memory of the negroes' threats. He heard them shuffle down the veranda, file across the plank and go up to the railway embankment like a flock of sheep.

He drew courage and straightened up, and three men, in the blue tunics and cork helmets of the French, entered the shop.

"Come on, Poveda," said one of them. "We can't let you stay here. You incite the labourers to riot. Hurry up—you leave for Panama at once."

A constable with the granulated eyelids of a San Blas albino was delegated by the chief of the *chantier* to escort Juan Poveda into exile.

Consulate

To the dusky throng silently gathered in the waiting room Leon Cabrol was the arbiter of life and death. He was the Consul's clerk. Clad in a pongee* silk suit, Cabrol was sitting at a long table behind the tall slatted railing. He was patiently putting the finishing touches to the papers of a cargo steamer due to sail at dusk from Limon Bay.

A middle-aged man of colour, Cabrol was a native of Demerara. He was heavily built, with thin, sandy hair, an aquiline nose and sunken expressionless eyes. Two years in the funereal climate of Colon had already begun to tell on him. He was sallow, yellow-eyed, white-lipped.

Having "despatched the ship," Cabrol came from behind the table and stood before the small square opening in the railing. A barely perceptible movement occurred in the room. A Negress who owned a fried fish and muffins stand on the Wharf Aux Herbes elbowed her way up to the railing. From a dirty blue handkerchief she emptied on the ledge a spate of golden coins.

From *The Spectator* March 20, 1936.
Reproduced with kind permission of *The Spectator*.

"Me 'fraid," she murmured, half-apologetically, "de Spaniards will steal it, sah." She dived into the flabby regions of her bodice and produced a passbook on a Jamaica bank. Pushing it over toward Cabrol she added, with a spirited, self-gratifying air, "An' if anybody gwine steal me money me radder them steal it in Jamaica!"

"How much yo' got heah?" drawled the clerk.

"Twenty pounds," she said, "Count um an' see, no."

But Cabrol had already done that. He gathered up the sovereigns and resumed his seat at the table. He entered the deposit in the passbook, recorded the entry in a ledger and handed the passbook back to the Negress.

"Next!" cried Cabrol.

Two men in baggy blue jumpers and mud-caked breeches came up to the railing.

"Oi's Eddie Culoden's half-brother," said one.

"Have you been to the French Consul yet?" asked Cabrol.

"No, but the patois man wit' he head split open is ovah there now, takin' out a writ."

"All right," murmured Cabrol, "just step round here."

He showed the men round the veranda and through a side door into the office. He drew up two chairs for them and sitting down himself, pulled out the table drawer and took out some sheets of foolscap.*

"Oi was in the rum shop," declared the man with Eddie Culoden's half-brother, "when the Spaniards rush down 'pon Eddie. Oi see him fall, holdin' his head, an' de blood runnin' down his face—."

"Good gracious!" interposed a Negress from the opposite side of the railing, "tek unna time."

With the foolscap spread out before him Cabrol began taking down the particulars of the case.

It was Eddie Culoden's first visit to the canteen. Newly arrived to take up a brakeman's job at "Kilometer 74"—a squalid, fly-by-night town on the French canal—Eddie was still more or less of a tenderfoot. Coming to the Isthmus from the island of St. Kitts, Eddie's brief apprenticeship at Colon—both in the railway yards and the dazzling night-life of Spanish Town—had taught him little beyond the art of standing in the path of a flying locomotive and safely easing himself up on the cow-catcher.* To hop a passing train or "buck" a fast approaching engine with style, grace and reckless ease was a source of great pride to Eddie.

He made directly for the bar. His arrival there coincided oddly with the end of Concha's patience. Concha,—a mestiza with an olive pigment, insolent wine-coloured lips and inscrutable grey eyes,—was the girl behind the bar. "*No hago negocio,*" snapped Concha at a buckra customer, "*soy la mujer de Pablo Pequeño.*" There was no reason for him to have confused her with the girls insinuating themselves like ticks in the fleeces of the lambs flocking into the canteen from the canal works; no excuse to insult her with his steady denuding gaze. "I have already told him I'm Pablo Pequeño's woman and still he keeps on annoying me. Pest!" All eyes at the bar turned on the buckra,—unshaven, green eyes burned a dull glow by a chronic excess of absinthe,* a cork hat awry, trousers of blue denim and yellow sabots.* With averted eyes the buckra started to slink off, bumped straight into Eddie. He spun round, facing the Negro. It was instantly clear that he approved of Eddie. "*Je suis royaliste, moi,*" he said, swaying drunkenly, "*et toi?*"* He reached out and grabbed Eddie by the shirt bosom. "Hey!" cried Eddie, "wha' you think you doin', ni? Man, unhandle muh!" Pablo Pequeño, a peon extremely adept at twirling a machete, quietly strode up. Concha ran from behind the bar and followed beside him. "*Da la palo!*" hissed one of the men at the bar. Suddenly, the curved steel blade of a machete flashed in the air; fell. "But Oi ain't do nutton," cried Eddie Culoden, reeling as in a daze, "Oi ain't do nutton—"

"Next!" cried Leon Cabrol.

A squat, unctuous Oriental with a naked dome and a curling pigtail, Melican Sam rose. Round him swarmed a small, doll-like brood of six yellow progeny. With a proudly paternal air, Melican patted the little ones along gently.

As Melican approached the railing, a Negress who had been sitting beside him got up and went and stood by the door to the veranda. She drew closer about her slender shoulders the black silk shawl that she wore and let her eyes travel slowly from the scarlet buds of the hibiscus and the white-spotted green leaves of the crotons lying between the young palm trees which fringed the gravel path outside the veranda, to the serene, silver-sunlit glimpses of Limon Bay beyond.

Bowing profusely, Melican handed Cabrol a passport.

"Where are you going, Sam?"

"Hong Kong!"

"Taking all these children with you?"

"Yes!" replied Melican with a grin.

"What about the children's mother," said Cabrol, affixing a stamp to the passport, "isn't she going, too?"

The Chinaman turned and glanced at the tall, willowy Negress standing dreamily by the door.

"No!" he replied, again grinning, "she no can go, too."

The clerk returned the Chinaman his passport, accepted the consular fee and Melican Sam with his exquisitely unreal little brood went out.

"Who's next?"

A large and bejewelled Negress, poised with incredible certitude on a pair of red, thimble-heeled shoes, swept up to the railing. She wore a "garden party" leghorn hat turned up in front and she carried a tiny parasol.

"What is it, Mary?" cried Cabrol sharply.

"It's dis yah gal, sah," whined Mary, turning to make way for Rhona. "Hurry up, gal, an' don't keep the Consul waitin'."

The girl crept forward with downcast eyes. A copper-coloured ad-mixture of Hindu and Negro, she was extremely slender, long-legged, fourteen years old.

"What has she done now?" asked Cabrol.

"She won't behave 'arself, sah," declared Mary. "All me beat 'ar, an' tump 'ar round, she won't change 'ar ways, sah. She still a go out at night time, till me can't stand 'ar no mo', sah. Me want yo' fuh send 'ar back to 'ar moomah* in Jamaica."

A puzzled frown appeared on Cabrol's brow. "You know, Mary," he said, "the Consul can't send her home against her will. If she doesn't want to go nobody can compel her." He gazed at shy, misty-eyed Rhona wincing under the accusation.

"Hold up yo' head, miss!" cried Mary, "befo' me box yo' heahs! An don't shub out yo' mout' like yo' is any woman!" She turned to Cabrol with a confidential air: "Me tell yo' de gal so rude me can't even speak to 'ar now."

"What's the matter, Rhona?" asked Cabrol, "why don't you want to behave like a nice little girl?"

"She na'h tell yo' de troot, sah," blurted out Rhona. "She want fo' send me back to Jamaica because me refuse fo' let 'ar chuck me down in Spanish Town among all the neygur men."

With his head slightly cocked on one side, Cabrol looked steadily at Mary.

"Lahd me Gahd!" cried the Negress, properly scandalised. "Look how de gal stan' up befo' de Consul an' trespass 'pon me character. Lahd! Yo' evah see such a bare-faced liad in all yo' bahn days! Gal stand up

308

befo' de Consul an' say me wahn send 'ar down in Spanish Town! An' hafta all me done do far 'ar. Hafta me tek de wretch out de buckra cane patch an' bring 'ar wid me own a money all de way from Cobie to Colon, an' clothes 'ar, an' feed 'ar till she fat like a mullet, two whole o' year now, an' dis is de tanks me did got!" She seized the child by the arm and dragged her off. "Come along yo' little tattle-tale wretch yo', me gwine show yo' how fo' stan' up befo' de Consul an' disgrace me character."

"Next!" cried Cabrol, scanning the slowly diminishing throng.

$\mathcal{M}$orning in Colon

The sun, coming up over the swamp, silvered the roof of the baker shop where the zinc was not yellowed with rust. A hen cackled. In the shop there was a burst of flame. There was a lazy swish and a prolonged jingle outside the door of a ground-floor room in the Ants' Nest.* A small Spanish boy had darted out of the room in haste. Up the alley he fled to the refuse yard behind the baker shop. Stepping over old rags, craters of dust and pieces of broken glass he came upon a white shinning egg under a cochineal clump. "Mama!" he cried, "it's a big one, a big one." He ran back with the egg, full of excitement.

"Yo' buy ten cents yo' get nutting
"Yo' buy de fifty cents yo' get *napa**
Say! me no wahn nutton but yo' money."

It was a piece of mockery, not a street-cry. The tenants in the Ants' Nest, all occupying one-room flats, were sated with it; none of them was in a position to exploit the promise of a baker's dozen. All this Natty Gumbs knew quite well. Opening the door he recoiled from the tongues

From *The West Indian Review* (Kingston, Jamaica) August 1940.

of flame licking the rose pink roof of the oven's mouth. His muscles bulged in his dirty singlet. His perspiring face and arms were a gleaming purple in the glowing heat and darkness.

"Wahn nutton but yo' money
"Say! me no—"

Back at the trough under the window he oiled and greased a row of baking pans; tore off, kneaded and patted hunks of dough, all in a mood of sultry unhurrying.

A child's cries floated down from the verandah of the Ants' Nest as if to offset the distant wail of a Moorish survival and the chatter of parokeets in the fustic tree in the yard. The child was sitting on a straw mat. Its brown virgin body lay on the fast encroaching line of the sun. At the sink a tall adz-faced woman* in whom the blood of Castile, the Guinea Coast and the Cholo aborigine was softly blended was brewing a cup of hot milk, passing it in a vertical flow from cup to cup until it cooled.

A woman, black and buxom, emerged from a bead-curtained door on the verandah peeling a ripe banana. She threw the skin on the roof of the baker shop and fed the banana to a macaw perched on the verandah rail.

"Eggs! Pullets! Fowls!"

The Negress leaned over the rail. "Senora!" she cried. "How yo' sell de fowl eggs?"

The vendor, saddled with a tray of poultry and a basket of eggs, paused. "One for five cents," she said.

"How much?"

"Two fo' ten cents."

"Tell me something," cried the Negress. "Is rob you want rob me, eh?"

The vendor shrugged. "If you don't like my price," she said, "you no can buy."

"But no mo'n de yadda day," declared the Negress, "me did got four fo' ten cents!"

"Yes," replied the vendor, "but the hens don't lay so much now." Her upturned gaze fell. She started to pick up the basket which she had put down on the ground.

"An' de fowl cock—him is not fi' sale, eh?"

"Which one?"

"The one up top yonder wid him comb red no cherry an' de blue feathers spread out 'pon him neck like yo' country uman *pollera*."*

311

The vendor ran her fingers along the edge of the tray upon her head. Bound by the legs and lying aslant the cock fluttered at her touch.

"This one?"

"Yes, how much the pound?"

"Eighty cents."

"Yo' must wahn me fi' t'ief, eh? Where yo' t'ink me gwine get eighty cents fi' pay fi' a scrawny, yallah-leg fowl cock? Off a ackee bush?"*

"Oh," murmured the vendor. "You Yamaica women no good."

"Why, only de yadda day," cried the Negress for the edification of all and sundry, "me buy a five-pound fowl—fomembah when me did got the gunga peas an' coconut rice, Miss Flamenco?" Sitting in a hammock gently rocking her baby, now pacified and half-asleep, Miss Flamenco stared at her icily. "An' all me did pay farrim was turty cents a pound. Now de dyam t'ievin' wretch wahn charge me eighty cents a pound fo' a lil' half-starve,' kiss-me-ears fowl cock."

She drew aside the curtain of glass beads and gazed at her white even teeth in the mirror hanging on the room door.

"Get yo' pullets," cried the vendor, vanishing down the alley. "Fowls! Eggs!"

❧

Jogging under the curving shadow of the verandah the donkey cart almost grazed the side of Rufus Nig's ice barrow.

"Why yo' don't look where yo' gwine?" shouted Rufus at the turbanned Babu* driver, "Yo' t'ink yo' own de road, eh?"

He removed the crocus bag from the ice and wiped the sawdust off the top. He unhooked the pincers from under the shaft and worked a chink between the frozen blocks.

"Lahd, it hot though, eh?" cried Rufus, mopping his brow.

He stood up, inhaling a whiff of something that smelt like water in a lily-crested tayche in an old sugar mill with the decomposing body of a bull-frog hidden in it. It was the swamp. The snipes flew low over it. The east wind had shifted. Clouds of egrets—silver specks in the tender azure of the sky—dipped and wheeled. A boy was exercising a horse in front of the stables. To-morrow was carnival. It was a rakish, toil-worn nag with a bandaged knee and a sore-razor-edged back. To-morrow there would be dancers on stilts and dark-eyed girls on floats and whirls of confetti and a Negro admiral with a land ship and rag-tailed urchins crying, "Aye, aye, conoce!" and, to crown all, horse races in the streets.

"Ice!" cried Rufus. "Ice!"

A Chinese half-caste girl at the canteen door hailed the ice man.

"Eh, eh," cried Rufus. "Is dat you 'New Dress'?"

Wheedling a new dress out of every man she met was the least of Rosie's accomplishments. "Hey!" she protested. "A body speak to one o' you neygurs an' the first thing all-yo' do is lose all-yo' place. Man, yo' bes' show yo' respect fo' me an' fomembah yo' ain't talkin' to none o' yo' low-class neygur women."

Rufus managed a wry smile. He bent down to the piazza and gazing past Rosie's gauzy knee-high skirt and bare legs glimpsed the white trousered legs of a couple of sailors.

"Yo' ridin' 'pon yo' high horse, eh?" he cried, straightening up. "Well, tek care yo' don't fall down an' brek yo' neck."

He started chipping the ice with a hatchet.

"Hey!" cried Rosie. "Anybody hear this red-lip, chigger-foot neygur man talkin' would t'ink me ah live wit' him."

With a goblet* in her hand she crossed the piazza and came and stood near him. "Quattie worth o' ice," she said.

Rufus demurred. "Me don't sell quattie worth o' ice," he said.

"Look, yaw, don't form fool!"*

"Me don't sell quattie worth!"

"Lahd! Wha' come over yo'?" asked Rosie, arms akimbo. "Mek say yo' don't want sell me quattie worth o' ice?"

"Dis mornin'," answered Rufus, laying down the hatchet, "when me went down to the Ice House yo' know wha' dem say to me? Dem say, 'Rufus, me boy, me 'fraid say me can't give yo' mo' dan fifty pound o' ice dis mornin'.' 'How day, Mistah Bombley boss,' me say, 'Yo' can't do dat, man! Didn't me pay yo' in exvance fo' seventy five pound?' 'Yes,' him say, 'dat are a fact, but since yo' was 'ere the Yankee fleet come in an' the captain leave a order so big, yo' see, de plant skasely big enough fi' hold it.' "

"Lahd!" cried Rosie. "What dis place a come to! Ev'ry blind t'ing a go up! Yo' know how much de Chinaman want fo' de macaroni now? Ten cents fo' two sprig! Imajing! Two sprig o' macaroni wit' de cobweb dust an' de worrum crawling' over dem—two fo' ten cents. It are a dyam shame."

"Tell me something—yo' go down the market yet?"

"No, me jes' get up."

"Yo' don't do* down to the market yet?"

"No, me jes' get up. Afta' yo' went way dis fo'day mornin' Beryl come call me meet some friends at the Ants' Nest."

"Well, wait till yo' go down to the market. Yo' know what de t'ievin' Spaniard want fi turtle now? One whole dollar! An' as fo' fresh fish an' seasonin'—gal, dere is some patois men wha' want fifteen cents a pound fo' bobo fish. Tink o' it! An' as for the baker—Natty Gumbs ah mek pappy show!* How long yo' tink him gwine go on askin' ten cents fo' a teeny weeny loaf o' French bread?"

"Yes, me know, Rufus. An' don't tink it confine to things fi' nyam* alone. No, don't tink dat. A man in the *Ants' Nest* was jes' tellin' me 'bout him properties. Him was tipsy, yo' see, an' him mout' run like fire. Seem like him own a bottle works in Chorillo an' next door to the bottle works is an empty lot and the owner o' de empty lot is one of dem craven Gatun contractors. Well, anyway, him need the lot fi' put up a next bottle works, yo' see, but him play shrewd an' wouldn't give the man the price him ask for it."

"How much him want fi' de yard?"

"A tous'n dollah."

"Pshaw! Him ah mek joke."

"Well, him hold out an' hold out, yo' see, tinkin' dat in time him will mek him sell fo' lil' or nutton. But, bwoy, the man run the price up to six tous'n dollah an' him ah run it up ev'ry time yo' turn round."

"No wonder the man come to Colon fo' ram him gut wit' white rum."

"Well, give me quattie worth o' ice an' let me go 'long 'bout me business."

"Me sorry, Rosie, but the smallest me can sell is five cents worth."

"Lahd!" she cried, giving him the goblet, "Yo' stingy wit' yo' ice though eh?"

$\mathcal{B}$y the River Avon

"What kind of nail polish do you use?"

"Vermillion."

"Not so good. You ought to try silver. It goes rather well with fair hair."

"Whoever did that ought to have a ring through her nose."

"Here, let me put this on."

"What is it?"

"Oh, just a little something for your wrist."

"Why, Pingo, it's white gold!"

"Oh, no. It's nickel."

"Whatever do I want with a nickel chain?"

"Just in case you get lost or something. It's like a soldier's identification disc or a dog's tag—"

I wasn't eavesdropping. I was merely standing, not far from a Negro soldier and a white girl, at the tail-end of a bus queue in front of the public gardens in Bradford-on-Avon, Wiltshire County, England.

A bus with standing room only came along and the queue moved

From *The Crisis* January 1947. Reprinted with permission.

forward. Nobody got off, one or two people got on and the bus drove off again.

When I looked around the girl had disappeared, but the GI had climbed on the garden wall and with legs dangling now sat under the dark, mauve-mellow cloud of a copper beech tree. Ranged about his legs were a couple of his Negro service buddies.

The movement of the GI's lips was rapid, unceasing. All of a sudden he threw his hands above his head and with the fingers outspread kept them up there quivering. Then, with as much ease as though he was sitting on a velvet cushion, the GI, who tended to be corpulent, even a little adipose,* quickly shifted his body from side to side.

"Look at them!" cried a white man passing by, "just like a lot of monkeys!"

Immediately ahead of me in the bus queue stood a tall, heavily built man whose black curly hair under the brim of a trilby hat* was fringed with silver. A dirty mackintosh hung loosely from his round sloping shoulders.

The big man was eyeing the two men in front of him with pity. "What I done in the Boer War?" he asked, speaking with a lisp, "Well, I will tell you. I helped Sergeant Wilson in the Market Place to enlist men in the Wilts Imperial Yeomanry. I wasn't big enough to be a trumpeter."

"What was it we were fighting for then?"

"I always understood meself—"

"Freedom and democracy?"

"—that it was a war for gold."

Under the two-pronged assault the big man faltered. His eyes widened out of focus. His astonishment was measureless.

He was no longer a solicitor's clerk in Bristol, the intimate of men whose daily concern was to interpret and administer the law. He was back in the county in which his parents, both devout church-goers, had first met, fallen in love and been united in wedlock; the county where he, his unmarried sister and his brother, who now kept a tavern in Derbyshire, were born and had grown up. Yes, on the eve of the pitiless hammering from the air which it was destined to receive the big man had kissed the old Negro slave mart goodbye. Now he was grubbing along in a ten-bob-a-week cottage in Avon Without, on the boundlessly sprawling hem of a hill-sited industrial town. His sister, a seamstress, shared the cottage with him, quietly sewing for the gentry. In his allotment, vital to the job of making ends meet, the couch grass, the flowering thistles, the dandelions and the clover vines had got a stranglehold. High blood pressure had compelled him to give up gardening. The sands were running out, but there was one consolation: he had managed, despite everything, to hang on to a white-collar job in a factory, a low-grade, poorly paid one but a white-collar one nevertheless.

Among some of the local folk the habit of prefixing "darkie" to the big man's name was current; but only behind his back, never to his face. Had he been tied, like most English "half-castes," to the squalid de-colonialized corner of a seaport town instead of to the rural heart of Old England the position would doubtless have been different; but for all useful purposes there had been nothing to prevent him from "passing," even though he was not so light-skinned a mulatto that he could have been mistaken for anything but a colored man. One of the reasons for the tolerance shown towards him arose from the esteem in which his mother, a God-fearing woman of unmixed African ancestry from Antigua in the West Indies, was still held by all who had known her and even by many who had only heard tell of her a quarter of a century after she had passed on. ("If anybody couldn't get along with she there must have been something wrong with they.") Toward his father, a Wiltshire merchant, the unspoken view was one of charity. In the Victorian era Britain's Negro empire was expanding. The adoption by a missionary society of a young attractive Negro girl with the aim of giving her the blessings of an English education and a Christian upbringing in the Mother Country had been nothing unusual. If the girl ended up by marrying a white man that showed that she was no longer a heathen.

The big man gazed at his companions as if he was seeing them for the first time. One, a storekeeper in the engineering works where he was employed, was slender and of medium height with a gay twinkle in his deep blue eyes. The other, short and stocky, old and feeble of step, a lifelong trade unionist, had spent forty years under the roof of a galvanized shed in close intimacy with hot metal and black sand.

The sound of the Avon River flowing over a weir,* cascading out in foam, harmonized with the big man's lisp. "I was in Bert Wilson's," he went on, "the night news came through that Mafeking* was relieved. A crowd quickly assembled in the market place with tin whistles and candles and a torch light procession started. There were a few Boers in the town and the crowd went after them. Then the crowd came back and went into Bert's to have a tot of whiskey with him. Old Bert soon had his hands full. Everybody wanted to join up."

He paused, aglow with a feeling of pride and patriotism. Nobody could say with justice that he was a yellow belly. "That's what I done in the Boer War," he said, "I helped Sergeant Wilson in the market place to enlist men in the Wilts Imperial Yeomanry. I wasn't big enough to be a trumpeter, mind!"

The storekeeper's eyes twinkled gaily. "I was in Singapore after the last war," he muttered, "and the Sultan of one of the islands in the Straits Settlements offered to give each white man in the British garrison an extra sixpence a day if they would salute his officers. There were then about 2,000 white troops in the garrison."

"No need to ask," observed the iron moulder drily, "what action was taken on the offer."

"That Sultan was prepared to spend up to twenty thousand pounds a year just for a salute, and I don't mind telling you there wasn't a man in the garrison who wouldn't have been glad for an extra sixpence a day. But our folks weren't having it, see. Oh, no. 'Twould have been too much for the prestige of the white man out East."

The curl of the storekeeper's lip, the bitter sarcasm in his voice and the quick up and down movement of his eyes all gave the big man a queer uncomfortable feeling. The big man moved to the edge of the pavement and craned his neck.

"This bus," he lisped, "is a deuce of a time coming."

A vehicle was coming down the road but it wasn't a bus. It was a jeep. Passing the public gardens in a cloud of dust the Negro GI at the wheel instead of proceeding on up into the town made a sharp turn at the entrance to the bridge. The river bank, a public swimming pool and a curving line of two-storey frame buildings wedged the car park in. The GI switched off the motor and the lieutenant beside him leapt out. The GI also got out, disappearing in the two-way flood of wheeled and foot traffic moving over the bridge.

The lieutenant mounted the pavement. He walked slowly past the doors of a blacksmith shop, a bakery. The queue on the pavement was two and three deep, long and winding. Passing behind it the lieutenant emerged at the bus stop outside a cafe directly across the road from where I was standing. He glanced up at the trinity of gables on the side of the roof of the 16th century stone structure. Quaint. The cafe, lying on below ground level, was dark, fly-blown. Its oak-beamed ceiling was low. There were no curtains on the windows. One was ajar. Through it the lieutenant, pacing to and fro, perceived Negro enlisted men from his unit (a service one, encamped on a hilltop outside the town in which all the officers were white) being served with tea and crumpets in a roomful of white folk . . . women and children evacuated from London, a couple of British tommies on leave, a British colonel of engineers sitting imperturbably with an elegant, grey-haired lady.

"Oh, hello."

The lieutenant was small, about 22 years of age and hailed from Georgia. A graduate of a military academy, he was the senior subaltern at the camp.

A question mark, like a column of black smoke had begun to billow up over the camp. Was GI morale all that it might be? The people in Bradford had begun to wonder. There wasn't much that they could do about it, but, even so, some of them if only from a feeling of national self-interest had decided to have a try. Every Saturday night a GI dance, organized on behalf of a local war charity, was held in the Town Hall. One Sunday morning a Negro soldier deputized for the Vicar, an Oxford M.A., in the pulpit of Holy Trinity Church. The wife of a political officer in the Sudan, a committee of ladies, a British naval officer and a popular young clergyman were the organizers of one GI party that I attended. The fraternization and schemes of "morale-building," not all of which were carried on on a basis of pink knees and jive,* were designed to accomplish one thing: to impress upon the Negro troops that all white folk did not believe in segregation, social inequality and the color bar; but in the process what looked dangerously like a new kind of egalitarianism was evolving and the white officers at the camp were not happy about it. Recoiling from the implied "affront" to the officers, the lieutenant was now going all out to dispel the shadow of a color line. He seemed anxious to demonstrate that as far as he was concerned a Negro was no different from a white man. He was charming in the process but he was trying too hard.

The driver of the lieutenant's jeep re-appeared on the horizon. He was walking on the chalk line that extended across the mouth of the car park. Ignoring the jeep, he kept on walking. When he skirted an overflow from the bus queue on the pavement I was certain that he was heading for the cafe, but I was mistaken.

Changing course suddenly the GI turned and, darting across the road at a jog trot, presented himself to the lieutenant.

From the viewpoint of size there wasn't much to choose between the lieutenant and the GI, but the GI was smaller and ebony-hued. He was trembling and seemed all worked up about something and looked as if he was itching to stamp his foot. The expression in his eyes was tearful.

"Lieutenant Perry!" he said with great vigor and in a tone of deep injury, "how come I passed you and you didn't salute me?"

The lieutenant touched his cap perfunctorily. "I'm sorry, Roger," he murmured, "but I didn't see you going by."

The GI scanned the lieutenant's face intently. A pacific mood flowed over him. "Okay!" he said merely; but it was as though he had granted

319

forgiveness coupled with a warning against a repetition of what he clearly deemed to have been a gross breach of Service etiquette. Then he turned and sauntered off, chuckling happily.

The lieutenant was in a daze. Then suddenly he came to. "Hey, you!" he shouted after the GI.

The men in the bus queue, the cluster of GIs under the copper beech tree, the long bulging line of people across the road saw the GI jump as if he had been shot. He turned and stood in the middle of the road facing the lieutenant. Had he overplayed his hand? Uncertainty was mirrored in his big, round, widening eyes.

The lieutenant took his time about it. Sloping his cap forward at an angle so that the pointed top stood over one eye, he fixed the GI in a steely gaze. His lips were firmly compressed. Then he brought his arm up smartly in a salute.

"Yes, sir!" cried the GI, his hand flying to his cap.

The big man, gazing with open mouth at the spectacle of the lieutenant and the GI, was on the verge of apoplexy. "Well, I never!" he murmured, a reddish glow spreading over his pale yellow skin. He stared anxiously at the iron moulder and the storekeeper. Then after an unbroken silence he declared solemnly:—"Now, that's something you'd never see in the British Army in a hundred years."

$\mathcal{P}$oor Great

Down through the thinning top of
a coconut palm whose trunk curved over the garden's zinc paling, there
was the flash of bronze skin in the sunlight. Persistently, again and again;
mingling with the dark bluish gleams of a road flanked by the waters of
the Lamaha Canal.*

I gazed down into the foliage of almond and fustic trees screening
the middle and the lower end of the garden. I watched in vain for a
glimpse of squat, mat-haired 'Buck' aborigines.* Then suddenly I heard
the sound of shuffling feet on the plank that stretched from outside the
garden gate across the Canal. The bell on the gate tinkled, the gate was
pushed open. . . .

Easing down the shutters, I backed away from the window. Then I
turned and fled through the hallway.

"Where are you off to, boy?" cried Clorinda, appearing in the dusk,
"I thought I told you to stay on the gallery."

" 'Bucks!' " I ejaculated, " 'Bucks!' "

"Where?"

"Coming through the gate!"

From *Arena* (London) September/October 1950.

Neither of us had any need to descend the long flight of steps. A glimpse from the top was sufficient.

Round the foot of the stairs the 'Bucks' had paused. They had passed under the house which was mounted on piles and they now stood with outstretched hands and upturned faces gazing in silence at us.

"Poor things!" murmured Clorinda, turning to go into the kitchen.

In the forefront of the gathering I saw an old man in a loin cloth; four or five small children—more yellow than bronze and with nothing to cover their pot bellies; an old woman and a young, full-breasted girl modestly attired in aprons of coloured beads.

"Hey, where yuh goin', soul?" drawled Vangie, the Negro servant girl, as Clorinda came out of the kitchen with half a ship's biscuit in her hand.

Vangie had migrated to Georgetown from a village on the East Coast of the Demerara River and there was little about the 'Buck' aborigines of British Guiana that she did not know. And it had always been Vangie's contention that unless the larder in the kitchen was well-stocked the problem of how to deal with 'Buck' Indian indigence was not quite so simple as it looked. One had to take into account the fact that, side by side with a high sense of communal cohesion, the 'Bucks' possessed a protective genius for witchcraft; and that they would not hesitate to use it against anyone who, however well-intentioned, had done anything that was likely to create friction or spread dissatisfaction among them.

"Yuh want fo' get a swell foot, soul?" she cried, intercepting Clorinda half-way down the stairs.

Eyeing the nutmeg on a string which Vangie wore around her neck to keep away the duppies, Clorinda, a Negro native of Barbados with roots deep in the Anglican soil of that island, frowned:—

"What's wrong with you, girl?"

"Yuh want fo' start wastin' away with a disease no doctor can cure?" asked Vangie gently.

"No, I don't!"

"A disease," pursued Vangie, "you'd have fo' cross the ocean three times before yuh could shake it off?"

"No, I don't!"

"Well, then, send them away, soul. Le' them go to the almshouse." She turned from Clorinda and, lifting up the tips of her skirt, gazed down at the red-skins. "Shoo!" she cried, shooting out a leg. "Go 'long 'bout all-yuh business. We ain't got nothin' today."

The upturned gazes fell. The hands dropped. A wave of leaden resignation swept over the 'Bucks'. Then they turned and moved in single file into the darkness under the house.

Squatting on her haunches, Vangie watched them penetrate deep into the sunlight. She waited until they had disappeared through the gate. Then she rose and came back up the stairs.

"If yuh ain't got enough fo' go round," she said to Clorinda with a lugubrious shake of the head, "Yuh must harden yuh heart against them, soul. Yuh must never give one be-out yuh give all, udderwise the naked vagabonds will think yuh does play favourites. Then, after all taking all yuh got to give them, they will go out through the gate without saying a word, but when they get back up-country they will start working obeah fo' yuh sure as sea-cows does graze in the pond in the Botanical Gardens."

II

Holding on to the bannister, I began the steep descent. Gingerly, I mustn't make any noise. No one must know that I was not still on the gallery.

When I reached the bottom of the stairs I again marvelled (I never ceased to do this) at the absence of vegetation under the house. Here and there on the black loamy soil a toadstool, white-hooded and 'ghostly', had come up in the night. Something for me to flourish under the servant girl's nose when, sated with the pleasures of the garden and an eyeful of the road, I crept back up the stairs.

"Oh, my Gawd! A *jumbie* tree!* Well, look pon my trial. Throw away de t'ing, boy!"

Poor Vangie! Although she had begun (upon Clorinda's insistence) to attend the Sunday evening services at Christ Church she still had, alongside of an unshakable belief in *obeah*, a horror of anything that embodied for her the spirit of the dead.

As I was about to emerge from under the house, I saw what at first I was almost tempted to believe was an apparition in the sunlight. I was six years of age but even so I had no faith in the existence of *jumbies* or *duppies*. So I looked again and saw, instead of a ghost, the motionless figure of a black man who had paused before the small wooden tray which Vangie had placed on a soap box outside the gate early that morning.

Lying upon the tray beneath a napkin was an assortment of fruits and home-made pastry. The coconut for the sugar cakes* and the corn pone wrapped in banana leaves had come out of the garden, but the custard apples,* the star apples and the sapodillas Vangie had bought in Georgetown Market. "Nobody ain't gwine t'ief nothin'!" Vangie had sworn when, on the previous day, Clorinda had—after much hesitation—decided to fall in with an old Carib custom which had spread to every Negro household along the road.

I hid behind one of the piles on which the house stood and watched. The Negro lifted up the edge of the napkin and, from beneath the shredded brim of his palm leaf hat, subjected Clorinda's first day's offerings to long, silent scrutiny. Eventually he selected a sapodilla and dropped a coin on the tray. The coin fell with a clink as though it had joined a small pile. Then he slowly turned and crossed the plank. As he sauntered down the road devouring the plum he spat the black shining seeds into the Canal.

III

Climbing on to the gate, I leaned over and glanced up the road. Hard by, under the scrappy shade of the coconut tree, I glimpsed the snowy plumes of a brood of ducks, fresh from a dip in the Lamaha, doing their toilet on the grassy verge. Halfway along the road two small Negro boys stood dangling pieces of string in the amber-hued flow.

"Sweet cassava! Sweet cassava! Poppin' round the corner! Put it in the pot and it burst like powder!"

I turned my head and saw, hurrying against the vanishing cool of the morning, a troop of Negro women coming up the road . . . their arms swinging . . . their white calico skirts, gathered up from just below the hips, swaying. Burdens lay upon the padded, kerchiefed heads: a long tray heaped up with ground provisions, a skillet shining as though newly arrived from the tinsmith's (*Tambrin syrup fo' de cold and cough!*), a basket filled with bottles of a greenish bitter brew (*Maubé! Get yo' Maubé!*), uncorked and foaming in the sun.

Nobody from the dwelling houses set in gardens on both sides of the road wanted any of the things they were crying. As it was, there wasn't a gate that did not have outside it a little unattended tray on which something was being offered for sale. And so the Negro women with their swaying skirts continued on up the high, blue-gleaming road.

IV

As the troop swung out of sight Mr. Underwood appeared at the top of the road.

I do not know how the old Negro had come by his afflictions but they were agonizing to contemplate. His bearded face, drooping lips and mournful eyes combined to mirror humility and distress. One of Mr. Underwood's legs was artificial. The other, scaly and puffed up across the instep, was so big—I'd heard Vangie say there was 'water' on it—that even with the aid of a stick Mr. Underwood could scarcely drag it along.

Clad in a preacher's old frock-coat, Mr. Underwood was a mendicant. He begged his daily bread. As he went from gate to gate, doddering along in the sun, weaving across the road, his hat outstretched in his hand, the response which Mr. Underwood evoked was furtive but fairly general. Housewife after housewife would lean over a garden gate or zinc paling and hand him the leavings of a meal which Mr. Underwood, with a "God bless you!" or a nod of silent gratitude would seize and instantly devour as if he, the paradox of a short, stocky man suspected of harbouring a maw-worm, could never get enough to eat.

"Br'r Goat comin' down the road!"

The crayfishing in the Canal abruptly ended. One of the two Negro boys, depositing the morning's catch in a tin can, moved with caution past Mr. Underwood up the road; the other boy seemed to be heading my way. When the distance between them and Mr. Underwood was approximately equal the boy coming towards me wheeled and shouted at the top of his voice:—

"Who stole the goat?"

Cried the other boy:—

"The man with the long coat!"

Hovering in defiance, the two boys moved round and round awhile. Then:—

"What smells so high?"

Back came the answering cry:—

"You mean like a billy goat?"

Suddenly the ducks, squawking, began to scatter from beneath the coconut tree. Some splashed into the Canal, while others flew straight on to the road, waddling in confusion and panic before the breathless onrush of one of the two boys. Not far behind the boy's flying shirt-tail Mr. Underwood was taking long, quick strides as though there was plenty of spring not only in his cork leg but in the other one too.

Retreating from the gate, I held my breath. There was the sound of a flying leap across the Lamaha. Then the scurrying of feet in the barrack yard next door. What if Mr. Underwood, thwarted in one direction, should turn in another? I stood still and listened. Then, from underneath the house, I saw Mr. Underwood standing on the road directly in front of our gate.

"You little poor great* vagabond!" he shouted, waving a stick at me, "You wait till I catch all-yuh. It's all-yuh that smell!"

Then he turned and, leaning heavily on the stick, limped back up the road.

*A*nnotations

A number of these notes were informed by different sources, including the *Oxford English Dictionary*, Richard Allsopp's *Dictionary of Caribbean English Usage* (Oxford: Oxford UP, 1996), Rosamund Grant's *Caribbean and African Cooking* (New York: Interlink Books, 1993), Bruce Kellner's *The Harlem Renaissance: A Historical Dictionary for the Era* (Westport, Conn.: Greenwood P, 1984), Basil Hedrick and Anne Hedrick's *Historical Dictionary of Panama* (Metuchen, N.J.: Scarecrow P, 1970) and Henry Fraser and others' *The A–Z of Barbadian Heritage* (Kingstown: Heinemann, 1990). I have listed a few of the more frequent variants of Creole words; meanings can differ widely throughout the Caribbean.

53 "Batouala": René Maran's novel of this title was also discussed by Walrond in *Negro World* July 22, 1922, and July 29, 1922.

54 H. L. Mencken: editor of *American Mercury* and *Smart Set*. His brutal honesty on social issues was admired by many Black writers. See Charles Scruggs's *The Sage in Harlem: H. L. Mencken and the Black Writers of the 1920s* (Baltimore: Johns Hopkins UP, 1984).

59 The young lady: Zora Neale Hurston, who published her own account of the visit ("Mr. Schomburg's Library" *Negro World* April 22, 1922: 6).

60 Baron De Vastey's 'Cry of the Fatherland in the Interest of All Haytians': Baron Pompee-Valentin de Vastey, author of *Le cri de la patrie; ou, les intérêts de tous les haytiens* (1807).

60 Spencer St. John: Walrond means Sir Spenser Buckingham St. John, the author of *Hayti; Or, the Black Republic* (1884).

60 Henry Calloway's personal copy of 'Zulu Folk Lore': Walrond means Henry Callaway, author of *Nursery Tales, Traditions and Histories of the Zulus, in Their Own Words* (1868).

60 Andrew Long: Walrond probably means Scottish writer Andrew Lang (1844–1912), author of *Myth, Literature, and Religion* (1887).

60 'Book of American Negro Poetry': Walrond praised the anthology in "The Negro Poet" *Negro World* April 1, 1922: 4.

61 Francis Baker: Jamaican-born Francis Barber, who was the principal beneficiary in Johnson's will.

61 Gertrude Atherton: American novelist (1857–1948), author of *The Conqueror* (1902), a fictionalized account of Alexander Hamilton's life.

62 Charles W. Chestnutt: Charles W. Chesnutt (1858–1932).

63 T. S. Stribling's Negro novel, "Birthright": Stribling was a white author whose depictions of Blacks in his works stirred controversy. Walrond, unlike most of the staff at *Negro World*, praised Stribling (see "Stribling on the Women of Trinidad" *Negro World* December 24, 1921: 4, and a review of *Birthright* in *Negro World* April 22, 1922: 4).

63 Miss Ovington: Mary White Ovington (1865–1951) was one of the founders of the N.A.A.C.P. She frequently contributed to *Negro World* and was the author of *Half a Man: The Status of the Negro in New York* (1911). She wrote a mixed review of *Tropic Death* (*Chicago Defender* Jan. 1, 1927).

64 Ira Aldridge: (ca. 1805–67) a famous Shakespearean actor who performed, largely in Europe, until 1865.

65 "In Dahomey": the musical show opened in 1902. Williams's command performance came the following year.

65 "Shuffle Along," "The Plantation Revue," "Liza" and "Strut Miss Lizzie": popular Broadway plays featuring Blacks. Walrond wrote a scathing review of *Strut Miss Lizzie* in *Negro World* June 10, 1922: 4; he favorably reviewed *The Plantation Revue* in *Negro World* July 29, 1922: 4.

65 Charles Gilpin: 1878–1930, a well-known actor who starred in Eugene O'Neill's *The Emperor Jones* at the Provincetown (Massachusetts) Theater in 1920, winning the N.A.A.C.P.'s Spingarn medal.

66 Henry O. Tanner, Alfred Smith: Henry Ossawa Tanner (1859– 1937) had an important influence on Harlem Renaissance artists. Walrond means Albert Alexander Smith (1896–1940), who, like Tanner, was an African American artist who spent many years in France.

66 Sorrolla and Zuloaga: The paintings of Joaquin Sorolla y Bastida (1863–1923) are known for their vivid colors and contrasts of shade and light. Ignacio Zuloaga y Zaboleta (1870–1945) was a portrait painter whose work was heavily influenced by Spanish folklore.

67 Montecelli: Adolphe Monticelli (1824–96), a French painter often classed with Daumier and Cézanne.

67 Pierre Loti, Lafcadio Hearn: Pierre Loti, pen-name of Julien Viaud, was a nineteenth century French author who set his novels in such "exotic" locales

as Tahiti, Algeria, and China. American-born author Lafcadio Hearn (1850–1904) also situated his writings in far-away locations, especially Japan, where he became a citizen. Robert Bone discusses the influence of both these writers on Walrond in *Down Home* (New York: Columbia UP, 1975): 185–94.

67 Gustav de la Touche: probably French painter and printmaker Gaston La Touche (1854–1913).

67 Erte: born in Russian under the name Romain de Tirtoff, Erté (1892–1990) won fame in France as a designer and illustrator.

72 the Black Star Line: established by Garvey in 1919; he raised significant funds for this Black-run shipping venture, but it soon proved to be largely a failure.

74 star-apple: a star apple is a purplish-brown fruit with a sweet pulp and seeds arranged in a star pattern.

77 I walk out: Although Walrond acknowledged connections between Jews and West Indians (e.g., in his essay "The Hebrews of the Black Race"), he sometimes depicted Jews in unflattering terms. For a succint discussion of the ambivalent relationships between Blacks and Jews see David Levering Lewis, *When Harlem Was in Vogue* (New York: Oxford UP, 1981), 100–103.

79 Montega Bay: Montego Bay, a popular resort area in Jamaica.

79 tinterillo: (Spanish) a low-level clerk; also a shyster lawyer.

79 La Prensa: a major Panamanian newspaper widely read throughout Latin America.

79 Guayaquil: the largest city in present-day Ecuador.

81 prado: (Spanish) a field or lawn.

81 callecitas: (Spanish) streets.

81 brujeria: (Spanish) relating to practitioners of witchcraft.

81 Babbitt: Babbitt was a dull-witted, middle-class realtor characterized in Sinclair Lewis's novel *Babbitt* (1922).

81 cebada: (Spanish) barley. In this context, an alcoholic drink.

82 Ambassador Crowder: General Enoch Crowder, sent by President Woodrow Wilson to Cuba in 1921 after the collapse of the Cuban sugar market. In 1923 he was appointed United States Ambassador to Cuba.

82 crocus bag: a brown sack made of jute, often used by poor people as clothing.

87 Dore's illustrations: Gustave Doré (1832–1883), a popular French painter and illustrator.

88 a white peacock: the allusion is to the White Peacock Café, a meeting place in Harlem often frequented by Walrond while he was working for *Negro World*. See "Books" (*Negro World* May 20, 1922: 4). A white poet, Joseph Kraus, worked with Walrond at *Negro World*.

94 cayukas: cayucos, small canoes built from tree bark and propelled by paddles.

94 *patois*: generally a Caribbean Creole, here especially one with a regional or rural dialect.

94 Monkey Hill: common name for the city of Mount Hope.

95 Louis Quinze: decorative furniture, architecture, and dress of the period of Louis XV of France (1715–74).

96 *obeah* man: a practitioner of *obeah*, a belief in supernatural forces used to achieve or protect against evil ends.

96 *bobo* fish: a flat, freshwater fish.

96 Aspinwall: The name that Americans gave in 1852 to the city that would later be called Colón, in honor of William Henry Aspinwall who was the founder of the Pacific Mail Steamship Company.

96 *alcadia:* (Spanish) *alcaldía*, the office of the *alcalde* (mayor).

96 jippi-jappa hat: a jipijapa hat is plaited from the leaves of the jipijapa plant; the hats are made in Ecuador.

97 *agente's:* (Spanish) an *agente* is an official.

97 *extranjero:* (Spanish) a foreigner.

97 "Chumbo": a *chumbo* (or *chombo*) is a derogatory term for a Black West Indian.

98 *cuartel:* (Spanish) barracks, perhaps Walrond intends *cárcel*, a jail.

98 *herido:* (Spanish) an insulted man.

99 *guardias:* (Spanish) members of the *guardia nacional*, the combined police and army of Panama.

100 *cordilleras:* (Spanish) mountain ranges.

101 "Old Sleuth," "Dick Turpin" or "Dead Wood Dick": fictional heroes enjoyed by Walrond as a teenager.

109 Dyer Anti-Lynching bill: Representative L.C. Dyer of Missouri, with the backing of the N.A.A.C.P., sponsored an antilynching law in 1921. The bill passed the House but lost in the Senate due to a filibuster by Southern lawmakers.

111 "Darkwater": *Darkwater: Voices from Within the Veil* (1920) a work of fiction, autobiography, and poetry by Du Bois.

119 first work of fiction . . . colored woman in these United States: a number of earlier novels subsequently have been discovered, including Harriet Wilson's *Our Nig* (1859). Walrond felt that Fauset, literary editor of *Crisis*, represented the conservative old guard.

123 Demosthenes: (384?–322 B.C.) often thought to have been the greatest of the Greek orators.

126 amalgamation: a term for racial mixing.

127 Herbert George DeLisser: an Afro-Jewish Jamaican author (1878–1944) whose work is often characterized by a conservative, elitist tone. De Lisser is best known for the novel, *Jane's Career* (1914).

130 Rudolph Fisher, Gwendolyn Bennett, . . . Esther Popel: Rudolph Fisher (1897–1934) was a physician and author of, among other works, *The Walls of Jericho* (favorably reviewed by Walrond in *The New York Herald Tribune* August 26, 1928); Gwendolyn Bennett (1902–1981) was a writer, painter, and educator who had attended school with Walrond at Columbia; Esther Popel (1896–1958)

lived in Harrisburg, Pennsylvania. Her poetry was frequently published in *Opportunity* from 1925 to 1934.

130 "flyest": best or greatest.

131 Mr. Lorimer: George Horace Lorimer (1867–1937), editor of the *Saturday Evening Post*, which catered to a middle-class audience.

131 Jurgen: title character in James Branch Cabell's novel (1919). After a series of fantastic, risqué adventures, the protagonist settles into a comfortable middle-class existence.

131 Lhassa: Lhasa, the capital of Tibet and a center for Buddhism.

135 "The Blind Bow-Boy" and "The Tattooed Countess": novels by Carl Van Vechten written in 1923 and 1924 respectively. Van Vechten, a controversial writer and photographer who befriended many of the Harlem Renaissance writers, often frequented Harlem nightspots with Walrond.

136 Striver's Row: an exclusive group of Harlem brownstones located on 138th and 139th Streets.

137 the Creeper's: the Scarlet Creeper (the alias of Anatole Longfellow), a character in *Nigger Heaven* who represents the more sordid side of Harlem life.

140 Dr. Ossian Sweet . . . depends: Sweet was represented in court by Clarence Darrow and Garfield Hayes, who won their client an acquittal.

140 Dr. Work of Tuskegee: Dr. Monroe Nathan Work (1866–1945) was the director of the department of records and research at Tuskegee Institute from 1908–1939.

142 the immortal Genoese's sail westward: Christopher Columbus, who led four voyages to the Americas between 1492 and 1502.

143 the Maroons, under Cudjo: Maroons were escaped slaves and their descendants who established isolated communities; Cudjo was a Maroon leader who in 1738 negotiated a treaty with the British establishing a free Maroon state in Jamaica.

143 on one isle: Haiti, which, under the leadership of Toussaint L'Ouverture, gained its freedom in 1804.

145 *las costumbres del pais:* (Spanish) the customs of the country.

145 *cazrip:* casareep, a thick, black cooking sauce and preservative made from the extract of cassava.

145 "pepper pot": In many places in the region pepper pot is a soup, but in Guyana it is more of a stew, using casareep, spices and meat, usually beef. It is a favorite at Christmas.

145 ill-fated penal colony: French Guiana, especially Devil's Island, which served as a penal colony from 1852 to 1951.

146 Ionia's: classical Greece.

146 Anancy tales: folk tales originating in West Africa and popular throughout the West Indies. Anancy (or Anansi) is a spider who must rely on his cunning to overcome his more physically imposing foes.

146 Small's: a popular Harlem nightspot.

149 trichological: medical terminology relating to the hair.

149 Mme. Walker's: Madame C.J. Walker (1867–1919), an entrepreneur and philanthropist, made her fortune by manufacturing hair care products for Black women.

150 "the nightingale of the race": perhaps Walrond is referring to operatic star Sissieretta Jones (1869–1933), known as the "Black Patti," after the Italian singer, Adelina Patti.

150 Camorra: an Italian secret society often noted for extortion and violence.

150 a four-flusher: someone who tries to disguise the truth.

151 I could smell it loud on his breath: the "it" is alcohol, which was illegal from 1919 to 1933 due to the passage of the 18th Amendment.

156 the Battle of Long Island: a British victory over Washington's forces in August 1776.

158 chirographic: pertaining to chirography, the art of handwriting; the suggestion may be that Miss Kenny cannot write.

158 lavallière: an ornamental pendant on a chain worn around the neck.

161 The following biographical sketch was included by Walrond with "The Godless City":

I was born on New Market Street, Georgetown, British Guiana, on December 18, 1898. At the age of eight, I remember boarding a sailing vessel bound for the West Indies—I remember that voyage distinctly. We were the only passengers on the vessel, I think, and it was a voyage that was not without its exciting moments. I slept on a bed that was always damp with the water of the sea.

I remember, five years later, being on another ship—this time a giant ocean liner. At St. Thomas, the Virgin Islands, we had to transship to another larger steamer going to the Isthmus of Panama. It was the most exciting moment of my life.

I think often of *Uncle Tom's Cabin* as I reflect on the awful possibilities yawning like a hideous abyss before us as the ship's surgeon examined us—first my mother, then Lily, then Annette, then me, then Claude. Tracoma—[trachoma, a highly contagious eye disease] did we have it? Needless to say, not one of us had it, *so here am I—in America!*

No matter where I go, how many countries I visit, *I love America!* I am spiritually a native of Panama. I owe the sincerest kind of allegiance to it.

For—

I grew up there.

I went to school there.

I began working there.

I had my early struggles there.

I had my first—and possibly my only—love affair there.

I studied and played truant—I rambled and roamed and adventured—all there.

And, for the purposes of this sketch, it was there that I experienced the life that I describe in *The Godless City*—a city whose destruction by fire I have seen time and time again.

There was a time when writing was a pastime with me. Now it is a trade. I have experimented with other things too long not to know what I feel best fitted to do.

I began as a reporter on the *Star and Herald*, of Panama City. I used to write up brawls, murders, political scandals, voodoo rituals, labor confabs, campaigns, concerts, dramatic affairs, shipping intelligence, etc.

Eventually I got to the point where I thought I must be moving out into a bigger world of endeavor. So before I knew it *I was on my way to America!*

I arrived here on June 30, 1918. And here's a list of the things I have been up to now:—salesman—porter—"dish slinger"—secretary—elevator operator—editor—longshoreman—stenographer—switchboard operator—janitor—advertising solicitor—houseman—free lance.

Then I went to sea. It is the easiest way to—to forget things. I was cook's mate on the *Turrialba*, the ship on which William McFee was chief engineer. I *lived!* I saw life lived!

Since I have been in America, it has been my privilege to know some of the finest people in the world here. Unheralded, unsung, untrumpeted, I go into the most amazing of places. Sometimes, I meet rebuffs; other times, I have had, after I got out on the street, to pinch myself and say: "*I must be dreaming. This surely is not you, Eric.*" Eric, the black boy from a race once in slavery!

I am still so much raw material—I owe everything to the encouragement of my mother and her determination (a determination that *just won't down*)—I have got to get there—there are so many reasons why I must find my place in the sun!

162 "Bedwardite": Alexander Bedward (1859–1930) was the leader of a messianic group in Jamaica in the early years of the twentieth century.

163 Preston's days: In 1885, Pedro Prestan led an insurrection in Colón during which he set fire to the city. Soon thereafter, Prestan was captured and hanged.

164 *Maube:* a bittersweet drink made from the bark of the mauby tree.

164 *callaloo . . . fungee . . . sling:* callaloo (calalu) is generally a green-leafed vegetable; fungee is spiced corn or cassava meal boiled down until jelly-like; sling is thick cane syrup often drunk or used in making pastry.

164 goat-bottomed chairs: chairs made from a variety of sugar cane with leaves that appear to be cloven like a goat's hoof.

165 "ginger beer": a popular beverage, especially at Christmas, made by either boiling or fermenting ginger root with sugar and various spices.

165 Delessep's: Vicomte Ferdinand de Lesseps (1805–94), a French engineer who supervised the construction of the Suez Canal. He led another company to begin work on a canal in Panama in 1881. The company, however, went bankrupt in 1888 and Lesseps was convicted, probably wrongfully, of misappropriation of funds.

165 Landaus: four-wheeled covered carriages.

165 "shimmy shawabbie": "Shim Me Sha Wabble," popularized by singer Ethel Waters at Edmond's Cellar, a Harlem club. The word "shimmy" is derived from *chemise*.

165 Paramaribo: capital of Suriname (formerly known as Surinam and Dutch Guiana).

165 the "Big Tree" men of Jamaica: the Maroons, who often lived in thick forests.

166 *chiggers:* chigo, a flea whose bite causes severe itching.

166 falernum: an alcoholic drink made from rum, lime juice, and sugar.

166 tamarind: a tall tree valued for its fruit, which has a brown pod. Inside are several seeds surrounded by a dark pulp. Tamarind is used in drinks, stews, desserts, and sauces. It is also used for medicinal purposes.

166 "Gatun Lambs": laborers from the city of Gatun, just inside the Canal Zone and the site of a large artificial lake.

166 III: There is no indication for section II in the original text.

168 *coco-bolo:* (Spanish, Panamanian) a bald head.

169 *danson:* presumably a dance hall, from the French *danser* (to dance).

170 garfish: a grey, saltwater fish with a long, narrow, spear-like snout.

170 Bomberos: (Spanish) firemen.

171 *spiggoties:* American slang, derogatory name for a Spanish-speaking native of South or Central America.

173 I'm a cage o' apes: I'm not to be trifled with.

173 the "Cotton Club": a popular Harlem nightclub on the corner of 142nd and Lenox Avenue. The club was notorious for excluding Blacks or assigning them to undesirable tables.

174 kopasettee: copacetic, or copesetic, or copasetic; all right.

174 Bandannaland: Walrond is satirizing the stereotype of Blacks wearing silk or cloth kerchiefs on their heads.

174 cinematograph: a motion-picture camera.

174 *ofay:* a generally derogatory term used for whites.

174 Bamville Nest: the Bamville Club, which was located at West 129th Street, had both Black and white clientele.

175 Al Brown, Tiger Flowers: Black boxers.

175 dickty: high-toned.

175 blue: very dark complexioned.

175 Bobby Something: a dancer who did a frenetic Charleston routine at the Bamville.

175 guilder: a Dutch silver coin, but also used as currency in British Guiana. Walrond probably uses it here to mean money in general.

175 Race horse touts. Bolita men. California jacks. Two storey guys: Respectively, people who gave tips on horses; numbers runners; common men; burglars.

175 Florence Mills, Johnny Hudgins, Sandy Burns, Johnny Dunn: Mills was a popular singer and dancer (in such shows as *The Plantation Revue*). Her death in 1927, at the age of thirty-two, was deeply mourned in Harlem. Hudgins was a comedian who pretended to be mute in his act; Burns was a vaudeville entertainer who often performed with Sam Russell; Dunn (1897–1937) was a cornetist who claimed credit for creating the instrument's "wah-wah" sound.

175 ink-toed mama: a dark-complexioned woman.

176 Ann Pennington: a white dancer who performed the "black bottom."

177 Spoof Moses . . . Camilia Doo Right: Two of the more notable names listed here are Miguel Covarrubias, a well-known Mexican artist (1904–1957) who illustrated two of Walrond's pieces in *Vanity Fair*, including this sketch, and Mary Stafford, a blues singer. Walrond's inclusion of himself is probably a playful reference to his frequent visits to cabarets.

182 water mout': dribbling.

182 fi': for, to.

182 picknee: picaninny, pickaninny, a term for a young child (usually of Black or East Indian heritage). While it is a pejorative term in the United States, it can be used with affection in the West Indies.

183 a next: another.

183 faht blue hice: fart blue ice (i.e., to do something impossible).

183 bittle: bickle, food.

184 coruscant: glittering.

189 cassava pone: cassava, also known as yucca or manioc, is a root vegetable with brown skin and a starchy white flesh; cassava pone is a baked desert made with cassava, coconut, butter, raisins, sugar, and spices.

189 buckra: backra, a white person, often used derogatorily.

190 ball of "cookoo": cou-cou, a pudding made from cornmeal and mixed with okra. Commonly served with fish.

190 gap: entrance to a road or a driveway.

192 Hard-ears: a stubborn person who will not listen.

192 roasting *cashews*: The hard shell around a cashew nut must be roasted to neutralize a poisonous oil.

192 breadfruit: a tree with large, green fruit that is roasted, fried, or boiled.

192 sugar apples: green, heart-shaped fruit with sweet, white flesh.

192 *bonavis*: bonavist, a legume with purple and white flowers and black and white beans.

196 "bill": a machete used for cutting sugar cane.

197 Assafetida: asafoetida, also called devil's dung, a foul-smelling folk medicine sometimes used to ward off evil spirits. It is also used as an antispasmodic.

197 go 'head: Walrond probably means yo' head.

199 farrad: forward, rude.

199 fastiness: facetiness, bold to the point of rudeness.

199 Wha' yo' ah try fi' do, leggo!: What are you trying to do, let go!

200 bos'n: boatswain, a petty officer in charge of many deck activities, including dropping anchor.

201 crash pants: pants made from a coarse cotton or linen cloth.

201 leghorn hat: a hat plaited from a distinctive wheat straw, chiefly imported from Leghorn, Italy.

201 Hawfissah: officer.

201 Cho: an expression of mild disgust.

202 Changuinola or the Cut at Culebra: Changuinola is a town in north-western Panama; the Cut at Culabra was the major trench being dug for the Panama Canal.

202 iced apples: apples imported from England and packed in ice because they quickly wither in the tropical heat.

203 sprat: a herring.

203 tea: can refer to any hot beverage.

203 quatty: quattie, a small silver coin worth a quarter of a sixpence.

203 gill: a liquid measure; also a British copper coin worth two cents.

204 donkey-engines: small, portable steam engines.

205 singlet: a man's sleeveless undershirt.

207 monkey jane: a derogatory term for a woman of Caribbean descent.

209 ready to peg at a lancing La Barrie snake: ready to hammer Jota. A labaria is a poisonous snake that strikes swiftly.

209 Aft: abaft, at the rear of the ship.

210 coombia: a popular dance in Panama.

212 ulcered girls: in Walrond's writings, ulcers are generally leprous.

212 Cholo: a South American Indian.

212 Sacre gache!: (French) Sacré gache is a mild oath.

213 rotie: roti, a baked, unleavened bread made from flour.

214 gamin: a street urchin.

214 abattoir: a slaughterhouse.

215 stand-pipe: short for standard pipe. The pipe was mounted on a concrete stand and placed at the side of the road for public usage of water.

216 fire hag: in folklore an old woman who sheds her skin at night and becomes a ball of fire seeking victims whose blood she sucks. Also known as a soukouyan in several islands and as an old-higue in Guyana and Jamaica.

218 "cracked licker" skillet: a pan used in processing cane.

219 crapeau: a large toad, whose glands contain toxins; a Creole variation of the French crapaud.

219 bateau: (French) a flat-bottomed boat.

222 "taw"-pitching: marble shooting.

223 Chagres: a river in Panama which flows into the Caribbean Sea.

224 gunga peas: gungo peas, dark green peas often cooked in stews; also known as pigeon peas.

224 unna: you, your, you all.

225 lorgnette: eyeglasses attached to a handle.

225 yampi or Lucy yam: varieties of yams. A Lucy (Lucea) yam is also known as a white yam.

226 prædial larceny: stealing from someone's land or landed property.

228 Mr. Thingamerry's hat: thingamerry is a substitute for a person's name who is either forgotten or thought of as being unimportant.

231 jook: to poke or jab.

232 sugar stick: penis, a great lover.

232 steal she guamazelli plum: take away her virginity.

232 *dounz:* a tree with light green fruit with white pulp and large seeds.

233 *bolonjays:* eggplants.

233 Demerara (Mud-Head Land): Demerara is the smallest, but most populated county in Guyana, in which the capital, Georgetown, is situated. Mud-Head Land is a term for Guyana, probably referring to the muddy coastland area where most of the people live.

234 *queriman:* a large grey saltwater fish.

234 Quakah Belly: a fish with a large stomach; a reference to a pregnant woman.

235 wall pockets: a wall-pocket is a hanging receptacle for small household items.

235 *conkee:* conkie, a dessert generally made from spiced cornmeal wrapped in banana leaves and boiled or steamed.

235 extafay: interfere.

236 matty: mattee, a friend or neighbor; "jookin' yo' hand in yo' matty saucepan" means to stick your nose in someone else's business.

237 sorrel: a flower of the hibiscus family; the bright red leaves are brewed in boiling water. Sugar and spices are then added and the liquid is served as a beverage.

237 de: Walrond probably means "me."

238 Sankey hymn: religious hymns taken from a book of gospel songs by evangelist composer, I. D. Sankey (1840–1908).

239 "big foot": a swollen leg, elephantiasis—a chronic skin disease in which certain parts of the body become enlarged.

242 Boer's: the Boers are South Africans of Dutch or French Huguenot descent. They were defeated by the British in a war that lasted from 1899 to 1902.

243 portcullis: a grating of wood or iron suspended over the gateway to a building to be let down to prevent entry.

245 duppies: spirits thought to be raised from the dead.

247 Soul: soulee, a familiar form of address used by one woman to another.

248 shying: throwing or flinging.

256 florin: small coin worth two shillings.

257 the pip and the yaws: fatal diseases affecting domestic hens.

257 tannias and eddoes: root vegetables.

258 *hossah* or *corass:* hassah, hassar, or cascadu is a very scaly freshwater fish with a cream-colored flesh; corass is a fleshy, grey saltwater fish.

258 maw worm: tape worm.

261 mahk an fi'-mee wud: mark my words.

261 trampoosin's: galavanting, tramping about.

263 rum goggle: Adam's apple.

263 *cabrons:* (Spanish) carousers.

265 *pacos:* (Spanish, Panamanian) the police.

266 Perro: (Spanish) dog.

266 coronation: the ascendancy to the throne of King George the Fifth of Great Britain in 1910.

266 banyan tree: an East Indian fig tree.

267 wine: a sensual dance that involves a circular movement of the hips.

267 Butt 'e down!: knock him down with your head.

268 fish tea: fish broth.

269 swanking: swaggering.

269 han': can refer specifically to the hand but also to the entire arm.

280 *vieux anglais:* (French) a pseudo-Englishman.

280 Froude: J. H. Froude was the author of the controversial travel book *The English in the West Indies; Or, the Bow of Ulysses* (1888). The book denigrated Black culture and maintained that white West Indians, because of their isolation from England, were not fit to rule.

280 Gallegos: someone from or of Galecia, Spain. An attempt was made by some American engineers to bring in Spaniards rather than Blacks to work on the Canal.

284 John Payne, Leslie Hutchinson: Payne was a baritone and conductor of the Jubilee Singers; Hutchinson (1900–1969) was a popular musician in the 1930s.

284 Coleridge Taylor: Samuel Coleridge-Taylor (1875–1912), popular Black British-born composer.

287 Emancipation Acts: several acts were passed affecting slavery in the British Empire. The most far-reaching was passed on March 25, 1833. The act declared "that slavery shall be abolished throughout British Colonies, on, from and after the First of August, 1834."

289 Jutland!: the British suffered heavy casualties in this naval battle with Germany off the coast of Denmark on May 31, 1916.

290 Eton: Founded with King's College, Cambridge University, by King Henry VI in 1440, Eton is the most famous and the largest of England's public schools.

291 Charles I: King of England 1625–49. During his reign the English Civil War raged, and Charles was beheaded in 1649.

292 Mr. Wright's new book: Although Wright's book was published in America in 1941, the first British edition did not appear until 1947.

293 Ode Ethiopissa: dedicatory poem to Governor George Haldane of Jamaica, published in Edward Long's A History of Jamaica (1774). This is Williams's only surviving poem.

298 comado: (Spanish) a comadre is a woman co-parent. Walrond likely means a male partner here.

298 forced-ripe brat: a child who acts older than his/her age, often in an offensive manner.

298 chopine: a chopin, a liquid measure ranging from a half a pint to a quart.

298 black puddin' an' souse: black pudding is a popular delicacy made of pig's intestines often stuffed with sweet potatoes, pepper and seasoning. Souse is made with the pig's head and feet, which are pickled and well seasoned. The two dishes are often served together, especially on weekends.

299 Trampo!: tramposa (Spanish), a thief.

300 sapodillas: apple-shaped edible fruit, brown-skinned with a sweet yellowish pulp.

300 "Allez . . . allez . . . rut!": (French) "Get out . . . get out . . . you animal in heat!"

300 contre-maitre: (French) contremaître, a foreman or supervisor.

300 fellahs: laborers or peasants in several Arabic-speaking countries.

301 chantiers: (French) building sites.

305 pongee: a thin, soft silken cloth, with a light-brown color.

306 foolscap: writing paper.

306 cow-catcher: a metal frame that is located at the front of a coach or a locomotive.

307 absinthe: a bitter liqueur flavored with wormwood.

307 sabots: wooden shoes.

307 je suis royaliste, moi . . . et toi?: (French) I'm a royalist, and you?

308 moomah: mother.

310 Ants' Nest: A six-story tenement in Colón

310 napa: (Spanish) imitation leather.

311 adz-faced woman: an adz is an axlike tool.

311 pollera: (Spanish) chicken coop.

312 ackee bush: an ackee is a pear-shaped fruit with black seeds and creamy, edible flesh; it is often served with saltfish.

312 Babu: derogatory term for an old East Indian man.

313 goblet: in this context, a clay vessel used to keep liquids cool.

313 don't form fool: don't act like a fool.

313 do: Walrond probably means "go." The repeated lines may be a printing error.

314 pappy show: poppy show, someone or something foolish; foolishness.

314 fi' nyam: to eat.

316 adipose: fat.

316 a trilby hat: a soft felt hat with a sunken crown

317 weir: either a dam used to channel or divert water, often for a mill, or a fence built to trap fish.

317 Mafeking: South African city besieged by the Boers from October 1899 until May 17, 1900. The bravery of the British defenders grew to legendary proportions over time.

319 pink knees and jive: an integrated gathering, often with white women and black men.

321 Lamaha Canal: a central manmade waterway located in Georgetown.

321 'Buck' aborigines: a derogatory term for the native inhabitants of Guyana.

323 *jumbie* tree: a *jumbie* tree (or *jumbie* umbrella) is a mushroom. A *jumbie* is an evil spirit.

324 sugar cakes: a confection made of grated coconut and brown sugar.

324 custard apples: small, heart-shaped fruit with a yellowish pulp that resembles custard.

326 poor great: poor but somewhat arrogant.

$\mathcal{B}$ibliography

Walrond published in such a wide range of publications, many ephemeral and in vastly different geographic locations, that it is not likely a complete listing of his writings will ever be forthcoming. The following bibliography, however, is by far the most comprehensive one available to date. Page numbers were unavailable for several works. For the most part, I have not indicated where individual pieces have been reprinted.

ARCHIVAL MATERIALS

Biographical material can be found in Walrond's applications for a Guggenheim Foundation Award in 1928 (the John Simon Guggenheim Memorial Foundation, New York City) and a Harmon Foundation Award in 1927 (Library of Congress). Correspondence is scattered in several locations including the Robert W. Woodruff Library at Atlanta University Center, the Moorland-Spingarn Research Center at Howard University, the Amistad Collection at Tulane University, the James Weldon Johnson Collection at Yale University, Fisk University, and the Schomburg Center for Research in Black Culture (New York Public Library). Margaret Perry's *The Harlem Renaissance: An Annotated Bibliography and Commentary* (New York: Garland, 1982) has additional information on archival material.

BOOKS

Tropic Death (New York: Boni and Liveright, 1926; rpt. New York: Collier Books, 1972). Contains:

"Drought" (first published New Age [London], Oct. 1925)
"Panama Gold"
"The Yellow One"
"The Wharf Rats"
"The Palm Porch" (published in a different form in Alain Locke, ed., The New Negro, New York: Albert and Charles Boni, 1925)
"Subjection"
"The Black Pin"
"The White Snake"
"The Vampire Bat"
"Tropic Death"
Black and Unknown Bards: A Collection of Negro Poetry. (Aldington, England: Hand & Flower Press, 1958). Compiled with Rosey E. Pool. Originally made for a poetry recital by the Company of Nine in association with the English Stage Society at the Royal Court Theatre, London, in 1958.

ARTICLES

"The Failure of the Pan-African Congress." Negro World (Dec. 3, 1921): 4.
"Discouraging the Negro." Negro World (Dec. 10, 1921): 4. Condemnation of European colonialism.
"Between Two Mountains." Negro World (Dec. 17, 1921): 4. Criticism of Blacks who refuse to support either Garvey or Du Bois.
"Stribling on the Women of Trinidad." Negro World (Dec. 24, 1921): 4.
"Art and Propaganda." Negro World (Dec. 31, 1921): 4.
"Negro Martyrs." Negro World (Jan. 7, 1922): 4. Criticism of the British government for its arrest of Black activist Prophet Enoch and his followers.
"The Voice of the People." Negro World (Jan. 21, 1922): 4. Describes the popular support of Marcus Garvey.
"The Word 'Nigger.'" Negro World (Feb. 4, 1922): 4. Attacks Carl Sandburg for his defense of the word "nigger."
"Marcus Garvey—A Defense." Negro World (Feb. 11, 1922): 4.
"The Morality of White Folks." Negro World (Feb. 25, 1922): 4. Notes Harold Stearns's book, Civilization in the United States.
"Jan Smuts—Dictator." Negro World (Mar. 4, 1922): 4. Criticism of the South African Premier.
"Portrait I: An Artist." Negro World (Mar. 4, 1922): 4. Discussion of pianist, Sadie Cohen.
"The Dice of Destiny." Negro World (Mar. 11, 1922): 4.
"Negro Artist [Cecil Gaylord] Stars in Waldorf Art Exhibit." Negro World (Mar. 18, 1922): 2.
"Visit to Arthur Schomburg's Library Brings out Wealth of Historical Information." Negro World (Apr. 22, 1922): 6.
"Developed and Undeveloped Negro Literature: Writers Desert Great Field of Folk-Life for Propagandism." Dearborn Independent (May 13, 1922): 12.

"D. Hamilton Jackson." *Negro World* (Sept. 30, 1922): 3. Focuses on the president of the St. Croix Labor Union.

"A Motor-Driven Parachute." *Science and Invention* (Oct. 1922): 536. Invention by a West Indian, Dr. Hubert Julian.

"Poushkin [sic] and Dumas." *Negro World* (Oct. 21, 1922): 4. Unsigned editorial credited to Walrond by William H. Ferris.

"Local Color Chasing." *Negro World* (Dec. 9, 1922): 4. Discusses a letter from Romeo L. Dougherty and club-hopping in Harlem.

"Florida Girl [Augusta Savage] Shows Amazing Gift for Sculpture." *Negro World* (Dec. 16, 1922): 3.

"Shop Talk." *Negro World* (Dec. 23, 1922): 4. Mentions Georgia Douglas Johnson's volume of poetry, *Bronze.*

"Junk." *Negro World* (Dec. 30, 1922): 4. On a lecture by Carl Van Doren at the 135th Street branch of New York Public Library.

"Dark Stars that Shine." *Motion Picture Classic* (Feb. 1923): 53, 94–95. Discussion of Reol Motion Picture Corporation.

"The New Negro Faces America." *Current History* (Feb. 1923): 786–88.

"My Version of It." *Negro World* (Mar. 31, 1923): 4. Discusses a controversial reading by Walrond at the 135th Street branch of New York Public Library.

"Bert Williams Foundation Organized to Perpetuate Ideals of Celebrated Actor." *Negro World* (Apr. 21, 1923): 4.

"West Indian Labor." *International Interpreter* (May 26, 1923): 240–42.

"The Hebrews of the Black Race." *International Interpreter* (July 14, 1923): 468–69. On Black Caribbean laborers migrating to the United States.

"The Negro Comes North." *New Republic* (July 18, 1923): 200–1.

"El Africano." *Crisis* (Aug. 1923): 168–69.

"The Negro Migration to the North." *International Interpreter* (Aug. 18, 1923): 628–30.

"The Negro Exodus from the South." *Current History* (Sept. 1923): 942–44.

"Aristocracy in the Virgin Islands." *Current History* (Oct. 1923): 121–23. Discussion of islands since their acquisition by the United States in 1917.

"The Black City." *Messenger* (Jan. 1924): 13–14.

"The Largest Negro Commercial Enterprise in the World." *Forbes* (Feb. 2, 1924): 503–5, 523, 525, 533. Discussion of Herman E. Perry, founder of the Standard Life Insurance Company.

"The Negro in Northern Industry." *International Interpreter* (Feb. 2, 1924): 1398–99.

"Inter-racial Cooperation in the South." *International Interpreter* (Mar. 29, 1924): 1652–54. Discusses the Commission on Inter-racial Cooperation established by Calvin Coolidge in 1923.

"Imperator Africanus: Marcus Garvey: Menace or Promise?" *Independent* (Jan. 3, 1925): 8–11.

"The Negro Literati." *Brentano's Book Chat* (Mar./Apr. 1925): 31–33.

"Growth of the Negro Theatre." *Theatre Magazine* (Oct. 1925): 20, 52.

"Black Bohemia." *Vanity Fair* (Nov. 1925): 125. Profile of the patrons of a Harlem nightclub.

"Charleston, Hey! Hey!" *Vanity Fair* (Apr. 1926): 73, 116. Attempts to locate the source for the popular dance craze.

"From Cotton, Cane, and Rice Fields." *Independent* (Sept. 4, 1926): 260–62.

"Introduction." *Earth: A Play in Seven Scenes* by Em Jo Basshe. (New York: Macaulay, 1927): vii–xiii. Walrond's evaluation of this play on Black folk life.

"Says Casper Holstein Is Champion of the Oppressed." *Chicago Defender* (Mar. 5, 1927): part II, p. 1. Discusses the contributions of the West Indian numbers banker.

"The Color of the Caribbean." *World Tomorrow* (May 1927): 225–27.

"Harlem." *Encyclopedia Britannica*. 14th ed. 1929.

"Harlem." *Lectures du Soir* (Paris) (Feb. 4, 1933). Harlem as the Black capital. Translated into French by Mathilde Camhi.

"Harlem, la Perle Noire de New York." *Voila* (Paris) (May 27, 1933). On Harlem cultural life. Translated into French by Mathilde Camhi.

"El Negro, Expulsado del Cabaret, Vuelve a Labrar la Tierra." *Ahora* (Madrid) (June 21, 1934). The effects of the Depression on Harlem.

"Como de Hizo el Canal de Panama." *Ahora* (Aug. 19, 1934). On the financial troubles involved with the building of the Panama Canal.

"White Man, What Now?" *Spectator* (Apr. 5, 1935), 562–63.

"200,000,000 Negroes Thank Britain." *Sunday Referee* (London) (Sept. 22, 1935). Praise of England for its assistance to Abyssinia in its struggles with Italy.

"The Negro in London." *Black Man* (London) (Late March 1936): 9–10.

"The Negro in the Armies of Europe." *Black Man* (Sept.–Oct. 1936): 8–9. History of Black soldiers in European armies.

"The End of Ras Nasibu." *Black Man* (Jan. 1937): 13–15. On the Abyssinian leader.

"Fascism and the Negro." *Black Man* (Mar.–April 1937): 3–5. The need for Blacks "to strike Fascism a mortal blow."

"Can the Negro Measure Up?" *Black Man* (Aug. 1937): 9–10. Discusses eighteenth-century freedom fighter and scholar, Henri Gregoire of Guadeloupe.

"The Negro before the World." *Black Man* (Mar. 1938): 4–5.

"On England." *Black Man* (July 1938): 18.

"That Emancipation Complex." *Keys* (London) (Oct./Dec. 1938): 11. Signed "E.W.," either Walrond or Eric Williams. The essay argues that capitalism led to the slave trade and to the continued oppression of poor people.

"White Airmen in England Protest Treatment of Negro Comrades." *People's Voice* (Dec. 9, 1944): 16.

"Britain Spurs Training of Negroes and Indians." *People's Voice* (Dec. 30, 1944): 6.

"West Indians Fight in Burma." *People's Voice* (Mar. 10, 1945): 9.

"Italy Leaves Trail of Terror in Ethiopia." *People's Voice* (Mar. 24, 1945): 22.

"Soapbox in Washington." *People's Voice* (Sept. 29, 1945): 5. On the growing socialist movement in England.

"Enosis in Cyprus." *People's Voice* (Oct. 20, 1945): p. 19 and (Oct. 27, 1945): p. 19. Enosis is the unification of all Greek-speaking peoples in the Mediterranean.

"Indian Troops Employed for British Dirty Work." *People's Voice* (Dec. 15, 1945): 13. Use of Indian troops in Greece, Cyprus, Indochina, and Indonesia.

"The Men of the Cibao." *People's Voice* (Dec. 29, 1945): p. 21 and (Jan. 5, 1946): p. 21. American occupation of Santo Domingo (1916–24).

SKETCHES, VIGNETTES

"A Senator's Memoirs." *Negro World* (Dec. 17, 1921): 6.

"A Black Virgin." *Negro World* (Feb. 11, 1922): 4.

"A Vision." *Negro World* (Feb. 18, 1922): 4.

"A Desert Fantasy." *Negro World* (Mar. 4, 1922): 4.

"A Rose." *Negro World* (Mar. 11, 1922): 5.

"Castle D'Or." *Negro World* (Mar. 18, 1922): 6.

"A Geisha Girl." *Negro World* (Apr. 8, 1922): 4.

"Regrets." *Negro World* (Sept. 2, 1922): 4.

"On Being Black." *New Republic* (Nov. 1, 1922): 244–46.

"I Am an American." *Negro World* (Apr. 7, 1923): 4.

"Ambassadors." *Negro World* (Apr. 21, 1923): 4.

"On Being a Domestic." *Opportunity* (Aug. 1923): 234.

"Vignettes of the Dusk." *Opportunity* (Jan. 1924): 19–20.

"Snakes." *Messenger* (Feb. 1924): 56–57.

"Romance of a Reporter." *Messenger* (Dec. 1924): 382–83.

"The Adventures of Kit Skyhead and Mistah Beauty: An All-Negro Evening in the Coloured Cabarets of New York." *Vanity Fair* (Mar. 1925): 52, 100.

"Adventures in Misunderstanding: A Personal Experience." *World Tomorrow* (Apr. 1926): 110–12.

"White Stranger." *Carolina Magazine* (Oct. 1926): 3–5.

"Harlem Nights." *Star* (London) (Sept. 26, 1935).

"A Fugitive from Dixie." *Black Man* (May–June 1936): 13.

"Morning in Colon" *West Indian Review* (Kingston, Jamaica) (Aug. 1940): 31–32.

SHORT STORIES

"Miss Kenny's Marriage." *Smart Set* (Sept. 1923): 73–80.

"The Stone Rebounds." *Opportunity* (Sept. 1923): 277–78.

"Cynthia Goes to the Prom." *Opportunity* (Nov. 1923): 342–43.

"The Godless City." *Success* (Jan. 1924): 32–33, 90, 104, 108, 111.

"The Silver King." *Argosy All Story Weekly* (Feb. 23, 1924): 291–97.

"The Stolen Necklace." *Argosy All Story Weekly* (Apr. 19: 1924): 628–34.

"A Cholo Romance." *Opportunity* (June 1924): 177–81.

"The Voodoo's Revenge." *Opportunity* (July 1925): 209–13.

"City Love." *The American Caravan*, Alfred Kreymborg and others, eds. (New York: Macaulay, 1927): 485–93.

"Tai Sing." *Spectator* (London) (Apr. 20, 1934), 615–16.

"Inciting to Riot." *Evening Standard* (London) (July 26, 1934): 22. Also published in French under the title "Sur les Chantiers de Panama." *Lectures du Soir* (Jan. 7, 1933). Translated by Mathilde Camhi.

"Consulate." *Spectator* (Mar. 20, 1936): 510–11.

"By the River Avon." *Crisis* (Jan. 1947): 16–17.

"Poor Great." *Arena* (London) (Sept./Oct. 1950): 40–44.

"Success Story." *Roundway Review* (Feb.–June 1954).

"Wind in the Palms." *Roundway Review* (Sept. 1954): 235–40.

REVIEWS OF BOOKS, SHOWS, AND PLAYS

"The Voice of Truth." *Negro World* (Mar. 4, 1922): 5. Review of George E. Carter's book, *Children of Folly.*

"Only a Nigger." *Negro World* (Mar. 4, 1922): 4. Review of short story collection *Carter* by Don Marquis.

"A Purifier of Fashion." *Negro World* (Mar. 11, 1922): 3. Review of the book, *The Glass of Fashion*, by Mr. Oliver.

"The Negro Poet." *Negro World* (Apr. 1, 1922): 4. Review of anthology *The Book of American Negro Poetry* edited by James Weldon Johnson.

"The Soul of a Poet." *Negro World* (Apr. 1, 1922): 4. Review of poetry collection *Colors of Life* by Max Eastman.

"Books." *Negro World* (Apr. 8, 1922): 4. Reaction to his review of Eastman's *Colors of Life.*

"Book Notes." *Negro World* (Apr. 22, 1922): 4. Review of the novel *Birthright* by T. S. Stribling.

"Missing Pages in American History." *Negro World* (Apr. 29, 1922): 4. Review of a "study of Negro history" by Laura E. Wilkes.

"Book Notes." *Negro World* (May 6, 1922): 4. Review of Claude McKay's volume of poetry, *Harlem Shadows.*

"Books." *Negro World* (May 20, 1922): 4. Notes on the books *The Trend of Races* by George Haynes and *In the Vanguard of a Race* by L. H. Hammond; also a discussion of the literary meeting place, the White Peacock Café.

"Strut Miss Lizzie." *Negro World* (June 10, 1922): 4.

"Ach!" *Negro World* (July 1, 1922): 4. Notes on *The Trend of the Races* by George Haynes and *From the Kingdom of the Stars* by A. B. Kinnimouth.

"Book Notes." *Negro World* (July 22, 1922): 4. Review of the short story collection *Vengeance of the Gods* by William Pickens and a note on reading René Maran's *Batouala* in translation.

"Books." *Negro World* (July 29, 1922): 4. Review of René Maran's novel *Batouala* and a note on Florence Mills's show, *The Plantation Revue*.

"'The Penitent' Shows Alexander Pushkin, Russia's Great Negro Poet, Was Influenced by Shelley." *Negro World* (Oct. 21, 1922): 3. Review of a book by Edna Worthley Underwood.

"Books." *Negro World* (Nov. 4, 1922): 4. Lists works by several writers including Edna Worthley Underwood and Georgia Douglas Johnson.

"Book Reviews." *Messenger* (Sept. 1923): 818. Review of the novel *Men Like Gods* by H. G. Wells.

"The Theatre." *Opportunity* (Feb. 1924): 60. Review of a folk play *Roseanne* by Nan Bagby Stephens.

"Negro Poets." *New Republic* (June 4, 1924): 53. Review of the anthology *Negro Poets and Their Poems* by Robert Kerlin and the novel *Veiled Aristocrats* by Gertrude Sanborn.

"Our Book Shelf." *Opportunity* (July 1924): 219–21. Reviews of the novel *Prancing Nigger* by Ronald Firbank and Eugene O'Neill's play *All God's Chillun Got Wings*.

"There Is Confusion." *New Republic* (July 9, 1924): 192. Review of the novel of this title by Jessie Fauset.

"Mistah Fish Kelly." *New York Herald Tribune* (July 13, 1924): sec. 11, p. 25. Review of a novel by Robert McBlair.

"A Negro Anthology." *New Republic* (Sept. 10, 1924): 52–53. Review of *An Anthology of Verse by American Negroes* by Norman Ivey White and Clinton Jackson.

"On Our Bookshelf." *Opportunity* (Oct. 1924): 309. Review of *Gone Native*, stories by "Asterisk."

"The Theatre." *Opportunity* (Nov. 1924): 345–46. Reviews of Noble Sissle and Eubie Blake's show, *The Chocolate Dandies*, and "Three Plays by the Ethiopian Art Players" (the plays are *Being Forty* by Eulalie Spence, *Cooped Up* by Eloise Bibb Thompson, and *Bills* by John M. Francis).

"A Negro Novel." *New Republic* (Mar. 4, 1925): 48–49. Review of the novel, *Fire in the Flint* by Walter White.

"Negro Folk-Song." *Saturday Review of Literature* (July 11, 1925): 891. Review of *The Negro and His Songs* by Howard W. Odum and Guy B. Johnson.

"A Poet for the Negro Race." *New Republic* (Mar. 31, 1926): 179. Review of *Color*, a volume of poetry by Countee Cullen.

"Mr. MacFall's 'Jezebel.'" *Saturday Review of Literature* (May 1, 1926): 756. Review of a novel by Haldane MacFall, *The Wooings of Jezebel Pettyfer*.

"The Epic of a Mood." *Saturday Review of Literature* (Oct. 2, 1926): 153. Review of Carl Van Vechten's novel *Nigger Heaven*.

"The Negro in the New World." *New Republic* (July 27, 1927): 260. Review of *Lonesome Road*, six one-act plays by Paul Green.

"A Rich Field." *New York Herald Tribune* (Nov. 27, 1927): sec. 7, pp. 3–4.

Review of *Plays of Negro Life*, edited by Alain Locke and Montgomery Gregory.

"Black Rambler." *New York Herald Tribune* (Mar. 11, 1928): sec. 12, p. 3. Review of the novel *Rainbow Round My Shoulder* by Howard W. Odum.

"Another Punishment If You Please." *New York Herald Tribune* (May 13, 1928): sec. 12, p. 5. Review of the novel *Condemned to Devil's Island* by Blair Niles.

"At Home in Harlem." *New York Herald Tribune* (Aug. 26, 1928): sec. 12, p. 5. Review of the novel *The Walls of Jericho* by Rudolph Fisher.

"Book Reviews." *Keys* (London) (Jan./Mar. 1935): 61. Reviews of the novels *Jonah's Gourd Vine* by Zora Neale Hurston and *The Ways of White Folks* by Langston Hughes.

"Reviews of Books." *Life and Letters* (London) (Aug. 1948): 160–64. Review of the novel *Adam in the Woodpile* by Ian McLeish.

"Reviews of Books." *Life and Letters* (Nov. 1948): 176, 178, 180. Review of the book *Twelve Million Black Voices* by Richard Wright.

"Reviews of Books." *Life and Letters* (June 1949): 257–60. Reviews of two works of fiction, *Three Seasons and Other Stories* and *They Fly South*, by Chun-Chan Yeh.

"Reviews of Books." *Life and Letters* (Nov. 1949): 174–77. Review of *Focus: Jamaica*, an anthology edited by Edna Manley.

"Reviews of Books." *Life and Letters* (Mar. 1950): 230–33. Review of Roi Ottley's history of Black America from 1619 to 1945, *Black Odyssey*.

"Reviews of Books." *Life and Letters* (Apr. 1950): 70–72. Review of the novel *South Bound* by Barbara Anderson.

$\mathcal{E}$mendations

The following changes have been made to the original texts. Page numbers are to this edition. The emendation is listed, followed in parentheses by what was given in the original text. Changes were made only when it was felt the original might be confusing to the reader.

55 administrative (administraitve)
57 movement's (movements)
57 grizzly (grizzily)
60 daguerreotypes (daguerrotypes)
71 transcendent (transcendant)
74 sends (send)
82 rocked (rock)
85 belligerent (belligerant)
85 tongue-tied (tongued-tied)
85 gargantuan (garguantan)
89 clearly!" she (clearly!" She)
91 shooed (shoed)
92 thoroughly (thoroly)
92 euphemistically (euphistically)
94 wore (worse)
95 crumbling (clumbling)
96 bruises (bruishes)
99 sat up (sat of)

102 paroxysm (paroxyism)
103 ofttimes (oftimes)
129 acculturation (accoulturation)
129 ghetto, of (ghetto, on)
130 Hurston (Hurstonk)
136 Hers (Her's)
164 ofttimes (oftimes)
165 merengue (meriengue)
167 timbre (timber)
169 asphyxiatedly (asyphxiatedly)
211 machete (machette)
244 "wha' (wha')
284 Douglass (Douglas)
304 flicked (flucked)
317 gauzy (guazy)
320 reddish (redish)
320 solemnly (solemly)
322 "Hey, where (Hey, where)

ℬooks in the African American Life Series

Coleman Young and Detroit Politics: From Social Activist to Power Broker, by Wilbur Rich, 1988

Great Black Russian: A Novel on the Life and Times of Alexander Pushkin, by John Oliver Killens, 1989

Indignant Heart: A Black Worker's Journal, by Charles Denby, 1989 (reprint)

The Spook Who Sat by the Door, by Sam Greenlee, 1989 (reprint)

Roots of African American Drama: An Anthology of Early Plays, 1858–1938, edited by Leo Hamalian and James V. Hatch, 1990

Walls: Essays, 1985–1990, by Kenneth McClane, 1991

Voices of the Self: A Study of Language Competence, by Keith Gilyard, 1991

Say Amen, Brother! Old-Time Negro Preaching: A Study in American Frustration, by William H. Pipes, 1991 (reprint)

The Politics of Black Empowerment: The Transformation of Black Activism in Urban America, by James Jennings, 1992

Pan Africanism in the African Diaspora: An Analysis of Modern Afrocentric Political Movements, by Ronald Walters, 1993

Three Plays: The Broken Calabash, Parables for a Season, and The Reign of Wazobia, by Tess Akaeke Onwueme, 1993

Untold Tales, Unsung Heroes: An Oral History of Detroit's African American Community, 1918–1967, by Elaine Latzman Moon, Detroit Urban League, Inc., 1994

Discarded Legacy: Politics and Poetics in the Life of Frances E.W. Harper, 1825–1911, by Melba Joyce Boyd, 1994

African American Women Speak Out on Anita Hill–Clarence Thomas, edited by Geneva Smitherman, 1995

Lost Plays of the Harlem Renaissance, 1920–1940, edited by James V. Hatch and Leo Hamalian, 1996

Let's Flip the Script: An African American Discourse on Language, Literature, and Learning, by Keith Gilyard, 1996

A History of the African American People: The History, Traditions, and Culture of African Americans, edited by James Oliver Horton and Lois E. Horton, 1997 (reprint)

Tell It to Women: An Epic Drama for Women, by Osonye Tess Onwueme, 1997

Ed Bullins: A Literary Biography, by Samuel Hay, 1997

Walkin' over Medicine, by Loudelle F. Snow, 1998 (reprint)

Negroes with Guns, by Robert F. Williams, 1998 (reprint)

A Study of Walter Rodney's Intellectual and Political Thought, by Rupert Lewis, 1998

Ideology and Change: The Transformation of the Caribbean Left, by Perry Mars, 1998

"Winds Can Wake Up the Dead": An Eric Walrond Reader, edited by Louis J. Parascandola, 1998